Family Interfaces:
Transgenerational Patterns

Family Interfaces:

Transgenerational Patterns

By

Jeannette R. Kramer

Center for Family Studies/The Family Institute of Chicago
Institute of Psychiatry
Northwestern Memorial Hospital

Assistant Professor of Clinical Psychiatry
Department of Psychiatry and Behavioral Sciences
Northwestern University Medical School

BRUNNER/MAZEL, *Publishers* • New York

Library of Congress Cataloging in Publication Data

Kramer, Jeannette R.
  Family interfaces.

  Bibliography: p.
  Includes index.
    1. Family psychotherapy.   2. Family therapists —
Family relationships.   3. Family psychotherapy —
Study and teaching.   4. Family therapists — Supervision
of.   I. Title.
RC488.5.K74   1984   616.89'156   84-15005
ISBN 0-87630-362-9

Copyright © 1985 by Jeannette R. Kramer
Published by
Brunner/Mazel, Inc.
19 Union Square West
New York, New York 10003

MANUFACTURED IN THE UNITED STATES OF AMERICA

Dedicated to my nuclear family:
Chuck, my husband,
and our children
Dan, Judy, Douglas, Greg, Chip, and David
who will carry
our heritage
into the future

Foreword

I first met Jan Kramer some 20 years ago after becoming friends with her husband, Chuck. Chuck was thinking about starting a family institute in Chicago and had visitied me in Philadelphia, and was looking over the Family Institute of Philadelphia. He invited me to present at The Family Institute of Chicago several years later, where I met Jan. At that time she was raising a family, and her family therapy work had to be ancillary to that of her husband. Like so many wives of well-known family therapists, she had to play "catch up," and indeed she has caught up. She is now an outstanding professional in her own right. There was a time when Virginia Satir was the only prominent woman in family therapy; Jan Kramer joins a number of women who seem to be making the most innovative contributions to the field.

A central part of her work deals with family of origin of clients who come for help. Transgenerational considerations are becoming increasingly important as perhaps the most fundamental explanatory concept for why there is so much distress in peoples' personal and marital lives. As a treatment method, work with family of origin of adults has proven to be, in my judgment, the most powerful therapeutic tool in any kind of psychotherapy endeavor.

Jan adheres to the treatment philosophy that therapists should be skilled at using a wide variety of techniques which can be pulled out for a specific, appropriate situation. She uses creatively many different experiential methods. Techniques for Jan do not consist of things one does to clients; she has made integrative use of her own therapy experiences, which are described in the book. I was particularly impressed with her courageous account of her own personal struggles with her family of origin issues. I tell my students all the time, "You should never ask clients to do what you are not willing to do yourself." Interspersing the theoretical material with therapy excerpts (including her co-therapist husband), as well as the case histories, enlivens the book. Her work with therapists who were exploring the relationship between their own family of origin experiences and their work with clinical families is a unique and valuable contribution.

It was gratifying to learn that I have been part of Jan's theoretical family tree. After reading her family history I thought it might have been interesting to have been part of her real family.

James L. Framo, Ph.D.
San Diego, CA

Preface

This book is, in a sense, an odyssey of my journey as a family therapist with client families, with my family of origin, and in the training of family therapists at the Center for Family Studies/The Family Institute of Chicago. The book is divided into the above three parts.

Chapter 1 explains the importance of the concepts of marital and family interfaces and the continuing thrust the family creates for growth and change as it moves through the family life cycle. The remainder of Part I examines concepts and methods therapists can use to help client family members find new ways to view their original families in order to change their own part in dysfunctional patterns. Transgenerational patterns are explored in Chapter 2, together with examples of an enmeshed family and a couple experiencing dysfunction in their marriage. In Chapter 3, following factual and relational information on diagramming, family diagrams are charted of the families of the marital couple introduced in Chapter 2. Chapter 4 follows the same couple through therapy, demonstrating the influence of the original family patterns on marital patterns.

Strategies for change are discussed in Chapter 5, including motivation and timing in bringing transgenerational issues into the therapeutic arena. Many of the case examples are of therapy that extended over a year or two, or even longer. Although I start interface work early, in first phase sessions, much if not most of the actual work goes on in the middle phase, which is the growth stage of therapy. Examples of dialogue in sessions with resistant family members are provided so the reader can observe how the therapists handle the client's hesitation to explore and change stereotyped interaction with family members. Experiential approaches are illustrated in Chapter 6, including gestalt techniques, redecision work, and family sculpture. Formats for meeting with extended family members are discussed and illustrated in Chapter 7, both for older parents inviting adult children in as consultants to their therapy, and for younger adults who invite their parents and siblings to one or more sessions.

Part II, which focuses on the therapist's own family, begins with Chapter 8, an explanation of the overlapping concept of therapeutic interface and its importance in understanding what family therapists bring from their own families into the therapeutic session. Chapter 9 is an account of the personal struggle to change in my family of origin. These efforts have touched a chord in students because my family's problems are both so common and so scary to confront. When readers understand these issues, then, in Chapter 10, they can also appreciate examples of how I not only got lost in a therapeutic issue, but also learned to use such experiences therapeutically. Numerous examples from cases are given in Chapter 11 of the therapist's use of self, both in the first and middle phases of therapy.

Part III is an exploration of the family and therapeutic interfaces of family therapists, drawing on work with 140 therapists in small, time-limited groups over a six-year period. The structure of the groups and the leader's involvement is described in Chapter 12, ending with a discussion of the question: Is this therapy or training? In Chapter 13, I attempt to bridge seemingly disparate theories to explain how a high percentage of group members are able to shift their perspectives vis-à-vis their original families, discovering for themselves changed attitudes and avenues for action. Chapter 14, on shaping interventions, gives illustrations of how second-order change happens, both from self-report questionnaires and from the group's process. Chapter 15 describes the influence of the group itself on the process, the curative factors in the group, and the importance of shared themes among members. Chapter 16 is based on Erik Erikson's individual developmental stages, with quotations from questionnaires of the participants' changes. Such examples demonstrate that when an individual can alter self's part in an interaction, that person may then move forward developmentally and function more appropriately in relevant interfaces. The final chapter describes my view of the transfer of learning between interfaces.

Writing this book has provided the motivation to go back over notes and tapes of therapy sessions and groups. It has forced me to evaluate both my words and actions, encouraging a learning process in which I was able to see my part more clearly. There is a crucial difference between treating troubled couples or families and working with family therapists in a training group, whose purpose is to explore the interface between their families of origin and their client families. Families in treatment are caught up in their current problem, usually not connecting it with patterns in earlier generations, and are often impatient with any such suggestions. In addition, the relationships within the couple/family are usually strained and, when members meet together, they are often fearful of making themselves vulnerable early in therapy. Such families may not understand interfacial connections unless/until they move into the middle phase of therapy, when the crisis has subsided.

Family therapists who volunteer to take part in a family of origin group, however, have usually had the experience of reaching an impasse with certain types of client families and realize that a process is in operation beyond their current understanding; they are often ambivalent about opening this Pandora's Box, yet they usually see that there could be benefit in learning about the forces interfering with their erstwhile competence. Their family members are not in the session; instead, there are supportive peers. In such a group they can explore their family history to discover patterns and rules they have been following, practice interventions, or plan how to change their own interaction with family members outside the group.

The self-report findings in Part III have been especially challenging. I have become increasingly aware, in struggling to conceptualize the process and outcome of Therapist's Own Family Groups, of how a short, focused experience, with an average of only two hours for each person's work, can resound for group members over a period of years. I have discovered, in sending excerpts of our work together to the therapist-participants for their comments, that they usually remember their work vividly and have continued to make and hold changes in their original families, which have often continued to reverberate into other interfaces in their lives.

Examples in Parts I and II are from both my own practice and the co-therapy practice that Chuck Kramer and I share; examples in Part III are from the Therapist's Own Family Groups I lead. The excerpts are authentic, although names, places, and situations have been changed. Permission for use of audiotaped dialogue has been granted by client families in Parts I and II and by group members in Part III.

Throughout the book I use Chuck and Jan when referring to Charles H. Kramer, M.D. and myself, since we have been called Chuck and Jan by client family members for years. How to introduce ourselves and what to call family members was an issue when we started working together as co-therapists. Using Dr., Mrs., Ms., Mr., or Miss in four-way communication was too formal for the intimacy that develops when one couple treats another couple. It seemed natural to use first names; soon we were also on a mutual first-name basis with children of all ages.

In Part II I have focused exclusively on my own family of origin, adding relevant aspects from my relationship with Chuck as it interfaced with my original family and with our co-therapy. I have not included the next generation, our children, although they have been an integral part of the interaction and have given me illuminating and useful feedback on Chapters 9 and 10.

Since there is, as yet, no umbrella pronoun that includes the person of both sexes, I have struggled to find a suitable way to represent males and females equally. The heavily male flavor of the manuscript, when the male pronoun was used throughout, was troubling; using only the female pronoun did not seem to offer a better solution. In experimenting with he/she and her/him in describing interface relationships, I became inextricably entangled and clarity suffered. My decision, therefore, has been to alternate pronouns, using the male in Chapter 1, female in Chapter 2, etc., skipping those chapters which have no indefinite pronouns.

ACKNOWLEDGMENTS

I want to thank those who have made this book possible:

My mentors and teachers, especially those who make up my theoretical family tree.*

Chuck Kramer, who, besides being a mentor and co-therapist and giving me invaluable feedback on the manuscript, put up with my withdrawal into my private world of writing on weekends for the last three years.

Betsy Ross Mills and Bob Ross, my sister and brother, who critiqued Chapter 9 and gave their permission to publish our family story.

The couples and families in my practice who have taught me how to use transgenerational patterns in therapy.

The therapists in the Therapist's Own Family Groups who filled out questionnaires and cheered me on.

Bill Motlong, for the last five years my co-supervisor of a Second-year Supervision Group which focused on cases and interface issues.

---

*See Fig. 1, p. xxii.

Bill critiqued the entire manuscript and gave me his counsel and encouragement.

Larry Feldman, John Schwartzman, and Sherry Tucker, colleagues at the Center, who read parts of the manuscript and gave useful suggestions.

Lynn Hoffman for permission to adapt her Time Cable for my use.

My editors, Susan Barrows and Ann Alhadeff, who, although they changed horses in the middle of the stream, kept me from falling in.

Contents

Introduction

As a "third-generation" family therapist, I have been influenced by diverse models. The pioneers in the field laid out specific theoretical frameworks within which to work, including psychodynamic, Bowenian, structural, strategic, behavioral, and experiential models. Many treatment formats are available, including therapy with individuals alone and in a group, with a couple, with a family, with couples' groups, and with multiple family groups, all of which I have experienced as a patient and used with client family members. Because I have been stimulated by a wide variety of models, it seems appropriate to describe these influences, since they form my professional interface and illumine the way I view family interfaces.

The dominant influence, both professional and personal, has been my husband, Chuck Kramer, whom I joined in leading a couples' group in 1970. We were then in the middle of launching six children, ranging in age from 14 to 24 years. We had already worked together professionally, he as Clinical Director and I as Administrator of the Plum Grove Nursing Home in Palatine, a suburb northwest of Chicago. I brought to our co-therapy 17 years of experience in organizing and managing a therapeutic community in a nursing home setting, working with families where the identified patient was either the aging parent or a chronically disabled younger person. I was familiar with inpatient systems and working with staff/patient/family interfaces. We were then in the process of writing a book on long-term care (1976) which combined an understanding of institutional and family systems with traditional medical and nursing care in a nursing home setting.

Chuck has a broad background, including the practice of family medicine, American Boards in Adult and Child Psychiatry, and graduation from the Chicago Institute for Psychoanalysis. He has been a pioneer in Chicago as practitioner, teacher, and integrator of therapies, and deeply interested in what it means to become a family therapist (1980). By 1968 he had launched The Family Institute of Chicago, which I attended as a student and then joined as a staff member in 1973. The Family Institute became part of the Institute of Psychiatry of Northwestern Memorial Hospital and of the Department of Psychiatry and Behavioral Sciences of Northwestern University Medical School in 1975, as the Center for Family Studies.

I learned basic skills in the co-therapy format, first as assistant therapist and later as co-therapist, as we continued to confront our therapeutic and personal differences. The switch to co-therapist was made in 1973 when we became aware we were both holding back: I, because he was the senior therapist and "knew more" than I, and he, to make room for me. We realized, following this breakthrough, the creative tension that can develop when each co-therapist brings full power into the therapeutic hour. Part of our success as co-therapists, however, has to do with our complementarity. Chuck's analytic base, his acute awareness of manipulation and resistance, and his dogged tracking of a theme were matched by my intuitive hunches, my visual and experiential sensitivity, and my comprehension of transgenerational patterns.

Experiencing therapy has been an important part of my becoming a family therapist, starting with psychoanalysis with Arthur Miller in the fifties when I was struggling to understand myself and to balance my need for both family and career. Over the years I have had a number of catalytic experiences in week and month-long therapy/training groups and in weekend and one-day workshops, some attended alone, many together with Chuck, and others with the family, either as a whole or with those who have asked me to participate.

Such experiences included a month with Bob and Mary Goulding and Ruth McClendon at the Western Institute for Group and Family Therapy at Mt. Madonna, California. Bob, through a short, focused gestalt, enabled me to understand my father's part in my conflictual relationship with my mother; this allowed me to shift perspective and reconnect with her in an empathic way. In a workshop with Bob Drye, an analyst who joined the Western Institute's faculty, I moved from an inflexible position of doing the "have-tos" before the "want-tos," a necessary step to free up time for writing.

When Chuck and I attended a Fight Fair Workshop, we volunteered to struggle together on a basic issue monitored by George Bach. Later, when we were in the middle of an important personal controversy, we again volunteered to be the in-person couple for a live interview with Ian Alger. We took our family to a one-week NTL Family Workshop with

Sonia and Ed Nevis of the Cleveland Gestalt Institute in the early seventies. Later, we attended therapy and workshop sessions with several of our children, including one memorable one with Stan Woollams, Director of the Huron Valley Institute in Ann Arbor. More recently, body therapy with Alan Richardson has facilitated my letting go of dogged messages from my father, enabling me to loosen up and focus so that I could engage in the lengthy process of writing this book.

Therapists who have influenced me professionally cut across radically different theoretical models. As I have traced their contributions, I have visualized them as my theoretical family tree (Figure 1), each supplying a piece of my clinical framework. Their effect on me has been amplified because I have known the members of this tree personally as well as professionally. Most of them have been guests in our home when they visited Chicago to lead conferences and workshops at the Family Institute in the late sixties and early seventies, before they published much of their work. The writings that are named in Figure 1 as their "children" are those that have been most important in stimulating my thinking. I want to make it clear that this professional family has been conceived strictly from my point of view. I am not making an assessment of where the members stand in the field but only where they stand in my head in terms of their influence on me. Nor has this tree relevance to the way the members relate to each other.

The four grandparental figures awakened my interest before I even knew I would become a family therapist. In the late fifties and early sixties, when Chuck was moving from a traditional psychoanalytic and child guidance approach to a family systems framework, I accompanied him to lectures by Murray Bowen, Don Jackson, and Virginia Satir; Nat Ackerman was the speaker at the Inaugural Luncheon of the Family Institute in 1968.

Bowen was a stimulating factor from the time I first met him. As I read his theories and heard him talk, I felt he was speaking to me, since I had been aware for years of tension within my family of origin and between my parents, myself, and my husband. Five years before Chuck and I started working as co-therapists, I had begun changing my relationship with original family members, using Bowen's theories and many of his techniques. This work continued, both with my own family and in work with client families. I found, however, that Bowen's method of working from a distance with a structured, multi-question approach was not a natural stance. I wanted to find another way.

Ackerman, a psychoanalyst and child psychiatrist like Chuck, was also his role model. Ackerman was a prototypical psychodynamic family therapist, involving himself actively with family members and working with

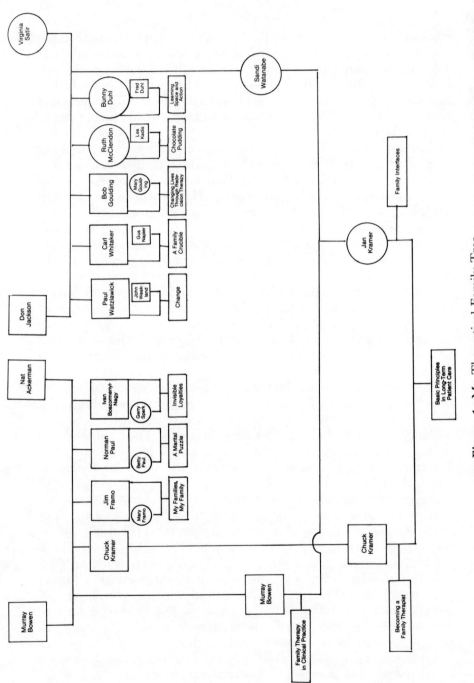

Figure 1. My Theoretical Family Tree

the developmental aspects of child and family life. His success in establishing the Ackerman Family Institute in New York encouraged Chuck to launch the Family Institute of Chicago.

Don Jackson's early tracking of family myths, patterns, and rules challenged my interest. His stance was emotionally distant and intellectually stimulating, like Bowen's. Satir's empathy and observation skills were always at work as she involved herself with families, enabling them to connect with each other. She used movements as well as words as a natural ingredient in the interaction, participating in the experience she was creating.

Sandi Watanabe, one of my teachers and supervisors at the Family Institute, was another important influence. Her forte was experiential learning which she evolved into an art with Bunny and Fred Duhl and David Kantor, who developed family sculpture at the Boston Family Institute. Satir was also a strong force at the BFI at that time. Watanabe helped me understand the inner life of families, their myths, patterns and rules. I learned with her to make visible the invisible by tracking a process in space, experiencing the past in the present, and exploring boundaries in relationships. She introduced me to the concept of interface and taught me how to use interfacial connections. Many of the concepts in this book are reflections of her ideas.

Working with Watanabe was an intense experience, engaging, creative and, at times, escalating. Bowen's coolness was balanced by Watanabe's heat. My reactions, as I was struggling to bridge their approaches, were an interface issue. I had grown up in a family polarized for years by my mother's intuition and intensity and my father's logical, calm behavior. In those early days, as Watanabe sparked my visual creativity, I needed Bowen's objectivity to keep me centered.

I attended two very different seminars concurrently in those early years. Watanabe presented a stimulating experiential group on innovative methods of working with family systems in which I sculpted my family, providing further insight. Michael Kerr led a family of origin seminar that reinforced Bowen's concepts. Its structure, predictably, was loose and did not confront the group's process. Participants were allowed to talk interminably and without focus in describing their families. When I spoke in the group of discomfort with the format, Kerr listened but did not see such remarks as relevant. I was faced with the contrast between the excitement and energy that were catalyzed in an experiential approach and the slowness of Kerr's intellectualized method.

Before knowing him personally, I was affected by Jim Framo's "My Families, My Family" (1968), a moving and personal description of the inevitable and natural interfacial process the family therapist struggles with throughout his professional life. I also share with Framo the excitement of bringing extended family members into the session to work together. Norman Paul's appreciation of the powerful influence of death and loss illumined the experiences I had had in the nursing home setting and gave me further tools for working with families. Ivan Boszormenyi-Nagy and Geraldine Spark (1973), in their conception of transgenerational loyalties and obligations, have supplied a framework for understanding fairness, justice, and balance in the extended family.

The Western Institute for Group and Family Therapy has provided yet another important area of learning. Bob and Mary Goulding, who combined transactional analysis and gestalt techniques in a time-intensive group format, structured training groups in which trainees took turns being patient and therapist, under supervision. Their method facilitated change in a relatively short period of time. Their co-worker, Ruth McClendon, who applied their concepts to work with families, taught me how to create a safe place in which family members can try out new behaviors. Her empathy, combined with gentle confrontation, enabled family members to discover new or unused parts of themselves. I have adapted their method for structuring groups, their creative use of gestalt, and the Gouldings' redecision work to use with members of families in therapy and with therapists in Therapist's Own Family groups.

Knowing Carl Whitaker and relishing his ability to "say it like it is" — outlandish, shocking, gentle, whatever — gave permission to the "good girl" in me to look at my own and others' absurd and distressing parts. Gus Napier, Whitaker's co-therapist at that time, encouraged me in 1975 to begin to plan this book. Paul Watzlawick and John Weakland, who together with Richard Fisch authored *Change* in 1974, introduced me to the theory of first- and second-order change. Although they do not see family of origin work as relevant and did not mention it in their book, it became obvious immediately that changing self in one's family of origin in order to change one's part in one's marriage, current family, and/or professional life was, indeed, second-order change and had universal application. This gave me a structure in which to see how changing self in one's family of origin automatically helped one change in other interfaces as well.

As I became comfortable with my own theoretical framework for helping families to change, I began conceptualizing my theoretical family tree. For a therapist like myself who wants to keep generational boundaries distinct, it is difficult to admit that the boundaries between generations in this theoretical family are breached. I see Bowen as both grandfather (first generation family therapist) and father, and Kramer as both uncle (second generation family therapist) and spouse. As I conceptualized Bowen as professional father and Watanabe as professional mother, then my aunts and uncles on the paternal and maternal sides came clearly into view. Kramer, Framo, Paul, and Boszormenyi-Nagy were children of Bowen and Ackerman, and Watzlawick, Whitaker, Goulding, Mc-Clendon, and B. Duhl were siblings of Watanabe on the maternal side and children of Satir and Jackson.

After I put my theoretical aunts and uncles in place, it became evident that they all had partners who were co-therapists and/or co-authors. Bowen, Ackerman, Jackson, Satir and Watanabe have each worked alone. The women on the paternal side are less dominant than those on the maternal side. Partners on the maternal side, as a whole, are equally dominant professionally. Thus, it became clear to me why I, as a woman, was not able to use Bowen's approach verbatim, but needed the feminine side, with its give and take between males and females.

In comparing my theoretical family to my personal family, I realized that the paternal sides of both tended to carry the logic and objectivity, while the maternal sides tended to carry intuition and intensity.* I needed both. As I had built connections with my own family members, I was also bridging for myself the differences in my theoretical family. This book was born out of the integration of these parts.

---

*I am aware there are many overlaps, as there are in "real" families; e.g., Watzlawick and Weakland are an obvious exception to "carrying intuition and intensity." Yet for me, they belong on the maternal side.

PART I

The Therapist
Treats the Family

CHAPTER 1

Family Interfaces

Interface is the area of overlap of two or more distinct psychological spaces. An interface can be as evanescent as two strangers glancing towards each other as they pass on the street. As their eyes meet, one may smile and, based on that fleeting impression, the other may begin to fantasize a relationship in the future based on hopes and memories. Or two people can grow up as neighbors, marry, and continue to live near their families as part of an intergenerational continuum. Interfaces develop between work colleagues, within religious and political groups, between friends and neighbors, and between therapist and patients, as well as within the family.

What is the difference between a relationship and an interface? A relationship is one person's connection with another, the condition or fact of their being related, and their shared interplay. Interface implies a more complicated interaction since each person leads multiple lives, as a self and also as a member of systems and subsystems, representing the groups' interests as well as his own. Thus, interface embodies not only the interaction of two individuals, but also the influence the systems exert on each member and each member exerts on the systems.

The term "family interfaces" narrows the definition. The family is

a group of persons with a past history, a present reality, and a future expectation of interconnected transgenerational relationships. Members often (but not necessarily) are bound together by heredity, by legal marital ties, by adoption, or by a common living arrangement at some point in their lifetime. Whenever intense psychological bonds and continuing emotional investments exist among intimates, the concept of "family" can be used, whether we are thinking of an unmarried couple living together, an intact two- or three-generation "blood" family, a one-parent family,

3

a foster family, a communal family, or even certain significant aspects
of an organizational or work "family" (Kramer, 1980, p. 43–44).

Family interfaces embody all the interaction and learning that occur in
the psychological spaces among individuals and systems. Each has its
own boundaries, with explicit and implicit rules governing transactional
patterns of acceptable behavior.

Two individuals, A and B, are shown in Figure 2, each with their own
psychological space and boundary, represented by the shaded area encircling each person. Where their psychological spaces overlap, a shared
interface is formed. This model applies to the interfaces of all the systems
described in the text: husband and wife, parent and child, sibling and
sibling, wife and mother-in-law, individual and extended family, nuclear
and extended family systems, etc. When two individuals meet, they form
a new interface which grows as their relationship deepens. With the
commitment of marriage, in-law relationships are set in motion. When
the spouses have a child, all four branches of the extended family are
affected by the other members' involvement with that child. Interfaces
become more complicated when families are blended, with "their" child
added to "his" and "hers," and with the need for families of origin to deal
with step-relationships. Because each transgenerational family system
has myths, beliefs, values, and rules going back in time, the joining of
families brings into focus the similarities and differences each system must
work out.

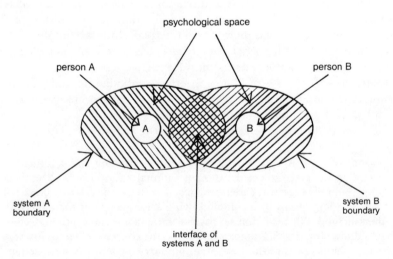

Figure 2. Interface

Meeting at interface allows individuals to define themselves in terms of differing systems and to develop strategies for interaction; once the commonalities and boundaries are known, the parallels can be explored. In practice, however, it is not easy to do. All individuals are the products of the families they were raised in and each tends to see the world through the lens the family provided. Whether they adapt to or oppose the family of origin, they continue to be influenced by it, and are vulnerable to being drawn into its mythology.

There are powerful forces that drive individuals towards emotional closeness and dependence, such as they experienced or wished to experience in their families of origin. There are also powerful opposing forces directed towards growth and individuality. Differentiation, that capacity of a person to develop his own uniqueness, can best be understood in relation to one's original family. The concept, a cornerstone of Bowen's theory (1978a), encompasses the ability to rebalance the transgenerational and current life commitments in the family interfaces. The maturing person, in evolving his own thoughts and beliefs, can develop further by letting himself be known, especially in the original family. He can search out the person of the other, whether father, mother, sibling, or extended family member, respecting the common ground they share. When the stubborn son of a stubborn father learns to respect his father's stubbornness as well as his own, he is then able to see that what binds them together (their stubbornness) is greater than what separates them (the content they fight over).

MARITAL INTERFACES

In the marital interface, each spouse provides the contact link between the family of origin and the marital system. As the representatives of two families unite, there is new input, both conscious and unconscious, into the generational patterns, forming a new interface. In looking outward from the family of origin towards a marital partner, each is searching for a complementary other. Attraction to a mate carries with it many things: a promise of gratification; an escape; a needed source of protection or continuity; an opportunity for experiences not encountered in the family; the possibility for growth and change.

The system that marital partners form can be understood by viewing it through the filter of their original contexts. Often they are not aware that they are caught up in a powerful, mutually reciprocal set of projection processes, with each spouse projecting traits internalized from his original family into the marital interface. A couple's development of a workable partnership requires understanding and respect for each other's backgrounds, values, boundaries, and learning styles.

The ability of each spouse to take a differentiated stand depends on the degree of each one's emotional emancipation from the original family during adolescence and thereafter, while at the same time maintaining emotional interconnectedness. If the maturing person can establish a separate emotional identity, he can become responsible for his own life and his occupational and marital choices. To "honor thy father and thy mother" is important, not just for the welfare of the parents, but especially for the growth of the adult child as he surmounts old patterns of adaptation and rebellion to create his own balanced life from his generational heritage.

According to Bowen, anxiety increases in one or both partners when they allow emotional forces to dominate intellectual functioning. If the partners are still intensely emotionally influenced by their families — and spouses usually pick partners who are at the same level of differentiation — they will bring unfinished aspects from their family interfaces into interactions with each other. When the ghosts of original family members hover about, direct negotiation between marital partners is blurred. When either partner copes with the original family's emotionality by merger into or cutoff from that family, he continues to carry those vulnerabilities to intense relationships into current life. If he allows self to be bound within the original family interface, he will be unable to free energy to plan for and live his own life. If he cuts himself off from the family, the emotional energy that was once invested searches for a substitute in which to invest, and the ensuing relationship recycles the old vulnerabilities.

BALANCE AND IMBALANCE

Each partner brings to the marriage the models of fidelity and fairness learned in the original family, which the partners struggle to rebalance together. Boszormenyi-Nagy and Spark (1973) conceptualize a multiperson systemic balance, in which family relationships are accountable generationally to standards of loyalty and justice. They envision a constantly shifting balance in a transgenerational ethical ledger, based on the family's rules, with credits for merit and fulfilling obligations and with debits for those unfulfilled. Clear rules for keeping the ledger contribute to basic trust. If the ledger is not balanced in one generation, the imbalance accrues to the next. Rebalancing of transitory imbalance leads to growth. Fixed, unchangeable imbalance over the generations, however, carries with it a subsequent loss of trust and hope.

Imbalance results from a series of social processes. The uncompleted actions of past generations impinge on relationships with the new generation as they interface. In the conflict between a partner's unresolved loyalty to his family of origin and loyalty to his nuclear family, past loyalties may take precedence over present loyalties. When this occurs, it will, if not corrected, influence his marriage and all succeeding stages of his family life cycle.

When one parent is allied with the child against the other parent, a perverse triangle (Haley, 1969) is set up which violates the developmental hierarchy and standards of fairness and accountability. Such imbalance can become entrenched, with the left-out parent partially or totally cut off. As both families' antecedents are explored in therapy, the existing situation becomes part of a larger context with recurring alliances and cutoffs from past generations forming the texture of involvement. For example, the current triangle can mirror a similar triangle in the father's family of origin, with father distant from paternal grandfather and allied closely with paternal grandmother. On closer look, it becomes evident that the grandparents' relationship is conflictual, with Grandmother closer to her son, the father, than to Grandfather, her husband. Thus, one can see that when a son learns to take his father's place with his mother and protect and be protected by her, he may have difficulty developing an intimate relationship with his wife, who may then use their son as an ally, carrying the pattern forward to another generation.

When imbalances are accrued over the generations, a family's image of itself is skewed. As individuals grow, they tend to look outside the family, especially to marriage partners, for compensation for those attributes they believe they did not receive in their own families. When a marriage begins with such oppressive expectations, it is difficult for the partners to develop a workable and intimate involvement.

REGRESSION AND PROGRESSION

Such spouses may function quite well in the normal course of events. Under stress, however, one or both go back to earlier patterns which helped them survive as children. There is a natural movement back and forth, from progression to regression to progression, as long as the old familiar behaviors are still useful. A person retreats to renew strength in order to move forward.

Freud (1963, pp. 339–341) conceptualized the process of regression in an individual in a migratory metaphor, labeling it as "regression in the service of the ego": that when an ethnic group moves out from home base, a series of outlying bases are established in enemy territory. When foreign troops are encountered and the advancing party is forced to retreat, their first move is back to the most recently vacated base because that was the latest safe encampment. After gathering strength, they move forward again. Or if the enemy onslaught is too great, they then fall back to the one before, and the one before that, as they flee before the enemy, until they finally return to home base. The unit withdraws in an orderly way to renew its strength in the service of survival and victory.

The process of the family under stress is similar: One or more family members move back to an earlier, safer stage in development in order to regenerate energy for a progressive move. This is not necessarily pathological; it may be the best way to move ahead.

The movement back may cause problems, however, in the marital interface. The spouses' attraction to each other, with conscious or unconscious promises of fulfillment, has roots in earlier experiences in the original families. Although they are attracted to the new relationship, there are powerful pulls to retain the old. Under stress, either spouse may regress to an earlier stage, trying to change the partner to fit the original family pattern in a continuing misplaced struggle to finish unfinished business with the original family. It is not a coincidence that the characteristics that attract spouses to each other are often those traits that become their battleground seven to ten years later.

FAMILY INTERFACES

When marital partners have a child, a new generation comes into being, creating new interfaces that tie the child through cultural, generational, and genetic bonds to the interfaces of the maternal and paternal families. The system increases in complexity as both families of origin invest emotionally in the child, invoking loyalty and assigning roles to carry on their traditions.

When the rules of these two powerful interfaces differ, the new parents struggle with the repercussions. In addition to adjusting their marital system to make room for the child, the new parents are called upon to rearrange their relationships with extended family members to include parenting and grandparenting roles. Individuals struggle with their own dilemmas. For example, now that the new mother is a parent, faced with problems similar to those her mother faced with her, will she become like her mother (the new grandmother)? Will the new father be able to continue the macho camaraderie he and his brothers have enjoyed now that he has agreed to take his turn caring for the infant? Will the new parents be able to move into an intimacy none of their parents have experienced, or will they center their lives in their children as their parents have done? The child is shaped by experience in the family of origin. He is enclosed within a family boundary that defines his family in contrast to others, discovering rules governing the family's movement within and across the boundary, and learning the consequences of entering and leaving the family's psychological space.

All family systems have rules forming a covert power structure of operational behavior. Moment by moment, through verbal and non-verbal cues, members are informed of the acceptability of their actions. Even saying or doing nothing carries a message. Every child discovers the rules he must follow in order to survive. He may adapt or rebel or carve his own course, but he must develop a way to live in his milieu. He observes the environment he inhabits, partakes of its ambiance. He forms values and beliefs; develops assumptions about how marriages and families are and should be; learns about the life cycle, including how to handle the changes of maturation and of aging and death. He learns about power and control and about the consequences of emotions, both his own and others. He is schooled in patterns of communication: what role to take in triangles; how to handle secrets; how to respond to pressure.

He is taught to perceive other people and their situations through the lens of his own family, and when the reality of the family is not congruent with the reality of the outside world, the child must somehow cope with this interface. Few children have intimate knowledge of families unlike their own, with dissimilar values and rules. Because this is the life the child knows best, the family's way of being is taken for granted, like the air he breathes.

In the normal course of events, differentiation starts early in life, as the child distinguishes his thoughts and feelings from those of others in the family. The course of his developing sense of self can be accelerated or slowed at crucial points in the life-cycle — when he starts school, approaches adolescence, or leaves home — by messages from the family and events from the outside world that influence the family's progress.

The degree to which family members are differentiated has profound importance in family life, where differences can be accepted and encouraged or where they can be suppressed. Thus, if spouses marry to "become one" and gloss over disagreements, they can blend into a united front. Such partners have no acceptable direct way to express dissimilar ideas and feelings and need to find someone or something outside themselves to concentrate on so that they can avoid the anxiety in looking at themselves. The most likely focus is a child in the family who becomes special, so that parental energy can then center on him. When a child is forced to be an extension of parents who are themselves unclear about their identity, he does not have the opportunity to develop his uniqueness. Family rules may be so omnipresent that the child loses touch with his own thoughts and feelings.

FAMILY LIFE CYCLE

Marital partners learn for themselves how to create a new system from the past lives each knew and from their common hopes for the future. It is useful if they can understand their own historical context, are aware of biases brought to the marriage, and are accountable for their own actions. Few are able to achieve such understanding and action early in marriage. The sequential phases of the life cycle, however, force all families to encounter new stages, giving the members continued opportunities for change and growth.

In the intergenerational spiral of the family life cycle, there are members in different stages of development, with opportunity for mutual interdependence. The continuing task is to support the growth and development of all individuals. There is a cyclical movement through stages, with the family's emotional balance subject to disruption by developmental changes, including marriage, birth, exodus of children, aging, and death.

Many problems arising in families grow out of failure to move in a timely way through these sequences. Family stress is highest at transition points, and anxiety and symptoms are most likely to occur when the family has difficulty bridging the transition. Carter and McGoldrick (1980) conceptualize the overall anxiety in the family system as flowing both vertically (as patterns move down through the generations) and horizontally (as the family moves through the life cycle). The ability of the family to manage transitions through life is affected by the degree of anxiety generated by stress from both axes where they interact.

The vertical stressors are entrenched styles of relating: family attitudes and rules, including patterns of emotional triangling passed down through generational interfaces. They are often covert, with such consequences as scapegoated members, psychosomatic illness, explosions of unexpected anger and violence, or cutoffs of individuals or branches of the family.

Horizontal stressors are both external and developmental. External stressors are unpredictable forces that disrupt the cycle, such as war, earthquake, fire, untimely death, and debilitating illness. Such stressors are the most obvious and can be devastating. Families and communities may pull together temporarily to overcome their effects. In later phases, however, the community spirit often breaks down, with growing resentment, frustration, and anger. Eventually individuals and families recognize that they must solve their own problems, and they begin to rebuild their lives.

Developmental stresses are like the seasons, moving forward in time through expectable phases. Everyone knows they are there; they are often taken for granted and not given the attention they deserve. Transition points, such as births, weddings, and funerals, are natural family crises; there is already developmental movement away from the status quo. Both during and immediately after such nodal points, the family is in flux and there is more possibility for change.

Each life cycle transition brings specific growth-producing tasks for the living generations (Haley, 1973). For example, as the late adolescent prepares to leave the family, the family also must deal with his leaving. This is the beginning of exits from and entrances into the family, with the parents truly the middle generation, caught between the emerging independence of children and the aging and death of the grandparental generation. The parents are faced with renegotiation of their marriage when the last child leaves and they are alone together. Room must be made for new members, as children choose spouses and grandchildren are born. Generational roles continue to shift as grandparents age, needing additional emotional, physical, and economic support.

As the adults in the middle generation go through the developmental stages with their children that their parents went through with them, there is opportunity for increasing peer-level contact. If such common sharing can be enjoyed, both generations can move more gracefully into the time when parents age and generations tend to reverse, with the adult children able to be a resource to their parents.

Even though death in the older generation is expectable, its occurrence has a powerful impact on the family. Emotions are intensely energized when the family system is experiencing loss. It is generally accepted that loss is followed by stages of grief and mourning. It is not generally recognized that a reorganization of emotional forces within the family is necessary following the crisis of loss (Kuhn, 1978). With the death of a member, especially a central figure, a vacuum is created which may be filled in any number of possible ways. Will one member, for instance, be designated to fill that role so that the family can move on with little disruption of the status quo? Or will the absence of a key member enable other members to shift their positions to fill the void? When a grandmother who has operated as the switchboard for the extended family dies, there will be a period of time in which change can more easily occur. The oldest daughter may move into this important role, with all communication going through her as it formerly was channeled through her mother. Or the adult children might decide to contact each other directly and eliminate that controlling role, thus changing an entrenched pattern.

Family systems that protect themselves by avoiding conflictual or sensitive areas may be caught unaware, with an emotional shock wave reverberating through the system, resulting in physical and emotional dysfunction and cutoff (Bowen, 1978b). Families whose members are emotionally connected and have reasonably clear communication can give and receive support, drawing in more distant members to form deeper and more functional bonds.

CHAPTER 2

Transgenerational Patterns

The developmental cycle of the family is ongoing, having evolved through preceding generations to come to its present balance at this moment in time. Each spouse has an internal image of the family of origin — the myth — which embodies the family's beliefs and its deep, commonly felt expression of emotions. The myth evolves out of traumatic, life-threatening experiences which elicit shared decisions that have survival value at the time. If the family continues to live by them, however, the decisions eventually become outmoded and interfere with the emotional and psychological growth of the members.

MYTHS, PATTERNS, AND RULES

The myth gets its power from: 1) the traumatic effect of the actual event; 2) the short-term utility of the decision; 3) the immaturity of those making the decision; 4) failure to reexamine periodically the decision and its growing inappropriateness; and 5) relegation of the painfulness of 1 and 2 to the unconscious where it remains alive indefinitely as a catastrophic expectation, since the unconscious has no sense of time as we consciously experience it. These traumatic events and the ensuing myths from each partner's past history influence the couple's current struggle to find a shared way to live their lives and raise their children, who become mutual participants in the process. This new family evolves its own shared myths, which then become part of the internal identity of its members.

Myths give rise to patterns, those recurring interactions in which family members mutually provoke and support each other in repetitive fashion, over time. Patterns are made up of rules and binds which reinforce the myth. Rules are unstated, covert guides for acceptable conduct which maintain the system and form the family's power structure (Jackson, 1965). Parents and children follow them automatically and are usually more conscious of rules than of myths. The family member has feelings associated with the breaking of rules — guilt, anxiety, knowing that if other members find out, she will be punished in some way. So she knows rules are there, even though they are not spelled out.

To see that rules are carried out, binds are instituted. Binds begin, for the child, as parental exploitation of dependency needs, constraining the child, for her emotional survival, through a sense of moral duty to follow the family rules. As children grow, binds are mutually interactive, binding parents as well as children. When families are caught in such binds, children have difficulty establishing their own autonomy and cutoff.

Discovering Connections

An exploratory process can be set in motion when a couple begins to understand transgenerational connections. Dan and Helen were in the middle phase of treatment (Kramer, 1968, 1980) following a marital crisis. They were seeing their interactions more objectively and began to explore a specific pattern that had been causing problems between them.

Dan: My mother came over the other day. She was repeating things three or four times — I mean, she *repeated* them. I can look at it more objectively now.

Helen: I could see how it was affecting me. I can accept her doing it more than I can accept Dan's needing it. When I tell him something and then he comes back and says, "Now, what did you say?" or "Tell me that again," I just think: "You baby! I told you! Damn it!" But, interestingly enough, and this is really fascinating, the school wants to test our oldest son, Jeff, for learning disabilities. They think he has an auditory difficulty — that he cannot process what he hears the first time.

Dan: Is it connected to my family? My family did not write notes and Helen's did. And there was the need to repeat and reinforce things from my side, versus Helen's side. It happens with my brother or sisters or mother. Marian will call me up and tell the story, then Ann will call, and then if I talk to my mother, she'll tell the same story — it's repeated and I can't say, even at this time, "I heard it."

Helen: She'll ask if you heard it and you'll say "Yes," and she'll tell it anyway . . .

Dan: . . . and it goes on and on to the point where I need less and less of that, but those patterns are still there.

Helen: Your mother was always there as the source of information. That wasn't true in my family—we were always coming and going so if you wanted to tell someone something, you wrote it down. And his dad did it, too, and his uncle did it.

Dan: Also, since the family did not read a lot, vocabulary was limited. We used words as simply as possible and as repetitively as possible to get the message across.

Helen: Did they repeat because they knew they needed to repeat because they all needed it? Because they had trouble processing auditory things? Or did they lose the ability to process things because they didn't use it? Which came first?

Jan: Then it becomes a pattern in which children are taught that it is so difficult to process things auditorily, even if it isn't difficult for you, that it really *is* difficult, like it is now for Jeff.

Dan: You are taught that the first time around you don't have to catch it.

Jan: It will come around again—as a matter of fact, if you catch it the first time, you're going to be bored!

Dan: That's it! Isn't that Judy!

Helen: Yes, our daughters—none of them are like that, but our son *is* like that.

Jan: It looks like it's coming down the male line.

Helen: Oh, yes. They couldn't be more different in terms of what their abilities are. Judy gets real annoyed when you tell her something twice. She says, "I heard you!"

Jan: (to Helen) But that's like you.

Dan: Oh, ho! The parallel's there!

Helen: I know she's a mirror. It's funny and scary at the same time.

As Dan and Helen were able to step back and see the patterns in their families, there bubbled up an escalating enjoyment in discovering the parallels and the process. As I was able to help them make explicit the implicit rules, they could see them more objectively. This gave Dan the choice to decide if he wished to continue to obey that family rule.

Understanding Repetitive Patterns

Although the actual traumatic event in Dan's original family is unknown, one can surmise that there was a time when, if words were not used as simply and repetitively as possible, an important message might not have been delivered and a catastrophe would have ensued. A myth evolved that if the family stayed together and repeated the shared message, they would all be safe. Thus, there was a short-term utility to the rule: "The message must be repeated to be heard." Dan's mother became the source of information and, long after the rule had lost its usefulness, his mother continued to enforce it and the family members automatically played their roles.

Now, in Dan and Helen's nuclear family, the rule applied only to the males and had become: "Don't listen to what is said the first time around." Dan had been bound by his unquestioned loyalty to his family, which had prevented him from examining the rule. For Jeff, an intelligent child in the next generation, the rule was not only inappropriate, but was also stunting his ability to learn. The girls were not affected by the rule, following their mother's family pattern of transferring information easily while becoming impatient with the males, who needed to be told again and again. This repetitive interaction aggravated the dominant female/passive-aggressive male pattern in the family.

Protections, Alliances, and Cutoffs

Rules and binds protect the family boundaries, making family members feel safe. Protections are appropriate when the child is young. As she grows, however, she becomes individuated by learning to protect herself in a gradual shift of power from parent to child. When parents do not transfer appropriate decision-making power to their children, status quo and stagnation are encouraged and growth and risk are discouraged. Often one or another individual in the family will feel compelled to break out. Symptoms may develop if she is unable to continue her autonomous growth.

Family loyalties bind members to each other in mutually reciprocal ways. Intense loyalty builds alliances between members, leaving other members out. As such alliances continue over time, imbalance occurs — for example, when loyalty is expected towards one parent and her side of the family and forbidden to the other. When carried to an extreme, relational cutoffs occur. A cutoff can be immediate and traumatic, such as a child's running away, a spouse's disappearance, or the suicide of a family member. A cutoff can also occur when one family member ceases to communicate, even though she remains nearby. Another type of cutoff is ritualized contact, characterized by families meeting for weddings, birthdays, or funerals in a routine, impersonal manner, exchanging little important information and not asking for or offering help.

Such cutoffs weaken support systems, leave fewer avenues for mutual exchange of feelings, and encourage intensity within the allied dyads. The more intense the cutoff, the more vulnerable that person is to duplicating the family pattern with the first available other person. She is also vulnerable to perpetuating alliances and cutoffs as she interfaces with the next generation.

Learning in the Family

As the child grows, she sees how her friends' families live, how teachers operate in the classroom, and how coaches handle their teams. When she finds her family rules do not work in another family or setting, she then has the opportunity to compare her own and other family rules. The child can bring these learnings back to her family and test her family's patterns against the reality of the other systems she observes. Gradually she may see her family's patterns more objectively and decide for herself how she wants to live, either now or in the future. If she does not recognize the patterns, she is likely to automatically either follow or oppose the rules, not only at home, but also outside the family at work, in social situations, and in therapy.

When a therapist treats a family and sees repetitive dysfunctional cycles, she can infer rules from these patterns and then determine how the family keeps itself in its dilemma by its rules and binds. She can then check out with the family member her hunches about the rules. The next step, if the member wishes to take it, is for her to test the myth by breaking the rule. The family member can expect a strong reaction from her family, calculated to force her back into line. As she withstands the family's reactions over time and stays on her own planned course, the reactions will eventually subside.

AN ENMESHED FAMILY

In the following case, the breakthrough in therapy came after Chuck Kramer, my co-therapist, and I explored with the family their rules and binds.

Twenty-two-year-old Sally Stone requested therapy for herself when she became worried about her drinking, her inexplicable rages that erupted towards her mother, and her lack of confidence, despite her success at school and work. We asked to see her with her widowed mother Gina and her sister, Brenda, who was a senior in college. Sally was single, slender and attractive, living at home and working in a responsible position in a business office. Her boyfriend, Dwight, was ready to get married. Her mother Gina was a beautiful but constricted woman, working in a routine office job; she said, "My children are my life." Brenda was a pleasant, overweight girl who had never dated and who seemed younger than her twenty years.

The extended family (Figure 3) had been enmeshed and female-dominated for several generations. Sally lived with her mother and sister in close proximity to three other households comprising her mother's family — her grandparents, two great-aunts, and her unmarried Uncle Alfred, who lived alone. Alfred and Gina were both sporadic drinkers. Sally's paranoid maternal grandfather had been hospitalized and had attempted suicide. This grandfather's mother had hanged herself when Sally's grandfather was nine, and two of her grandfather's siblings had also committed suicide. Her grandfather rarely related to the family, leaving the field to Sally's grandmother, who was allied in a contentious triangle with her two sisters, Sally's great-aunts. These three women had cut off from their younger brother when he had married, years before. All three idolized the beautiful Gina, Sally's mother, whom they called "the Queen." Sally's father had died of a heart attack when she was 12. He was an alcoholic, 20 years older than Gina, who had cut himself off from his own family, and had never been accepted by the older generation of women in Gina's family.

There was a dull, smothered atmosphere in the sessions, with all three — Sally, Brenda, and Gina — evading talk about anything important. Although Sally and Gina momentarily touched real issues, including Sally's ambivalence about marriage and her frustrations about living at home like a child, they quickly retreated. Gina lectured, Sally was hostile, and Brenda was silent. At home, Gina's drinking brought her fears to the surface and Sally's drinking allowed her to express her anger. If the situation did not change, I could see in the future the three of them settling down in a tight hostile female triangle similar to the one already operating in the grandparental generation.

Adding a Family Member

We terminated treatment after the fourteenth session when Sally refused to come in and Gina and Brenda were unwilling to talk about themselves. Alfred, Gina's brother, after persuading them to return, joined the sessions at our request. The therapy immediately became livelier, with Alfred and Gina's relationship becoming an important part of the treatment, a sibship that paralleled that of Sally and Brenda.

Alfred described the family atmosphere as reminiscent of that in *Cat on a Hot Tin Roof* (Williams, 1955). Their lives seemed to be planned in unending dullness, bickering, and blaming. Everything was pretend: Real feelings were stifled; life was seen as it "should be." Gina had al-

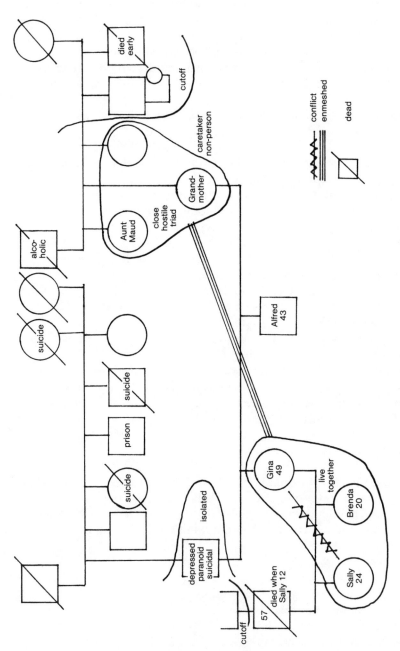

Figure 3. Stone Family Diagram

ways been on a pedestal; no one touched her; no one was intimate with her; she was not even aware that she was not expressing her real feelings.

Sally continued to be involved in erratic, violent episodes—an automobile accident, a drunken fight—and periodically refused to attend sessions. She was fired from her job following unexplained absences from work. Gina continued to allow her to live at home without a job and without paying rent, giving her money for expenses.

Sally was appalled at the things she was doing; she did not know why she did them or what awful thing might happen to her as a result. She felt that she could not control a part of herself—that it kept escaping. She was more afraid of *not* coming to the sessions than of coming, but she worried that she might sometime stop coming.

Gina began to realize her own contribution to Sally's problems when Gina became furious with her own mother's intrusiveness and saw the situation transposed to herself and Sally, with herself in her mother's shoes and Sally as herself. Suddenly she knew how Sally felt when Sally was furious at her intrusion. For the first time she saw that Sally needed to change for herself, not for her mother.

Brenda described herself as "more of a puppydog than a person." She felt she and her dog just existed and no one noticed them. Her communication with Sally had stopped when Sally had left for college and their interaction was on an adolescent level. The message Brenda heard from her mother was "You can't do anything right."

Alfred was anxious and upset with "a mountain to uncover," which he had been unwilling to talk about before. He was now willing because he could see parallels and connections in his life to Sally's problems; he now thought she might be in a worse position than he had been.

Identifying Rules and Binds

In one session with Brenda, Gina, and Alfred, when Sally overslept, we began to talk about family rules. It became clear that the "Constitution" of the family had very firm guidelines about feelings. As they described the rules and binds, I wrote them on the flip chart:

Rules

Don't tell anybody your true feelings.
Don't believe what others tell you.
If you feel you have to tell someone your feelings, lie about it.
Pretend agreement because no one knows how others feel.
One's obligation is to the family; non-family individuals are always
    outside.

Binds

Members of the family tell you how you feel.
If this continues long enough, you really don't know how you feel.
The family organization works to keep certain members helpless, like
children.

Problems

How to be intimate with outsiders and still be a part of the family.
How to bring someone new — a marital partner — into the family.

As they talked, they began to understand the powerful transgenerational forces that were shaping their lives. Death-laden traumatic events
permeated the family's history; their reaction had been to pull in, hide
feelings, focus on others, and pretend everything was all right. Women
controlled the family, tied together in hostile alliances, while men remained cut off and isolated. Rules perpetuated enmeshment within the
family and a chasm between family members and the outside world. The
myth could be stated: "Only the family is to be trusted. If you trust anyone outside of the family, a catastrophe will happen." This left no way
for members to move out of the family and control their own lives. It
would be necessary for each of them to test these rules in the family to
see if the myth was, in fact, true.

In addition, the family rules placed binds on our therapy. Members
had to break the rules to talk about their feelings with the therapists, which
explained why the atmosphere was so closed and smothered when we
first met together. The rules also kept them from believing others, which
included the therapists. Our task was to help them differentiate from each
other and to form a bridge between the world inside the family and the
outside world.

Moving Past the Impasse

Discussing the rules openly had a different impact on each family member. Although Sally was the one who had requested therapy, she refused
to come back, sitting around the house, drinking sporadically. Alfred
dropped out to go into individual therapy. Gina and Brenda continued
to come and began to make changes.

Gina had spent so many years pleasing and caring for others and living up to their expectations that she did not know what was right for her.
She wanted to find out what she really believed, to act on those beliefs,
and to stop feeling so responsible for Sally. She realized that she had

taught Sally how to be a tyrant, perpetuating a three-generation process. Each generation contained a pair of tyrant/non-person roles. Alfred
and Sally were each tyrants in their generations, as her Aunt Maude was
in hers. Gina also saw that Brenda, her mother, and herself had accepted
the role of "non-person." Gina started a training program which could
lead to a more interesting job.

Brenda described the split in herself—the fat child part who wanted
to stay home and watch TV, and the smart, thin, adult part who wanted
to plan her own life. The child part kept thwarting the adult part and
she had never been able to get out of her rut. She found an apartment
with several friends, set a date to move, began losing weight, and, at
a later point, quit her job to take a year's technical training. When her
training schedule prevented her from coming regularly to sessions, she
was satisfied to continue her changes by herself. Most of the energy in
the family had been turned in on itself when we started therapy. Now
Gina and Brenda were turning some of their energy outward.

Sally, who had been feeling competitive and left out, returned after
Brenda left the sessions. Gina and Sally's relationship was still primarily characterized by Gina lecturing and Sally responding hostilely, with
little rapport between them. Gina began making decisions to reduce Sally's dependency on her, setting limits to how much longer she would give
Sally money, let her drive Gina's car, and let her live in the family home.
Gina was now ready to stand her ground, despite Sally's anger.

I pulled out the family rules that Brenda and Gina had made and
showed them to Sally, since she had not been present when we had written them down. She added "obligations," which were binds, protecting
the family rules:

Obligations

If you tell people about weaknesses or problems, they will give you advice whether you ask for it or not, and you are obligated to follow
their advice.

When family members do things for you, you are obligated to accept
them.

Sally's category of obligations fit into the rules and binds the other three
had described. One of their rules was: "One's obligation is to the family." For Sally, it was a one-way obligation, and she was on the receiving end. When Gina let her live at home without paying rent and also
gave her spending money, she felt obligated to accept. She had remained
in a helpless, childlike role from which she had periodically erupted. Testing the rules and alleviating these binds in their interaction formed the
basis for continued renegotiation between Sally and Gina.

Understanding Failure

I made a "Circle of Failure" chart (Figure 4) several sessions later, which showed Sally's repetitive, destructive patterns. In the A cycle, she had dated Dwight and agreed to marry him although she did not really want to, and kept telling herself "I can always back out." Since it had been a pretend agreement, the situation had escalated as she began fight-

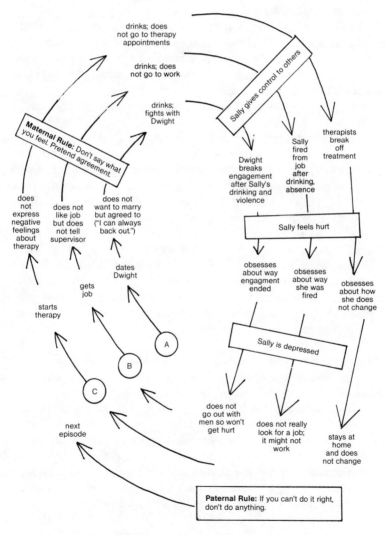

Figure 4. Circle of Failure

ing with him and drinking. When he broke the engagement after a violent episode, she continued obsessing and decided she did not want to date anyone again so that she would not be hurt.

In the B cycle, Sally had taken a job which had a lot of clerical aspects she did not like. She did not discuss her reservations with her supervisor, continued drinking in the evening, found it harder and harder to get up in the morning, was late for work, missed a number of days, continued drinking, and was subsequently fired. She obsessed about her situation, remaining out of work and not applying for other positions, since she might not like them.

In the C cycle, the same pattern happened in therapy. Sally had many negative thoughts and feelings she was not expressing. She began drinking at home the night before our scheduled appointments, came late, and missed sessions. When we broke off treatment, she stayed home, obsessing about how she was not able to change.

In each case she had been following the maternal family rule, "Don't tell anyone your true feelings. Pretend agreement." This fit the family myth, "Don't trust anybody outside the family." In doing so, she put herself in an untenable position. As her tension rose, she began drinking and acting out, precipitating an abrupt ending to the relationship, which left her feeling helpless, and pulling her even further back into the family cocoon. She began to see how she continued to set up situations over which she would have no control and then acted in an uncontrolled fashion, which made her prediction come true.

Sally added another rule she had learned from her father: "Either do it right, or don't do it at all." This rule explained why she did not feel much discomfort in staying home without a job and in not coming to sessions. Since she did not seem able to do anything right, according to her mother's family rules, she was better off following her father's and not doing anything at all.

The Stone family illustrates the way enmeshed family members begin to change at different times and in different ways while taking part in the same therapy. When therapy began, each was focused on others, since family rules did not allow the possibility of change for oneself or for trusting therapists, who were outsiders. Gina changed first as she recognized the transgenerational grandmother/mother/daughter parallel; only later was she able to seek change for her own sake and to set limits for Sally. Brenda followed her mother in discovering her own personhood, and it was only after Brenda had left home and stopped therapy that Sally returned and began to work to help herself.

CHANGING MARITAL PATTERNS

When one partner has a lifelong history of enmeshment with family of origin and has not shifted primary loyalty from parent to spouse, difficulties are likely to start with marriage, a family event which, developmentally, should signal emancipation from the original family. The following case shows how a transgenerational approach can activate a belated launching phase from family of origin and resolve a marital crisis.

Therapy with Stephen and Mary focused more on Stephen's changes with his family of origin than on Mary's with hers. This is often true when working with couples who have polarized into an underadequate/overadequate pattern. Stephen, who assumed the underadequate role, was the one who requested therapy, was more able at the beginning of treatment to see the value in changing, and was more willing to work on change with his family members. His membership in a lively, interactive family of origin and his training as a psychotherapist increased his capability for change. As long as the therapist holds a systems view, she does not have to insist rigidly on equal work by both partners. If the less active partner is kept fully informed and involved in the changes, both benefit, and sabotage is minimized.

The myth in Stephen's family of origin, "If conflict and anger are expressed directly, a catastrophe will happen," set up a multigenerational projection process, with indirect hostility between husband and wife, enmeshment between mother and son, and distance between father and son in three succeeding generations of triangles (Figure 5). No destructive myths were uncovered in Mary's family. Her problem was naïveté, since she had not been exposed to triangling at such a rampant level and had allowed herself to be drawn in, as a pawn. Both were able to shift positions, however, with Mary detriangling herself from Stephen's family and Stephen confronting his family's myth.

When therapy started, Mary had wanted to focus on problems in the marriage; Stephen had hoped to change his relationship with his family of origin. As we worked back and forth between their goals, we dealt with patterns of triangling and conflicted loyalty bonds which formed the interface for the crisis between the spouses. Their struggle was intensified by their move, with their daughter's birth, into the new-family stage of the life cycle, with its more complex tasks.

The reader can observe in this and the following two chapters how family rules moved from each family of origin to the marital interface; how each partner functioned under stress, regressing to continue their progression; and how the spouses differentiated from original family

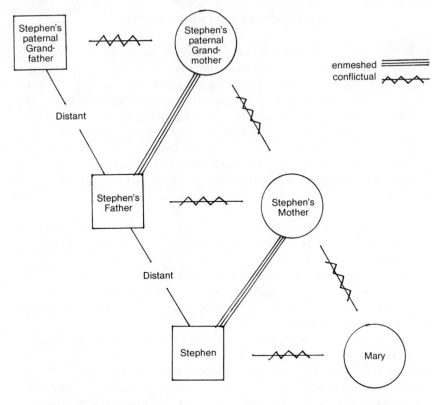

Figure 5. Transgenerational Projection Process in Stephen's Family

members and in the marriage, learning to keep emotional forces from dominating intellectual functioning.

A Marital Crisis

Stephen and Mary had been married for eight years and had a 16-month-old daughter Patty. They were competent professionals, Stephen as a psychotherapist in private practice and Mary as an administrative manager at a university. Both were dedicated to sharing duties to make a dual-career marriage work. The therapy covered 14 months with a total of 22 sessions. The first phase, working actively on the crisis, lasted three months, with 11 sessions. As they were accomplishing their goals, we increased the time between sessions, meeting seven times during the next five months. We continued to taper off, meeting four times in the last six months, until a second visit with Stephen's parents had been success-fully completed.

Stephen made the initial phone call. He sounded upset and wanted an immediate appointment. They had been having repetitive fights which had escalated since they had heard, a few days before, that his mother was coming to visit. His wife claimed he was sabotaging the marriage and she was talking about divorce. He admitted he had many problems with his family which he wanted to confront. I set up an appointment for both spouses the next day.

In the initial session, Stephen spoke first about his family situation. He saw his mother, specifically, as the problem, saying she was para-noid and manipulative and that everyone had problems with her, includ-ing both his brothers and his sister. He got along well with his father and was able to talk to him. His parents, however, had never had a good marriage; Stephen had difficulty seeing how his father was able to cope.

Mary wanted to talk about the current situation in the marriage, not about his family. They took turns describing the crisis, with Mary be-coming flushed and angry and Stephen avoiding her eyes as he hunched into his chair. Stephen's sister, Laura, who lived nearby, had received a call from their mother in California that she was coming alone to visit at the beginning of the next week. Laura had called Mary at work with the news, asking that Stephen and Mary help her arrange "every hour" of mother's visit. Mary had become anxious and upset; she and Stephen were leaving at the end of the following week for their first vacation alone since Patty's birth. She had no time to entertain his mother.

Stephen had dismissed Mary's feelings, saying he was willing to go along with Laura's plan. Yet he did not call either his sister or his mother to discuss the arrangements. His mother had finally called and they talked to her together until she made a nasty crack at Mary, whereupon Mary hung up abruptly. Since then she had been feeling frustrated and angry. Stephen acknowledged that he always became anxious as he listened to the barbs fly between his mother and his wife. Afterwards he and Mary would start to fight. Mary said, "He isn't himself where his mother is concerned."

It was hard for Mary, as an only child, to understand Stephen's large chaotic family because hers was quiet and fairly healthy. She added that their life had changed when Patty was born. Both had cut their work hours to share care of the baby for the first four months. In the last year they had gradually increased their schedules to nearly full-time, adding child care at home and sometimes leaving Patty in a nursery. They were experiencing increasing conflict and had grown apart, leading separate, busy lives.

From Mary's point of view, the problem was between Stephen and herself. When she and Stephen made plans together concerning his family, he did not carry them through; when she reminded him, then she became the "heavy." In recent months, when Stephen talked to his mother, Mary had joined him on the phone because Stephen did not defend her to his mother. Laura and Stephen rarely talked to each other because Laura claimed it was easier to talk to Mary.

We made a plan for the next week when his mother would be in town. Since he had given up control to both his mother and Mary, my focus was on how he could stay in charge of his own actions. I told him, "Your mother believes either *she* is influencing you, or *Mary* is influencing you — that you cannot stand up as an adult by yourself." And I said to her, "You are an active participant in the dysfunction by allowing yourself to be *so* involved."

I suggested specific tactics they could use. He agreed to start saying "I" instead of the marital "we," taking responsibility for his own decisions. He decided to phone his mother and tell her clearly when he would be able to be with her during the next week, a plan he would work out with Mary before he called his mother. Mary agreed to stay off the phone and out of the middle. When I raised the possibility of Stephen's inviting his mother for lunch alone, Mary reacted with anxiety: Would they talk about her? He acknowledged the problem, but said he would not allow it to happen. I suggested ways he could keep the interaction between himself and his mother. If he kept in mind a video camera, he could focus in, as with a zoom lens, then back out when it got too intense. He realized that his brother backed out in this way to stay in control.

As Stephen was leaving, he asked if he should tell his mother they were in therapy. I said it sounded to me as if his family operated under a family rule that allowed women to manipulate men. If this were true, then his mother would think his woman therapist was pulling the strings. I told him to take his own responsibility for his changes.

Triangular Interaction

Balance is a key concept in understanding family interface. No one person can dominate without someone else letting it happen. Stephen came to therapy feeling at fault in the marriage and focusing this fault on his mother, yet refusing to take a stand with her. When Mary allowed herself to be his buffer, it weakened her position without helping him. Stephen's mother could not wield her power in a vacuum; she needed the compliance of her family system, including Stephen and Mary, who unwittingly encouraged her dominance. Therapy consisted of helping them to recognize the parts they played in the patterns and to develop new strategies for disentangling themselves, while maintaining connection.

Stephen's relief was visible in the second session. He had been calm as he talked to his mother on the phone, able to set limits and decide what to do. Then, 12 hours before his mother was to arrive, his sister had become apprehensive, calling her mother's trip off. I was not surprised; this system induced intense reactions in its members. I explained that there was a basic amount of anxiety in the system; as his tension had decreased and Mary had kept herself from becoming involved, I would expect Laura's anxiety to increase.

I used the flip chart to show them how triangles had been operating (Figure 6), giving them a copy of Hogg's (1972) article to read at home. Mary had been an unwitting relayer of covertly held hostile feelings between two others who formed a split field and were not communicating directly with each other: Stephen/his mother in one triangle (A), and Stephen/Laura in another (B). Each person in each triangle had continued to act as if in a two-person system. Mary had become a messenger between the figures in the split fields, developing symptoms of anxiety as she had lost her power in the system.

I drew another triangle (Figure 7) to show them a different way of looking at the situation. Stephen's mother talked negatively about Mary

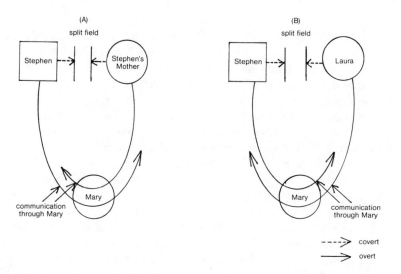

Figure 6. Stephen's Communication through Mary to his Mother and Sister

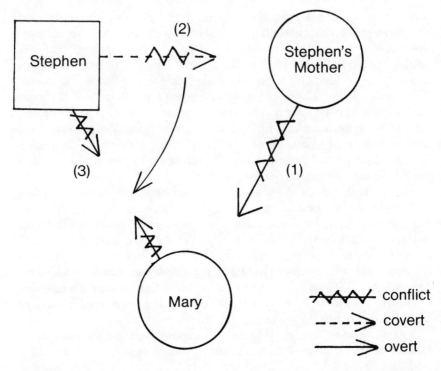

Figure 7. Communication Triangle: Stephen, Stephen's Mother, and Mary

(1), and Stephen listened passively, feeling uncomfortable and not standing up for Mary or telling his mother about his negative feelings (2). When his mother left and they were alone together, Stephen still had his unexpressed negative feelings and Mary felt unsupported. They then began to fight (3).

As we discussed the next step, it became clear that, until his planned telephone call to his mother the week before, Stephen had rarely initiated or terminated phone contacts with her. His passive behavior invited her to pursue and set him up to be a reactor. To correct this, we looked for ways he could take charge. He decided to initiate phone calls with both mother and sister, planning before calling how long he would talk and how he would end the conversation, discovering in the process that he equated setting limits with being unkind. I suggested it was similar to setting limits for their daughter, Patty, who needed kind but firm boundaries. He could learn by practicing on his mother and sister.

Although Mary was relieved, she was also conflicted about their relationship. There had been a communication block between them for more than a year. He used to talk to her and listen to her point of view about his parents. When he had stopped listening, she had tried harder to talk to him and he had still refused, saying her talking was not helpful. He agreed that he had stopped; he did not know why her comments were no longer useful.

I wondered aloud if his *not* talking might be connected with Patty's birth; starting a new generation often increases the new parent's identification with his parent and there can be a concomitant emotional investment from the new grandparent. This tightening of generational bonds may have pulled Stephen back into his family so that he was less able to listen to Mary.

While she wanted to work on their marriage, he wanted to change his relationships in his family of origin. Both saw these goals as compatible. I suggested diagramming their families to understand their backgrounds.

Communication Block

Stephen arrived at the third session dishevelled and anxious. He had not been sleeping well. His father was coming to town and his sister was anxiously scheduling things again. Mary was also upset; she had brought a list of complaints and started in with a tearful tirade, more concerned with his lack of listening than with the content of her concerns. He sat with his eyes down, squirming in his chair, talking about how much better he was doing than he used to do.

I commented that he was giving a demonstration of not looking at her and not listening to her feelings. Would he look at Mary and just listen? Both these actions were very difficult; he became more anxious and was unable to concentrate. I reminded him that he had said he protected himself from his mother when she was pursuing him. Was he able to look directly at his mother? That was difficult, too.

I changed the subject, since their upcoming vacation had been on my mind, and asked how their vacations usually were. Both agreed they usually went well. I observed that they had been arranging their lives to see very little of each other lately; that sometimes, before spouses were going to spend a lot of time together, such as a vacation, they regulated their distance with each other by fighting. I told them of several incidents when my husband and I had picked fights before intimate times together, before we had become aware of the pattern. They looked thoughtful, agreeing they had fought before vacations in the past, also. Following this exchange, he made an effort to listen to Mary's feelings. I again suggested, before we stopped, that we diagram their families to identify patterns, including triangles in the earlier generations that were being repeated now.

Towards Direct Communication

Before the fourth session, Stephen and Mary had had dinner with Laura and Stephen's father. Stephen was now observing his family more closely, reporting his discomfort with their interaction. Laura acted like a little girl with her father, who treated her like a child. Although she was usually anxious with Stephen, she did not appear to be anxious with Father. I asked if Father also protected Mother and treated her like a little girl. Stephen said yes. I suggested he initiate moves with both Mother and Laura, staying in control and stopping the interaction when he had had enough. He hesitated, afraid that Mary would feel left out if he did not include her in his contacts with Laura. Mary disagreed: She really did not enjoy such contacts.

Four or five different times during the session Stephen said he was afraid of Mary's reaction if he did what seemed right to him. As I pointed this out, Mary said that she often did not know what he meant. For instance, she had asked him earlier that day if he was feeling distant and he had answered her ambiguously. He remembered the instance, acknowledged his distance, and said that he had been afraid to tell her even though his feelings had nothing to do with her. She assured him that if he had said, "Yes, I feel distant. Just give me time; it has nothing to do with you," his distance would not have bothered her. I asked about the patterns in Stephen's original family; both his mother and father used this equivocal type of response.

Stephen then asked if we were ready for sessions every other week. Mary vetoed his request. I was alert to his resistance as well as to his need to not become dependent on another woman. I expressed my willingness to meet less often; first, however, we needed to diagram their families. I was not willing to space out the sessions until they both knew what changes they planned to make with each other and their families of origin, and were carrying them out. I wanted to meet with them for at least a year so that I could monitor several visits with their families and we could see the effect of their de-triangling over a long period.

It was difficult not to focus on the more obvious contributions of Stephen, who came from a large, intense, emotionally volatile family and was hurting, blaming himself, and wanting to change. I believe, however, that couples who stay together over time have approximately the same level of emotional involvement, even if it is not always apparent. Although Mary's eruptive blame turned the focus away from herself and she had little to say about her small sedate family of origin, she was equally involved in the marital dysfunction. She had not been tested, until recently, in triangulating behavior and she became more and more mired as she plunged into his family system with solutions that only entangled her further.

Mary brought Stephen to therapy with her escalating anxiety, forcing both of them to look at their dysfunctional relationship with his original family. In dealing with pathological triangles, the therapist needs to be active and directive, explaining the dysfunctional process and giving clear messages about how to correct it. As Stephen began to focus, Mary's overinvolvement also became clear to her. As he concentrated on his family, she kept focusing back on the marriage, keeping the tension high for continuing change. They were both able to make and hold changes after the first session, an early indication that they would be able to accomplish their goals.

CHAPTER 3

Diagramming the Family

The process of diagramming is a mutual exploration of transgenerational issues, giving the therapist an opportunity to highlight interfacing parallels easily missed in verbal history-taking. Children are usually present when a family diagram is charted if the children are involved in the therapy. Children may know very little about their family history and often enjoy the process. When a child is the identified patient, diagramming shifts the focus to the parents and their view of the larger system, often providing clues as to how one specific child has been identified as special. Such a child may feel relief as the parent focuses on unresolved family of origin issues, easing the downward pressure.

I bring up the idea of diagramming early in therapy to generate interest and let family members know that it is part of my diagnostic and therapeutic plan. When the family is focusing on the crisis that brings them in, however, they are anxious, often in pain, and not yet committed to therapy. Under these circumstances they find it difficult, if not impossible, to concentrate on a discovery process, so I wait to implement the plan until they are ready.

The therapist asks for a spouse to volunteer to go first; usually one is more ready than the other. If they are extremely competitive, it may work best if they alternate and share the time, with the family of one diagrammed for half of the session, followed by the other. The volunteer is in charge of communicating information about his own family. Although the working member may turn to the spouse for "how it is," or the spouse may want to take over, the process works best when it is clear that the working member is taking full responsibility.

Although diagramming is usually a satisfying and integrating experience, it is a powerful tool and, for some individuals, it may be upsetting, bringing up unresolved grief and feelings of hurt and anger from the past that they have spent years burying. It may be necessary to go very slowly and provide support, deciding with the individual when to continue and when to wait. If one of the spouses is likely to have psychosomatic symptoms, the therapist should watch for eruptions. One man reported feelings of "dis-ease" after I charted his family, saying that he felt like he had opened Pandora's Box. He subsequently developed diarrhea, which necessitated hospitalization for an extended period. Such events, although not common, call for caution on the therapist's part.

The therapist can usually complete a diagram of one individual's family of origin within a fifty-minute therapy session. The diagram, which covers at least three generations, details not only facts, but also relational vectors, including alliances, cutoff, and the resulting triangles. As each spouse looks at his own family system in this more objective framework, he is usually able to begin to observe the systemic aspects, especially if the therapist asks questions that lead him to see repetitive and connecting interactions in the family interfaces.

COLLECTING FACTUAL INFORMATION

Factual data (Table 1) are filled in first, using factual symbols (Figure 8). The use of consistent symbols substitutes for descriptive words, becoming a shorthand which makes charts easy to draw and read. Most of these symbols are in common usage and many have been published in journals and books.* I find it useful to write in quotes on the chart descriptions given about specific members, such as "the dowager," "the brain in the family," or "John couldn't do anything right."

I usually start by asking for the number of siblings in the individual's family of origin and draw them in, after determining if they were from one marriage or more, in order to adjust the spacing on the flip chart. As I place each family member, I fill in factual information about that person. Then I move up the chart, gathering facts in the parental generation before I move to the grandparental level.

When the therapist gathers information verbally, the family member tells him only what he knows. Yet what he does not know is as important as what he knows. When the family is diagrammed, what is not known stands out in bold relief. Such lack of knowledge is indicative of a cutoff in the family that can be explored. The therapist can also point

---

*See Bradt, 1980; Guerin & Pendagast, 1976; Hartman, 1978; Jolly, Froom, & Rosen, 1980; Lieberman, 1979; Orfanidis, 1979; Pendagast & Sherman, 1979; Stagoll & Lang, 1980; Wachtel, 1982.

TABLE 1
Factual Data to Include in Family Diagram

Include major family events, with dates:
  birth and age at present
  death and cause of death
  adoption
  marriage and where live
  divorce and whom children live with
  serious illnesses (physical and mental); describe dysfunction
  geographic moves, to where and precipitating factor, if relevant
  dates family members leave home
  accidents and losses in addition to the above
  miscarriages, abortions, stillbirths, and children who died in infancy

Also include:
  occupations
  special interests
  ethnic backgrounds
  religious affiliation
  education

Look for parallels through generations, such as:
  names
  occupations, including family businesses
  marrying out of religious, racial, national or cultural group
  divorces
  children born out of wedlock
  achievements in education or business
  sibship order

---

out parallels which become apparent and repeat in succeeding generations, such as names, level of education, occupations, geographical moves, and divorces. He can look for similar sibships and the birth order of children (Toman, 1976), commenting on the characteristics of firstborn, middle, lastborn, or only child.

If there are large families with many aunts, uncles, and cousins, the family member may want to pass over them to go on to "more important" matters. If the therapist does not chart them, however, he will not have crucial information about family size, male/female distribution, never-married, divorce, abortion or miscarriage, early death, or whatever else may form the important patterns for that particular family. Some families increase in progeny as generations go by; others tend towards extinction (Christofori, 1978). The birth of a child holds different meanings, depending on the context in which he is born.

GATHERING RELATIONSHIP DATA

When most of the facts are on the chart, then the questioning turns to relationship information (Table 2 and Figure 9). Knowing the facts elicited so far and the problems the family faces, there are already themes becoming apparent, such as patterns of illness, violent or early deaths, clustering of families geographically with specific members migrating, or marrying out of the family religion. Questioning about the relationships in the family expands on these perceptions and adds new direction. Information usually flows more easily if the therapist reverses the direction and moves methodically down the chart, starting with the grandparent generation, about whom the family members can usually be more objective. As patterns emerge they can be recorded and then noted as they appear in following generations.

The therapist asks questions about the relationships as the family member has understood them over time — between husbands and wives, among siblings, between parents and children, extended family and children, and with in-laws. In some families triangles form basic themes, often interlocking through succeeding generations. If the member reports no conflicts or problems, I will comment on this, asking, "How come there are no skeletons in your closets — or maybe your family doesn't let you know?" United front families mask profound differences, which come out in symptomatic behavior. It may take many sessions before members in such families can admit the problems they knew were there but were constrained to hide.

Questioning moves down the chart to the current generation. Dates are important in order to see how events in several generations cluster. When a daughter mentions a time when her mother was hospitalized for several months, then the therapist can look to see what ages the children were and what other events in the extended family preceded and postdated that trauma. Nodal events typically cluster, with stress building and the family members vulnerable to further trauma. The therapist can inquire about events before or within a year or two after the identified patient was born, which can give clues to the parents' preoccupation at the time the infant needed total care. The stress of concurrent family life traumas — for example, grandparental death before or after childbirth — may impede mourning and parenting processes in the middle generation (Walsh, 1978). It is not uncommon to find clusters of traumatic events in each generation of the family; these can be explored in terms of their repetitive features, especially if the current problem is part of such a cluster. How did the family master earlier traumas? What is necessary for them to master this and future ones?

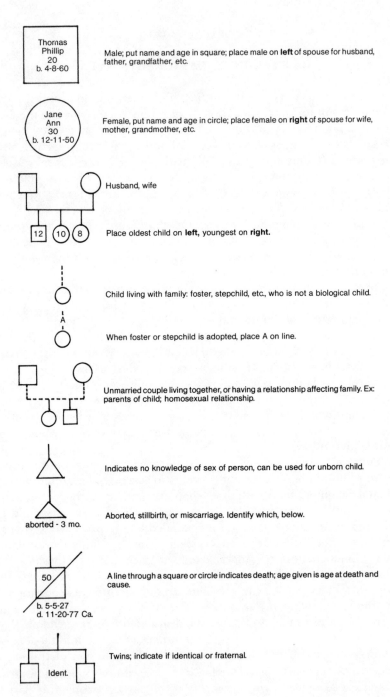

Male; put name and age in square; place male on **left** of spouse for husband, father, grandfather, etc.

Female, put name and age in circle; place female on **right** of spouse for wife, mother, grandmother, etc.

Husband, wife

Place oldest child on **left**, youngest on **right.**

Child living with family: foster, stepchild, etc., who is not a biological child.

When foster or stepchild is adopted, place A on line.

Unmarried couple living together, or having a relationship affecting family. Ex: parents of child; homosexual relationship.

Indicates no knowledge of sex of person, can be used for unborn child.

Aborted, stillbirth, or miscarriage. Identify which, below.

A line through a square or circle indicates death; age given is age at death and cause.

Twins; indicate if identical or fraternal.

Figure 8. Symbols for Family Diagramming: Factual Information

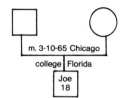

Indicate on line connecting spouses when each couple was married and where they live.

If child is living away from home, give place and occupation.

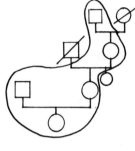

Many families have unusual living arrangements. When diagramming households covering more than 2 generations, draw a line around those in the same household. It is useful to use a different color to outline a household.

This diagram shows a 4-generation household.

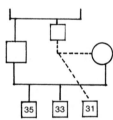

Many families have unusual constellations. Find ways to diagram them, such as:

This diagram shows that mother's last child was fathered by her husband's younger brother.

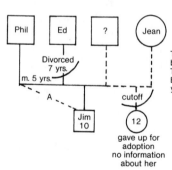

This diagram shows that Jean had a daughter, fathered by an unknown man, whom she gave up for adoption. Two years later she had a son Jim by her first husband Ed, whom she divorced 7 years ago. She married Phil 5 years ago, who adopted Jim.

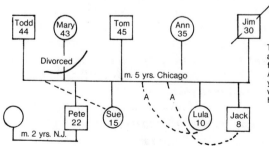

This diagram shows that Tom and Ann married 5 years ago, following which Tom adopted Ann's daughter and son. His younger daughter Sue lives with his former wife Mary and her current husband, Todd.

Figure 8 (continued)

TABLE 2
Relationship Data to Include in Family Diagram

Look for patterns, such as:

    balance in nuclear family and with extended families, including alliances and cut-offs. Does the nuclear family relate in a balanced way to both branches of the extended family?

    triangles
    male/female issues
    patterns of illness
    communication patterns
    clusters of crisis/dysfunction, especially around loss

    identify relatively concurrent births and deaths (within a year of each other) and trace the effects

    listen for unspoken family rules and binds as the family members describe their interaction. Write these down and encourage family members to discuss them.

What is important in gathering family history is the underlying message — the myths, rules, and binds — that still influences the member in automatic and dysfunctional ways, controlling his thoughts and actions in the present. The therapist's task is to help him gain a sense of his unique experience in his family — what his role has been — so he can decide about his own future. Is he a replacement child (Legg & Sherrick, 1976)? If so, what were the circumstances around both his birth and the life and death of the individual he has replaced? Does he feel loyalty-bound to carry out certain obligations in the family? If he is the burden-bearer, caretaker, or sacrificial object, where is the rest of the support system — his siblings, aunts and uncles — and how might he be able to share his burdens with others to achieve more balance in the family?

The therapist asks about the systemic functioning in the family as crucial areas emerge. Who is the ostensibly powerful one and how is his power balanced by the apparently helpless spouse? How do members pressure each other and respond to stress? How do they maintain their boundaries? How does the family handle secrets? Is each member obligated to honor each confidence or do all family members have a right to know what is going on? As the family member responds to such inquiries, the therapist can listen for unspoken family rules as members describe the interaction, and he can write them on the chart, encouraging family members to discuss them.

The therapist can now observe the differences and similarities between the maternal and paternal generational sides of the family. Are they

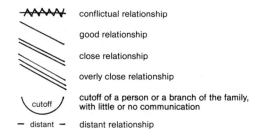

conflictual relationship

good relationship

close relationship

overly close relationship

cutoff
cutoff of a person or a branch of the family, with little or no communication

— distant — distant relationship

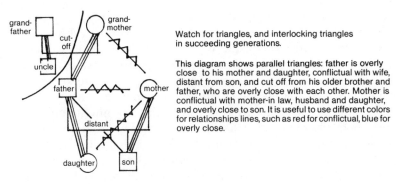

Watch for triangles, and interlocking triangles in succeeding generations.

This diagram shows parallel triangles: father is overly close to his mother and daughter, conflictual with wife, distant from son, and cut off from his older brother and father, who are overly close with each other. Mother is conflictual with mother-in law, husband and daughter, and overly close to son. It is useful to use different colors for relationships lines, such as red for conflictual, blue for overly close.

Figure 9. Symbols for Family Diagramming: Relationship Information

equally dominant and involved? Has one grandparent or parent cut off from his family to join the family of origin of his spouse? Does the nuclear family relate in a balanced way to both branches of the extended family? These are important questions. When a woman, for instance, does not want to associate with the family she was born into and, through marriage, joins a family she considers better than her own, the spousal relationship is already skewed and she is negating that part of her family that is within her and, hence, negating part of her heritage and her own self-esteem. Will she make up for the loss of her parents and siblings by binding her children to her? Does she fear they will cut her off, as she has done before them? And how will her husband play into this? However they handle it, the children see one side of the extended family accepted and the other side rejected, which gives them a message which they may follow in the future.

When one partner's diagram is completed, the therapist moves on to that of the spouse, usually in the next session. When they are both completed, the diagrams can be taped to the wall and the couple or family can explore together how the patterns mesh and conflict with each other. I keep the charts in the office to come back to again and again, adding and revising until the patterns are clearly understood, while helping family members to think systematically.

DIAGRAMMING STEPHEN'S FAMILY

Diagramming was essential for me to understand Mary's and Stephen's background, yet I did not want to start the process until they were calm enough to explore family patterns with me. I had suggested diagramming to them at the end of the second, third, and fourth sessions, tying my suggestions to patterns I saw in their interactions. The next four sessions, which included diagramming both their families, shifted us into a solid therapeutic alliance. There was a synergy to those four sessions, starting with charting Stephen's family and understanding how his patterns had developed. This is not unusual; diagramming families, when it is strategically planned, will often move therapy to a new level.

As I diagrammed, I not only elicited facts, but also fed back to them what I saw in terms of nodal points, triangles, parallels, and family rules, checking out my impressions with them. I was interested in creating a mutual discovery process in which each of them could step back and take a more objective view of the family's process.

Stephen was ready for this new stage by the fifth session (Figure 10). Both his parents were from middle European backgrounds, creative and talented, both starting artistic careers early which had provided self-fulfillment. Stephen's mother, however, had given up her career to concentrate her energies on her children. Stephen was the third of four siblings, with his two older married brothers, Edward and Leonard, living in California near his parents and his unmarried younger sister Laura living near Stephen.

Father was dominant when the two older sons, who became "Father's boys," were born, before his mother was hospitalized for depression. Following her illness, there was a restructuring of the power balance between the parents, and his father retreated. The split between the parents was reflected in the alliances formed with the children. Stephen, who considered himself his mother's favorite, and Laura were born after his mother's depression. They became "Mother's children," cutting Stephen off from the other males in the family and allying him with his mother and Laura. Father treated "his boys" harshly, even beating them at times, and he sent them to public schools. Mother bound the two youngest to

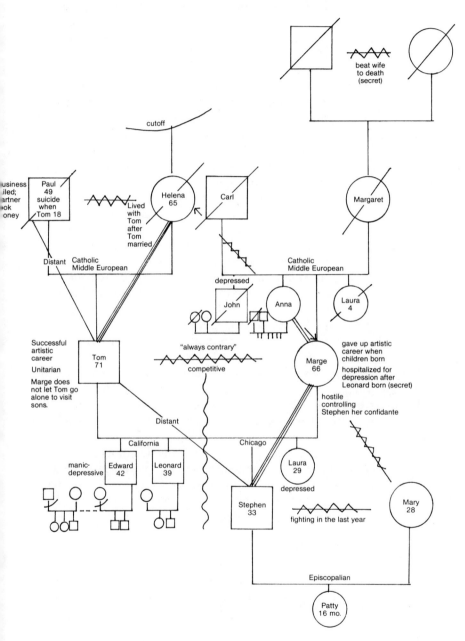

Figure 10. Stephen's Family Diagram

her by loyalty and obligation, providing private schools, music lessons, and special treats. The oldest son, Edward, was a manic-depressive, controlled by lithium. He and Laura, the youngest, had experienced more dysfunction than the middle sons.

Stephen spoke of his parents' relationship as "always contrary." There was violence on both sides of his family. His maternal great grandfather had beaten his great grandmother to death during a fit of bad temper, a family secret Stephen had only recently discovered. His paternal grandfather had committed suicide when Stephen's father was 18, contributing to a three-generation interlocking triangle that Stephen was struggling with. Stephen's father, an only son, had been distant from his father and allied with his mother, which contributed to the strained relationship with his wife, Stephen's mother, who then turned to her son Stephen for closeness. Stephen was the third of four siblings as his mother was before him. He and his mother each had a younger sister Laura, although his mother's sister had died as a child, and each also married an only child.

Stephen had been caught between his parents, loyal to his mother although resentful of her domination, and yearning for more contact with his father and brothers. His method of coping was to withdraw from her, screening out what he could not handle. He had not learned how to resolve conflict because he had no models for resolution. One can surmise that there was catastrophic expectation of violence and death on both sides of this family, if anger were to be expressed.

Religion had become one stage where family members could play out their roles. Stephen's parents were brought up in the Catholic faith. His mother continued as a Catholic, while his father left the Church when Stephen was 13 to become a Unitarian, thereafter disparaging Catholics. Father could act out his hostility to Mother indirectly through the Church. Stephen followed his father in this arena, showing disloyalty to his mother by joining his two brothers in marrying non-Catholic women, while Laura continued in her Catholic faith. Mary had been a Methodist in a family in which religion had not been emphasized. She and Stephen had compromised by joining the Episcopal Church.

Understanding Stephen's Family

The legacy of violence from earlier generations, including the restructuring of power between his father and mother after his mother's depression, had fed into the painful splits in Stephen's family of origin, dividing father and older sons from mother and younger children. The splits were internalized and were part of Stephen's self image. To survive as a child, he had developed a protective part in himself which directed him, at specific times, to withhold his attention and not to look or listen, as he had done with Mary in the first and third sessions, and as his mother had done before him, an interface he had been unaware of as he started therapy. This protective part had become entrenched, existing alongside a creative, thoughtful, efficient part that most people saw.*

The multigenerational projection process, described in Chapter 2 (Figure 5), was evident from Stephen's father's original family to Stephen's, with distance and conflict between paternal grandfather and grandmother, an overly close bond between Stephen's paternal grandmother and Stephen's father, and a distant relationship between Stephen's grandfather and Stephen's father. The same triangle was repeated between Stephen's father and mother with Stephen, forming interlocking triangles over three generations. Generational boundaries were breached, with Stephen's paternal grandparents colluding to designate Stephen's father to take Stephen's grandfather's place with his grandmother. In like manner, Stephen's parents also colluded to designate Stephen as a child-substitute for his father with his mother.

Since another generation had come into being with Patty, distance and conflict had been increasing between Stephen and Mary, with the beginning of a projection process which, if not changed, would doubtless continue into the next generation, especially if they had a son. If such relationships cannot be rebalanced, they lead progressively to more explosive tension, as primary loyalties remain entrenched with earlier generations.

DIAGRAMMING MARY'S FAMILY

Although we had planned to diagram Mary's family in the sixth session, we detoured to resolve a marital conflict, a not unusual occurrence. We came back to her family (Figure 11) in the seventh session to understand her background and explore how patterns from the two extended families both enhanced and interfered with their lives together.

Mary came from a quiet, cool and self-paced family, in marked contrast to Stephen's. She was attracted by Stephen's intensity, as he was by her calm and organized manner. Mary was the only child of parents of German heritage who met and married in their late thirties. She was

---

*Gestalt techniques can help clients reconstruct and consolidate such parts before changing their actions with their families. With Stephen, this was unnecessary. He was able, during therapy, to integrate the regressed parts by changing his actions directly with Mary and then with original family members.

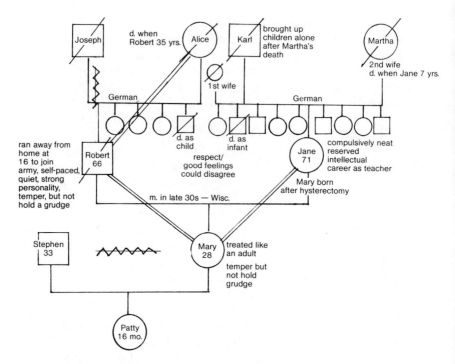

Figure 11. Mary's Family Diagram

also a very special child, born after her mother, who was then over 40, had had a partial hysterectomy and had given up expectations of child-bearing. Mary's mother, who resumed her career as a teacher when Mary was two, was compulsively neat, socially reserved, and intellectual. She pushed Mary academically and Mary excelled.

Mary's maternal grandmother had died early when Mary's mother was only seven, leaving her maternal grandfather, who had lost two wives through death, to bring up ten children by himself. Mary's mother, who was lost in the middle of the ten, had always felt strongly about family ties. She was now retired, living alone in her hometown and enjoying her daughter's family during occasional visits.

Mary's father had died six years before. He exhibited a strong personality and was warm, friendly and outgoing, idolizing Mary. Although he had a quick temper, he did not hold a grudge. When she was upset, Mary had always exploded like he did and had then been able, until recently, to resolve her anger. Her father was the oldest son with three younger sisters, close to his mother and competitive with his father, who also had a strong personality. Her father had run away from home at 16 to join the army, which he made his career. He had lived overseas before his marriage, although he had returned home several times to see his mother and did reconnect, to a minimal extent, with his father.

Mary's parents had had quite a good relationship and an enormous amount of respect for each other. They had also trusted her, treating her as an equal, allowing her the right to her opinion and not questioning her decisions. In this open atmosphere she had learned to listen and respond. She had not felt she needed to please her parents because her behavior pleased them automatically. This made it difficult for her to understand the approval-seeking in Stephen's family.

Mary's Interlock with Stephen

Mary came from a much more balanced family than Stephen did. She had grown up in a pleasant but controlled relationship reflecting her German heritage, with older parents who had already had interesting and fulfilling lives, and were settled in their ways. They let her into their world, but she had not experienced the excitement of a large and intense family from a middle European background, or the give and take of siblings and young parents which Stephen had known. Her mother had lost her mother early in life and no doubt had had to grow up prematurely, making the best of it by achievement in her career. Mary's father also had learned to make it on his own, leaving home at 16 and creating his own success.

Since Mary's parents had met and married after many of their goals were accomplished, they brought to their marriage the personal skills of partners who enjoyed working together. Mary had moved into their partnership in a child-adult role. This set her up for the overadequate role she later played in her marriage. All three accepted her role naturally because both parents had had to function as adults before they were grown. She learned to trust and be trusted and to listen and respond.

Mary had been attracted by the emotionality and creativity of Stephen's family, although she had little experience in dealing with the interlocking triangles which both excited and overwhelmed her. She retreated in the marital interface to old ways of responding with anger and tears.

Mary had naively believed that all problems could be worked out rationally because that had been her early experience. She had not been exposed, on an intimate level, to irrational, exciting people like Stephen's family and she had followed him into the entanglements. Part of their marital energy was bound up in this interface and unavailable for their forward movement through the family life cycle.

Uncovering, through diagramming, those early family patterns that still influence the present illuminates for the family member his position in the larger system and may give him a sense of the direction he wants to take. The process also contributes to his spouse's and children's understanding of the special pressures he is under. Thus diagramming can become for the family a shared experience, deepening their understanding of themselves as a system and giving the therapy a forward thrust.

CHAPTER 4

Influence of
Family Patterns on
Marital Patterns

Marriage brings diverse patterns from each partner's family of origin into a shared arena. The marital partners are called upon to define their new commitment vis-à-vis the values they learned in their original families, while each original family struggles to incorporate the new member. The joining of families through marriage gives both partners the opportunity to establish their individuality vis-à-vis a chosen other, a second chance to confront areas they did not complete in their original families, and an opportunity to experience aspects of life not encountered in their growing-up years.

If trust is to grow between spouses, a shared understanding of what is just and fair must evolve, with both partners becoming accountable for their own actions. Original family members may exert pressure on their adult child — the new spouse — if there have been unfulfilled obligations in past generations. Conflict may erupt between parent and child over loyalty to original family members. If past loyalties take precedence over the new marriage, further enmeshment may occur, continuing the imbalance. When either partner copes with the original family's emotionality by merger or cutoff, that spouse continues to be vulnerable to intense relationships in current life.

Stephen's difficulties stemmed from his enmeshment in his family of origin. Having learned to triangle in his family, he had used Mary to buffer his actions with his mother and sister. She had cooperated, trying to be helpful, and the system had boomeranged in escalating triangles. When she exploded, as her father had done before her, demanding Stephen's attention, he withdrew, screening her out as he had screened out his mother.

Differentiation was crucial for them both and can best be understood in relational terms as it includes the ability to rebalance generational and spousal commitments. Although Stephen usually functioned well in most parts of his life, including the professional area, he had not effected an emotional separation from his family of origin, was reactive to their automatic emotional system, and was easily stressed into dysfunction. Thus, he had not, in his intimate systems, established what he needed for his own development and growth. His family background had set him up for an underadequate role in marriage, as Mary's had set her up to be overadequate.

Although Mary's need for differentiation was not as obvious as Stephen's, she was, at the beginning of therapy, as tied to her family's way as he was to his, with her perfectionism, her obsessiveness, and her lack of spontaneity. Mary's anxiety was a red flag when she became mired in his unresolved interface.

RESOLVING A MARITAL CRISIS

It was predictable that when Stephen spent a whole session diagramming his family, Mary would want the next one to work on a major marital issue. They had been angrily avoiding each other for two days when they arrived. This sixth session, sandwiched between their family diagrams, was a major breakthrough and turning point in which, for the first time, they solved a problem in the session, breaking his family rule of letting things go on and on. Stephen highlighted this session in follow-up as the most significant event in therapy.

The incident was typical of their fights. When Len, a divorced mutual friend, had stopped by, Stephen had invited him to dinner. Mary was pleased and enjoyed the evening. Stephen was irritable, upset that he had asked Len, because he also wanted time alone with Mary and she was enjoying Len instead of him. Mary felt he was punishing her.

As we explored the situation, additional factors emerged. He had talked to his sister on the phone, feeling anger, which was new for him, but not letting her know. He had also initiated a satisfactory call to his mother and had stopped at the time he had planned. I expressed several thoughts: Just having contact with his sister and mother might make him susceptible to a current triangle; his new anger at Laura, his not expressing it, and the success with his mother might have made him more vulnerable. Sometimes people regress after success; it may be more scary than failure. After considering my ideas, he thought they might be correct.

I began to explore the boundaries they set for each other: Did he have any women friends? Was Mary jealous of them? He had women friends but both agreed Mary was not jealous. How about his relationship with

Len? He admitted to being jealous of Len's attention to Mary, though he liked Len, too. But Len was macho; Stephen did not trust him because Len viewed women as sex objects. When I asked Stephen if he trusted Mary, he wasn't sure.

At this, Mary's anger flared. She was trustworthy, she protested, and had been for nine years. She also liked Len; he was her friend. Stephen wanted to run her life; he had done it for years. She broke down in angry tears. Now it was hard for him to look at her and she was again complaining that he never listened.

As I watched his face, seeing him avoid her eyes, I saw his old familiar pattern emerging and knew there were ghosts in the room. I asked him if jealousy was a pattern between his parents. He was not aware of it. I taped his family diagram to the flip chart and looked for connections. Sure enough, his mother would not let his father visit either of Stephen's older brothers without her. If he grew up in a house where one partner limited the other, such restriction would probably seem normal. It was the old familiar triangle again, but this time he had transferred the triangle between his mother, father, and brother to himself, his wife, and their mutual friend.

There was silence as he absorbed the parallel. Then he nodded, agreeing that was where the jealousy was rooted. His mother was more jealous than he was but they both controlled others. He had not wanted father to visit his brothers, either, because he was jealous of their relationship with his father. He took the audiotape, which we used throughout the therapy, to replay at home. Then he hugged Mary and suggested they go out to dinner and talk.

WORKING TOWARDS CHANGE

After diagramming Mary's extended family, we had a thoughtful and productive eighth session, without blame. They now trusted the process, were willing to talk openly about their differences and vulnerabilities, and were establishing a new pattern of communication that Stephen had not experienced in his family, building on the healthy core of their marriage. They were increasingly becoming resources for each other, using skills they had already mastered in their professional lives. The fact that they kept regressing allowed them to relearn over and over the irrefutable basic premise of each person's responsibility for his own change. They needed to learn through experience that either could initiate new action and change old patterns, and that their working changes out together could move the process forward at a faster pace.

Stephen started the eighth session by talking about the striking differences between their families, with hers cool and slow and his polarized and intrusive. Despite the triangling and confusion, he admired the productivity and creativity in his family. His and Mary's parents had never liked each other. When he had told his mother he was getting married, she had cried, felt jealous and left out. Their parents had only seen each other at the wedding. I said their parents' antagonism would be a problem only if Mary and Stephen allowed themselves to be used as relayers in triangles between the families.

The central theme of family contact, as well as its key role in the differentiation process, was raised when I inquired as to whether Stephen had ever visited his family alone. He had not and, in the last year, had even left it up to Mary how often they visited his family. Neither was comfortable with the plan. As his parents were getting old, it was important to Stephen to see them. Mary did not want to be responsible for their visits to his family, but she was not satisfied with how Stephen handled them. Mary's central complaint was Stephen's adaptive role, reflecting his father's stance, resulted in more contact than either was comfortable with, and prevented them from spending time with friends, other family members, or by themselves.

I encouraged him to consider a visit to his family for a limited period without Mary as his buffer. He could practice in person those principles he had been using via phone: spending time alone with each family member, initiating and ending contacts according to his own plan, not talking about anyone not present, being aware of his anxiety, and moving away voluntarily when anxiety increased.

I pointed out the imbalance in the way he perceived his relationship with his father and mother. He saw his mother as the problem, with his father helplessly adapting. Stephen was not aware of the part his father played in letting his mother dominate and by not setting his own limits. I surmised that his father must be more comfortable hiding behind his mother's intrusiveness, which was not surprising if one remembered the tragedy Stephen's father was faced with when he was on the brink of adulthood. His father allowed his mother to take the heat off of him, and Stephen had followed his father's example with Mary. It relieved both Father and Stephen of taking responsibility for their own actions and had its parallel in Stephen's manipulating Mary into a limit-setting position with his parents.

I asked Mary if there was anything she wanted from Stephen. She would like Stephen not to let things go on and on. Was it a practice in his family to go on and on? Yes. I put this family rule on the flip chart and he added two more. I added what it would take to break the family rules:

Family Rules
let things go on and on
approach others expecting anger
rush, yet never be on time

Break Family Rules
take initiative and make the first move
pace self and take your time

I commented that the model for breaking his family rules must have been one of his out-of-awareness motives for marrying Mary, yet she often complained he never used her as a resource. She did not think she would be angry if he took initiative.

I asked what Stephen wanted from Mary. Her goals for him were too high, she was too perfectionistic, and she wanted him to change too fast. He wanted her to slow down and respect the way he was. She admitted what he said was true, and that these were traits she had learned in her family. She agreed to watch and pace herself.

At the end, she had a final request of him: She would like him to tell her how *he* felt, not how he thought *she* would feel when he approached her. He did not respond, but it was clear that he had heard.

PROBLEMS IN PARENTHOOD

As Stephen and Mary had approached parenthood, they had been even more deeply out of phase with the family life cycle. Birth is a life cycle event which rallies opposing forces to battle for primary loyalty, if the new parents have not already resolved these issues in their original families. In the ninth session they reported conflict between them for two days after the previous session, stemming from their long-standing conflict over spending vacations with his parents. I acknowledged that I had stepped into the middle of their old conflict by encouraging Stephen to visit his family alone before Mary was ready to trust how he would handle it.

Mary described their worst visit to his family, which occurred one month before Patty was born. They had made plans for a day's outing with friends when Stephen's mother had announced she had not had any time alone with Stephen and wanted him to stay at home with her. Stephen had given in when she became hysterical, and Mary found herself sent off to the beach with her friends. Mary had lost that battle to the unwilling coalition of Stephen with his mother. That day had been terrible for Stephen, too, who had felt helpless as his mother continually criticized both him and Mary. Mary was angry when she returned, pressing to leave town that night. When Stephen refused, the tension had increased; they had left early the next day.

Stephen, caught between the two women, had backed off. This was when he had assigned to Mary the job of planning future visits to his family. His reparation, in giving Mary control, further unbalanced the ledger, setting wife and mother against each other. I underscored the closeness of his mother's blow-up to Patty's birth and identified Patty as the start of a new generation, making room for new pathological triangles to evolve unless they consciously detriangled themselves.

Because Stephen's family's pattern was to put the mother/child relationship before the couple relationship, there was a regressive pull for him to put mother before wife, which foreshadowed a future parallel, when he might place child before wife. Any movement in this direction raised alarm in Mary, who was sensitive to and expected equality between spouses because of her own family experience. Yet, because of his family experience, the parent/child relationship (or the flip of child/parent) was more familiar and easier for Stephen than that of spouse/spouse.

Mary was also upset with Stephen's desire to spend all his vacations with his family. Both her parents had been self-contained and independent, not especially close to their families. Her pattern from childhood had been for the three of them — mother, father, and daughter — to enjoy themselves together. She wanted this for Stephen, Patty, and herself.

Over the years, and especially after their child was born, Stephen had longed for the old closeness with his family. Yet he felt safer when he had a buffer, and he had drawn Mary in as a relayer to his mother and sister, in the same way his mother had used him with his father when he was a child. The same process, the relayer triangle, that I had explained to them in the second session also applied to Stephen when he was a child in his family of origin (Figure 12). Stephen had come from an entrenched system where mother and father had ceased talking to each other about important controversial issues. He had learned as a child to relay covert antagonistic feelings from his mother to his father, which kept him distant from father, although he longed for closeness. When he married, although he distanced geographically from his original family, he was still emotionally triangled, not communicating directly on important issues with family members.

With the birth of a child, however, Stephen had unwittingly induced Mary into the position he had occupied as a child. As Mary had accepted this dependent position, she resonated to the conflicting messages with increasing anxiety and then anger. Discharging her anger, however, did

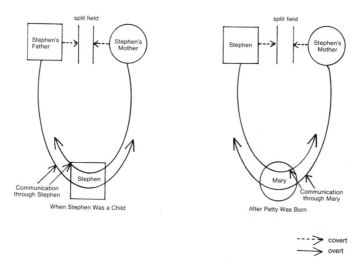

Figure 12. Two-Generation Relayer System

not give her relief, as it had in her family of origin. She felt helpless and scared, unlike her usual competent self. There had been a power shift; she had lost her equal position with Stephen, as well as his attention and support.

As Stephen withdrew, screening Mary out in the same way he had screened out his mother, he also felt the change in his interface with Mary. He became emotionally reactive to her, as he was to his mother, did not carry through on commitments he made, and left her to fend off his family. In struggling to relieve the anxiety of the moment, both gave up control of themselves.

The same imbalance that had existed between Stephen's father and mother, which I pointed out to them in the eighth session, had also become increasingly evident between Stephen and Mary since Patty's birth. As Stephen continued to see Mary as his mother, he avoided looking at or listening to her and misinterpreted how she would react and what she would do.

Both had increasingly polarized. She stressed her logical and reasonable part and wanted everything to be neat, orderly, and predictable. She expected to have fights and to have them blow over quickly. She felt blameless in the way she listened to him, and she responded with anger when his actions did not meet her expectations. He yearned for life to be multifaceted, spontaneous, unscheduled, and exciting, all without anger. He withdrew and became depressed and helpless when her expectations overwhelmed him, and then he would stop listening. They had not been able to find a satisfactory way to be together.

TRIANGLE WITH A SIBLING

Both Mary and Stephen had allowed themselves to be caught in this web, coping with his original family members on his family's terms, with Stephen maintaining the imbalance by triangling and manipulating as the family members did. Their current problem in the ninth session was whether to invite Laura for Easter, an important Catholic holiday for Stephen's mother and sister. Stephen considered holidays as family days, and they usually invited Laura to whatever they were planning. Mary liked to spend holidays with friends.

They described Laura as nervous and unpredictable; she did not decide if she would accept invitations until the last minute. When she appeared, she often acted like a little girl; then Stephen would become anxious, pushing her to grow up. I saw it as an old family game, designed to keep contact and distance at the same time. Stephen admitted that his mother expected him to invite Laura, which he had not disclosed to Mary before. This, of course, set up a triangular situation with Laura and his mother, and a double triangle with Mary, preventing him from dealing directly with Laura. I wondered aloud if his mother was playing her role in the family's religious drama, pulling Stephen over to her side.

I asked for an example of a visit with Laura that had gone well. Recently, he had been fixing his car and she had dropped by. They chatted while he worked and neither had been anxious. The problem arose when they asked her for dinners and holidays. At my probing, he remembered how tense dinnertimes at his parents' house had been for both of them. He was realizing how pervasive his mother's wishes were in his relationship with his sister and how guilty he felt when he did not carry out those wishes.

His guilt was especially strong with his mother, leading him to let her go on and on, without stopping her. He knew his oldest brother Edward left when he had had enough from his mother. Mary added that his other brother Leonard used humor to keep distance. I commented that Laura also left when she had had enough; that Laura did not come to Stephen's house if she was too upset, and left early if she became anxious. He was realizing he could learn from all three siblings.

I wondered aloud how to change the context so he would not be triangled with Laura and his mother. Could he take the initiative, asking Laura to go to a movie or concert on neutral ground, something both of them would like? Could he remain cool and honestly not care whether she went, thus getting out of dutiful family patterns? The steps became clear: 1) take initiative; 2) plan with Mary so both agreed whether he could go alone or both would go; 3) ask Laura in such a way that he would be comfortable, whether she went or not; 4) enjoy themselves, with or without Laura; 5) do not expect Laura to change. Stephen and Mary made a decision together that he would invite Laura to a concert the Friday before Easter, and they would not invite her to the house on Easter day when they were entertaining friends.

ANOTHER MARITAL CRISIS

Mary was flushed and angry as she arrived at the tenth session. The issue was still Stephen's adaptive role in his family; he had broken the agreement they had made in the last session. He was withdrawn again, not meeting her eyes. When Stephen had called Laura to go to the concert on Friday and found that she had already decided to go to church, he invited her to drop by for a drink on Easter. He had not told Mary because he did not think Laura would come. On Easter Laura called, wanting to drop off packages for their parents. Stephen again invited her for a glass of wine. He did not understand Mary's anger; there were only two calls from Laura; she had only stayed five minutes. Why did Mary have to be in on every little thing?

I stopped him, reminding them they had made an agreement together last week and he had changed it unilaterally. The number of calls and length of time Laura was there were irrelevant. They had made a decision not to invite Laura for Easter; if he had wanted to change their plans, he needed to talk to Mary.

There was silence as he assimilated my words. He saw how he undercut himself by saying one thing and doing another. Even more important, he recognized that he had given lip service in our previous session to not inviting Laura for Easter when he had not really agreed; he still considered Easter a "family" time. He was more deeply tied into his mother's family and religious traditions than he had admitted, even to himself.

At this point Mary exploded. She yelled that they had spent a whole hour on this subject the week before and she thought they had agreed. She might as well leave; he wasn't ever going to hear her; she couldn't trust him; she would never know where she stood.

Now he was upset. He said he knew he had been at fault by not following through, but he was only now coming to grips with what the holiday meant to him. Then, as he tried to think it through, she got demanding and started threatening and it was hard for him to think. He said she wanted too much too soon. I told her that, although he had broken his agreement, now she was overreacting. I pointed out that when it heated up between them, they both became dysfunctional.

EVALUATION

Mary and Stephen were beginning to evaluate their changes by the eleventh session. Their fight at Easter, they decided, was a regression in an upward swing. Stephen described changes in Mary: She was taking better care of herself, not pushing him. When he was in a bad mood and could not hear her, she left him alone. Mary agreed she was changing and described how much more decisive Stephen was with his family. Laura, in an unprecedented move, had asked them for dinner and he had not felt anxious or angry during the evening.

Stephen saw himself as more effective; he had been elected to an important office in a professional organization. He was paying attention to his anxiety and the intensity he felt, monitoring it, and backing off when it escalated. He also knew he was working too hard and was not getting enough exercise and recreation. He was now recognizing his difficulty in saying "no," finding himself going places and not wanting to be there. Both agreed they liked doing things by themselves as well as together.

I raised the question of spacing their sessions out to every other week as we moved into middle phase (Kramer, 1968b). It was not necessary to see them often as it was to see them over time to monitor their changes. They decided to play tennis together on alternate weeks, replacing our sessions.

We continued to explore their changes in the twelfth session. Stephen described Mary as more sensitive to his bad moods; as she remained uninvolved, he came out of them sooner, appreciating her afterwards. He had been calling his mother at irregular intervals and found she was not always prepared to talk to him. He realized she got into bad moods, too, becoming overly intense and not knowing how to shut it off. As he understood her worry and struggle, his anxiety diminished. He recognized the contagion for him in her free-floating anxiety and saw that he needed to remain uninvolved, as Mary was doing with him.

He was conscious, however, of a need on his part to worry about money, as his father did. He recognized that if he stopped worrying about money, he would then worry about something else. His mother was now worrying about whether to go to the beach for the summer. In seeing his parents' endless anxiety more objectively, Stephen was finding it easier not to get involved.

Stephen and Mary had asked Laura to events they both wanted to attend. He still felt angry when Laura decided at the last moment not to come. When I asked if his anger had to do with his parents' expectations, he said yes. Especially at holidays he felt "poor Laura" should be taken care of. Mary reminded him, to my surprise, that Laura was a beautiful woman, intelligent and talented, with a responsible job. Laura had recently called Mary about a book publisher and Mary had related to her efficient side. Mary said Laura furnished her own transportation so she could leave when she wanted to; that Laura liked to "stay on the edge" with the family and not be counted on. I agreed that she probably got too intense, like her mother.

CHANGES WITH FAMILY OF ORIGIN

As Mary understood his family's influence on Stephen, she recognized she had not been as understanding of him as she could have been. She also saw how her efforts to help had aggravated the problem. He was realizing how much he was reacting to his family rules — putting mother before wife, avoiding conflict at all costs, and not talking directly to the person he had a problem with — rather than depending on his own considered decisions.

As Stephen began to take direct action with each family member, he became responsible for those actions and began to correct his part in the generational imbalance (Figure 13). It took courage for him to defy the covert family rule of primary loyalty to the original family and to be accountable for decisions he knew were fair. His first move had been to take responsibility for beginning and ending phone contacts. He rented a car while visiting his family so that he could come and go, free of subtle obligations. He was alert to his and Mary's need for space, staying in his brother's house rather than his parents' and firmly asking that his parents stay in a hotel when they visited him so he could remain more objective.

Mary had changed as well, moving out of her overinvolvement with his family as Stephen put her first. She realized that she had also overinvolved him with her family; he was relieved when she did not expect him to visit her mother's relatives with them, as he usually did. On her last visit to her mother's she had been able to be more objective, recog-

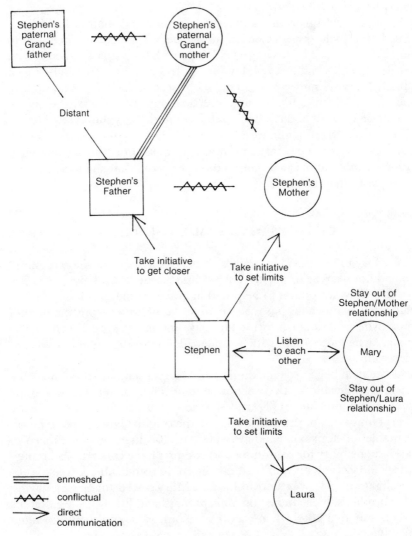

Figure 13. Interruption of Transgenerational Projection Process
in Stephen's Family

nizing how compulsive her mother had become, walking around cleaning up after Patty. Her mother used to be tempered by her father, who had been permissive and easygoing. Mary saw in herself some of the same compelling need to organize her life, which she knew irritated Stephen.

Stephen's father was a model for him. It appeared, as we talked, that there was a family rule that one could be efficient as an individual outside the family but not inside. Inside they were to remain unclear, make assumptions, and avoid direct dealings. This rule clarified his family's unpredictability and Stephen's regressive behavior with his mother, Laura, and Mary.

Stephen was learning not to follow the rules automatically, becoming more objective, able to give more appropriately to his parents and his siblings. His ability to view them in a more balanced way, seeing both strengths and weaknesses, allowed him to accept those strengths and weaknesses in himself, repairing his own self-esteem. Although his mother at first resisted his efforts and had sometimes made threats, she eventually accepted his changes and his firmer stance.

I often discuss with couples the possibility of bringing in members of their families of origin to our sessions, either to address issues they find difficult to handle by themselves or to acquaint their families with our process. Stephen brought up my involvement with his family of origin in the first session when he asked if he should tell his mother they were in therapy. I challenged him to take his own responsibility for his changes, saying that if his family operated under a rule that allowed women to manipulate men, then his mother would think I was influencing him instead of her. We did not discuss either family attending sessions. If their progress had stopped, I would have raised the possibility. The subject of having parents and/or siblings attend sessions as consultants to the therapy will be discussed in more detail in Chapter 7.

CHANGES IN THE MARRIAGE

As Stephen began to control himself in his relationship to his mother and Laura, and as Mary disentangled herself, both began confronting each other on their marital issues. They had moved from a pattern of her pursuing him and him avoiding her (a game Stephen's mother and Stephen had played for years) to a more functional pattern of negotiation and willingness to change.

In the fourth session Stephen checked out several times his fear of Mary's reactions and, at her prompting, acknowledged his ambiguity around his need for distance. In checking out his fears, he began finding that his assumptions were often unfounded. When he questioned her trustworthiness in the sixth session, she became angry and he reacted to her as he did to his mother. In the eighth session, after Mary had asked him not to let unresolved issues go on and on, he told her that her goals for him were too high; that he wanted her to slow down and respect the way he was.

After learning to set limits with his mother, he was able, by the fourteenth session, to set limits with Mary, telling her he had been embarrassed when she told her friends how upset his mother had been when they had gotten engaged. When he asked her not to talk about his family, she agreed he was right and apologized; she had not realized that it bothered him.

By the eighteenth session, when I brought up termination, they were talking seriously about alternative approaches to unblock their communication. Mary was still uneasy about their interaction, continuing to maintain that Stephen did not hear her concerns. She wanted more help — both a cleaning woman and an additional half-day of daycare for Patty — so that she could have more time for herself. For Stephen, there was more to it than that; he was bothered by the way she presented her problems to him; she had solutions before she ever told him about the problem. He insisted that he did listen now when she brought him problems at the beginning stage and they could brainstorm together.

We talked about how they still became blocked. She had a tendency to duplicate her mother's pattern, planning far ahead and organizing her life; he liked new ideas to emerge and life to unfold. They made a plan that led to a new level of interaction: For the next few weeks she would bring problems to him and he would listen, with each challenging the other if he or she was not satisfied.

They were each able to reveal their polarized parts. Stephen had begun to feel anger rather than anxiety towards Laura and also experienced anger towards his father. In the fourth session it was Stephen who was worried about Mary's reaction if he left her out of his interactions with others; yet, in the twentieth session, Mary was concerned that Stephen might take it personally if she left their bed early in the morning to have more time alone. Stephen was planning ahead, anticipating reactions. When they celebrated his birthday while visiting his parents, he insisted they all go out for dinner to avoid the tension of special preparations at home. Mary was increasingly flexible, willing to consider moving to the west coast if she could find a suitable job.

In this last phase of therapy, Mary and Stephen were dealing with transitory imbalance, negotiating better ways of living together, and resolving situations that had caused resentment between them. Instead of automatically reproducing familial patterns in their marital interface, they experimented with a variety of ways of being together. They also planned activities alone, each claiming more freedom for self, and found they both enjoyed it. They were solving problems as they came up and were using the sessions to look at differences between them. Stephen complained in the nineteenth session that she rushed too much; that she was too busy. She defended herself; she liked to be busy. Then she became thoughtful, talked about her periodic migraine headaches, and admitted that she did push herself.

Neither Stephen nor Mary wanted a long therapeutic experience; it was important to both of them that they do as much as possible for themselves. They were effective professionals and had been able to use their resources everywhere except in the family, a stance following Stephen's family rule, which he had discovered in the twelfth session, that family members could be efficient as individuals outside the family but not inside.

Follow-up questionnaires indicated that marital changes continued after the therapy ended, even in areas that had not been addressed. They had not raised sex as a problem and I had not pursued it. Yet Stephen's ability to initiate closeness with his father and limit-setting with his mother paid off in his sexual relationship with Mary, in which, shortly after termination, he was able to initiate sex and tolerate refusal from Mary. Within six months Mary was pregnant with their second child, planning the delivery so she could take maternity leave at the most convenient time.

FOLLOW-UP

I had been looking for a way to evaluate therapy with couples like Mary and Stephen, where there was a strong emphasis on the interface with family of origin. I had developed a follow-up questionnaire for members of "The Therapist's Own Family" seminar that I had been leading for five years.* The seminar and basic questionniare will be described in Part III. Using that questionnaire as a base, I developed a similar one for therapy with couples which I gave to Stephen and Mary at termination. Stephen returned his three months after therapy ended and Mary sent hers after eight months, saying in an accompanying note: "I put it off because it felt like objectifying the experience and I didn't want to evaluate it."

---

*See Chapter 12.

Stephen's Changes

Stephen described his most significant event in therapy:

"Probably having a fight *in the session* and seeing 1) that it could be resolved; 2) that Mary could have *another* resource — in the middle of a fight — besides me; 3) that the fight could quickly end and I could quickly feel better after a few perspective-restoring words from the therapist. This was significant because it proved that things *can be resolved*, and quickly. Also, the therapist's gentle support and genuineness at that time (even her own frustration) was helpful."

Stephen described the impact of his changes with members of his family, in his work situation, and with the therapist:

With Mother: "I am able to distinctly separate *her* anxiety from my own — that is, I can remain calm, or even empathize, without becoming fused. Also, I do not have to 'zoom' in so close or remain that way. I can easily shift to a comfortable distance now. This is extremely important if we are to have good visits. I have less guilt."

With Father: "Though I did not feel I needed to work on this much, now I feel I can get angry at him to his face (in fact, I never got angry — I always thought he could do no wrong). This allows for a much more real adult-to-adult relationship."

With brothers: "Although I did little work with them during therapy, our relationships have been changing since. I recently stayed with my older brother for a week and he was not the threatening person he used to be. I am now relating to my next older brother like a peer; we can talk about our problems together."

With sister: "I'm not anxious around Laura anymore. This is a BIG change. I get more openly angry, but not irresponsibly, with her. For a while, I found it hard to continue unilaterally working at this relationship, since she never initiated anything, yet appeared to want me to. In the last few months I have been getting along with Laura much better. We now have lunch weekly. Not long ago I asked her for advice about layouts for a project of mine, which is her area of expertise. We have been working on it together."

With wife: "Our life together continues to get better. Situations are so much clearer to me. I am more tolerant of her, less angry, and able to plan better. But, most importantly, I realize how I had subtly been assigning *her* decision-making responsibilities while I seemed to make decisions (I was quite clever that way!). Then I would blame her for the decision. Now we are no longer sticking our noses in each other's business. Improvement in sex life and communication in this area: shortly after termination I was able to directly initiate sex and tolerate refusal without feeling bad or angry."

In work relationships: "I am more open/self-disclosing with my patients; more optimistic in my private beliefs and behavior with them; and, at times, more structured in sessions. My career is moving well."

Reactions, pro and con, about the therapist: "She was always willing to work on issues with us — any issues. She conveyed the impression of *really* listening — and obviously she did hear the real issues at hand. She moved along at a comfortable pace. I liked her self-disclosure regarding her own marriage."

Overall, Stephen liked the predictability and familiarity of the three-way meetings, the safeness of it. He said he had matured greatly and wished they had had therapy eight years before, when they were first married. He described change he thought might enhance the format:

"Opportunities for individual sessions — perhaps one required session built into the format. I felt sometimes that I monopolized the sessions — without much empathy expressed by Mary at those times — hence my assumption that she did not care to be there then."

Mary's Changes

Mary described her most significant event:

"Two things: 1) The acknowledgment that there *was* a problem in our relationship. I'd been complaining about it for years — but thought maybe my expectations were just off the wall; that I could never expect any more from Stephen than he had been giving; that he would always be what I saw as hopelessly tied to his family. It was significant because as soon as I knew that my complaints about lack of attention and involvement with me were indeed valid, and began to understand the reasons for them, I was able to start to trust Stephen again and not be constantly angry at him. 2) My ease in being able to pull out of improper communications with Stephen's family and how quickly that had an impact on things. I really felt proud and hopeful when I saw how fast the impact of my getting out of triangled relationships with Stephen and his family made me feel better and helped Stephen be more responsible, which made him feel better."

Mary also described the impact of her changes with members of her family, in her work situation and with the therapist:

With Mother: "I think we have a more comfortable threesome now — with Stephen, my mother and myself. It was never bad, but I think that Stephen functions more comfortably with fewer 'shoulds,' which makes the visiting easier on me. Stephen and I don't triangle each other in dealing with my mother — an added bonus from all the specific work of dealing with triangles in his family."

With husband: "I feel much closer to Stephen now. He's more responsive and in touch with my feelings, often by his own observations, not always needing to be told. He becomes less responsive when he's overworked, ill, or having family of origin problems. But at those times I try to leave him alone and arguments are much less frequent and tend not to escalate. I am usually able to catch his occasional guilt-inducing remarks very quickly, responding in some humorous manner, and don't get hysterical or resentful about them. I am now working on trying to talk about differences, schedules, complaints about housework, etc., more in terms of my feelings, without blaming Stephen. I think I've gotten better at that."

With daughter: "I think my relationship with her has improved as a result of therapy. I feel closer to her and pleased that Stephen and I are really working very hard together to raise her and provide a healthy environment."

In work relationships: "I'm no longer distracted by home issues as I was for a while. I frequently meet Stephen for lunch and it's a great break and good time for us to have meaningful conversations when we're alert and don't have to get a babysitter. I've also had a second important promotion at work."

Reactions, pro and con, about the therapist: "She was very supportive of both of us, able to acknowledge our feelings as valid, while at the same time helping to instruct us in ways to change patterns so we could communicate better with each other and with our families. I very much appreciated the times she was self-disclosing — referring to her own family of origin, getting cleaning help, having family back to visit, etc. That made the therapy more comfortable and human for me and implied a trust and bond between her and us. She was clearly concerned about each of us and our progress. I really liked the diagramming and cognitive instructive approach to learning about what goes on in families. On several occasions I would have liked some quicker intervention in a session when we were at a deadend in a conflict with each other."

Overall, Mary liked the combination of current and family issues. She liked the instruction — family diagrams, triangling diagrams, etc., which made her feel that they were not unusual, which in itself was a hopeful sign, especially at the beginning of therapy. She liked the special instruction for changing patterns of communication and being able to work on immediate problems within the framework of a long-range plan for the therapy. She felt from the beginning that they were really responsible for their own changes. Mary described changes that would enhance the therapy:

"I wish we'd brought Patty with us once as we discussed. Not so much to do any work involving her, but because I feel so strongly that she will benefit all of her life from the work we did in our therapy."

I was conscious throughout of the therapeutic interface — those issues from my own family that overlapped with Stephen's and Mary's experiences in theirs. I referred briefly at times, as I often do in the later stages of therapy, to parallel processes that have been problems for me, both with my family of origin and in my marriage. In follow-up both commented on my self-disclosure, with Mary saying that it implied a trust and bond between us, which I also believe is true. Those areas I referred to explicitly in our therapy were only a small part of the therapeutic interface that I was aware of. Having changed my relationship to my own parents and siblings, I was sensitive to many nuances of their struggle. After I describe my own family interface in Part II, I will refer back to the therapy with Mary and Stephen in Chapter 10 and fill in those relevant parallels from my own background.

CHAPTER 5

Strategies for Change

Families define their problems in many ways. They may be conscious from the beginning of therapy, as Stephen and Mary were, of dysfunctional patterns from the family of origin which interfere in the marriage. Spouses may resist creating a functional marital system by holding onto the security of the family each knew as a child. Anxiety and fear are aroused when departing from the old familiar ways, even though habitual patterns have been painful.

Spouses who enter therapy are often not aware of their unrealistic expectations of and their intense focus on each other. It seems so simple to each — if only the other would change! They may be highly conflictual, each insisting he or she is right. As therapy begins, each is focused on the therapist, hoping the therapist will see the situation through her eyes. There may be a dominant partner, with the acquiescent one feeling hopeless, depressed, symptomatic, and uncertain that she will be heard. Or both spouses may unite in an enmeshed twosome, focusing their efforts on influencing the therapist to help them change a child who is carrying the symptoms for the family.

MOTIVATION AND TIMING

To the question, "When should I begin working with families on extended family issues?", I answer that it depends on a number of variables: whether the family's goals include problems obviously related to the family of origin; whether the therapist and family can solve the existing problems quickly through other methods; and the therapist's ability to provide a safe atmosphere together with the family's readiness to enter un-explored areas.

Therapy is most effective when it starts with the problem the family brings. If members see no connection between their extended family and their current problems, they will be resistant to or uninterested in even talking about their original families and will present those relationships as satisfactory with no problems, or as fixed and unchangeable and not worth spending time on. The first task is to deal with the current situation and help them find immediate relief. In this context the therapist can build a therapeutic alliance and be aware of those areas where current problems are likely to be manifestations of transgenerational patterns, connect these to the problems, and bring them to the family's attention as they emerge.

As Therapy Begins

When family members mention their parents or siblings in passing, I ask for more information. I start with whatever they bring, comment on it, and connect the observations they give me. If they make no reference to their original families, I may observe, "I haven't heard you mention any member of either of your families," and see what this elicits. If a husband mentions his mother, I may say, without expecting an answer, "Sometimes I will want to understand more about how your mother fits into your marital problems." I reflect on connections I see: "My hunch is that the problems you are having with your wife are reminiscent of problems you had as a child with one of your parents"; or I may ask, "Was there a similar issue for you in your family as you were growing up?" As I know them better, I may make a prediction: "If you remain cut off from your father and your son sees this as a continuing pattern, is it possible that he may someday cut off from you?" I explain family diagramming as a tool for understanding family patterns and look for an opening to engage them in this process.

If the presenting problem can be solved in a few sessions and they are satisfied, it may not be necessary to go more deeply into family of origin issues. I work with many families who stop after short-term treatment and who are not interested in further exploration. In the final session, however, I give them feedback on both the positive changes they have made and areas that may become problematic in the future, including comments on original family patterns that may be interfacing with their current relationship. I let them know I will be available if they want to come back at some future time.

During Middle Phase

When therapist and family are able to solve the immediate problem, a number of families find that new issues have emerged that they want to explore. Then therapy can move into a middle phase, where the goal is growth and differentiation for each member. Working with original family issues fits naturally into this growth phase. In fact, it may be only at this stage that individuals can begin to acknowledge or even to recognize that extended family dynamics are influencing their current lives.

Family of origin work is a natural second stage with conflictual couples. As the therapist helps them separate emotionally from each other, the fighting subsides and the emptiness that was masked by their conflict emerges. Both spouses need to live with this emptiness rather than focusing on the other, using their energy to further develop their adult selves, which can be done effectively in relation to the extended family.

When spouses are seen together in sessions during this phase, each can better understand the problems the partner has in his or her own individuation and how their patterns fit together. In this way they can continue connecting intrapsychic and family of origin work with the current issues in their relationship. As each differentiates, sooner or later each knows whether he or she wants to reconnect and recourt or to separate and divorce. Since each has watched the other's progress, both are more ready for the outcome.

If the presenting problem has not been solved after 10 or 12 sessions, the therapist can be more emphatic in recommending that the next step be family of origin work. If a therapeutic alliance has developed, family members are often willing to take another tack and begin a cooperative exploration. However, when a family is still in crisis, the therapist may lose rapport if she concentrates on issues concerning the original family when the members do not see these are relevant. I am more likely to follow the family's lead, waiting until the crisis is settled before such exploration. Yet, sometimes I wonder if the crises continue to escalate to keep us from investigating further into these crucial areas.

BRIEF THERAPY AS A FOLLOW-UP TO CRISIS THERAPY

The Browns, whom I saw 13 years ago with Chuck as co-therapist, were caught up in one crisis after another. Joe and Edna had been married for 18 years and had four children, eight through 15. Joe had worked with his father and brother in the family business for many years. The couple came to therapy when Edna discovered Joe had been gambling compulsively for years and was deeply in debt. We had 47 treatment sessions over the period of a year. During this time, in addition to his giving up gambling, their teenage daughter Anna ran away, and Joe had a heart attack and by-pass surgery, followed by a traumatic reaction to medication. As he recovered, he decided to leave the family business and start on his own as a freelance writer. At that point, therapy was terminated for financial reasons.

We had talked about their families of origin from time to time without much effect. There had always been a crisis that took center stage. Four months after termination they returned for three follow-up sessions. Although they were not in crisis at this point, neither was satisfied with the way their life was moving. Joe had gotten a number of freelance assignments and his future looked good, yet he was not finishing the assignments and delivering them. He had no time or energy left for Edna and the children. We saw his old script as a loser being reenacted and began probing into his relationship with his original family:

Joe: Something is preventing me from completing the jobs.

Edna: Your work patterns are changing, but since you work in the house, it takes discipline.

Joe: Am I going to be able to make it? It's the first time I've not been supported by my brother, and the money we're living on now has not come from writing. We have yet to exist for a month on my writing.

Jan: If you allow yourself success in freelance writing, will you also allow yourself additional success enjoying your family?

Joe: This worries me.

Chuck: I wonder what this has to do with your feeling of dependency on your own family.

Joe: It had not occurred to me.

Chuck: When you were a loser before in your work, your dad or brother picked you up.

Joe:How does it apply here?

Chuck: That's what is happening.

Edna: I never thought of that. It's the first time you're totally independent.

Jan: What have your contacts with your father and brother been recently?

Joe: Miniscule. Once in a great, great while. It's not much of a personal relationship. We don't know how to relate to each other. Dad is old and sick and ready to die. He's living on half a heart.

Chuck: How does that sit with you? How is it related to your own heart?

Joe: There's no relationship.

Chuck: I'm thinking of the parallels there, too.

Joe: He follows what I do. (He gives examples.)
Chuck: Who's modeling for whom?
Joe: I model for him.
Jan: When did the switch come?
Joe: He had a pushy style. I followed him. (thoughtful pause) The switch
     came when we got married. He was jealous about losing his son.
     He was angry at Edna for about six or seven years. He was a free-
     lance writer when I was a kid. The roles are reversed.
Chuck: The parallels have a lot to do with what is going on now.
Joe: Where will it get us to know it?
Chuck: To figure out who you are and who he is and what you can do
     in the relationship with you and Edna.
Joe: My goals are a better sex life and to enjoy our times together more.
Chuck: One of the things that keeps you from doing that is your hook
     to your family. It's stronger than you realize. Your father and
     brother are always in the background and you deal with them by
     avoidance. You don't tell your brother what you think and, with
     your father, almost never. When it's tough to deal with them, then
     it also hangs you up in your relationship with Edna.

Joe was enmeshed in his family of origin, with diffuse boundaries between him and his father in which they interchangeably played child/
parent roles but did not meet each other as adults on equal ground. This
same muddiness permeated Joe's relationship with Edna, interfering in
their development of a satisfying sexual relationship and in his handling
of the financial responsibility for his family.

Joe's skepticism gave us an opportunity to explain the connections.
We encouraged him to become aware of his fear of success and his dependency on his family and to recognize that the pattern between his
father and himself, in which each modeled for the other without knowing how to relate to the other, had kept them hooked together and had
affected his relationship with Edna.

DIFFERENTIATION

Bowen speaks of opposing life forces — those towards growth and autonomy and those towards dependency and emotional closeness. To differentiate is to achieve a balance between these forces. When a person
defines self in her family, she remains emotionally connected and also
observes herself, controlling her actions according to her own plan, thus
changing the part she plays in the family process. The assumption is that
if at least one person can change his or her emotional functioning in the

family of origin, then the system will shift so that previous dysfunctional patterns can change and that person will be able to function more flexibly in current and future relationships.

There is a three-step process that Bowen describes, which is helpful for clients to be aware of. The first step is the client's differentiating move in her family. When she makes this move, the second step comes into play: the knowledge that she should expect to run into opposition from the togetherness forces in the family, pushing her back into her former automatic way of being. The third step is to prepare herself—to plan ahead what she will do as a result of the family's onslaught. She needs to be aware that when the family tries to reestablish the status quo, it is a sign that her changes are having an impact on them. If she keeps on her own calm course, eventually family members will give up their struggle and accept that "that's the way she is." At that point it often happens that another member of the family, following her example, may make a differentiating move.

A plan is made in therapy about how to begin the process. With the client the therapist looks at the family system with an eye to balance and justice. Does the client know and relate to all the branches? Is she equally fair to all, including self, with acceptance of members although not necessarily approval of the things those members do? The plan is basically a lifetime one. A family system can be so powerful that, unless the client is serious about permanent change, there is not much point in starting. Thus, moves are planned to be steady and slow, and when there is pressure to go back to the old way, the family member is prepared to resist and hold her steady course. When old feelings surface, such as hurt and anger, the client can use them as signals that she is getting sucked in and recalibrate herself.

After family diagrams are constructed and patterns reviewed, a decision can be made about whom to contact. It may be easier to contact peripheral members first to gather information before making contact with the central figures, especially if there are long-term cutoffs. This can provide the family member with practice in new ways of relating and give her confidence as she proceeds.

Planning Change

Later in the same session with Joe and Edna, we focused on Joe's relationship with his father and changes he might want to make.

Edna: His brother Gerald would like to have a relaxed relationship with Joe. It's tense. Sometimes I have to explain to Joe what Gerald says because Joe feels Gerald is attacking him.

Chuck: It's important to get to this kind of leveling with Gerald, but it's even more important with your Dad, because you have limited opportunity.

Joe: I was thinking about this last night. If I could go out with him alone . . . (pause). What would I say to him?

Jan: What do you want to tell him about yourself?

Joe: (pause) If I really level, I would say, "Dad — why do we always talk about baseball? What do we really want to say to each other?"

Edna: The other night he wanted to touch you and you backed off. (to therapists) There's tenseness when his father is there.

Chuck: (to Joe) What are your reactions inside?

Joe: Sad.

Jan: Say more about your sadness.

Joe: I'm blocking it. I have no idea what to do about it. He has a limited amount of time to live. It's silly to go on playing games.

Chuck: If you can change your relationship to him, his will switch.

Edna: Can you fit in time to stop there and be with him?

Joe: I don't even have the strength for my own family. And there's no way to get rid of my stepmother.

Edna: I don't mind taking her out to lunch.

Joe is now conscious of their game-playing. He is intrigued by the idea of really talking to his father, yet resistant, citing his lack of time and strength and his inability to pry his father and his stepmother apart.

Change Begins

A month later, at the second follow-up session, Joe reported that he had called his father and told him that he wanted to talk to him alone.

Joe: I took your suggestion. I called him. I cried like a baby before I got there, thinking about all the things that hadn't happened, and he cried.

Chuck: You'll have to slow it down.

Joe: I made a decision to contact him. I said, "There are certain things we know for sure: I'm your son and you're my father. We have a problem — a difficult time expressing ourselves." I gave him an example — that we want to kiss each other, but we don't. He said, "Yes, you're right." He started talking, then. He said if the relationship with Mother had been OK, things would have been better. He cried. He was happy at the end. I felt the beginning of a freeing up in my relationship with him. It had an effect on my nuclear family. I recognize the connection between the two — one I had not recognized.

I went to him almost blind, based on your and Edna's prodding. It was a very emotional thing, but he didn't have a heart attack.

Chuck: And you didn't have a heart attack.

Jan: You were worried about him?

Joe: The doctor scared me; I was worried.

Chuck: Did he put it on a realistic basis?

Joe: He had a bad heart after his heart attack. I was afraid high emotions would have an effect. But now he's walking around OK.

Edna: Things did change a lot. Joe had been talking about dying. It was very tense. I didn't know about his added tension until he said, after we left here and were riding home in the car, that when you said he was confusing him and his Dad, that he still was worried about dying. When he went to see his Dad it was a stormy day. I was tired. I didn't want to see any crazy superplanning. I said, "Do it." I didn't take his stepmother out. And after he came back from talking to his Dad, I was angry. I listened. I was glad for him, but I thought, "Well, so what?" There was a big emptiness in terms of my feeling for him. I was exhausted. Eventually Joe just got more relaxed and I became more relaxed and I went through a lot of things. I've been putting so much energy into Joe rather than myself that I've gotten lost. Where am I? My mind is still trying to do things. What's to be done? This last week I've been saying to myself, "He can do it." I don't have to watch what he is doing. (Long pause) The day after he went to talk to his Dad, I didn't meddle in it. I saw I was afraid he couldn't do it. I don't want to help him in his freelance writing either. I've put so much energy into him. I've been centering my whole life around Joe and Joe's survival. I want to take care of myself and do things on my own. We've spent 24 hours a day with each other. We've had no separate lives.

Joe had been worried about and protective of his father and confusing his problems with his father's, all inside himself. When he was able to express his fear and his love, he freed himself up. As Edna saw this happening, she was able to begin separating herself from Joe in a similar process, realizing how much she had been protecting him and how she had lost her own direction in the process. She began planning her own differentiating steps.

Taking an "I" Position

When family members take an "I" position in the family, as Joe did with his father and as Edna did with Joe, they take responsibility for their own feelings, thoughts, and actions without blaming others for the way they are. They take responsibility for writing or calling, asking themselves if they are following dysfunctional patterns or saying honestly what they think and feel. If they have trouble initiating or ending phone calls, as Stephen did in Chapter 2, they plan ahead and follow the plan. They arrange each visit carefully, determining how long they will be able to relate without getting sucked back into destructive patterns. They learn to move in on their own volition to an intimate distance and out again before it becomes smothering. If, like Joe, they do not let feelings show, they can test themselves by revealing parts of the self in one-to-one exchanges with family members. If they have always let feelings tumble out indiscriminately, they can practice self-control and monitor the flow of feelings so they will not overwhelm themselves or be overwhelming.

The differentiating person decides where to start her changes. She needs a long-term plan which can be implemented slowly in an ongoing campaign. It may be easier to start at the edges of the family where there is less tension — with cousins, aunts, uncles, or grandparents — rather than in the center with the father or mother. Family members are not always as receptive as Joe's father, who also wanted to break through the barrier dividing them. If we had been working with Joe and Edna over a longer period of time, I might have encouraged him to change his relationship with his brother before talking to his father. However, time was limited — both our therapy time with them and time available for contact with Joe's father, who was critically ill.

In many families adult children only see their parents together, never alone, in a replication of their childhood family. If this is the case, as with Joe, then a plan is made to see each parent alone. Triangling is avoided by insisting on direct one-to-one communication, by not taking sides, by refusing to listen to talk about others, and by defining self in the "I" position. This is difficult to do when the parent is accustomed to talking about others and not about self. The client has to be active, as Joe was, who said to his father: "We have a problem — a difficult time expressing ourselves."

The client can also ask herself, as Joe did, "What do I want to say to my parent that I have never said?" If she has always appeared strong and self-sufficient, she may decide to talk about her fears and doubts; if she has always shown her weak side, she may want to let the parent know how well she has handled some important aspect of her life. Often words of love are notably lacking from such relationships. If the client does not know how to say what she wants to say, she can rehearse in the therapy session by visualizing her parent in an empty chair, and talking to that parent as if she were there. With feedback from the therapist, the client can practice various ways to change her manner of relating.

When one spouse takes an overly-intellectualized position, the partner often assumes an overly-emotional stance and carries the anxiety for them both. An anxious parent is prone to relieve her anxiety by allying with a child in a loyalty-seeking dyad in which the child suffers by compliance or by acting out. Thus, the imbalance is projected downward, with serious consequences to the system. Joe had been the over-intellectualized spouse and Edna had carried the anxiety, seeking an ally in Anna, the oldest daughter. Joe, whose mother had been dead for years, saw his father and brother from time to time, but had been distant and emotionally cut off from both. Joe's difficulty with intimacy in his family of origin and Edna's alliance with their daughter stood in the way of a balanced relationship between Joe and Edna.

Reverberations Through the Family

It was much later, in the same session with Edna and Joe, when I asked about secrets:

Jan: What is going through my mind about your father concerns secrets. Did you ever talk to your father about your gambling?
Joe: No. What's to be gained by it?
Jan: I have a fantasy your father had a secret life he didn't share . . .
Joe: . . . with my mother? We opened up new areas. He talked more than I did.
Jan: He's testing you out. Then you can integrate it in order to put the past behind you.
Joe: Gambling is not a secret. How would this have an effect on him? I told him most of the things I protected him from. I was protecting me, not him. And that is also true about gambling.
Jan: Why does it have to be a secret?
Joe: I don't feel it is a secret. My brother advised me against it because of Dad's health.
Chuck: How would it hurt him to have him know you gambled, now that it's over?
Joe: He identifies so much with me. (pause) It would be a burden he's responsible for and he would have guilt feelings. He said if things had been different between him and Mother, we wouldn't be like this. He took the blame. I said to not worry about the blame. (pause) I have more hesitancy about other things than gambling.
Jan: I hear hesitancy.
Chuck: I'm not getting my point across. I'm not talking about one conversation or another. I'm talking about changing your relationship

with him for the rest of your life, a piece at a time. I'm talking about a growth experience rather than a therapeutic one.

Jan: To bring your secret life and your real life together into one life that is open.

Joe: The two people I've told are my wife and brother and the repercussions on their lives were fantastic — like an atom bomb.

Chuck: There's no guarantee. (to Edna) What do you think?

Edna: I don't know. At one time he was *so* controlled by his Dad, I just wanted to get rid of it. I think the relationship is much pleasanter now. Before his talk with his Dad, I wanted to say, "And why don't you tell him about your gambling?" But he wouldn't have understood.

Joe: I'm not sure mystery isn't better than telling him.

Edna: Well, those things are your decisions.

Joe: I don't feel I have to protect myself from him.

When secrets are withheld or differentially shared, old patterns are perpetuated and cutoffs fostered. The secret forms a boundary between the secret holder and that person in the family who is unaware. Until our sessions, Joe had not trusted his father with important information about himself. Joe had told his wife about his gambling, and his brother had advised him against telling their father because of his health. Joe's scare about his father dying and fear of his own death were intertwined; it was hard to tell if Joe was protecting his father or himself.

Later in the session Joe and Edna talked about the emerging changes in their relationship:

Joe: I wanted to hire someone to help with the typing and Edna didn't want to spend the money. Finally she agreed.

Jan: So that's another area in which she's getting off your back.

Chuck: Not just getting off your back — she's establishing an independent identity for herself.

Edna: When the bomb dropped about his gambling, there were such financial responsibilities I had to assume — so many burdens and responsibilities.

Chuck: (to Jan) He's willing to let her be a separate person.

Joe: She's genuinely independent. I'm delighted. I'm in favor of it. I don't want a financial bomb now, either.

Edna: This is the first month in two years that Joe has met all our monthly payments. I feel great. The kids are excited. They know we've been living off government money and insurance and borrowing. But the most important thing for me is my attitude change. I'd like to keep it for the rest of my life.

Evaluation and Termination

A month later, at the third and last session, Joe had progress to report:

Joe: I did talk to my father, by the way. I not only told him about the gambling, but about Anna's running away the second time, which we were also hiding from him. I waited 24 hours after telling him and wondered why he hadn't called. It took him 48 hours. The trouble was, he couldn't stop thinking about it — about what would happen in the future. Would I gamble if he left me his money? I had another talk with him and I told him, "Only I know and I'm not worried about it. Anyway, I don't want your money."

Later in the hour the therapist checked out with Joe how he saw his change with his father:

Chuck: I want to ask you two things: What did you learn about yourself and him and how has it changed your relationship?
Joe: There was something very complicated in one of our conversations. I told him about the feelings we have when he comes into our house. Our friends are more relaxed; they take off their coats and get coffee and he doesn't. But the second time I went there I said, "Do you realize you and Edna are the two people I can confide in? Even though with friends I'm more relaxed, now with these talks we've had, you and Edna are the only two people I can really talk to."
Chuck: I wonder if this ties in with your feeling that we are a crutch — two more people you depend on and confide in. Do you feel you're going to become dependent on us so you can't let go?
Edna: Maybe I'm afraid of it because of my past relationship with Joe. There's always been an authority figure to relate to to solve problems and I want to get to the place where we solve problems on our own.
Chuck: If you forget about the past and think of the sessions this fall, they have been fruitful.
Edna: Yes, they have been productive. We were ripe for doing it. And because things have gotten to this point, we're going to be able to progress on our own.

Jan: One of the things you have been doing is working continually between sessions.
Joe: I have worked after the last sessions.
Chuck: I don't see much of a crutch operating in our relationship.
Joe: It's contradictory. We won't know the lasting power of the therapy
until we're not coming here. On the other hand, we won't really
know what we haven't done yet unless we keep coming here and
see what happens. I have mixed feelings.

It was predictable that Edna and Joe would feel differently about the
ending. Joe had begun to change his relationship with his father and he
had inner knowledge of the powerful step he had taken and of the resulting reverberations throughout the system. Even so, he was a beginner and not at all sure that he could follow through.

If we had insisted that they look at these patterns earlier, would it have
changed the escalation of the crises in the previous year? I have no
answer. My guess is that the family was already into the escalation when
they came for therapy and were not trusting enough or interested enough
in family of origin issues to be ready to openly explore and change the
patterns, even though it might have helped. I, also, was not as knowledgeable or persistent at that time. The groundwork had been laid in the early
sessions, however, for Joe to move out of the family business and to adopt
a more objective stance. At this point, despite his skepticism, he was ready
to work on his own differentiation from his family, and Edna was ready
to work on her differentiation from Joe.

Brief Family-of-Origin-Oriented Therapy

Our work with Joe and Edna was, in effect, brief therapy as a follow-
up to a long-term crisis therapy. Some presenting cases, however, can
be resolved to the satisfaction of the family or individual in brief therapy
of four to 12 sessions, using almost exclusively family of origin techniques,
as we did with this couple. I am collecting data on these cases for future
evaluation.

A common misconception about and drawback to work with family
of origin issues is that it is long-term therapy, taking months and years
to complete. Some individuals and couples are only looking to become
unstuck; once out of their impasse, they want to continue without therapy. I find transgenerational therapy compatible with brief therapy, especially in those situations where a decision needs to be made and spouse
or individual finds self unable to move. The impasse may well be primarily with the preceding generation; resources to solve the problem may

not become available until irresolutions with that previous generation have been addressed.

RECONNECTING CUTOFFS

When there is an inflexible imbalance in family loyalties, there is a concomitant development of pathological obligations (Boszormenyi-Nagy & Spark, 1973). Imbalance results from a series of social processes over time, as unfinished business from past generations is woven into the fabric of a new marriage, with the possibility of projection into the next generation. Intense loyalty tends to build intense alliances within the family, and when these become extreme, relational cutoffs occur.

Bowen (1978) has conceptualized a useful theory about cutoffs in families. He believes that the unresolved emotional attachment to parents parallels the lack of differentiation that must be managed in a person's life and in future generations. When there is an excess of unresolved emotional attachment, differentiation is low and anxiety is high. The problem is seen by the younger generation as being "in" the parents. The adolescent or young adult who is inclined to impulsive behavior may make a physical cutoff by becoming angry and running away to gain independence rather than acting in an independent and responsible way before leaving home. The more passive young adult, feeling a necessity to isolate self or deny the importance of the parental family, may cut off emotionally while still continuing to live with or near the family. Or there may be a combination of emotional isolation and physical distance, with others being triangled in to prevent intimacy.

A person who runs away can be as emotionally dependent as the one who never leaves home, and she becomes vulnerable to duplicating her impulsive behavior with other important people in her life. She needs the closeness, yet is allergic to it. The one who stays at home maintains the supportive contacts but many develop internalized symptoms, such as depression or physical illness, under stress.

When people cope with intense emotional systems by fusing into them or avoiding them, they continue to carry their vulnerabilities to intense relationships with them wherever they go. The individual whose emotional energy was once invested in the family of origin is now searching for another person to attach herself to. The more intense the cutoff with the past, the more vulnerable the individual is to duplicating patterns with the first available other person. If the intensity continues into marriage, she is likely to precipitate an exaggerated version of her parental family problem in the marriage.

When family of origin connections are cut off on one side but not the other, the cutoff spouse often joins the partner's family of origin and continues the imbalance, with a loss of self-esteem in the cutoff spouse. Children may know uncles, aunts, and cousins on one side of the family and not hear about or hear only negatives about relatives on the other side. One side may appear lively and interesting; the other, boring or dangerous. Children may be trained to go through one parent to get to the other parent and this triangular route may seem to be the only way to contact that other parent's extended family. When both families of origin are cut off, then the unresolved emotional attachment is directed downward and intensity increases in the nuclear family. Such a concentration may become too intense for the children, one or more of whom may then be likely to repeat the pattern.

As individuals follow family patterns, they are often not conscious of the problematic nature of cutoffs. In constructing a family diagram, they become aware that they do not know the names of extended family members and may then realize that they have been subtly directed not to be curious about them. When such an individual is cut off from parent or siblings, it may be easier to begin a process of reconnection by making contacts with more distant cutoff parts of the family first, where she can be more objective. This helps her understand the family's rigidity and diversity and how the family patterns have become unbalanced.

Attitudes and prejudices often get in the way. The common perceptions people have of family members they do not know are often based on family myths. It is usually easier to accept other members' perceptions of one's family than to formulate one's own opinion by getting to know relatives personally. Often the blackballed relative has retained a different point of view, was not willing to live under the family rules, or has inside information about family secrets. The family's stereotyped perspective of those who are ignored or put down—for example, the black sheep, the playboy, the one who is not very bright, the one who has cheated the family, or the one who "thinks he is too good for the family"— is balanced by the total acceptance by the family of the "in" group, those known as good, hardworking, and intelligent, whom the family member may also know only superficially and take for granted. The "in" group may contain alliance-makers and trianglers who blackmail the unwary in order to maintain the status quo.

The greater the unresolved emotional attachment to parents, the greater the difficulty young adults have in maintaining intimate relationships. Yet many, unaware that their problem with intimacy has its roots in their family of origin, are only interested in working in therapy with their intimate partner. The therapist must be patient and persistent in helping such individuals accept a transgenerational perspective. An example will illustrate both the problem and the solution.

Resistance to Change

Amy, a college professor, requested therapy for herself and her husband Gene, an executive for a large corporation, because of a lack of intimacy between them. Amy had been in analysis for three years before they married and had continued analysis for two years after. Gene had not been in therapy before. Both were in their thirties and they had a two-year-old daughter, Donna. Both reported feeling closer to Donna than they did to each other. Amy, who was attracted to suave and nonchalant older men, had started an affair with Loren, who lived in another part of the country. Gene, although upset by her liaison, did not want to separate or divorce; he wanted her to stop seeing Loren and recommit herself to him.

Amy had been her father's favorite as a small child, accompanying him on fishing trips. He left home when she was seven, following a violent argument with her mother, who never spoke about him after he left. Amy had no idea where he was or if he was still living. This cutoff had dominated her life without her knowing it. She and her mother had a distant, strained relationship, and she was also distant from her older sister.

Gene was equally unwilling to look at his family, which he considered an ideal one. He had escaped into a prosperous life, leaving his ineffectual younger brother, who had difficulty holding a job, still at home with his parents. Everything in the family revolved around his mother. When he visited, which was fairly often, he fitted back into his former role as the oldest son who was successful outside the home.

In the first phase of therapy it became clear to me that Amy's difficulties in the marriage were connected to her father's abrupt departure as a child. Since she had resigned herself to the fact that her original family members would never change, however, she did not want to focus on any changes she might make with them. Chuck and I, as co-therapists, waited until we had established a therapeutic alliance before making family diagrams in the seventh and tenth sessions. We found, as we expected, that there were numerous cutoffs in Amy's family and a rigidly closed system in Gene's. Whenever there was an opening, I kept edging both of them towards family of origin work. It had reached a point where, when Amy made a comment about her family, she would look at me and say, "I know what *you* are going to say."

Although we were in the middle phase of treatment, they had not yet committed themselves to a transgenerational approach by the twentieth

session. Halfway through the session I asked Amy about her early recollections about her father; she said she thought her parents' argument,
before her father left home, had been about her:

Jan: You mean he left for good right after that fight with your mother?
Amy: Yeah, I think so, but I'm not absolutely sure. He was very angry
   at me.
Jan: That would be interesting for you to check out with your mother.
Amy: I don't really feel like talking about it with my mother at this point.
   (silence) It may be some kind of a prototype for what happens to
   me, but I'm not sure. (another silence)
Jan: I guess one of the things I find hard to understand is how you make
   decisions such as, "I don't want to check that out." I have a picture
   of a door closing. You make these comments from time to time,
   around your family. I don't think you make them around anything
   else. And I think, she is telling me to get off this subject — to go on
   to something that's . . .
Amy: Well, I'm not telling you that. I just feel prescriptions to talk to
   my mother are probably not going to be followed by me.
Jan: That's what I hear.
Amy: It's not that I'm saying I wouldn't discuss it with you. I'm not closing
   the door to *you*.
Jan: And I just want to say that I'll keep bringing up things which seem
   important to me, whatever you do.
Amy: I haven't felt inclined to talk to her without some evidence of re-
   ceptivity on her part. Anyway, that's a tangential matter as I see
   it right now.
Gene: Well, I don't think it is, because I get that kind of feeling Jan got,
   in some ways — that you're being compliant and you're not being
   compliant. I think you're going to have to approach your mother
   sometime or other. That's a prescription we've got to hear. When
   you say "I have to know if she's receptive," then it rings a bell in
   my brain when you tell me I have to do something before you'll
   do something. And I don't think that will ever happen in the case
   of your mother.
Amy: I think both of you are overstating how I am in that regard. I don't
   understand why we're getting off on whether I discuss this with my
   mother. I think the focus of this discussion should be you and me.
Gene: When Jan responded after you said you're not going to talk to your
   mother about that, it reminded me of a lot of conversations we've
   had about a lot of topics. (silence)
Amy: (to Chuck) What do you think? I think we're off on a tangent.

Chuck: We're stuck.

Amy: I'm trying to get things back on track.

Chuck: I guess it doesn't seem to me that we're as far off the track as it seems to you. I think that an important way to change the relationship here is to change the earlier relationships that have a connecting causal link, or that we think might have. And I think that to operate on the basis that your mother has to be receptive gives her a lot more power than she really needs to have if you want to change the relationship with her, because you can change your relationship to her even if she doesn't want to do anything. And that could reverberate into this relationship. So it may seem like it is off the track, but I don't really think that it is.

As I told Amy my thoughts about her family, she dismissed them as tangential, making sure I knew she was not dismissing me. Gene kept the subject open, focusing on a parallel process he saw in their relationship and criticizing her part in it. Since she felt on the spot, Amy brought in Chuck, who had been quietly observing the interaction. This gave him an opportunity to frame our interchange more objectively.

Triangular Relationships

The discussion moved to the therapeutic interface,* focusing on Amy's attraction to Chuck as an older man, and Chuck's identification of her with his daughter. They agreed to track their feelings in the sessions. Gene also was intrigued as he saw the possibilities in and the complementarity of the co-therapy format. He began to speak for himself, rather than for Amy, identifying an upset feeling that he had had all his life when someone he was close to got close to somebody else. Amy was now much less defended, and admitted that though her affair was, in part, sexual she thought the real issue was about her being close to anyone.

Amy spoke of her need to spend time alone and her envy of a single male friend who went on vacation by himself. She felt restricted by Gene's need to spend all of his free time with her. She thought he did not have enough interests of his own, outside of his work. Gene found it difficult to appreciate her position.

Jan: Two adults can live together and move in and be very close and move out and be like your friend, who spends his vacation alone.

Amy: That's always very hard to do with Gene.

---

*See Chapter 11 for the part of the session dealing with therapeutic interface.

Jan: That's what I'm getting to.

Amy: He feels awfully guilty if he goes off for a weekend. (to Gene) You've always had that problem that you can't go off and do what you want to do, so it's hard for me to do what I want to do, too.

Jan: (to Gene) That's an important area to work on because that has to do with the closeness in your family.

Gene: We're skimming along the surface of these issues. I'm not sure, though, where to go next.

Jan: I'm aware, with these kinds of issues between the two of you, of how your marriage has become more of a burden to you, rather than a context for being yourselves yet having support. I don't think I ever saw that as clearly as today. When you say we're skimming along the surface, I don't think we are. We're not resolving anything, but we need to see things in context.

Amy: Gene's and my psychological burden is rather persistent.

Chuck: (to Jan) Maybe that has something to do with why they arranged for an affair.

Jan: Uh, huh.

Chuck: To liven things up.

Jan: To get out from under the heaviness of the burden.

Amy: I'm interested in getting out of it. I don't know if Gene is, but I certainly am.

Gene: As long as you have an outside source for goodies, I think it's inevitable we won't work on those issues.

One direct consequence of emotional cutoff and enmeshment is the burdening of the nuclear family system with equivalent overinvestment of feelings and expectations. The unresolved emotional attachment both Amy and Gene had to their parents moved with each of them into the marriage. Amy wanted unencumbered freedom in their relationship, while Gene was overly invested in spending time together, as his parents had done.

The underlying dynamic was that both Amy and Gene had difficulty with intimacy. Since being involved in a triangle cuts down on intimacy, Amy had triangled in Loren to relieve the smothering togetherness that Gene interpreted as closeness. She was as emotionally dependent as Gene, but was running away from it. Amy had carried her intense unresolved attachment to her father into her marriage, triangling in older men to defuse the intimacy. The co-therapy situation made an excellent format to examine Amy's relationship to Chuck and vice versa in a safe setting, with both Gene and myself present.

Breakthrough

There followed a heated argument between them before Amy broke it off abruptly.

Amy: I need to discuss with Gene if I can see Loren. How do you resolve something like this when you have a difference of opinion?

Jan: At the risk of being redundant — one of my ways of going about it is to go at it from another angle, but you aren't interested in other angles. You want to go head-on.

Amy: No. I want to hear your other angle.

Jan: Well, I think it has something to do with your father. I think this would be a great time to think about how you could get in contact with your father. That's where my mind goes. I don't know what you'd find out, or if you'd find out anything, but I have a feeling that it would open some doors for you and it's there to be done if you want to do it.

Gene: You wanted another angle and you've got one! (All laugh.)

Jan: I think another way of working at it is with Chuck, in here. I'd like to see you work at it in a number of different kinds of ways. But I hate having you leave one of the basic ways out.

Chuck: (to Jan) Amy has things in such nice little compartments. Why do you have to go around messing up her plans for herself?

Gene: The way things are . . .

Chuck: The trouble with advice is — you mess up people's plans.

Gene: *I* know that. I mean . . . (to Amy) I didn't know that about you — well, my mouth was as much agape as yours was at that particular piece of advice. But I know the pressures to do things — pressures to get on airplanes and visit people, and they're all overdetermined, and also about myself . . .

Amy: What are you talking about?

Gene: About your need to go see Loren. There's more there than meets the eye.

Jan: I guess we're talking about two different trips, aren't we? Which trip?

Amy: Well, I'd like to get in touch with my father, but when I think about what's stopping me, it's not really my family's possible objection but really how I feel about it.

Chuck: Right!

Amy: And I think that I'm afraid I'll find out he's already died or something. Just the thought is very upsetting to me. Just as long as I don't find out, then I can imagine him alive and well . . .

Gene: . . .and having affairs all over the world, and getting compliments for being the perfect father.

Amy: I don't like everything in my life, and especially my relationship with Loren, completely reduced to me searching for my father.

Jan: I'm not saying it's completely reduced to that. I'm saying . . .

Amy: I know *you* aren't. But Gene is.

Jan: . . . that if there is a search in you going on for your father, it may continue going on until you find your father, whether it is with Loren, or another man, or Chuck. I don't mean that if you find your father it will stop you wanting relationships with other people, but you may be able to understand . . .

Amy: Right on! Right on!

Jan: . . . what it's all about and to maybe give some of that feeling over here. (motioning towards Gene)

Amy: You're a very wise woman. Because if there is anything I don't like, it's people who are reductionists in a way that's quite unreal. But I like what you say. And I'm interested in doing that.

Gene: Did you get the whole thing?

Amy: Oh, yes, I heard it and it's quite different from what you're thinking I think.

Chuck: What are you thinking he thinks?

Amy: I think that Gene is a reductionist, and when he views this he likes to think that if I analyze away everything that has to do with my father, I'll never be interested in another man again.

Chuck: That sounds terrible.

Amy: Yes, it sounds awful. I don't think that's likely to happen. And I don't want Gene to undergo this kind of process with me for some kind of mistaken notion about what the upshot of it is likely to be.

Gene: I hope the upshot of what we do here is that we'll solve some of our problems we have that bring us here.

Chuck: I agree with that.

When Amy brought up her wish to see Loren, I again moved in with an idea, but this time I dismissed it before I presented it. When Amy asked to hear what I had to say, I knew she would listen. Gene was completely surprised by my plan and became somewhat incoherent for the next few minutes. Chuck spoke to me in a half-humorous way of Amy's compartmentalized plans, pointing up the contrast.

Amy answered me directly, in an honest, forthright way, admitting for the first time how upsetting it would be to her to find out the truth about her father's whereabouts. After Gene moved in provocatively, I thought her reductionist comment applied to my statement. As I continued, however, she cheered me on. She was finally understanding what I had been saying all along. Chuck and I kept the emotional reactivity between the two of them, keeping ourselves detriangled and staying with the larger context. Amy made it clear that she did not want to start a search for her father if Gene had a mistaken idea about her aims. Gene calmed down as he understood that she was making a serious decision.

Follow-up

This was a crucial interview. Amy began looking for her father, a search that lasted two-and-a-half years. She started by calling her sister, who was curious and interested and who had asked an uncle about their father in a coincidental move a month before. Her mother surprised Amy by getting in touch with relatives on her father's side of the family. No one knew where he was; he had never used his social security card; there were rumors that he had left the country.

Amy attended a reunion of her father's family before the thirty-seventh session. His relatives described him as a quiet, charming person. They said it was unlike him to leave, that something awful must have happened. Only one aunt did not whitewash the past, describing him as restless, a drifter and a gambler. In the search for her father, Amy had to come to terms with the knowledge that she feared meeting her father: What if he did not want to see her? What if she did not like him when she saw him? Amy began to fantasize about how to make enough money to hire a detective to find him. By the fifty-eighth session she signed a contract with a detective that would cost her $15,000.

For the next 15 sessions, while Amy pursued her search, Gene began to communicate with his family of origin, culminating in his family's joining us for two sessions.* Three months later Amy brought her mother to a session, and then her sister. During this time, as Amy and Gene's relationship deepened and Amy's search for her father continued, we spaced out our sessions to once a month. Amy was now seeing her family as a support system.

Five months after our family of origin sessions, the detective found Amy's father; she flew to Canada to see him and he agreed to visit Chicago to meet her husband and child and attend a session with us. Her father was charming and verbal on first meeting. He said he got along well with people outside the family but not with people he cared about. Amy reported that his charm wore thin during the visit and she

---

*See Chapter 7 for sessions with Gene's family of origin.

saw him as self-centered and shallow. Her mother and sister refused to see him.

We held our final session a month later. Amy reported that finding him had had a tremendous effect on her, in that she felt centered, calm, and sure. She realized that many of her earlier decisions were influenced in a negative way by her father's absence. Now, as she felt complete, she needed to rethink these decisions and decide if they were still valid. Amy could now see her mother's commitment to her children clearly and felt love and respect for her; she was able to ignore the things about her mother that she did not like.

Two years later Amy and I met for lunch. Finding her father, she said, had been the most important event for her. Even though he really was not what she wanted in a father, there was still an affinity and he filled a need. She continued to be attracted to exciting older men who were loners, but with an important difference — she was both in it, enjoying the experience, and also watching herself, knowing the feeling was transient and had nothing to do with her real life with Gene. She was still restless, but it was a contained restlessness. And, most of all, Gene understood this part of her and was not worried about it and they both knew it would not destroy what they had together. A year and a half later, Amy wrote that her father had died. She found his death surprisingly easy. For her, she said, the grief of not knowing was always worse.

Motivating a couple who are having problems in their relationship to focus back on their original families is often difficult to accomplish. The therapist needs to be persistent, coming back again and again as relevant issues surface, until the client sees the connections for herself. Developing a plan for change may happen quickly if the family member can grasp its meaning and is motivated to make a change. In other cases the planning process is slow and seemingly endless.

When the therapeutic effort can be directed towards an orderly differentiation of self from the extended family, it helps to loosen up relationships in the nuclear family. The goal is to be autonomous while also maintaining connection with all branches of the family. This allows one to take the family's rich heritage and use it equitably in one's own unique way. The more the nuclear family members can maintain balanced, emotional contact with past generations, the more harmonious and asymptomatic life processes will be in both generations.

CHAPTER 6

Experiential Approaches

Because status quo functioning in the family is so effectively self-maintaining, the therapist needs to make powerful interventions to interrupt entrenched patterns, after which family members can reintegrate their relationships with altered experiences of self and other. The therapist can introduce such interventions when members begin to feel safe within the therapeutic experience. A trusting atmosphere depends on a number of variables: the family members' prior knowledge of or participation in therapy, their trust in the therapist, their ability to take risks, and the therapist's ability to challenge while responding empathically.

Words, especially words describing past events, are most often used as the medium in psychotherapy. This process can be expedient as long as therapist and family are moving toward their goal. As a family member talks about a past event, however, the therapist may sense that it is a stale retelling and that the client is reinforcing old patterns through repetition, rather than discovering the crucial aspects of his experience.

The therapist can shift or sharpen the focus at this point, cutting through verbalization to allow a new understanding to emerge. There are many ways to do this. One of the simplest techniques is to ask the person to tell his experience as if it were happening now by using the present tense. He may feel uncomfortable with this shift, as it changes his focus, forcing him to reexperience the event by dealing with the past in the present. The therapist may need to coach him as he begins and later if he falls back into reporting, by rephrasing his sentences in the present tense. Usually the immediacy of the experience will emerge. At some point he may feel affect such as anger, sadness, or hopelessness. His hands may clench, his voice shake, or tears fill his eyes. As his experience intensifies, other family members' reactions are also heightened, and they are able to see his dilemma more clearly. The therapist now has, in the family member's emergent processes, the unfinished problem from the past coming to life in the present. He can highlight those areas the person is avoiding and move him toward an experiment to increase his awareness and his options.

Experiential techniques lead individuals into alternative kinds of experience. Because the context is changed, each person is required to rethink his point of view and his part in the interaction. Experiential ways of working have evolved in different schools of therapy. Gestalt, role-play, and redecision therapy are used, for the most part, in work with individuals, often in a group setting. Together with family sculpting, which originated in the family therapy field, they provide different ways for family members to achieve greater self-awareness and self-direction, and to develop more choices for action. When used in a marital or family context, a further goal emerges. The experience itself becomes a means of communication within the intimate system, as the family member is able to conceptualize and then to express his inner experience in a unique way.

GESTALT TECHNIQUES

Gestalt principles, which apply both to a person's inner life and to the family's life as a system, are concerned with the process of struggle. The tension is between polarities, with the basic conflict the pressing and often distressing undulation between separateness and merger. The child internalizes the struggle he experiences in the family as he grows and brings it to the new family he marries. The conflicts inside self gain further meaning as they are seen to interface with the family's struggle.

Contact and Awareness

The experiential therapist focuses on contact and awareness, leading to encounter. Each person has awareness of his own need for distance and closeness but may not know how to claim it for self or how to contact the other. Family members, as they enter therapy, may be paralyzed and afraid to make contact, or may be intrusive, impulsively invading the other's space. To be in contact is to test boundaries. If appropriate contact is modeled by the therapist and encouraged in the session, family members usually feel safe enough, over time, to take risks.

Barriers to contact can be erected by words and body position. Examples of using words to deflect include talking in generalities, talking *about* rather than *to* another person, telling the other person what he feels or does rather than speaking for self, ascribing blame to the other rather than describing one's own dilemma, using passive rather than active tense, and using "you" or "we" when meaning "I." Body language is equally important, as when a family member does not look at the person he is talking to, or when he smiles inappropriately, or moves away when someone speaks to him. The therapist can watch for such deflections, calling attention to them to heighten the contact:

Therapist: Say it again, in one short sentence.

Therapist: Turn your chairs and look at each other. Tell him.

Therapist: Put your mother in the chair and tell *her*.

Therapist: Your smile is telling me one thing, while your words are saying something else.

As contact is established, family members are encouraged to be aware of self and to identify their own process. The therapist asks such questions as: "What are you aware of now?" and "What do your tears say?" If contact is lost, the therapist reports what he sees, checking out his experience: "Your eyes are wandering and I sense I have lost contact with you. What are you thinking?" Heightening contact furthers the differentiating process, helping spouses understand their differences and realize that the goal is not to make the partner like self. When the need for contact is met and the gestalt completed, both participants are free to move on to new contacts. When the gestalt is incomplete, a part of that person's energy remains bound in that event.

New awarenesses, called "figures," are constantly arising from the "ground," that indistinct background that is made up of the past (unfinished business from one's prior living experiences), the present (flow of present experiences), and the future (plans and fantasies). As one figure is finished, another will emerge from the ground and fade in its turn, to be replaced by whatever new process has the energy to surface. This flux is basic to all experience.

The figure, the dominant process at the moment, is a never-ending series of polarities with the two parts struggling within the person and/or split between family members. Complex interrelationships exist between individual and family needs. As family members take on different affective roles and reinforce polarities — controlling and dependent, powerful and weak, angry and placating, emotional and intellectual — interaction can rigidify into a ritualized playing out of functions, rather than contact between people important to each other. The therapist's task is to help each person to integrate the parts within self in order to move more flexibly between the polarities.

The Experiment in Gestalt

Gestalt principles are used in therapeutic interaction between family members to heighten the experience. A further application is an exploration of the emerging figure in a dramatic form, a technique using chairs or roleplayed interactions to heighten polarities. In an exercise with empty chairs, an individual family member can experience his internal ambivalent parts struggling towards balance. If the individual's battle is with a person not present, such as a parent, the empty chair may also be used. If the struggle is between two family members, then the therapist can work with the two and their polarized positions. A completed experiment includes the struggle between polarities either within self or with a significant other, affect congruent with the situation, and an affectively worded acceptance of one's current position in the struggle. As a gestalt experiment is experienced in the context of the family system, it becomes an avenue towards differentiation, which means moving beyond one's usual role in the family to claim a larger vision for oneself.

The moment for a gestalt arises out of the process of the session, starting with a current issue. When an experiential technique comes to mind, I think about it for a while, test its parameters against the family members' expressions and imagine how it will fit. I then introduce the idea to the family and see if anyone has energy to pursue it. If we have not done any experiential work together before, I am exploring their trust level in presenting a new possibility. I ask for a volunteer to work with me, telling him he will be free to stop anytime he wishes. If no one wants to try, I let it go, commenting that I will ask again at a later time when someone may be interested in taking a risk. When an experiment is handled as an exploration rather than as a performance, whatever emerges becomes new information to work with.

When a person begins an experimental process using chairs, I move to the floor, out of eye level, so I can guide the work. If the volunteer becomes hesitant or I am not sure what he is thinking or feeling, I may bring him back to the present by asking "What is going on with you right now?" to check if the process is working for him. I resume the exploration if assured there is motivation and mutual trust.

Time is left for feedback after the experiential work is finished. The volunteer can be asked if he wants a response from family members at that time. It may be best to let a person sit quietly with new self-knowledge and not contaminate it with discussion. Other members can be asked, however, what the work stimulated in them about themselves.

Some therapists, including Bowen, do not encourage individuals to experience emotions in the therapy session. Yet some clients, although saying they want to change their relationships with their families, do not make the move, despite planning and encouragement. They may have to recover the affect from the past, if feelings were repressed at an earlier time, in order to break through the block. If they are unaware of how they communicate, rehearsal during the session of a proposed conversation with a parent allows the therapist to suggest different approaches which he can practice until he has a grasp of what he wants to do. The experience can be reinforced by self feedback through audio or video playback.

My experiential work with family members is predicated on the premise that the experience in therapy is a first step towards completing the work with the actual family member—a parent, for example. If the parent is no longer living, a gestalt experiment can foster mourning and help complete unfinished business, so that the adult child is able to be more accepting of the parent. The therapist can help the family member identify those in his current situation (a boss or supervisor, for example) who have been filling a place in his life similar to that of the dead parent. He can then be coached in differentiating from that person.

Empty chair work is useful in expressing and getting beyond strong feelings that keep the individual from accepting his parent—for example, to actually express aloud to the parent in the empty chair all of the accumulated rage that has been stored up inside over the years. Once it is let out, he is better able to decide on the next step. Sometimes the discovery is made that there is more than anger there, as the following vignette illustrates.

Moving Beyond an Impasse

Wendy, a woman in her early thirties, entered therapy after her third intimate relationship broke up. She knew that her problem in establishing a viable long-term relationship with a man was related to her loss of her father. Her parents had divorced when she was seven and she had continued living with her mother, visiting her father from time to time after the divorce. Her most intense memory was finding out at 15 that he had left town without saying goodbye. She believed that reestablishing contact with him would help her, but she was so angry at him that she could not bring herself to start the search. Her expectation was that he would continue to reject her. I asked her to be 15 and to put her father in the empty chair:

Jan: Tell him what you see, sitting there in the chair — how he is sitting, how he is looking.

Wendy: It's funny. Even when I think about . . . (She stops.) I'm aware of feeling sad right away.

Jan: Tell your father about your sadness.

Wendy: It's hard for me to even see you right now because when I see you, I just automatically get sad and I'm not sure what that is all about. (pause) Funny, I feel better just having said that. (long pause. Then, to Jan) I'm not sure where to go. Just talk to him like a 15-year-old? Part of me wants to talk to him *now*.

Jan: Is there anything you didn't say to him at the time he was leaving? You can always come back to the present.

Wendy: Maybe the reason I'm having difficulty is that I didn't know he had left until almost a year later. It's like he just disappeared. Like I must have gotten some message from my mom not to ask any questions. He just disappeared.

Jan: Tell *him* that.

Wendy: I didn't even know you had left. You didn't tell me anything. You never sent me an address. You never even said goodbye. And I guess Mom didn't know where you were either. And I guess I just didn't ask. And I feel bad about not asking. (sobbing) I just never asked where you were. That's just hard for me to believe. I guess I just feel bad about that.

Jan: Do you think his leaving has to do with you?

Wendy: Yeah. I just wasn't important enough to you. (pause) I guess I really don't know that for sure.

When Wendy questioned her own statement, I realized she was ready to take her father's chair. I touched it, asking her to be Father.

Wendy (as Father): I think it was just too dangerous for me to talk to you. I just couldn't seem to do it. To say goodbye to each other was just too much for me. And I think I was angry at you and at your mother and at the whole situation. You didn't come to see what I was doing. You weren't that interested in me. You were angry at me. (Wendy moves back to her chair.)

Wendy (as self): It's not really true. I *was* interested in you. I just couldn't say it. I felt like it would be disloyal to my mother. She had told me so many things against you. She kept slamming you. And it wasn't *you* so much as it was telling me things and I guess it just makes me very sad that I missed you. Now I know that I distanced myself because of things that went on, and right now I'm going through a time feeling more critical of you. Yet I don't want you to go away. (sobbing) I want you to stay. (Wendy is breathing heavily. There is a long pause.)

Jan: (softly) Maybe you would like to be him now. (Wendy moves to the other chair.)

Wendy (as father): I guess I didn't know. I felt badly — I've never heard you say things like that before. I wasn't sure. It's difficult to keep going. I've been trying to reach out to you but I'm afraid of reaching out because your mother is so angry at me.

Jan: (gesturing towards Wendy's chair) Is there anything more you'd like to say?

Wendy (as self, after moving back): I guess I really didn't realize. I thought that the reason you didn't involve yourself more was that you just didn't want to, rather than realizing that what was going on at home and how I was influenced by my mom affected how *I* related to you and how difficult it was for you.

Wendy was able, sitting in her father's chair, to see his side and thus to realize that she had rejected him before he rejected her. With this new knowledge she was ready to begin her search to find him. Another important aspect was her acknowledgment of her intense loyalty to her mother and its effect on her relationship with her father. It was now possible for her to talk directly to her mother about her search, which changed her relationship with her mother to a more equal one and allowed her to start her search on a more realistic basis.

REDECISION AND CHANGE

Goulding and Goulding (1979) developed a regression-integration technique called redecision therapy in their work with individuals and groups of individuals. Starting with a painful feeling in the present in response to a problematic situation, the therapist helps the individual to get in touch with his current affective state and then identify one or more times in the past when he has had similar feelings, leading to a decision to act in a specific way. Such a decision is usually made because of a catastrophic expectation having to do with the individual's survival, and it results, over time, in rigid behavior. Reexperiencing in the present that affective state from the past can reveal repressed material, which then opens the door to redecision in the present — and change.

A person traces the feeling back through situations having similar processes. He may recall an incident as a young adult, then go back to another in high school, then back to grade school, and often to a time at home, before starting school. Or he may go directly back to the early childhood dilemma. The object is to reexperience the feelings from the original trauma, when the person decided how to order his life so that the traumatic situation would not occur again. When such a decision is made by a child in a highly emotional state, the child may continue to live by that decision, even after he has grown up and the context that required the decision has changed. The occurrence, which is extremely important to the child, may not be remembered at all by other members; only the person affected can rate its importance. When the therapist can help him recreate and reexperience the early decision, then the therapist can observe the fixed and grandiose limits of that early position. By accentuating those limits, he helps the client to recognize them, freeing him to make a new decision in the present which fits the current context, and to take responsibility for his own feelings, thoughts, and actions.

Often it is not what parents consciously "do" to children that causes them to make early decisions, but rather the generational patterns the child is exposed to which were part of the life of the family. In the same situation, different children in the same family make different decisions, which then become reinforced and imbedded in the way each member lives and acts. Each takes the decision for granted because it worked for him as a child. When he joins a different system, however, such as committing himself to marriage or a new job, such functioning may cause interactional problems in the new interface. Since such inflexible child positions interfere with reciprocity in marriage, it is mutually growth-enhancing for a spouse to be present when the partner makes a redecision.

Tracking the Early Decision

Lucy and her husband Roger were in treatment with Chuck and myself as co-therapists. Lucy was describing a current dilemma. Friends had offered their children a puppy from a new litter and both the children and Roger were excited about the prospect of a pet. Lucy felt overwhelmed, having just started a full-time job, and knew she could not handle one more thing. Yet she had found herself being very reasonable and agreeing that the children should have a dog. After the decision had been made she had panicked, calling her husband at work, and they had had a big fight.

Lucy: I was going back and forth. I thought there was no way out. If I didn't keep the dog, they would hate me. If we kept the dog, I couldn't hack it. I'd yell at the kids all the time. Roger was too involved in it. I felt trapped. (a long pause) And it reminds me—it's the exact thing that happened with my mother when she came to live with us.

Lucy identifies her dilemma.

Lucy brings up a situation when she had similar feelings

Chuck: The process is similar because you know you are going to have trouble and that you shouldn't do it.

Lucy: I know. I hate what I do to myself and what I put my family through.

Chuck: But you set it up in such a way that you feel bound and trapped.

Lucy: I know.

Chuck: Once you said "yes" to having the dog, against your better judgment, then you were in a bind where it was going to be painful, no matter what you did. Just as once you said "yes" to your mother coming, you were in a bind, no matter what you did. The thing is that you don't do what you know you should do. Instead, you please somebody else.

Chuck identifies how Lucy sets herself up.

Lucy: Right. (pause) But why would I do that?

Chuck: Because it comes from childhood. (There is a long silence.) What comes to mind? (Lucy begins sobbing uncontrollably. She sobs for a long time.)

When Chuck speaks of the connection between Lucy's current feeling and her childhood, Lucy immediately makes the emotional connection.

Chuck: You sound like a little girl crying. (Her tears continue to flow as her painful sobbing eases.)

Chuck identifies her affect as that of a small child.

Lucy: (struggling for breath) What comes to mind is that my mother was sick and she made me stay with her all the time.

Chuck: Get the picture in your mind.

Chuck encourages her to imagine the scene.

Lucy: (talking through her tears) My brother belonged to my father. It was all so crazy. I didn't know what was going on.

Chuck: Put into words how you feel as a little girl when things are so crazy.

Chuck asks her to put her child feelings into words.

Lucy: Helpless.

Chuck: You feel helpless.

Lucy: I wonder what's going on with my mother and father.

Chuck: What does Mother want you to do?

Chuck asks her to identify in words the demands made on her.

Lucy: To be everything to her. To fill all the voids for her. To take his place. (Her sobbing gets stronger.) I can't do it.

Lucy identifies the origin of her helpless feelings and her inability to satisfy her mother. In asking her to tell her mother the words she had never said to her as a child, Chuck helps her to visualize her mother in front of her.

Chuck: (motioning to a spot in front of Lucy) Tell your mother that.

Lucy: (to her mother) I can't do it.

Chuck: Tell her again—I can't fill all the voids in your life.

Chuck again emphasizes her helplessness as a child and encourages her to put her feelings into words.

Lucy: (to her mother) I can't.

Chuck: Even if you want me to.

Lucy: It's not fair to me. I can't be a little girl and go out to play. I can't be close to Father. I'm not close to my brother because I'm jealous of him because he has my father completely and I have my mother.

Chuck: Tell us what you decide to do.

Lucy: (crying softly) To try to please everybody. To do what my mother wants me to do. I thought I had to . . .

Chuck: Tell your mother that.

Lucy: Because she was ill.

Chuck: Tell *her* that.

Lucy: I had to please you or you would die.

Chuck: (in a low voice) I'm so afraid you're going to die, Mother, that I'm going to do whatever you want me to do.

Lucy: I need you so badly.

Chuck: I need you so badly I'll do anything you want me to do. If you want me to please everybody for the rest of my life, I'll do it. No matter what they want, I'll please them. (There is a long silence.)

Chuck: (speaking in a conversational tone) You've been working off that decision ever since.

Lucy: Yeah.

Chuck: You made a promise that was impossible to fulfill and then you've tried to fulfill it ever since.

Lucy: I had to do it to survive.

Chuck: It was a good decision to make then. Do you want to change it now? What would you really like to have said to your mother at that point?

Chuck gently moves her towards her early decision to find out how she will satisfy both her mother and herself.

Now that he knows the decision, Chuck asks her to speak those words *to* her mother.
As Lucy avoids telling her mother, Chuck persists.

Chuck echoes her voice, encouraging her to continue.

Chuck is still speaking in a low hypnotic tone. He emphasizes Lucy's responsibility for her own feelings and exaggerates her decision so that she will recognize its grandiose and ridiculous aspect.
Chuck now brings her back to the present.

Lucy speaks of the necessity of her position.
Chuck agrees, reinforcing that her decision as a child, in response to the situation, was normal. Then he moves on to help her renounce her victim posi-

tion. Now that he is clear about
what she had decided to do, he
takes her back to her child position to find out what she gave
up by making that early decision.

Lucy: (speaking in a soft voice to
her mother) Leave me alone.
Give me room.
Chuck: Say it again, like you
mean it.

Again, Chuck has her emphasize
her position so she hears it
clearly.

Lucy: (speaking in a full voice to
her mother) Leave me alone.
Give me a place of my own.
Give me space to be. I don't
want to be part of you. I don't
want to always feel guilty because you're sick.

Lucy moves from asking Mother
to change to an "I" position. A
redecision is possible when the
person sees the situation in a different light and realizes that the
other—in this case, her mother
—did not "make Lucy feel that
way."

Chuck: I want to hear what
you've decided about yourself
now.
Lucy: I'm not going to . . .
Chuck: (interrupting) I don't
want to hear what you're *not*
going to do. See if you can put
it in one sentence—where you're
at, right now, in relation to
yourself.
Lucy: (in a quiet, full voice) I am
going to be true to myself.
Chuck: Tell your husband.

Chuck is now ready to move to
the present for a redecision.

A redecision is a positive statement. Chuck refused to hear her
negative version.

Chuck now directs her to confront her husband with her redecision in order to immediately
begin the process of change.
Once her victim position has
been exposed to both herself and
her husband, they will not be
able to automatically cycle
through it.

Lucy: I'm going to do what I feel
is right about the dog and I wish
to Hell you'd get off my back!

If Lucy's mother were still living, the next step would be for Lucy to plan a contact with her mother in which she would function with an awareness of being true to herself. Since her mother was dead, she would, instead, test her redecision with other important people in her life — her brother, her husband, her children, and with us, as therapists.

PARALLEL GESTALT EXPERIMENTS

A gestalt experiment is indicated when a family member begins, in the course of a therapy session, to talk about polarized parts of self. The therapist can then help the member identify the parts and explore the struggle between them.

The following excerpt is taken from a middle phase interview in which Larry and Marianne, husband and wife, are in therapy with Chuck and myself as co-therapists. They experienced parallel gestalt experiments in the same session as they both worked individually on their own changes in a couple format. Each was struggling with similar issues, taking steps towards integrating discrepant parts of self. Neither one had done experiential work before. The husband, Larry, at the start of the session, was talking about his promotion at work and a successful speech he had delivered at a national conference. Yet every time he spoke of success, he followed it with comments about his anxiety and worry.

Larry: I have been negotiating with myself. I wake up at 5:30 in the morning. Everything is going well, yet I worry.

Jan: Maybe you always have to have something to stew about. (long silence)

Larry: Well, yes, OK . . . uh . . . so . . .

Jan: Perhaps, whatever you do, you need to stew. And, if so, you have to ask yourself, "How come I need to stew?"

Larry: I'm asking myself that, yeah.

Jan: Because, when you focus on the content of what you've been stewing about right now, you really lose the point.

Larry: Right.

Jan: Because content is not important. The important thing is that everything is going well and you still have that old syndrome.

Larry: Of worrying. Yes.

Jan: The question to ask is, "What would I do if I'm not stewing?"

Larry: I'd have fun. I'd enjoy myself.

Jan: And what is so scary about having fun and enjoying yourself that you have to stew?

Larry: Damned if I know.

Jan: I'm thinking about your doing a gestalt experiment with these two parts of yourself—the part that is stewing all the time and the part that wants to have a good time. To let them talk to each other. (pause) You used the words a few minutes ago, "I have to negotiate with myself."

Larry: Uh huh.

Jan: What I'm talking about is to negotiate with yourself by dividing yourself up into the two parts which you are describing. Are you clear on those two parts?

Larry: Yes. The one side of me says, "I am not worthy of having this job." When I stood at . . .

Jan: Is that the chair you are sitting in now? (I interrupted him because his comment was going to take us back to the interminable discussion about success and worry.)

Larry: This is my bad side. That is my happy side. (pause) What is the purpose of this? To help me clarify?

Chuck: To negotiate . . .

Jan: . . . between these two parts because you're stuck in the middle and your movement is impeded because when you get in one part and start moving, the other part of you comes in and pulls you back.

Larry: I'm not sure what this will do.

Jan: It's an exploration. I'm not sure what it will do either.

Larry: I get anxious. I guess I don't like games. I feel comfortable with the process of therapy when it is like what we usually do, but whenever we do something different like this, I feel I'm being manipulated.

Jan: One of the things I see is that you understand and understand and understand but have problems with putting that into action.

Larry: Right.

Jan: And one of the ways we can put it into action is to change the format so it's not quite so comfortable. Then sometimes you get new learning.

Larry: Right. This is the bad side, then. I feel not worthy of my job.

As he talked I knew that Larry had indeed intended to recycle the endless discussion. As he raised objections, I answered them but I kept firmly on course. There was already trust in the relationship and I intended to have him explore these polarities in a new way. Although he was skeptical, Larry was now willing to take part in this new experiment. I welcomed his skepticism, which kept a check on our work. I also realized that he was reenacting his typical pattern with us and I expected that, following his anxiety about the technique, he would be able to experience some success.

The chair Larry was sitting in became his "worried" side and I set up another chair for the part that was successful and allowed him to feel good. As he sat in the "successful" chair, he immediately needed to put himself down. As he alternated between the chairs, he realized how he alternated roles, jubilant in his successes, then overtaken by anxiety. After his successful speech for the national audience, he described his fear of being too successful, which precipitated a lonely all-night tour of the city; after experiencing closeness with his brothers in planning the care of his senile father, he berated himself for not caring for his father in his own home.

Working Towards Integration

Larry: And all these happy and good things I feel I can't share with anybody because Mom is dead and I would always write home all kinds of things to Mom. Dad never acknowledged good things.

Chuck: (putting out a third chair) Try this chair. This is Larry's observing chair. (Larry moved to the observing chair.) Now, take a moment and remember what it was like in each of these chairs. Is there any possibility of negotiation between these two chairs?

Larry: I don't know what you mean.

Chuck: I'm just using your words. You said you had to negotiate with yourself. Is there any way those two can be merged so you can use the valuable parts of both? Does that seem at all possible to you?

Larry: As I think about the two chairs and what I did, I think I was in that chair (the worried, unworthy one) more than I was in the other chair. I tend to always look on the gloomy side.

Chuck: Always?

Larry: No, I don't always.

Chuck: Some possibility?

Larry: Yes, of course.

Chuck: I'd like you to try another one of these explorations. (Chuck was beginning to lay the groundwork for a hypnotic trance to help Larry integrate his two discrepant parts.) Look at that chair for a moment. Think about what it was like when you sat in that chair and the thoughts that you had. Can you see yourself?

Larry: Yes.

Chuck: Now, look over at this chair. Do you get a sense of what it was like in this chair?

Larry: Uh huh.

Chuck: This may be harder to do, but it's possible. Do you see an image there? Worthy Larry? Worried Larry? (Larry answers "Yes" to both.) Now close your eyes for a moment. Now I want you to take the mental picture on your left side that you have of worthy Larry and on your right side that you have of worried Larry—see them there?

Larry: Uh huh.

Chuck: All right. Now in your mind's eye I want you to gradually bring those images closer and closer together. Worthy Larry comes in from the left; worried Larry comes in from the right. Are they getting closer? Do you see them? Closer?

Larry: Um.

Chuck: Closer—they're almost touching—and now they're beginning to merge.

Larry: OK.

Chuck: See it happening?

Larry: Yeah.

Chuck: What does it look like as they begin merging into each other?

Larry: Whole. A whole person.

Chuck: What does it feel like?

Larry: Complex.

Chuck: Anything else?

Larry: Yeah, it feels good. I think that would be good. A little unbelievable.

Chuck: Now hold that image. Just hold it. Hold that good feeling. (silence)

Larry: You know, I . . .

Chuck: What's happening?

Larry: You know, I feel embarrassed about what I'm doing, yet I felt good when I felt myself as being all of that.

Chuck: You were able to bring them together as a whole?

Larry: Yeah, when I concentrated on it.

Chuck: That's what the kids call "getting yourself together." (There was a burst of laughter from Larry.)

Marianne: That's interesting. I always thought one action would come out on top. I do this when I iron, I talk with both halves and it's always that one is convincing the other one so that one is gone and the other one ends up there. (She glances up above her head.)

Chuck: But you lose part of yourself when you do that.

Marianne: Yes, but I never really thought of that.
Chuck: There's value in both sides.

There are many ways to change: One is to alter one's part in the external system, another is to alter the internal experience. In helping Larry to reorder his internal experience, we first needed to create trust and rapport, using what Larry presented to us. We began with his own language — the worried part and the worthy part, and his comment, "I have to negotiate with myself." Larry's gestalt brought into clear focus his alternating pattern, which echoed his experience in his parental home, where he shared with his mother good things that he felt his father never acknowledged. Chuck then slowly put him into a trance. As he began to come out of the trance, although he was still self-conscious, he had had the experience of wholeness, which he could hold when he concentrated on it.

Exploring Polarized Parts

The work with Larry stirred parallel feelings in his wife, Marianne, who had been sitting quietly, watching with intense interest. When she began to talk about her "halves," this was a sign that she, also, could benefit from gestalt work, and was waiting to be invited.

Jan: I'm wondering if you will explore those two parts inside yourself that you have in your head while you are ironing. It won't go at all like Larry's. I never know how it will go.
Marianne: Yes, my parts are different. Oh! I can feel myself getting real nervous and feeling helpless.
Jan: OK, which is the helpless part?
Marianne: I'll probably only need one chair.
Jan: There's a putdown! So you're sitting in the helpless chair when you say that.
Chuck: She probably won't even be able to do it.
Marianne: I probably won't! See, I just want to sit here and cry. I really can't put things into words in this chair.

Marianne complained that others could do things better than she — they knew more than she did. She said she never volunteered to talk, yet became angry at herself when someone else said what she was thinking and took the credit, while keeping herself from saying it first. As her thoughts went back to childhood, I had her move to her observing chair.

Marianne: Dad would always be right, because he was the man and the father and the teacher and you can't beat that. It was a triumvirate that was like a Mack truck. (sigh) I felt happy in my bedroom when I was a kid because I liked to be alone.

Marianne's competent side had been evident in her grades at school, yet she was happiest when alone in her bedroom. She became tearful, wishing her competent part had the guts to speak out. She pictured her helpless part parked like a Mack truck on top of her competent part.

Marianne: My mother just let Dad run right over her. I was angry at her for never trying to get out because when I look at her, I don't know whether she's got that competent chair inside of her. I just feel her in that helpless one.

Jan: So the face on that chair (pointing to helpless one) is your mother's. See her in that chair? (pause) Do you have anything to say to your mother?

Marianne: I think I can deal with my mother. But what am I to do with myself? I wish she'd find a way to get out of that chair.

Jan: Tell her.

Marianne: I wish you would find a way to get yourself out of that chair. I'd like you to be a person I'm proud of but it is hard to be proud of you when you don't like yourself.

Jan: Tell your mother, "I won't be proud of myself until you are proud of yourself."

Marianne: I won't be proud of myself until you are proud of yourself.

Jan: Is that true or false?

Marianne: I never thought about it, but I guess it is true. (Marianne is crying.)

Jan: Be your mother and see Marianne over here.

Marianne (as her mother): You've already passed me up. You've gone to school more; you draw and paint better than I do. I always did what my mother told me to do. I envy you.

Jan: Answer your mother. (Marianne switches chairs.)

Marianne (as herself): Sometimes it feels, from what you say, that I have everything put together and that I'm not afraid of anything, and that whatever I want I just do, but inside I don't feel that way.

Jan: Will you say, "I'll keep you thinking I have things put together, while I really won't put things together, and that way I'll have the best of both worlds." How about that?

Marianne: (slowly) I'll keep you thinking I have things put together while really I don't, because then I'll have the best of both worlds. (pause)

It's true in that way, I can have one part that looks put together and one part not put together.

Jan: Will you entertain the thought that as long as you're telling your mother about only one side of yourself she is probably only showing you one side of herself?

Marianne: I guess that's true. Yeah, in our family we usually only show one side.

Chuck: So you only know half of the person.

Jan: (to Chuck) And since she's showing the strong side to her mother, then she has to keep the helpless side to herself. She hasn't brought it out so that she can look at it and decide if she wants it or not. It's all tucked away. She keeps it powerful by keeping it tucked away.

As Marianne sat in her observing chair commenting on her competent and helpless parts, she began exploring the place of helplessness in her family of origin. The helpless chair became her mother and I used the technique of feeding her a line that I believed to be the key to her block, asking her, after she repeated it, if it were true. In doing so, she discovered she was loyally waiting for her mother to change from helpless to competent before allowing herself to show her own competence publicly. My last comments were spoken to my co-therapist because I thought Marianne would hear me better in overhearing me than if I talked to her directly.

Afterthoughts from the Couple

During this stage of therapy Larry, Marianne, and both therapists were writing weekly notes following each session and mailing them to each other before the next meeting. This was an experiment, designed to cut through the obsessional reporting in the sessions and move the therapy along at a faster pace. The idea had occurred to us when Chuck asked me one day if I would be willing to share my notes, written after each session, with this family.

As I thought about it, the idea seemed useful since I focused on the process rather than the content, but I knew my notes were colored by my own perceptions. I agreed to participate if Chuck and each spouse would also take part. All three agreed to record their impressions. Marianne's note, written the same evening, read in part:

"This morning . . . was very difficult. I find myself reliving it often. I still can't quite comprehend it all and find myself surprised at what came out of my mouth. I am angry at my father, then I put Larry in his place. I am disappointed in my mother and put myself in her slot. I've never seen it so clearly. And all of it is inside me. . . . Not liking myself seems most connected to Mom, who never did, still doesn't like herself. I have thought about her a lot since our session and I realize that she has always blamed her lack of confidence and ability on someone or something — on Dad, her mother, having so many children, her role as teacher's wife, and now her age. She has never taken that responsibility on herself. And I'm a carbon copy — still trying to blame. The words that Jan had me say to the mother-chair really hit me. I want Mom to like herself and feel confident so that I can like myself. I had been wondering just where to continue working with my folks, but now I have some direction.

I felt real affection for Larry while he was dialoguing with his two sides. I've always had trouble believing that he actually feels powerless and fearful — it became very real on Friday. Chuck's speaking of merging the two selves was a new idea and a helpful one."

Larry's note, following the session, described an emergency trip to move his father from his younger brother's house in one state to his older brother's house in another. "My trip, like myself, was two-sided," he wrote. He was successful in calming his father and in experiencing a certain acceptance of and peacefulness with his father for the two days. His other side was revealed when they reached his older brother's house. Larry felt his father became allied with his older brother, as he always had, and Larry missed his mother and her attention. "The two sides are often in tension," he wrote, "and again, this week, I tried to accept both sides of myself."

FAMILY SCULPTURE

To participate in family sculpture (Duhl, Kantor, & Duhl, 1973) is to experience an alternate language composed of space and action expressed both nonverbally and verbally. The family is accustomed to using the same words and phrases and automatically taking part in the same interactional games. When a family member is forced to translate his feelings and thoughts into action in space, it encourages him to explore his frame of reference in an unfamiliar way. This stimulates his thinking both as he sculpts and as he translates the sculpture back into words, motivating him to pull together unformed thoughts about the family's inner life.

Family sculpture is never "the way it is"; it is only true as a representation of the sculptor's inner reality, which may not fit the ideas of other family members. The sculpture, however, encourages understanding of and respect for the other's way of being and emboldens others to also show it the way they see it. The experience encourages all family members to see themselves as a unit, each affecting the other, while at the same time seeing each as an independent entity. The enactment makes visible the space-time dimensions in the family's life and opens up new areas for consideration, stimulating exploration, insight, and action.

Sculpting in the First Interview

A simple sculptural technique is to ask the family members to physically move about the room to clarify their relationships. This type of intervention works best when members are already talking in terms of distance and closeness, and using spatial words in describing their experiences with each other. The Randall family, with four adolescents from 14 to 17, was approaching the launching phase. The last part of the initial interview will exemplify this simple structural technique.

Chuck: Father seems to be on the edge of the family.
Father: I like to look at the family. Everyone is more comfortable on the outside, looking in.
Mother: I'm "in" all the time.
Chuck: I'd like every family member to move anywhere in the room in relation to all family members.
Father: Who I feel closest to?
Chuck: Place yourself in physical space in a way that demonstrates how you feel about the emotional relationships. (Mother moves over next to Father, and sits on the floor.)
Father: That makes me uncomfortable. (Mother leaves the floor and sits in a chair next to Father.)
Mother: It's better up here.
Father: I don't suppose I would have picked you to sit next to. What concerns me is that sitting next to one kid would signify I didn't like the others . . .
Chuck: That's like it is in families.
Father: If I were to move, I'd go back in front of the whole group. (Father moves so that he faces the family.)
Chuck: The same distance from everyone. How does that feel?
Harold: (13 years old) I don't like it. It seems like he's the teacher— that he handles all the problems.
Chuck: I thought of him as the orchestra conductor.
Harold: At home he should react as part of the family, not a teacher. (to Father) You try hard to become part of the family.

Father: It makes you feel how?

Harold: Uncomfortable.

Father: Where would you like me to be?

Harold: Not necessarily next to Mom.

Father: I don't want to play favorites.

Jan: So it is more important not to turn someone off than to turn someone on?

Father: I would feel bad if I offended anyone, bad if I made one happy at the expense of others.

Tom: (16 years old; recently returned home from residential treatment after a suicidal depression) I try to stay away more.

Chuck: So you will change your chair.

Tom: It's hard to do. My feelings change a lot.

Chuck: How do you feel right now?

Tom: I would be sitting about there. (He points to a spot on the floor between his parents and then sits there.) I'll stay where I'm at.

Chuck: How about you, Jeannie?

Jeannie: (14 years old) It was funny with Mom over there next to Dad. It wasn't right when she was on the floor. She was like a clown. Dad felt more normal. Tom there is normal. I could be anywhere.

Chuck: In lots of different places.

Jeannie: Any place is normal, but I'm equally distant from everyone. (Stays where she is.)

Chuck: Ann, where are you at? How is it for you?

Ann: (15 years old, currently identified patient because of sexual acting-out) I'd walk out of the room. (She does not move.)

Chuck: Are you sitting in the right place for now, between Mom and Jeannie?

Ann: No.

Chuck: Is there anything you can do to make it seem right?

Ann: Nothing.

Chuck: How can you move to make it right? (There is a long silence.)

Chuck: Were you reluctant to come today?

Ann: Yes.

Chuck: Then let's talk about that.

During the sculpture, family patterns began to emerge. When Mother took the initiative in moving closer to Father (Figure 14-A), tension between the parents became evident. Father, including Mother as one of the "kids," explained his move away from Mother by saying that his goal was to treat all family members equally, a statement that ignored generational boundaries. To Father, being close to one member, even his wife, signified rejection of the others.

A. Seating before and during sculpture (a semi-circle because session was videotaped):

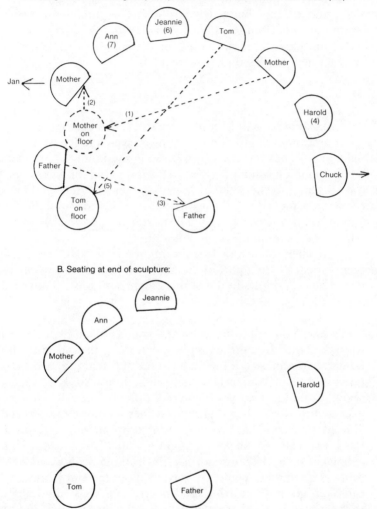

B. Seating at end of sculpture:

Figure 14. First Interview: Family Movements During Sculpture

Harold, who described Father's position as like that of a teacher's, was the only one who challenged Father, yet he also stayed in a distant position, like Father's. The two older children, Tom and Ann, who were approaching the launching stage, spoke of their need for distance, yet seemed powerless. Tom was uncertain, lowering himself to the floor like a child, equidistant from Father and Mother. Ann was angry, wanting to leave the room, yet not moving, and feeling that nothing could make things right. Jeannie served as commentator, saying she could be anywhere, and did not change her position. The family ended up with females on one side close together and males on the other, with Tom, who had recently reentered the family, on the floor between and equidistant from Father and Mother (Figure 14-B).

Roles in the Family

After a year, Father and Mother were still concentrating on the children, who continued to provide problems on which to focus. The identified patient role was moving down through the family. Tom was still on the edge, making some progress, yet unprepared for leaving home. Ann was speaking for herself and was no longer the identified patient; Jeannie had now moved into the acting-out role. Harold continued as the "good" child, yet he realized he might be next in line: 14 was the age when his siblings had become problem children.

Father, Mother, Ann and Harold attended the 47th session. The adolescents spent the first part of the hour in a heated discussion about the roles of boys and girls in the family, their positions exemplified by the following exchange:

Ann: (to Father) You still won't listen and you act like it's not true when we talk about the differences between the girls and guys in this family. Mom picks out the faults in me and Jeannie, and hates us for it, and when Tom or Harold are at fault, it's A-OK-Man, everybody has faults! And you! You're a different way. Tom is never expected to work—like Tom never does anything and everytime Harold does something wrong, Mom jumps in there—"Now don't touch my little boy here—he might get hurt!" So me and Jeannie get picked on and Tom is downstairs drinking Schlitz and walking upstairs on tiptoes. You're so worried about me and Jeannie. How can Tom go out and drive fast and you don't say anything?

Jan: So there are different standards in the family for boys and girls?

Ann: Yes! Dad doesn't agree because he doesnt see it. It's normal to you. To Jeannie and me, it's not normal. We deserve to be treated just like they are.

Mother: There is a difference between males and females. Males are bigger and stronger and can overpower females.

Ann: So what? You talk about women's lib and then you get upset about Jeannie and me. You won't tell me what you're mad about. You're really snotty to me and it goes on all day.

Mother: I don't agree. I think you cook it all up.

Father: I can see how you feel that way. I think perhaps I treat you girls different than I do the boys — yes, I think so.

Ann: OK.

Jan: Will you say in what way you think you do that?

Father: I suppose I come on together with Harold in having common interests. We like to do things together. Let me see if I can get this figured out. I guess — Harold's doing things I like him to do — see? And you're doing things I don't like you to do.

Ann: Even if I do things Harold does, you wouldn't like it.

Harold: I guess it's that — the way me and Tom do things. We don't get all defensive about it and we don't scream and yell about it. When Mom and Dad say, "Where are you going tonight?" we don't say "It's none of your damn business!" You girls tend to get bitchy but you never hear Tom or me get mad and bitch at Dad and Mom.

Role expectation for the adolescents was an important issue and needed airing but, as the fight continued, the atmosphere became one of blame and defense. I decided to shift the focus to sculpture, which we had not done in the family since the simple technique during the first session. I wanted to understand the family interfaces and help family members get perspective on their relationships. I knew that sculpting would put current issues in a more objective framework.

A Member Sculpts the Family

Jan: I think it would be helpful at this point to do a sculpture and find out in a different way your view of how things are between yourself and the rest of the family — how close and distant. Would you be willing to do that? Who wants to start?

Ann: Do what?

Jan: I'll coach you, whoever wants to do it.

Harold: I'll do it.

Jan: What we are going to do is a sculpture in space of how you see yourself in relation to the family — how you see the family right now. (to Harold) Stand up. Push back the chairs. You can use chairs in it, you can put people on the floor, you can have them standing on chairs, you can have them anyway you like. Like you were saying, "The girls are here and the two boys are here." That's a space concept. And what I want you to do is take the space here and put your family members in the space in such a way that it shows us how you view who's close to who and their relationship to each other.

Harold: Let's see. There's Jeannie. She's sometimes . . . well, before,

when we were younger, we would sometimes get along and sometimes wouldn't. So I'd put Jeannie . . . she's away from me now . . .
we're not close at all.

Jan: This can be a moving sculpture too. You can have her move in and
out, or you can have her stationary.

Harold: I'd put her about there — sitting there — at a distance.

Jan: All right. How will you show Jeannie?

Harold: Jeannie will be a chair.

Jan: Which way does the chair face?

Harold: I'd put Jeannie this way, looking away from the family, or trying
to. She's halfway away from the family. (He places the chair partially facing away, on the other side of the room. See Figure 15-A
for his sculpture.) And then sometimes me and Ann get along and
then sometimes we're at each other's throats. So I'd put Ann in the
same place. (He places a chair next to Jeannie's.) But Ann, you're
not trying to get away from the family. Or at least, I don't think
you are. Though it's not for me to judge.

Jan: Do you want to put Ann in this chair?

Harold: I guess, if she'll sit there.

Jan: Ann is clay in your hands. Everybody will do exactly as you tell
them to do because this isn't the way Ann sees it. It's the way *you*
see it.

Harold: OK. And then I'd put . . .

Jan: Wait a minute. Is Ann — is this right for Ann? (Her chair is facing
Harold.)

Harold: Yes, that's fine. I'd put Jeannie about here. (He moves Jeannie's
chair a little away from Ann's.) At times you two really get along
and at times you want to kill each other. And then I'd put Tom —
I'll really have to use two chairs for Tom. Because in a way, Tom
is in the family and in a way he's not. He'd be over there, too. (He
places two chairs on the other side of Ann, one facing him and one
facing away back to back.) We're not real close. And then I'd put
Dad right next to me because me and Dad get along a lot. (He
moves a chair next to him and Father sits in it.) And then I'd put
Mom here. (He places a chair a distance from Father, on Father's
other side.) And there's another chair there, behind her, looking
out. (He places another chair, backed up to Mother's chair.)

Father: So Mom's two people, too, looking in and out.

Jan: OK. Now . . . wait a minute. She sits there and then she comes
around and sits here?

Harold: Yeah. It's just two sides. In some ways Mom is close to Dad
and in the family and in some ways she looks out on the things she
wants to do outside the family.

A. The family as Harold sees them now

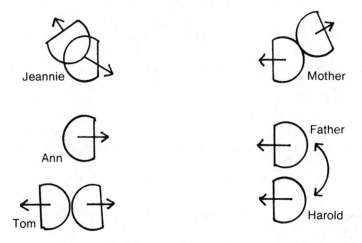

B. The family, as Harold would like it to be, with "the family looking at itself, correcting itself, and looking out, and looking at things as separate individuals"

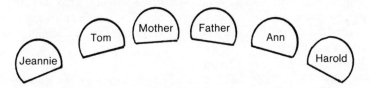

Figure 15. 47th Interview: A Member Sculpts the Family

Jan: At the moment where is she? Here, or here? (pointing to each chair)
Harold: I'd put her *in* the family. (Mother sits down.)
Jan: All right. Now, how about you?
Harold: Me. This is where I am. (He is sitting next to Father, on Father's left.)
Jan: Who are you looking at?
Harold: I'm looking at the other kids.
Jan: Where is Dad looking?
Harold: At the kids. Because — you know, me and Dad switch roles quite often. I'm Father this minute and Dad's father the next minute.

Jan: So actually you two could be switching chairs, and Mother could be going from her in-chair to her out-chair, and Tom could be going from his in-chair to his out-chair. (pause) Is there any relationship to when you're in which chair to which chair Mother's in and which chair Tom's in? Does that have a pattern to it?

Harold: Well, I would think that when Mom's outside the family . . .

Jan: (points to Mother's chair facing away from the family) She's in this chair . . . OK.

Harold: I would be in this one, in my role as one of the kids in the family. Then I would say that I am. . . . When Mom is outside the family, Tom is normally inside the family and I'm inside the family as myself and Dad's the father.

Jan: And then, when Mom gets in *this* chair (Jan points to inside chair), what happens?

Harold: Then it stays the same and Tom often is outside the family. But normally, when I get to be in the father role is when Jeannie starts switching back and forth inside and outside . . .

Jan: Jeannie has two chairs, too, then!

Harold: Well, just about. It seems like she's always looking at the family, except sort of over her shoulder.

Jan: So, when Jeannie looks at the family, what happens to you?

Harold: Normally it's OK. But it's so often now that she's almost one-sided, that she's trying to get herself so depressed and so beat up. And that's when I become the father figure, when she's out fucking around and comes back home and Mom and Dad and Ann and Tom and everybody else are so. . . . I'm the father figure when everybody is *in* the family and the whole family is focused in — when there's a fight.

Jan: Then what happens to you?

Harold: Then I'll be Dad, in Dad's chair. Yes, that's pretty close to what the family's like, in my eyes.

The youngest child is often an excellent observer of family dynamics. When he is also a "good" child, like Harold, sculpture allows him to express his fears and burdens, which are often not obvious to his family. This sculpture is an intimate look at how Harold experienced the family interfaces. He saw his parents, along with himself as parentified child, in a united front, focused on the three older children, who had been or were identified patients. He described the different scenarios when Father was in his role as Father and Harold in his as a child. If one or more of the three — Mother, Tom, or Jeannie — were out of the family, Father was in charge and Harold could remain in his role as a child. If *all* of them were in the family, then conflict and chaos escalated and Father moved out to an uninvolved distance. Then Harold, as Father's stand-in, felt he had no alternative but to take Father's role and try to calm the chaos.

Sibling Patterns

Harold saw his siblings lined up on the other side in an uneasy scapegoat alliance. He stayed on the parental side, allied with the parental power and avoiding the identified patient role.

Harold: I'm closer to my parents than I am to any of the kids and nobody else is in the family, I guess.

Jan: So they could be jealous of that role.

Harold: I don't know if it's jealousy. It just looks like favoritism.

Jan: Something special. Where is Mom looking?

Harold: At the kids and I'm looking at the kids, and even if I'm in my kid role, it sometimes comes on as a looking-down, almost, though I try to control that, so it happens as little as possible, but still too much. Sometimes it's like I'm standing up, looking down at everybody (he stands, arms folded) and sometimes it's all three of us (he motions, including Mother and Father) standing up looking down at them, and sometimes it's all three of them (he motions towards the other three children) standing up, and me not standing up, and I'm out of the picture and everybody is looking down at me — well, mostly Ann and Jeannie. Then I'm on the floor and they (pointing to parents) are in chairs and Ann and Jeannie are standing up. There are so many different roles . . .

Jan: Try that one. Try sitting on the floor and see how that feels.

Harold: (sitting on the floor) Then Ann and Jeannie would stand up (Ann stands) and that's the time when everyone is pissed off. Because this is how it *looks*. When Ann and Jeannie are pissed off with me, it really looks like I'm hiding underneath my parents.

Ann: Why do you keep putting me with Jeannie? I don't get pissed off that much at you.

Harold: Oh, no, no. It's when you and Jeannie are mad at me for favoritism. It looks like favoritism because Mom and Dad don't bitch at me and I'm closer with them.

Ann: I don't get mad at you. I get mad at Mom usually, mostly for favoritism. Jeannie's mad at you, not me.

Harold: You get pissed off at Mom and you get pissed off at me.

As Harold had been able to identify his father figure position, he then moved to a safer focus — that of conflict between himself and his sisters which he identified as favoritism. He developed variations on that conflict as he experimented with the many ways the three "parents" (Father, Mother and Harold) interacted with the three older children. Then Harold returned again to his relationship with Jeannie and Ann, which was a stand-in for the emotional triangle of Father with Mother and Tom.

Sculpting Change

The focus on Ann and Jeannie had brought Ann and Harold close to a resumption of their earlier fight about male/female roles. I interrupted it because I had one more sculpture I wanted Harold to do and I wanted to save time for feedback.

Jan: I'd like you to take it a step further. Would you arrange the family the way you would like it to be?
Harold: That's easy enough. Let's see. (pause) I'd move it like this. (He arranges the chairs in a row, with Mother and Father in the middle, with Tom next to Mother and Jeannie next to Tom, and Ann next to Father, with Harold next to Ann. See Figure 15-B.)
Father: This is the way you want it to be. Are we all looking away?
Harold: At each other — it's pretty hard to do. Just as a family, as a whole one single unit.
Jan: Who looks where? How do you relate?
Harold: Well, it's the family looking at itself and correcting itself, and looking out, and looking at things as separate individuals, is what they do. (pause) And that's how I see it. Cause now, mostly, one big thing is the relationship between Mom and Tom which Mom really wants to solve and I can understand that, and then there's the relationship between Dad and Mom which seems to be so complex. How can I even start to go into that? And then Jeannie and the whole family, too, because Jeannie, she's having a lot of her own trouble right now. (pause) That's how it comes out. (another pause) Sculpture works out better than I thought it would. It takes a minute to figure it out, but once I understand it, it works.

I had had Harold sculpt the family as he would like it to be to enable him and the other members to see their current situation in a framework of change. His former sculpture allowed only rigid, stereotyped ways that members could look or move towards the outside, depending on triangular forces. His wish was to move them from their two camps, watching and opposing each other, to a family unit, allowing each one the freedom as an individual to look at the others or outside, towards each one's own interests. He placed himself on the end, next to Ann, showing his wish to get out of the middle.

This is one of a number of sculptures we could have done, depending on the family context and the time available. Once the stage is set in the present, it is relatively easy to move the same group of family members into a critical time in the past to explore the roots of the problem or into the future to test out various ways to change the current pattern. I could have asked Harold to sculpt the family at an earlier important nodal point, such as before the current pattern of in-and-out behavior, finding out his impression of when and how it started. I could then have had him collapse the time between that earlier occasion and the present, shifting the family members until they were in their present places again. Or I could have had him experiment with physically moving himself away from his parental position to see how that would change his interaction with the other members, giving him options for changes he could make in the future.

The Family Gives Feedback

There was one last task, however, still to be done in Harold's sculpting session. Since other family members now had a common metaphor against which to compare their own images of the family, I wanted to give them an opportunity to voice their reactions.

Jan: What are the thoughts and feelings the rest of you have in relation to Harold's sculpture?
Father: The strange thing about it is that I can see the sculpture the way he does. I guess what I'm doing is putting myself in Harold's shoes. This is how I think he would see it. I'm not saying I would sculpt the family this way. (silence)
Chuck: I'd like to know what the others' reactions are.
Mother: I'm thinking. I'll pass right now.
Ann: I agree. I think it's pretty true, really. I'd do it differently though.
Chuck: How did you feel over here, so distant from the other three? There were three on one side and three on the other.
Ann: Far away.
Chuck: How did you like the two spots — way over here and over there? (He is making a distinction between Harold's first sculpture and where she is sitting now, with all the family.)
Ann: Well, I like this way better, but . . .

Chuck: But what?

Ann: But that's the way it's got to be.

Jan: Got to be?

Ann: Yeah, for now. Because I'm not going to change the way I am, that's for sure. Well, I *am* going to change the way I am because that makes you a better person but the way *he* feels about me (nods at Father) and *she* feels about me (nods at Mother) I *know*, and there's nothing I can do about it because that's the way it is. I can't change the way they are.

Jan: (to Mother) Is there anything you want to say before we stop?

Mother: Well, there is this so-called favoritism that I feel the pull of—I do. I'm glad you brought it up because I hear it constantly and I really stop and think—is this favoritism? It's almost like treading on eggs.

Jan: You're becoming aware of it? Is that what you're saying?

Mother: I've been told it, all the time. But I really don't think it's fair. I don't see it the way she sees it. The girls are like tigers—you really fight. You identify with me and I'm a fighter.

Chuck: I think that Ann's observations are accurate as far as our sessions together are concerned. There have been a number of sessions when parents and girls have been fighting bitterly. When similar episodes come up with the boys, especially Tom, it doesn't turn into that kind of fight. For instance, when Tom got drunk and wrecked the wall with his fist, he didn't get any criticism from the parents. He was looked on as sick or that he couldn't help himself.

Mother: But the girls are more out in the open and fighting.

Ann: Our house is as big as a boat and Tom is at one end and Harold at the other, and me and Jeannie are stuck in between together, and that makes it a lot harder, too. If I lived where Tom does, I wouldn't have as much problem.

Jan: You're talking in space concepts, too. So maybe next time we can get into some of your ideas about where the family is. We have to stop now.

Two weeks later, we asked Harold to repeat his sculpture for the absent members to show them the process and stimulate their thoughts, so they could each sculpt the family as they saw it. As he began to sculpt, Harold became aware that the current situation had changed in the intervening time. Jeannie was now in her outside chair with her back to Ann and Tom. Harold moved Mother's and Father's chairs nearer to Jeannie, as they watched her closely. Harold said, "Mom and Dad aren't worried about anyone else, now" as he moved away from them and closer to Tom.

The adolescents, one by one, had been caught up in the unresolved issues between Father and Mother in a homeostatic process which kept the family energy focused on the children. Tom filled the role first, struggling to bridge the tensions between the parents. Such a struggle, however, was doomed because a child cannot find a solution to that which is not resolved between the parents. Our strategy as therapists was to help each adolescent stay out of the middle and take responsibility for self in order to be able to separate from the family in an appropriate way when the time came.

The more methods of approach the therapist has at his disposal, the more likely he will be to be able to join a client family. Introducing new experiments into therapy enlivens the therapeutic hour and allows discovery to become part of the process. The best intervention is one that is congruent with the presenting problem, uses the language and images of the family member concerned about the problem, and gives that member a multidimensional view of reality. Experiential techniques provide powerful tools to help a member, who is stuck in what he sees as a no-win position, to shift his perspective so that the possibility of new solutions becomes a reality. Such approaches can also be used to help other family members understand the dilemma of one of its members. As that member's inner reality is portrayed and then understood by other members, an understanding grows of the potential in the shared family relationships.

CHAPTER 7

Family Members as Consultants

Family conferences can help both young adults and their parents explore ways to keep in meaningful contact while still maintaining their autonomy. A new framework can be established for transgenerational openness if the therapist can establish an atmosphere which allows them to hear, accept, and, finally, respect each other's feelings and opinions. There is often mystification between parents and children, with neither understanding why the relations between the generations have not continued to grow or have deteriorated since the children left home. To express their confusion and their fears and to have all clarify their points of view, whether they agree with one another or not, can provide relief and the basis for a more honest dialogue.

As the two generations become more comfortable with each other in a family meeting, they may discuss important family events including areas previously off limits, clarify misperceptions, and mourn both recent and past losses together. Because they have dared to move beyond the old boundaries, further exploration now seems possible. They may experience, on either side, a new sense of being needed or a freedom to seek more distance or to come closer. There may be a growing confidence in the process of change. The client who has initiated the conferences usually evolves an increased sense of self as she clarifies the situation which prompted her wish for a meeting.

FORMATS FOR FAMILY MEETINGS

When only one generation has identified a problem and asked for help, convening the original family requires special consideration. The other generation may approach the session expecting to be blamed for whatever problems the client family member is encountering. A workable approach is for the adult child to ask her parents, siblings, or other extended family to come in as consultants to her therapy to help her. Or, if the clients are older parents, they ask the adult children to be consultants to their therapy. In this way, it is clear from the beginning that members of the other generation are free to speak but are not focused on as the problem. Siblings are important in providing objectivity and relieving intensity. Often a breakthrough will happen when siblings begin to act together on common concerns.

Whom to Invite?

When one partner plans a meeting with family of origin, that partner needs to decide whether to include the spouse. If she is triangled between parents and spouse, if the spouse has been filling the role of buffer, or if the original family members are inhibited in front of in-laws and will have difficulty talking freely, it is preferable to meet alone with the therapist and original family members. If the decision is made to include the spouse, the role of observer is most appropriate, and from this position the spouse may be able to make useful connections. These decisions can basically be left to the person who is bringing in the older generation. I usually audiotape such sessions and, unless the members refuse to give permission, the spouse can listen to the tape.

In a similar manner, when older parents plan to invite their adult children to a conference, the therapist raises the question of whether to include the spouses or live-in partners of their children. The issues the parents want to discuss and the acceptance of in-laws into the family are important variables. The presence of spouses may inhibit initial discussion; not inviting spouses may raise a barrier. Spouses may choose not to come even if invited. Parents may decide to have an initial meeting with their children, followed by another to which spouses are invited in order to integrate the new understandings. The effect on the system of the varying combinations needs to be explored before any steps are taken.

When members live in the same area, it is relatively easy to set up family meetings. A single meeting or a series of meetings can be planned, with the family itself becoming a part of the planning process if meetings extend over a period of time. When members are widely scattered geographically, a great deal of planning may go into a session. Often whole families are together during holidays; this may be the best time available. I find the most workable format is a series of sessions over a two-day period — a one-hour meeting both before and after lunch on the first day, with the same sequence repeated on the following day. This gives us time to get acquainted before lunch, and then have additional time after lunch to move into the crucial areas the client wants to discuss. There is an opportunity for everyone to mull over, talk about, and sleep on their common experience before they return to continue working their differences through. By the second session I initiate "rounds," asking that each in turn give her reactions to the last session as well as identify additional issues she wants to discuss. When enough time is available, usually all participants are willing to give their views at some time during the sessions.

Another, less leisurely format is to meet for an hour, take a short break, and then meet for a second hour. The break, whether for lunch or just to stretch and have a cup of coffee, allows the second hour to be a separate session. I always start the second hour by getting the reactions, positive and negative, of all members to the first session, and then giving my own reactions, setting a model for openness. I honor any member's expressed reservations or refusal to talk, checking in with her once or twice to see if she has changed her position. Her presence and her attention, even without verbal participation, can make a profound difference.

The client who invites her family to a therapy session should plan the meeting so that she is reasonably comfortable with the format. It is preferable to see the whole family together for the first visit, so that the system can be seen in action. This may not be possible, however, or the client may have other ideas. Sometimes, because of geographic distance, the only way to see family members is one at a time. Or the client may want to meet alone with parents or with siblings or with one member of the family, as a first step to work on a one-to-one relationship.

Levels of Motivation

Some clients welcome the idea of a transgenerational family conference. They may have identified issues they want to discuss with the family in a neutral setting, not having found the courage to raise them alone. Or they may have already changed relationships to the point where they feel more satisfied, yet not know what they may have overlooked. The conference is an opportunity to gain further objectivity about family patterns and to share the experience of their therapy.

If therapy has reached an impasse, the therapist may ask for a family conference to enlarge the field. Introducing new members stresses the system and increases interaction, since the consultant member sees the ongoing therapy from a different perspective and can often provide new information or give direction.

Family conferences are sometimes not necessary and may even be contraindicated. For example, if the client's parents have been dominant, considering the client dependent and unable to make her own decisions, and the client has already changed herself with her family members, taking responsibility for her changes, the client may decide not to have a family conference. Also, members of the family of origin may have had previous negative experiences in therapy and refuse to come in.

Many clients, however, are sure that members of their family will not be interested or that they will refuse to come. There is often a complicated process that begins when the question of bringing in another generation is raised in therapy. As she thinks through the process, the client may be painfully aware that she has avoided telling family members about her problems; in fact, she often has not even told them that she is in therapy. Planning to ask them to come in as consultants, therefore, may involve a number of preceding steps, forcing her to review her relationships.

GOALS FOR TRANSGENERATIONAL SESSIONS

When one generation invites the other to a session, they open themselves to honest, two-way communication. Such a conference not only provides the opportunity to change the current relationships into a more balanced older adult to younger adult framework, but also can be a modeling for the future of the possibilities for change in a long-term relationship. It is crucial that the inviting generation takes leadership by focusing on self—one's own hopes, fears, and changes—rather than on blaming the other generation or asking them to change. This is more easily done when the inviting generation has been in therapy over time and is clear about the ways they are changing in their family. When family members meet with a therapist without such preparation, there is a greater possibility that conflict may erupt, with members reinforcing polarized positions.

The Young Adult's Goals

The young adult can tell her family about her own problems, how she is solving them, and how they interface with her experiences in her family. The therapist can encourage the parents to share what it was like for them at parallel times in their lives. Siblings can be encouraged to give their point of view, which widens the context and provides new information. Siblings can often provide objectivity, relieving the intensity. There may be painful affect attached to the events both generations describe, which provides a moving experience for all participants. Almost inevitably there will be reactions from family members of resentment, disappointment, anger, or sadness. Sometimes bitter accusations of unfulfilled obligations and injustices emerge, leading to an impasse. Or there may be a protective defensiveness that keeps meaningful dialogue from happening. Even if a mutual acceptance is not possible, it can still be beneficial to the client to have stated her position and accepted that of her parent, in terms of her own acceptance of self.

Confrontation alone does not change deprived and warped views. A process needs to occur on both sides in which those who feel they have been treated unfairly can speak of their hurts, fears, and rejection. The hope is to move beyond blame to a deeper level of reciprocal discussion so that the client will be able to accept her parents more objectively as real persons doing the best they can, and to see her own contribution to the problems for which she may blame her parents. The therapist provides support for all participants, seeing that no one gets scapegoated. Some clients begin to develop a peer relationship with parents, which can provide mutual support so that misunderstandings can be clarified and caring can be identified in its own right, apart from agreement and approval.

The Older Parents' Goals

It is more common for younger adults to ask their families of origin to attend sessions than for older parents to convene their adult children as consultants. When older parents have either resolved their issues in therapy or come to a mutual acceptance of their differences and agreed on ways to handle them, they are then ready to meet with their children. Adult children often view their parents as literally the same people they were when the children left home, years before, and have difficulty seeing that parents continue to mature and grow as do their children.

The older parents can discuss the differences between them, the problems these differences have created, and the changes they have made. They can speak of the difficulties they have had in separating from their own parents and accepting them. They can be open to questions from their children about past family happenings, share family secrets, and clarify misperceptions. Most of all, they can hear and respond to their children's concerns and accept their positions, even while stating their own.

Usually, meeting three to four hours over a two-day period is sufficient to open up areas of discussion that can be continued within the family. Occasionally, however, a family conference raises issues that parents and children want to continue resolving with assistance from the therapist. The adult children may enter their parents' therapy for a number of sessions on a weekly basis, or joint sessions can alternate with their parents' sessions. Another alternative is to plan a number of sessions over several days to work on specific issues.

Whatever the issues or format, the goal is open and honest communication, including respect for the autonomy of each. There is an important difference between the concepts of *acceptance* and *approval.* Parents and children are often not satisfied with acceptance; they require that the other generation approve of what they are doing. When two stubborn generations lock horns, then differences become accentuated and similarities fade away.

I work towards helping each generation to think in terms of acceptance, rather than approval, of the other as a person who can take the consequences for her actions. When there is a lessening of the need for conformity, then rebellion subsides and honest differences in beliefs, values, and styles of living can be acknowledged and understood. It is then possible for family members to evolve a new sense of identification through the rebalancing of obligations, with a renewed sense of fairness on each side.

Issues for Transgenerational Sessions

Some of the issues that have been discussed in family conferences are listed below:

> *Differences in values between generations —*
> *what to do when family expectations are not met*

Work values: Status vs. fringe occupations; importance of making money vs. competing values; importance of education; issues involved in family business, if relevant.

Religious values: How the family accepts a member who leaves the church; how the family tolerates different religious beliefs.

Marital and sexual values: Living together vs. marital commitment; how to bring the live-in partner home; divorce and remarriage; abortion; conception of children outside marriage; homosexuality.

Use of alcohol and drugs: How can family members state their concerns while allowing each individual to take his/her own consequences and be responsible for self?

*Differences in power relationships in the family —
how to balance them*

How to be unique, separate, different, and still belong.
How to have one-to-one relationships in the family.
Who is in the switchboard role? How does this get in the way of direct communication?
How to be a younger adult to an older adult rather than a child to a parent.
How to handle decision-making when it concerns the whole family.
How to stay out of early family roles (smart one, hysterical one, wild one, mother's helper, clown, etc.).
How to accept in-laws into the family.
How to relate to divorced family members.

Resolving emotional differences

What is "fair" and how to deal with situations some members think are unfair.
How to resolve a situation when obligations are perceived differently from each side.
How to understand the other's feelings and point of view.
How important issues get smoothed over; how to allow angry feelings to surface, and then resolve them.
How to respond to the pain of others.
How to share grief and sadness in the family.
How to affirm others.

Different perspectives

How children born at different stages in the family's life cycle viewed the family differently, and how this colors their present view; parents' views when they were the age their children are now.
How the aging of the parental generation affects all family members; sharing of information about retirement, health changes, housing needs, wills, etc.
How the generational splits that grew out of the changing milieu in the sixties and seventies are still alive in the present, for both generations.

THE THERAPIST SETS THE STAGE

I usually start the session, after introductions, by speaking to the group as a whole. Both generations may be tense and uncomfortable; I want to establish a framework in which they can express themselves. I may start from a family life perspective to normalize the therapeutic situation, placing it in a growth, rather than a pathological framework. I may say something like this:

> "I see families going through developmental stages — all families. There was the time when you (to the parents) got married, when the first child, John, was born, when the children began school, and when they entered adolescence. There was a big shift when the children left home for college or jobs, which I call the launching phase. And through all these phases, and as the children moved out into the world, the family members kept changing. If is often helpful to look at one's own family and see how those changes have gone, to see if everyone is satisfied with them, and if you are each able to say to other family members the things you want to say. I think it is useful — and it certainly has been useful for me in my own family — to take a look at where the family members are with each other, now that they are adults. John has asked you to come in today as a consultant to his change, but that does not mean that you are not free to say whatever you want to say about your family. As a starter, I'm curious about how you see yourselves as a family."

Or, if the older parents have invited their adult children, I may introduce the session as follows:

> "I have been seeing your parents for the last six months as they have been working on their relationship. I find it useful to both generations when adult children come in as consultants to our therapy. You have all spent years together as a family with many shared life experiences, yet you haven't lived together for any length of time since the last child left for college. You have all made many changes since that time. I hope today will be an opportunity for you to share some important thoughts and feelings with each other. Your father and mother have items for the agenda; perhaps you, too, have issues you wish to discuss."

By opening the session to all members to talk about how they see themselves as a family, it is possible for us to become acquainted, to relax, and to test out this strange new experience. During this time I establish rapport with each member, sharing a laugh together, possibly referring briefly to an experience in my own family that matches their own. I also gain important information about each member that I can use later in the hour. When the members feel relatively safe in the overall setting, then it is easier for the client to bring up her own issues.

ADULT CHILDREN AS CONSULTANTS

When parents have focused their joint energies on work and on their children over the growing-up years at the expense of their own relationship, they may find it difficult to regain a sense of meaningfulness and joy in being alone together after the children have left. Such parents may enter therapy to revive their marriage. After they have made a commitment and are in the process of change, their adult children can be involved to give input to the process.

A typical couple would be in their fifties or early sixties, with a successful workaholic husband who traveled extensively while his wife raised the children and was involved in the community. As the children left home, she felt increasingly neglected. Although both have developed their own talents and each is competent in separate spheres, they have not explored common interests or nourished intimacy, and their marriage lacks growth and excitement.

Exploring the patterns in the families of origin often gives insight that can lead to useful interventions. A common pattern involves a husband who left humble beginnings to become successful and, in the process, cut himself off from nurturing roots. He has continued to "do his duty" for his original family as a caretaker, supporting them instrumentally while cutting himself off emotionally, a pattern he has also followed in his marriage. He continues to appear strong, not admitting weakness, hurt, or grief in his family of origin or to his wife or children. He knows how to give practical help and keep distance but not to receive emotional support or to move closer. Approaching retirement for such a man can be a difficult adjustment, as he prepares to give up his superior position without resources to put in its place, and without any practice in revealing his vulnerability.

During the successful and busy years of middle life he may have felt little need for family support. As he ages and his children leave, however, he may have second thoughts, coupled with a conviction that his family members will never change. He may not see that the change can come from within himself, in a deeper sharing of his own personhood with his wife, his aging parents, his siblings, and his own children.

The wife of such a man is often overinvolved emotionally with her family of origin. She is familiar with an enmeshed system and is often intrusive. She speaks for others, including her husband, not having learned in her original family to respect innate differences. His under-involvement and her overinvolvement result in transgenerational im-balance.

The mother's family has always been part of the children's world, while they have hardly known father's, absorbing his view that, because his fami-ly has problems and is not successful, they are really hardly worth know-ing. When transgenerational involvement is limited to one parent's side, the intensity in that side increases and the refreshing diversity that comes from two different family lineages is lacking. Alliances and polarization result.

Two Generations Meet Together

The Petersons, Pete and June, invited their five married children, Ellen, Tina, Elsa, Jana, and Gordon, and their spouses, all of whom lived out of state, to meet with them for two double sessions over one week-end, with Chuck and myself as co-therapists (Figure 16). Elsa and Gor-don did not attend the first session. After introductory statements, we made an agenda of the issues the family members wanted to discuss, list-ing them on the flip chart.

June started the discussion, saying she wanted all of them to say openly what they thought and felt. Her statement became a theme for the day, because her mother, Grandma Bea, the matriarch of the family, had a "Be perfect" motto and had strongly discouraged conflict. Grandma Bea's notion, according to Ellen, the oldest daughter, had been that when you got married you didn't have to work on issues. Ellen said she and her husband Marvin fought out their battles all the time.

The children said it felt good to see their parents now working on changing themselves. They had heard Mother find fault with Father dur-ing their childhood, with Father ending up the butt of family teasing and jokes. Although the girls had participated, they admitted they had felt uncomfortable about their part.

We talked of the transgenerational pattern of female dominance in both the grandparental and parental generations. The two older daughters' husbands, Marvin and Arthur, had fathers who had died be-fore their sons were grown. They had both joined the Peterson family, as Pete had joined June's. Marvin acknowledged that he felt conflicted as he saw himself in his father-in-law's position. He wondered if there really was a place for an outside man in this family.

Pete said he was viewing his original family differently now and could be straighter with his brother and sister. He spoke movingly of a recent

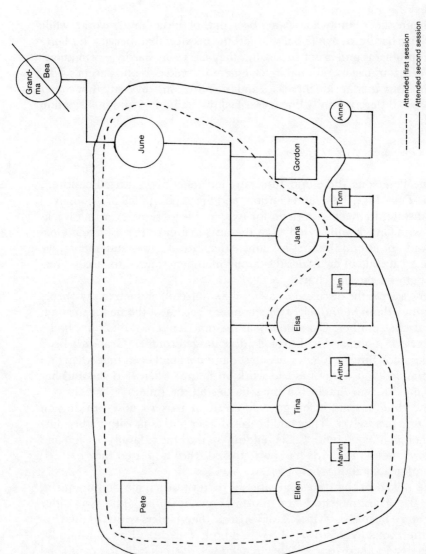

Attended first session

Attended second session

Figure 16. Peterson Family Diagram

trip he had taken with Tina and Gordon to visit his brother, who now lived in the family homestead. An important insight for Pete had been when Tina and Gordon had told him on that trip to the farm that they thought it would have been hard to live with their mother as a spouse because she had been so "right." Ellen spoke of her father's recent visit to her home, the first visit he had ever made alone without her mother, and how her relationship with him was changing.

Pete told him about his insight into the three past stages of his life and how he was looking forward to the fourth stage now, with June. The first stage had been with his original family when he was a child. The second had been during his and June's early struggling years, when he had become alienated from his family of origin. In the third stage, although he had been very successful in business, his self-esteem had not risen accordingly, and he had thought he needed business success to feel personal satisfaction. Now, even though he was experiencing a gradual tapering off in his business life as he faced retirement, he and June were more comfortable together and he was experiencing more peace within himself.

The adult children reminisced about the past. Ellen, as the oldest child, had felt she never did anything right and had decided to enjoy her "bad girl" status. Tina, coming second, had been the good child and had gotten better grades; as a typical second child, she had seen, from what happened to Ellen, what would get her into trouble. Jana, the youngest daughter, called herself the clown. Tina, however, did not see her that way — only that she lightened the atmosphere with her humor. There were good feelings and give and take among the siblings.

Marvin, Ellen's husband, who had stated when the session began that he came to observe but not to talk, said he had been struggling for a long time with how to handle the family discussions that were ostensibly about politics or other outside issues, yet were personal to him. He felt two levels of communication were going on, and no one was addressing the personal friction underneath. His theory was that there were rules against confronting each other or getting to basic issues and so, to alleviate tension when the family was together, everyone teased Pete, and Jana became the family clown. Family members acknowledged the tension, and Pete and June spoke of what they were doing to change. The children were grateful to hear their parents talk.

Second Session

Grandma Bea, who had been admitted to a nursing home a month before, died the night after the first session. Pete called to tell us of her death and that the family had met together and decided they did want to go ahead with the second session. Her death heightened everyone's emotional level and was the precipitating factor in bringing Elsa, her husband Jim, and Gordon to the second session.

After talking about Grandma Bea's death and welcoming Elsa and Gordon, we continued by asking each member to give his or her reactions to the earlier meeting and to put items on the agenda for this one. The third daughter, Elsa, who had stayed with her sick child the day before, replied first, saying she had wanted to come and understand the family. There were two issues for her: the pain in her parents' relationship that she sensed was still there for her mother, and the issue of "belief vs. wealth," which was a difficult area for her.

Gordon, the youngest child and only son, had also missed the first session. He looked uncomfortable but purposeful as he asked, "Who is the patient?" His father answered that the patients were June and himself and their marriage; that they wanted the children to understand what was happening in their marriage and the changes they were making. He also said he would like to hear from Gordon and the others their thoughts about the family and how they would like family interactions to change.

Areas of tension centered around money and religion. Elsa saw a discrepancy between her mother's expressed beliefs about the unimportance of money and the affluent way in which her parents lived. In recent years June and Pete had been generous, giving gifts freely to their children. It became clear that the siblings' birth order had had an influence on the way they viewed money. Ellen gave an example. When she, the oldest, had gone to elementary school, she only had two dresses. When she had asked her mother why she didn't have as many as her friends, her mother had said, "You don't need any more — just one to wear and one in the wash!" and that had satisfied her. When Tina had started school, she had three dresses and mother's answer was: "We don't have enough money for any more." When Elsa had reached school age, the answer was, "Someday you'll have more dresses." For Jana, however, she had all the dresses she wanted, and with Gordon, Mother had asked, "Wouldn't you like more clothes?" Gordon and Jana had accepted the gifts readily without guilt, but, after hearing the older siblings' comments about money, wondered, "Does that mean we owe our parents something?" The answer was not really clarified during the session. The question was posed, however, for further discussion later.

It was clear that a lot of assuming was going on. In many ways the children saw their parents as they used to be when the children had left home. The parents had also not seen or recognized changes in their children. When they visited, especially at the maternal family's summer home, which was shared with Mother's family of origin, the children often got sucked back into childhood behavior. This year, when Ellen short-ened her yearly summer visit to spend some time alone with Marvin, it was, she said, her best home visit ever. She had been upset, however, when her mother had written later, asking if something was wrong.

Marvin asked June if her religion was important for her alone, or if she needed the others to believe as she did. She answered that when the children were young, she had indeed wanted them to believe as she did; now it was not so necessary, although she got so much joy out of her religion for herself that she would like to share it with them. Several of the girls said they were turned off by religion, while Gordon, who was a minister, shared his mother's beliefs. It was obvious that Gordon was feeling tension, but it was not clear where the conflict was.

Pete had spoken firmly about his looking towards the future; Elsa asked if her mother had anything she was looking forward to. June said she was most enthusiastic about her religion and all of her activities connected with it, many of which were now shared with Pete. She said it had stood by her during the bad years when her marriage was falling apart. She still sounded bitter about those years, but she said she did not change fast. Pete protected her, saying, "We've been dumping on your mother." I asked if she felt they had. She was not sure; she had not been surprised at anything that had come up. She said she had asked for it and she wanted to think about it.

Tina especially expressed her urge to help her parents. She said that she had felt she should "do" something when her mother had talked to her about the problems Mother and Father were having and about get-ting help. Chuck spoke of the changes both parents had made, adding that the children did not need to be therapists; there were already enough therapists. I spoke of Grandma Bea's death and the vacuum that it would create. I asked June, "Will you fill your mother's shoes as matriarch for the extended family now that she is dead?" June said, "No," explaining to her children that that was a lonely role she no longer wanted.

Follow-up Comments

The family felt no need to schedule additional sessions. The meetings opened up discussion that would be continued by both generations in an ongoing dialogue as the family members met together in the future. Jana wrote us a note immediately after the session:

"I just wanted to say thank you for your warmth and love. We have no-ticed the effect on our parents of your wisdom, but it was a great help to me to meet with you two and experience these things first hand. You've given me a way of trying to assert myself with the family, a fresh approach. And I think everyone else in the family came away with other new perspectives. Best of all, though, it looks like Mom and Dad have discovered a new direction for themselves and their marriage and we're (or at least I am) more hopeful than ever about the two of them."

June wrote her impressions of the aftereffects of the sessions when I sent them the preceding section from my manuscript for their comments:

"We were all (except Gordon) together at Ellen's when Pete arrived with your manuscript. So, we each had a crack at it and read it through, discussed it, and were entertained by the recollections of those days and what it all meant. By and large we concurred with your account. Sometimes the discussion revealed that certain ones wandered from the emphasis of its being the parents' therapy and not theirs. So, wistfulness about getting more direction for their own relationship to us got in the way of the main purpose of its being the parents' therapy. . . . The breaking down of the barriers to communication has been good but had some hard, hard effects immediately. In the long run it's made the children much closer, I think—also more open with each other.

"Gordon's misreading of his relationship with his sibs was quite a revelation to him and after the first devastating realization of it, he took steps to correct the misunderstandings, which, I think, contributed to his interest now in family counselling. . . . Marvin was encouraged, as a result of the session, to get therapy on his own and was in it for a couple of years after that. He, incidentally, has been greatly helped.

"You know, I listened to the tapes one day and took notes and then spoke with each of the kids on subjects that came up in their conversations at that session. That was *very* good and has helped. I no longer feel the need to explain Pete and they no longer ask me to and that's nice. So there have been some good results."

Tina wrote that she had not understood the children's roles as consultants to their parents and wished we had explained ourselves at the beginning:

"At the time of the meetings I experienced tremendous confusion about our role in the process. I have had many years of therapy with several different therapists and I had been acquainted with several people who had convened their own family reunions within a family therapy context. This background seemed to hinder rather than help me. I wish that you had been clearer about our role as consultants early on. For some reason, I had been expecting to be more in a patient role, or part of the whole family as a patient. I, at least, would have felt better oriented and more able to contribute appropriately had I been told the context in which I was invited to the sessions. . . . I also want to say that I believe our sessions with you did help us identify some family issues, bringing them out of the closet for airing."

I realized that our depending on Pete and June to explain the context of the session to their children was not enough; that we should have restated it clearly as the session began. It was not until the beginning of the second session that Gordon had asked "Who is the patient?" and his father explained. This was an omission on our part and a learning experience for us.

PARENTS AND SIBLINGS AS CONSULTANTS

As couples move into the middle phase of treatment, the intensity of the acute problems that brought them to therapy has diminished and each begins to work on differentiation. They move at different paces, dividing the time between each one's individual needs, family of origin issues, their relationship, and parenting problems.

Amy and Gene, a couple in their thirties with a two-year-old daughter, Donna, were in the middle phase of therapy* with Chuck and myself. Amy had made some important moves in her family of origin by the sixty-second session. She had altered her relationship with her mother, sister, and extended family members on both sides of her family. After hiring a detective to find her father, who had disappeared when she was seven, she stated clearly that she wanted to invest her energies in continuing to work with her family of origin for the time being. She was willing to come to sessions, but she wanted us all to understand that she would not be participating in couples work for a while. Her position left a void since she had been using more than her share of the therapy time over the past several months.

It was obviously Gene's turn to take center stage, but he wanted to work on their relationship, not on himself, and she refused to work with him, backing her chair out of the circle. Gene turned towards me, saying that it was more comfortable talking to me. As I listened, I began feeling burdened, imagining that I was his mother, and realizing that he was excluding Chuck. As I spoke about these feelings, Chuck replied that he had become sleepy as Gene started talking to me. Gene defended himself, saying that he knew where he was with me and that Chuck

---

*See Chapter 5 for a therapy session with Gene and Amy a year and a half earlier.

did not give him either verbal or nonverbal feedback. So I turned my chair around and faced the window in a move which paralleled Amy's, leaving Chuck and Gene to talk together for the rest of the hour.

As I sat there, I thought about the dynamics that had just occurred. Gene wanted to concentrate on Amy or me, and not work on himself or with Chuck. This told me that the unresolved male/female issues in his family were surfacing in the therapy with the therapists. He was enmeshed with his mother and distant from his father, without a satisfactory relationship with either of them. I resolved to have him bring his family members to a session so we could help him rebalance these relationships. As it turned out, it was several months before this came to pass.

Getting the Family In

At the beginning of the next session I told Gene my thoughts about asking his parents to come in as consultants. He was reluctant, although he said he might be willing to come with his younger brother Philip, who, at age 32, continued living in the parental home.

By the next week he was willing to rehearse in the session various ways to ask his brother to accompany him. He became tearful as he talked to Philip in an empty chair. Chuck asked, "What are your tears about?" Gene replied that he was sad that he had grown up being so far away from his family members. When I asked, motioning towards the empty chair, "Will you say that to Philip — that you want to be closer?" he answered, "Not now," adding that he feared if they were closer it would be too sticky — or they wouldn't be close at all.

By the next session, Gene and Amy had spent a day at his parents'. Philip had suggested he and Gene wash dishes, which gave Gene a chance to talk to Philip about coming to the session. Philip said he would think about it, which usually meant that he would not come. Gene was realizing how much Amy had been serving as a buffer between him and his family. He began visiting his parents' home alone or with his daughter Donna. He found he said very little and usually felt excluded. He reported that no one ever talked about anything important.

A month later, when Gene still had no plan to bring his family in, Chuck worked with him on a childhood incident when his early decision was, "I don't expect anybody to understand me and I won't ask for help. I'll do it myself." Following this, Gene asked Philip again if he would come. Philip replied, "It's a crazy idea," and turned him down. When Chuck inquired what it meant to Gene for his brother to refuse to come in, Gene responded that it looked like he could not count on any of them emotionally, although they would do anything instrumentally, such as give him money.

The next week Gene announced that "someone" from his family would be coming in two weeks. He had invited himself to join his mother and brother for lunch. He had fumbled around when Philip asked "What's up?" until Philip finally told his mother that Gene had asked Philip to get the family to come to therapy. Mother instantly said "yes," without expressing curiosity or asking any questions. Philip had given several reasons why he might or might not come. Gene thought this time he probably would. His father was not mentioned in this whole conversation.

Gene predicted that none of his family would have anything to say. He said they felt easily criticized and that Philip had been offended when Gene told him that Chuck thought his reluctance to come in was connected with a fear of something hidden coming out in the session. Amy decided to stay home, although she wanted to listen to the tape of the session.

The equivocal process that Gene went through to bring his family in is typical of many families. Although he was a successfully functioning executive, he acted like a little boy as he went about setting up the family conference. His early decision, "I don't expect anybody to understand me and I won't ask for help," was still ruling his actions. He was not seeing any of his family members realistically and was not understanding what he was contributing to the lack of communication. He dutifully visited and phoned but there was little sharing of thoughts or feelings.

Although Chuck and I like to start with the entire family at the first session, we had been willing for Gene to bring his brother first since his anxiety was so high and Philip seemed to be a key member. A meeting with Philip could serve as a lead-in to having all members come. As he thought about how to approach Philip in the empty chair rehearsal, however, Gene had found himself tearful, recognizing his distance from his family and not seeing any possibility for establishing a middle ground somewhere between enmeshment and cutoff. As the weeks went by, he had felt increasingly awkward and unable to accomplish his purpose in his family of origin, in contrast to his usual ease at work. He was relieved when Philip finally came to his rescue.

First Session and Its Aftermath

Philip brought Father and Mother to the first of two family sessions. Mother obviously came to help; Father was uncomfortable, looking away most of the time, nodding his head and agreeing. When any friction arose, he changed the subject. Philip was also ill at ease and silent. I actually kept forgetting that he was in the room, which revealed his ability to erase himself.

This first session was an introductory one as they looked us over. Mother spoke of both her and her husband's families of origin and of incidents when Gene was a child. As she became more comfortable, she said it was hard for them to believe that Gene could need therapy. He replied that if he and Amy had not had a baby and then therapy, he did not think they would still be together.

Towards the end of the session, when Gene was feeling emotional, Father changed the subject to talk about his grandchild, Donna, and everyone followed his lead. I intervened at this point to make them aware of their deeply engrained pattern which kept them from talking about important emotional issues. I described the process: When someone (in this case Gene) was feeling deeply, someone else (in this case Father) changed the subject. When I asked if this process happened often, Gene replied that it did. I told them that one thing I had had to learn in my own family was to keep quiet and let other members experience their emotions. Father said he would not have changed the subject if he had known that Gene wanted to talk about it. Gene acknowledged that he could have returned to the subject.

We scheduled a session alone with Gene and Amy in the week between Gene's two family of origin sessions. Not surprisingly, after Gene had made the big move to bring in his family, regression was triggered in both Gene and Amy and they were fighting like they had been when they first came to therapy. We told them that we were not surprised, that sometimes sessions with extended family members are like major surgery and threatening to both partners.

I asked Gene: "Will this scare you off?" His answer was "No," but he admitted that he had thought about calling off the second meeting. Amy said she did not want to come in, that she did not have the time, energy, or money. She suggested that she come in once a month and Gene work with his family the rest of the time. Chuck said she needed to think about how she was going to bring in the members of her family, which might be even more difficult since they lived at a distance.

I realized that Amy felt left out of the excitement with Gene's family. I told her I thought she was on the right track in taking care of herself, but that we needed to keep a balance in our sessions. I added that I thought she was being provocative about not coming in, and suggested that she could take care of herself in all the other hours except for the one we had scheduled for therapy. She agreed, saying she felt understood and close to me.

Second Session Begins

In the second meeting Father was not present, although he had agreed to come. Philip was spokesman for the family, in striking contrast to the earlier session when Father attended and Philip had hardly spoken at all. The theme of family patterns, which initiated this session, continued throughout.

Chuck: Your Dad said last time he would be here today. He must have changed his mind at some point.
Philip: No. I don't think he had any intention of being here.
Mother: Grandpa used to say of my husband, "He's a good man. He always says yes. He doesn't do it, but he always says yes."
Philip: I always say yes, but then I always do it.
Jan: (to Mother) Did you think about staying home today?
Mother: No, I said I was coming. If I promise, I'll come. I do as I say I will.
Jan: If you didn't want to, how would you handle it?
Mother: Well, even if I didn't want to, if it would help, I would still come.
Jan: I'm fascinated, Gene, about where you fit into all this.
Gene: I'm like my father.
Jan: You say yes and then you don't do it. (He nodded.) So these two (motions towards Mother and Philip) are more alike in this and you, Gene, and your father are more alike.
Chuck: And that has the effect of keeping the hassle down in the short run, but in the long run it may not be so good because people don't know when you mean it and when you don't. They have to read your mind as to whether it's a yes-yes or a yes-no.

Both Philip and Mother felt more comfortable in this session. I wondered about Philip's position vis-à-vis Father. When Father was present, Philip was invisible; when Father was absent, Philip took over as family leader at the beginning of the session. Another factor was also operating; it was the second meeting and families are usually more relaxed the second time around. Father's absence provided a beginning focus, as Philip and Mother described his style of communication in relation to their own. The therapists then made explicit two related family rules and their consequences: 1) Father and Gene say yes but do not follow through; 2) Mother and Philip say yes and follow through. These rules provided a key to the difficulties Gene had had in setting up the meeting in the first place.

Reactions to the First Session

I was curious if my confrontation of Father in the first session (pointing out his protective pattern of changing the subject) had made it difficult for him to return.

Jan: Did anything happen last time that was upsetting to him?
Philip: Well, first of all, I don't think he's used to sitting around, talking to people. And, second of all, I think it's the things that people don't usually talk about. And that's a formula for upsetting people. Right?
Mother: I was uncomfortable and very uneasy because I never knew there was any kind of a problem between Gene and Amy. That makes you a little sick when you think about it. They kept up a good front. When you think everything is all right and everything isn't all right — and their beautiful child! Donna would be hurt most of all. I wasn't even aware of it — that's frightening.
Jan: You'd rather be aware of it when things are going on with Gene?
Mother: Right.
Chuck: That's where you and your husband are different.
Mother: Yes. He'll brush it off. "It's not so! It's not so! You're imagining this."

Mother identified her concern about Gene's marriage and especially her wish to know about serious problems. She acknowledged the difference between herself and her husband, who would rather not know.

Things That Don't Get Said

Following talk of Father's absence, Philip led the conversation into a long discussion about Amy's absence and we got stuck there, with Philip obviously hurt by Amy's avoidance, not only in the session, but during recent visits to their home. Gene told him to ask Amy, trying to stay out of the middle. Yet the focus continued on Father and Amy, safe topics since neither of them was present. The therapists each identified the impasse in different ways, but we remained stuck until Gene began to speak for himself.

Gene: (to Philip) You have a different agenda than I have. And really, what I'm interested in is not the things between you and Amy, but the things that don't get said among us, that have been going on for years. I think that's part of the reason why there's a lot of talk between you and Amy, for example. The kind of talk we're doing today is absolutely unlike anything we ever do at home. There are times that none of us can get past talking about what we're having to eat. And sometimes that just makes me tense because I feel like we're all just wasting time. There are things that go on that no one ever talks about. You know, Philip, when Mother was sick, I didn't even know about it.

A discussion followed about the time when Mother had high blood pressure and dizzy spells and no one let Gene know, even though he continued to call and visit. Weeks later, Philip had told Gene when Mother was diagnosed at a clinic.

Jan: (to Mother) It sounds like Philip takes care of you.
Mother: I guess so. He panics.
Philip: No, I didn't panic. That's why I didn't tell him before.
Mother: It was stupid. If I wasn't feeling well, I should have looked for help.
Chuck: But you didn't want to bother anybody, either.
Mother: Right. But it wasn't getting any better.
Jan: Did you tell your husband about it?
Mother: Oh, yes. I guess I can't avoid it. He gets scared after a point. Usually he thinks it will be all right.
Jan: But somehow, when you're not feeling well, it's just not OK to tell Gene, when he comes over.
Mother: No, I guess I would hide that. Maybe it will pass. To not bother him.
Jan: It must make it difficult for you to decide when you should tell somebody something.
Mother: Right.
Jan: If you tell them, it's like you're expecting them to *do* something about it. It doesn't sound like you can just tell them because they're close to you.
Gene: There are lots of things I'm not told about.
Philip: I do normal average things that I don't have to think about, but you do other things that take a lot of thinking, so we all say, "Why bother you?" It's not absolutely necessary. You have enough to worry about. And your job is important. So why bother you unless it is important?
Chuck: (to Gene) Apparently they see you as a very busy, preoccupied person.

Gene: Unnecessarily, I think.
Chuck: And they feel protective towards you — they don't want to burden
   you.

As Gene began to speak of his agenda and raised the specific issue of
Mother's illness, the session became focused. It was clear that there was
a complicated caretaking ritual going on involving all four members of
the family in rigid roles, defining not only what was said, but also what
was done. When Philip identified Gene as important, a hierarchy began
to emerge, with the identification of Philip as unimportant made by implication. Father and Gene were the powerful and uninvolved family
members who were protected; Mother and Philip were the involved ones
who did the protecting. It was also clear that Philip and Mother had the
same rule with Gene that he had with them: I don't expect anybody to
understand me and I won't ask for help.

Identification of Patterns

Gene: I think of another example. This may not be how it happened, but
   it's how I remember it. And that is your graduation from college
   that I didn't know about.
Philip: What?
Gene: I remember very clearly because I really felt badly I wasn't there.
Philip: Why weren't you there?
Gene: I didn't know you were graduating.
Philip: Who didn't tell you?
Chuck: Apparently everybody didn't tell you.
Philip: Well, I wasn't home at the time; I was in college. Who is the cul-
   prit on that?
Mother: That's me, I guess. I'm the culprit. And there's Father, too.
Jan: Oh, so you're supposed to tell Gene about what happens with
   Philip . . .
Mother: That's it!
Jan: . . . and Philip is supposed to tell Gene what happens with you!
   (Mother is laughing in a delighted way at my discovery.) And no-
   body tells Gene about themselves!
Mother: Right!
Chuck: That's why they expect Gene to tell them about Amy.
Jan: Right. Because that's the way it happens in the family. (to Gene)
   And you're really changing a family pattern if you say, "Ask me
   about me and ask Amy about Amy." (to Chuck) It's really clear that
   Mother was supposed to tell Gene about Philip's graduation and

Philip was supposed to tell Gene about Mother's illness. (Mother is laughing again.) Isn't that fascinating?

Gene: Do you realize that's happened all our lives when people are relaying messages?

Philip: It's bizarre!

Chuck: It's more than bizarre, it's inefficient! (Everyone laughs.)

Philip: That's like the story that they tell funny jokes down the line. You start at one end and it gets all garbled when it gets to the other end.

Chuck: That's exactly right. It's bound to be mixed up in some way by the time the last person hears it.

As Gene stayed with his agenda and brought up another example, this time about Philip's graduation, another connected set of inefficient and time-consuming rules became clear. Misdirected loyalty bonds kept Mother and Philip allied in maintaining a triangle, protecting Gene, the special child. Mother was to tell Gene what happened with Philip, and Philip was to tell Gene what happened with Mother; neither was supposed to tell Gene directly. We connected these rules with Gene's failure earlier in the session to get Philip to talk directly to Amy. By now the family members were working together as a team, interested in and curious about tracking their own patterns. Since the rules were being acknowledged, change was possible.

Acknowledgment of Feelings

Gene: I didn't ask, "When is Philip graduating?" And when we talked later, he said he'd already graduated, and I knew he felt bad.

Mother: I was hurt, too. He knew his brother was graduating and he didn't ask.

Philip: (to Gene, his voice rising) You acted like it was a crime that I pulled it off—the graduation. Everyone acted as if it was some kind of joke that I finally mastered it. That I went to that place and I came through. The first two years were the hardest thing I ever did.

Mother: I didn't know that, either. Their schooling was not my business. It's none of my business until it's too bad.

Jan: It sounds like you're all suffering from not hearing about things at the time.

Philip: I think some of that is your own business and you shouldn't sit there and say, "I'm really having a tough time."

Gene: What's wrong with that?

Philip: What's wrong with that is that then you'll complain all the time.

I could hardly get through school. What was I to do? Could *you* get me through there any better? I had to do that myself.

Jan: But you're talking the same way your mother was talking about her illness by saying, "Why would it help to tell anybody about it?" And yet, there she was, worrying inside herself.

Philip: But with me, it wasn't an illness.

Jan: It's not always that somebody else can *do* something . . .

Gene: I think you've hit one of the real critical things in how our family gets along—that when you *say* something, you're supposed to *do* something, rather than just listen. It's come up time and again today. (to Mother) If you told me about his graduation, then I'd have to go. But I could have said "No" or I could have called him and told him "No." There's no reason why I should be protected from making my own decisions about whether I'll go to his graduation or to anything else.

Chuck: In a communication problem like this, usually everybody is playing a part. Gene could have asked, Mother could have told him, and Philip could have invited him.

Jan: And, Gene, your pattern was to say "yes" and not to do anything. And my hunch is that it would have hurt you more, Philip, to have told him and to have had him say "Yes" and then not show up than to not tell him. That may have played into it.

Gene led the way to a deeper level by acknowledging both his own failure to ask about graduation and Philip's disappointment when Gene missed the event. The family had the courage to follow Gene's lead, moving into affectively loaded areas. Mother acknowledged her hurt and Philip was able to admit his bitter frustration at his family's disqualification of his efforts and accomplishments, railing at the injustice of being the unimportant one whose graduation was seen as a joke or as a crime he had pulled off. Mother was then able to admit her parallel ineffectual feelings in only being involved when something went wrong. As each spoke for self without protecting the other, they were exorcizing old myths by breaking the rigid rules and sharing their emotions in a new way.

Philip, having revealed his feelings, began to cover them over by assuming a stoical role, mirroring Gene's old early decision: "I'll do it myself." Gene challenged this stand. I noted the parallels between Philip's and Mother's attitudes, in that they both said, "Why would it help to tell anybody about it?" Gene restated as crucial a rule that had been identified earlier, that when you *say* something, you are also supposed to *do* something, rather than just listen, and he identified ways he could change his part in this communication. He also challenged their protection of him, defining his right to make his own decisions.

Chuck identified the options available and I pointed out how one set of rules reinforced another. As they revealed their feelings and positions, there was an increase in empathy and a possibility for a changed response: Anyone could ask for help or say that he or she hurt and the other could be free to do what was requested or just to listen and respond.

Recognition of Caring

Mother: We knew what was going on to a point and Gene was interested, and then he no longer called and he no longer came. When your child no longer cares what goes on, this is it. He is through.

Chuck: And so Amy's not communicating with you is a parallel to times when Gene wasn't communicating with you.

Mother: Right.

Jan: And that is scary because it means . . .

Mother: . . . that he doesn't care anymore.

Jan: And when you say, "People don't talk in the family," it's like they're scared to talk because maybe someone will withdraw and they won't have any more to do with you?

Philip: No, I don't think that could happen. I don't think this hurts any-thing—what we are doing, talking here today.

Gene: No.

Philip: (to Gene) How could that affect me with you? That's impossible. That won't change, no matter what.

Chuck: You're saying you care about him, no matter what.

Philip: That's right.

Jan: It sounds like Gene can say what he wants to say in the family be-cause . . .

Philip: Well, he gets too upset. He upsets me because he's upset. And when he comes to our house with Amy, he's very uptight. And if I try to be clever or to get along with her, it upsets him. And then he turns around and says, "You're picking on me," and he's not kid-ding—he means it. And I don't know what to do. I can't talk with her; I can't joke with her. Or that's a conspiracy against him. She wants to talk to me when she's there. We get along just fine when she decides to show up. And it bothers him that we get along just fine. Then we're picking on him.

Jan: You're talking to me, but you're really talking to him.

Philip: I know . . .

Jan: It sounds like you want an answer from him.

Gene: I can take it, Philip. You don't have to worry about me getting up-
    set. I do get upset, but . . .
Philip: Do you know what I've learned in the two times here? I don't know
    if you *can* take it.
Gene: Well, I can. Right?
Jan: You have to ask? (Everyone laughs.)
Gene: What kind of a person am I? Sure, I get upset. Do I need to be
    protected? I'm not going to flip out or anything.
Philip: Are you sure?
Gene: Yes.
Philip: All right.
Chuck: That's good to know.

After the frustration and the hurt were acknowledged, then Mother
could speak of her fear that Gene no longer cared. Philip affirmed the
importance of talking together as we were doing in the session, and his
caring for Gene. Philip's caring, however, was encumbered by a fear
which he now revealed, a belief that Gene would get so upset he might
flip out and become mentally ill. The reason for Philip's protection of
Gene now became clear.

The exchange between Philip and Gene was important in rebalancing the family's obligations. The interlocking alliances had kept all the
members from growing and developing autonomy. Gene was already
moving more freely, challenging the old rules and taking responsibility
for self. If Philip could give up his protection of Gene, he could then put
more energy into his own life. Gene had been overadequate and successful outside the family home and underadequate and upset in the
home. Philip, on the other hand, had been underadequate and unsuccessful outside the home and overadequate and protective in the home.
If they could move into a peer-to-peer relationship, developing mutual
give and take, each could gain.

Sibling Reconnection

Chuck: I sense that talking together is something both of you have wanted
    to do but have not known how to do.
Gene: But what you have to understand is that everyone feels — that there's
    no permission for me to say anything because it might upset some-
    body, and when I get there, my mind goes totally blank.
Philip: Really?
Gene: Yes.
Jan: I'm thinking about your saying that you don't feel permission or that

nobody gives you permission. I don't think it's possible for anybody to give you permission. You have to take it.

Gene: I know it. And Philip doesn't believe it, but it costs me great courage and energy to . . .

Philip: I believe that. I just don't understand why—why it would take you so much courage to say something like that to *me*.

Gene: I'm not like you, Philip. It does.

Philip: Maybe you don't talk enough to me.

Chuck: He's got something there.

Gene: I don't know how to talk to you.

Philip: You don't try.

Chuck: (to Gene) He's saying, "Try me."

Gene: My thought is that that's one of the reasons why we're here.

As Chuck encouraged the brothers to talk together, Gene disclosed his part in the family's protection myth by revealing his fear that anything that he said might upset somebody unless there was permission. Although fearful, both wanted more connection, yearning to fill the emptiness with a more differentiated family belongingness. Gene had protected himself by blanking out his mind, a counterpart to his father's pattern of doing nothing. I could see looming behind the brothers a similar dyad in Father and Mother, who had given up their autonomous energies for an interlocking "we-ness." Gene and Philip now had the opportunity to lead the way with a different type of relating. They began the journey in this session, which was essentially a reworking of old hurts and fears, resulting in reconnection.

Sibling relationships have had less focus in family of origin work than those between parents and children. Yet the sibling system is an integral part of the family, balancing the marital system and influencing the family's course during the entire life cycle. When children are young they form a support system with its own loyalty bonds that can continue beyond the lives of the parents as they identify with, care for, learn from, and differentiate from each other. Relating to siblings provides early training in peer-to-peer communication. There is continual interplay between the sibling subsystem and the parental system, with siblings often assigned roles by parents, such as the "sick" one or the "well" one. Bank and Kahn (1975) describe how the well sibling reacts to such role assignment by flight or avoidance, siding with the parents, forming a coalition with the sick sibling, or becoming a go-between.

When children leave for college, they often, in fact, leave their families behind. They develop a new work life, marry, and form their own nuclear family. When they return to their original home, they often return as if they were still 18 years old, to the old games and the old conversations with both parents and siblings. They may see this regression as something the original family imposes on them; because they fear their parents and/or siblings will probably not approve of their new life, they therefore decide not to bring it home. Or they fear that their family members, being uneducated or economically deprived, are not capable of understanding their chosen life. The parents, on their side, may still see themselves as parents, responsible for their offspring, especially since the young adult still acts, when she comes home, in the immature ways she did before she left home.

When both sides play this game, the adult child still acts and is treated as a teenager in the family and the parents retain their caretaking roles. This may continue until the parents become so old that the roles flip and a reversal of generations occurs. When neither parents nor siblings choose to reveal their real thoughts and feelings to each other and allow roles to predominate instead, much of the meaningfulness that both parents and adult children find outside the family with their spouses, friends, and in their jobs is not available to be shared between siblings and between the generations, within the family.

Sibling reconnection can often carry the nucleus for change. As children reach adulthood, they can be increasingly influential with their parents, a condition that young adults often do not realize. Energy which has been tied up in protecting, holding back, or opposing, as it was with Philip and Gene, can be released for support and constructive action. When parents are observer-participants of this process, they can follow if they choose.

When a framework for transgenerational openness can be established by the client members and therapist, then invited family members can come voluntarily, drawn in by their own curiosity, rather than maneuvered by the other generation. With this format they can come together on a more honest basis, encouraging curiosity about commonalities and respect for differences, with caring identified in its own right, apart from agreement and approval.

PART II

The Therapist's
Own Family

CHAPTER 8

The Therapeutic Interface

When the therapist meets with a family, he brings his unique learnings from his own background, as the family members bring theirs. The therapist is also a member of a family with a tendency to repeat the same patterns in different systems, just as client families do. He carries his own bias, like a filter, so that he is susceptible to setting up the reality he then treats. When a family comes for treatment, a therapeutic system is formed in which all parties must struggle within the common arena where the two systems overlap. This is the therapeutic interface (Figure 17).

The term "interface," used increasingly in family therapy, is broader than the psychoanalytic concepts of transference and countertransference, although it includes them. They are dyadic terms, used in one-to-one, individually-oriented therapy and are too narrow when more than two individuals are involved. Although transference and countertransference can be, and often are, present in family therapy, the purpose of working with the family is to help each member learn to deal directly and autonomously with other members, as well as with the therapist. The systemic aspects, therefore, distinguish the concept of therapeutic interface from the creation of one patient's exclusive transferential relationship with the therapist and the therapist's counterreactions to that patient.

Working with a family is crucially different from working with an individual in ways that affect the therapist's objectivity. A family is an already established system and includes, in addition to the dysfunctional member(s), members with adequate and excellent functioning in their daily lives. There is not the distinct separation between the dysfunctional patient who requests help and the functional therapist who offers it. For instance, an overadequate adult who accompanies the underadequate spouse to therapy usually sees self as a nonpatient and is likely to stir up a power struggle in the therapist if the therapist has not resolved similar

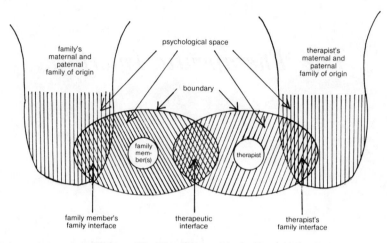

Figure 17. The Therapeutic Interface

power issues with his own parent. Likewise, if the therapist's own family has pathology similar to that of the family he is treating, he is vulnerable to induction by that family into their dysfunctional system.

There are many family therapists working in a task-oriented, here-and-now framework who do not consider the therapeutic interface as relevant. Such therapy can be effective and efficient, especially if it is short-term and carefully structured so the therapist's internal experiences are not likely to be triggered. It ignores an important arena, however, where learning can take place.

Donald Williamson (1981) explains how the therapist's family of origin affects the person of the therapist and the context of therapy:

> A major contribution of family therapy has been the notion that the family therapist has to deal with his/her own family. To put that in simple terms, it means that there are at least three families in the consulting room. You need the permission of your own family to be and to do family therapy. It means that we are forever at work on the multiple levels, and that every time you work with a family you are trying to improve your own family of origin. There have been others who have talked about the humanness of the therapist, but family therapy has given that an impact which is more powerful. The family therapy movement has brought the dethroning of the therapist, conceptualizing the therapist as being thrown into therapy him/herself, struggling and working on everything that the clients are working on. . . . I do not think that clients coming to a marital and family therapist experience the same sense of gap as they do with other practi-

tioners . . . . there is more of a sense of reciprocity. . . . Family therapy generally tends to look at human conflict as the stuff of life rather than as pathology, and that it is somehow not to be gotten rid of. I think that makes for an empathy with people at large. (p. 9)

A central theme for this book, in addition to an exploration of family interfaces, is how the therapist both influences and is influenced by the client family systems he treats. All of the concepts presented in Part I also apply to the therapist as a member of his own family. When he works with a client family, his own family experiences frame how he interacts. When the therapist continues dysfunctional relationships with his own family members, his ability to treat certain other families is limited. Although professionally competent, he may find himself unable to use his skills and experience effectively when a family with a process similar to his own enters therapy.

PRESSURES FAMILIES EXERT

The family's entry into the therapist's office tests the boundaries of both therapist and family. There are fears and expectations on both sides. Families can have very strong boundaries and resist the entry of a stranger. In addition, each individual within the family has a spatial field in which he feels comfortable. His sphere is not just physical, but also affect-laden and can be tested by having another person push against the boundary. Family members have pushed each others' boundaries to arrive at this place. Now they must also deal with an outsider. How will the therapist begin? Where will he push on the boundary? Family members watch the therapist: Is this a safe place to talk about what is troubling me? Can I talk to him? Will I be blamed? Will he protect me? Will he care?

Families give weight to the therapist's position and watch for a response, reading their own expectations into his actions. If he does nothing, they may interpret this as either approving of or disapproving of what is happening. The therapist needs to carry his own weight to match the family's system. A member may ally with the therapist to triangle him in, struggle to get the upper hand to control the therapy, or turn to the therapist and put him in charge. A family member may say, "Tell us what we should do. We heard you were the best family therapist in town," and then sit back and wait to be told what to do, so they will know how to beat him at his own game. Therapists are often vulnerable to contagion by the family's manipulation.

Since family members repeat the same patterns in the different systems in which they interact, they will eventually act in the therapeutic session as they behaved in their families of origin and demonstrate in therapy those dysfunctional patterns with the therapist. If the therapist is not caught up in the family's personal system, he can give them a new experience in the therapeutic interface that will help them break the repetitive cycle. It will be especially effective if they can then complete this action with crucial members in their families of origin.

THE THERAPIST'S REACTIONS

The therapist brings to the sessions experiences from his family of origin which shaped him and which, as a child, he considered normal; the manner in which they handled life cycle issues; the survival tactics they used; their view of males and females; the way they handled triangles, secrets, stress, anxiety, depression, sex; the patterns, assumptions, beliefs, and cultural values they accepted.

The therapist also brings to the interface his current life struggles: the physical, emotional, and intellectual problems he is grappling with in his marriage, with his children, with his aging parents, or in the community; issues of illness, death, divorce, of injustice and imbalance. When such problems are current in the therapist's own life, it is often harder for him to deal with the same problem in the families he treats.

When there is contagion from family to therapist, the therapist's feelings are stirred up. Each therapist has his own set of regressive reactions which interfere with his technical competence. He may become anxious or confused and find himself talking too much or too little, or he may become paralyzed, with his mind going blank. He may find himself becoming untypically authoritarian, telling people what to do, or he may become angry and find himself lashing out, or wanting to. Reactions can also take the form of physical symptoms such as headache, upset stomach, or a recurrence of earlier psychosomatic symptoms. The therapist usually has a physical clue at that point that he can utilize if he pays attention to his internal signals. It may be a tightening at the back of his neck, in one of his temples, or in the pit of his stomach; he may find himself pushing his chair back, away from the family, or tapping his fingers on the arm of his chair.

If the therapist is experiencing such reactions, the next step is for him to ask himself if he is inexperienced in setting up the structure, whether he lacks the skill in understanding the presenting problem, or if he is deficient in suitable techniques. If none of these seems to explain his reaction, then the situation in the family he is treating is probably exacerbating a personal, unresolved family issue in his own life.

When interface issues get stirred up, they can also create tensions in the broader system. A co-therapy team, seeing a conflictual couple, may find themselves fighting and not resolving issues. One of the co-therapists may find himself picking a fight with his wife, like he used to do with his sister when his father and mother fought when he was a child. It is easy to revert to earlier ways of coping, even if one is aware of one's vulnerability in familiar family interfaces. If one is not aware, the reaction may be automatic.

THERAPISTS' INTERFACE ISSUES

Family therapists are usually aware of the areas in which they have problems when they treat families. Some see the similarities to their vulnerable areas with their own families; some do not. As a supervision group begins, I routinely ask therapists to describe their interface issues as they see them. The following comments are typical:

"I never get intense and I don't understand intensity in families I treat. My family doesn't know me very well and we never talk about important things, so it's difficult for me to maintain relationships, not only with my family but with friends."

"I don't know what it's like to live with sibs since I never had brothers and sisters. It's also hard for me to treat mothers of young children; maybe that's too close to my own situation."

"I'm a middle child, a go-between, and I find myself defending and talking for individuals who are in the same place I am in in my family."

"I'm still very angry from years ago about my domineering father, and also with my husband. I feel bounded by both of them. I wasn't so aware of it until I began to treat families."

"I'm most effective in analyzing communication patterns and in helping to solve couples' disagreements with solutions both can tolerate. I have problems with impasses like my parents are now in, where people don't fight fairly and winning is the only goal."

"I have an overidentification with children, especially males, in divorced families. I was very close to my father and never got the attention and time I wanted from him."

"I'm not sure about my role when I work with families where the anger is up front. My anxiety level rises and I want to put a cap on it. It seems

alright to me when men act out, but not women. I sometimes wonder if
I encourage adolescents to act out."

"I can resolve immediate crises with clients, but then I don't know what
to do next. I have a vague feeling that my panic is related to the many
triangles I am a part of in my own family. I guard against expressing negative emotion with my own family, which transfers to work with my clients.
I wait too long to intervene and by the time I do, I'm mad or angry or
numb."

Such family interaction needs to be dealt with. The problem is: where
and how to confront these issues? The choices are usually between supervision and therapy. Most supervisors, however, rarely know enough
about the supervisee's family life, transgenerational patterns, and individual problems to see the connection between the supervisee's life and
his work. On the other hand, therapy rarely focuses upon cases; indeed,
supervision and therapy are routinely separated in many training programs and the student/client is on his own to make the connections between. He is often not able to be objective enough to do this by himself.

Family therapists and family therapy supervisors who work from a
transgenerational systems perspective and have applied the principles
to their own lives have the tools to help the beginning family therapist
look at the interfaces and make the connections. Then, when the therapist
starts to solve a problem in one area of his life, he can apply his knowledge to similar interfaces. In the following example, a therapist-trainee
was able to see such a connection and then to assert his own authority
in therapy:

Paul asked to talk about an interface issue in a family therapy supervision group. He had become aware, during the week, of an important
connection between the family he was treating and his own family.

Paul's parents had been divorced five years before and his father had
left the area. His mother and 19-year-old sister, Marie, who had a close
hostile/dependent relationship, still lived in his hometown. Marie and
her boyfriend lived together in an apartment near her mother; they had
been engaged for over a year, and the boyfriend had ostensibly become
the "man of the house" for Marie's mother. Paul and his brother lived
in different cities, several hundred miles away.

During the past week Paul's mother had called hysterically, raving that
Marie had left her boyfriend and gone to live with another man. Mother
said Marie was "just like her father, bull-headed — they both do just what
they want to do!"

Hearing those words, Paul remembered five years earlier, after his
parents' divorce, when Marie ran away and his mother had reacted hys-

terically in the same way. At that time Paul's father and brother were both unavailable and Paul, who was still living at home, had been the intermediary between his mother and Marie.

Paul saw the parallel clearly. He told his mother he thought she was reacting to Marie as she had done five years earlier, as if his father were leaving all over again. He said to her, "What's the big deal? She's 19 years old and has to live her own life. Why are you so upset?" As his mother saw the connection, she also calmed down.

As Paul left the phone, another parallel flashed into his mind: the case he had presented to the group over the last few months and with which he was currently in an impasse. His case concerned an 18-year-old borderline girl, Francine, who had been hospitalized four times since her parents had divorced when she was 13, the most recent hospitalization because of a serious suicide attempt. There was an older brother who was unavailable, as was her father. Francine's mother who was unstable, alcoholic, and depressed, had also spent time in mental hospitals.

Paul had been trapped between Francine and her mother as they were deciding where Francine should live after discharge, in the same way he had been caught in his earlier intermediary role between Marie and his own mother. He now realized that his anxiety in treating this family came from his earlier personal need to keep the fragments of his own family together, and his view of that role as being indispensable. Because of his experience with his father and brother, he had lost sight of the larger system of the client family, including the father and brother.

Paul's view of his role with this family changed. He had been working harder than either Francine or her mother. He became less willing to bend, insisted on regular meetings and began to seriously plan how to contact and involve Francine's father and brother, strategies that had been suggested in the group but which he had not been able to hear. As the therapy began to move ahead, it was clear to him why he was so fascinated with this family and why he had put up with all of their manipulations.

THE THERAPIST'S ACCOUNTABILITY

The therapist is accountable for his own actions with the family he treats. When he keeps the family focused on itself and promises no advantages apart from the members' own efforts to learn and change themselves, he is then able to avoid their attributing undue importance to himself. It is useful for him to ask about other therapists they have seen and find out why the family did not return. He can say, following negative comments about previous therapists, "I expect you may feel that way about me, too, one of these days." He can plan periodic evaluations in which he asks for feedback, both negative and positive, and models for them by telling them his reactions.

As the therapist takes responsibility for the session, he defines family members as responsible for themselves and for each other outside the sessions. This is especially important in terms of suicidal threats; the therapist needs to know when a family member should be hospitalized and when he can remain in the family. Drye, Goulding, and Goulding (1973) have developed an effective no-suicide decision that gives clear guidelines for any life-threatening situation. Thus, the therapist can have the patient determine in the session for himself, his family, and the therapist what risk actually exists so that safety precautions can be decided on in the session.

The therapist can carry a combination zoom/wide angle lens in his head. He can zoom in close to taste the feelings of one member and then, using the wide angle lens, zoom back out emotionally to a point where he is sufficiently distant from the family members so that he can watch the systemic flow of the emotional process between them, keeping self out of the current. Bowen has said that the best place for him is halfway between seriousness and humor, where he can shift either way to facilitate the process in the family.

The therapist can also back out emotionally and tune in to his own feelings at the moment. He can develop a language that cuts through the silent tension or noisy conflict to reveal his feelings in a graphic way, a process that keeps him from absorbing the feelings of individual members by handing them back to the family. He is also modeling for them the freedom to express themselves. He can say: "Wait a moment. This is how I am feeling right now. I am churning inside. I feel very anxious, as though some awful catastrophe is going to happen. Does anyone else in the room feel like that, or is it just me?" He can push his chair back, get up and walk around, putting words to his action: "I can't just sit quietly in one place when there is so much tension."

He can ask to change places with a family member, seeing how it feels to sit between the two conflictual ones, and then comment on his feelings, sitting in that hot spot. He can be direct in his interactions, apologizing for having hurt a family member's feelings, owning his part in having allowed himself to be triangled, and also holding firm when a member is trying to manipulate him.

Most of all, however, he can learn to recognize himself as a bridge between the client family in his office and his own family inside himself. He can identify the current feelings stirred up within, recalling times in his earlier life when similar feelings were triggered, and focus on the connection between those feelings and what is happening in the session. It may not be possible to do all this while the session is in progress. If the therapist routinely audiotapes, he can replay the part where he lost his bearings and was sucked into the family's system, recalling his feelings in the session as he listens. He can then analyze the interaction from a more objective stance, asking himself: How was the behavior that upset me valued in my family of origin and how was it handled? What is the parallel between my reaction (helpless, angry, psychosomatic, etc.) and patterns in my family? What can I do about it?

If he is not able to make the connections by himself, he can talk with a consultant, add a co-therapist, or join a small supervision group that routinely presents family of origin information and deals with interface issues. In such a setting he can receive feedback from his peers as well as from the leader, and learn to focus on the interface parallels. When he has experienced the disquieting yet energizing reality of changing himself in his own family, he usually finds he is able to work more effectively with families like his own; it may even become an advantage, since he has firsthand knowledge of their anxiety and empathy for their position.

CHAPTER 9

The Therapist's Own Family: Case Study

My change in my family of origin is the subject of this chapter. Recounting my own story is based on the premise that when a therapist writes on family and therapeutic interface, the most apparent and credible examples she can use are her own efforts to change and her understanding of how that change interfaces with her experiences as a therapist. There is a problem, however, since a therapist cannot get outside of her own family and therefore cannot, in fact, be objective. Yet, as I have been slowly changing my relationship with original family members over an 18-year period, I have seen parallel changes in other relationships and in my work with families. From my experience in training family therapists, I have become convinced that understanding how other therapists change is a catalyst to further change.

My parents both came from a long line of Scotch Presbyterian farmers who arrived in this country during the 1700s. Both were middle children of middle children for several generations back. Religion and education provided both a solid value base and a social framework for their lives. Ancestors in both families helped to found religious colleges in the middle 1800s in the middle west, with many of their grandchildren, including my parents, working their way through those institutions, although both families lived in rural areas where such initiative was unusual.

My mother, although trained in public speaking and teaching, was a traditional housewife, emotional, social, outspoken, and artistic. My father was a university professor and on the governing board of his church for many years. He was a man of few words, tolerant, hardworking, and conscientious, with an unexpected sense of humor. He rarely revealed his feelings. A series of traumatic events created an emotional shock wave that reverberated through the family over a four-year period, resulting in my parents forming a child-centered united front.

TRAUMATIC EVENTS

I was nine years old and my sister, Betsy, 11 when the crisis started building. The time was the depth of the Depression; my father, while teaching full-time, was working against a final deadline for completing his doctoral dissertation. Following the sudden death of a staff member, his Dean had asked him to take on an additional time-consuming traveling assignment. He accepted without telling the Dean of his thesis deadline, putting himself in an almost impossible bind. At the same time, my paternal grandparents were asking Dad and his siblings for help: Farmland they owned was in danger of foreclosure, which could also threaten their home. My grandfather wrote to my father's older brother: "The most important thing is to save your mother from worry as she had a nervous breakdown after your sister's birth and she fears worry might bring trouble back to her."

During this crucial period, Mother, who was nearing 40, became pregnant and needed more of my father's attention because she was feeling unwell. Then, three months before his thesis deadline, my father's mother died of a heart attack. He took no time to mourn, although he attended the funeral and continued to give support to his father, older brother, and younger sister.

My father finished his thesis on the day of the deadline, having slept less than four hours a night for the previous several months. The family, however, was already in trouble. Mother was in and out of the hospital with complications and fever before labor was induced in August, when twins were born two months prematurely. The smaller twin, Ruth, died the following day; again, no one took the time to mourn. Bob, the long-awaited boy, survived in an incubator and became the focus of attention.

This series of events started a cycle of dysfunction as illness rotated through three members of the family — Bob, myself, and Mother — with Betsy joining Dad in the caretaker role. Bob had digestive disorders, requiring Mother to take him to a hospital in a larger city. I had facial and stomach tics which were diagnosed as St. Vitus' Dance, although I suspect that my susceptibility to the family stress was enough to cause my symptoms. I was nine years old when the doctor ordered me to bed for total rest for five months.

As I returned to school, Bob had developed asthma and was often sick. The focus finally settled on Mother, who was withdrawing, losing weight, and becoming depressed, with constant migraine headaches. When Mother's weight fell to 80 pounds, the doctor diagnosed a "nervous breakdown" and sent her to a sanitarium for six months. Dad was told not to visit, and the family regrouped without her. Betsy, now 14, settled into the position of substitute housewife and mother, a role I resented. I yearned for Mother, fought with Betsy, and played with Bob.

My parents' reactions to this cycle of events had roots in identifications, illnesses, and deaths in the past generation. My father had chosen a woman with the same name, Mary, and birthdate as his mother. History also repeated itself when my mother had a "nervous breakdown" after her third living child, like her mother-in-law before her. When Dad had been sent overseas in World War I, his mother had developed heart problems from "worrying about him," remaining an invalid for the last 13 years of her life. When he was similarly unavailable to his wife, she had also become ill. Both his mother and baby daughter had died within months of each other and he was fearful his wife would not recover.

My mother's original family experience, however, had given her a different expectation. My maternal grandmother had become ill with tuberculosis after her three sisters had died from the same disease in a cluster of traumatic events similar to that my mother experienced. Mother had seen her mother recover, however, to live a hearty and robust life and Mother expected to recover. She told me, years later: "I was fighting with myself when I was ill. When I put myself in God's hands, then I was able to get well."

Before Mother came home from the hospital, Dad told us she had been very ill, had almost died, and that we should be careful not to upset her. Betsy heard the message as "Don't make your mother unhappy," and her answer was to escape on her bicycle to the country from the house and Mother's depression. I took his directive as a clear message, "Don't upset your mother or she may die," and it shaped my adolescence. I decided not to do anything that might displease her and to wait until after I left home to experiment with what I wanted to do.

My father must have also decided not to upset her. His pattern of carrying the load himself and not asking for help had developed in his family of origin where he had learned to protect his mother and sister. When his father had been ill, he had managed the farm while going to high school. So it was in character when he did not tell the Dean about the bind he was in, even though it placed him in an untenable position with Mother, who was left to carry the emotional burden alone. A stable dysfunctional equilibrium evolved in which illness became the family's mode of coping.

When Mother returned from the hospital, Betsy was allied with Dad, opposing Mother's authority indirectly, often through procrastination, and never winning. I remained close to Mother, continuing to do what Mother wanted before she asked, and thus avoided the constant criticism Betsy elicited. My parents were stabilizing into a united front. I felt the tension but there was no way to talk about it. I wrote in my diary when I was 12:

> "Why is it that sometimes I wake up tense? All day today I have been kind of worked up. Betsy and I had a fight this morning. Why is it that sometimes the sight of her makes my blood boil and I just can't get along with her? Others can. And Mother, with her cool, calm hardness, with a surface it's hard to get through. What makes her so I-want-to-be-loved and yet so unfeeling? And yet, I love her so much, but I guess she sometimes strikes the devil in me. And Daddy follows her lead in everything. If she says to scold us, he will. My only real friend in the household is Bobby, though everyone is kind."

The tension continued at home as the situation stabilized, with my focus shifting outward towards friends and my social world. Through high school and college I continued to be close to Mother, pleasing my parents by being a "good" girl and excelling in school and extracurricular activities.

NEED FOR CHANGE

When I married, my mother expected our old pattern to continue, with her influence still primary. She dominated the family, with Dad allied with and protecting her; I had distanced from him, considering him stolid and boring. Dad had led the way with his protectiveness and passivity, yet I also allowed and encouraged Mother's intrusiveness since my contacts with my father, sister, and brother were still going through her. I had promised myself to start living my own life when I left home, yet I was still protecting Mother (and myself) by not telling my parents about the changes I was making that they would disapprove of. Thus, after I married, Mother saw my actions as influenced by my husband, not as my personal decisions. There was truth in her view as well, since I did not, at that point, know what I wanted; I was in love with and influenced by Chuck, and was consciously shutting my parents out in order to build a new life with him.

Predictably, negative feelings surfaced from Mother to Chuck as my interaction with my parents became oppositional and increasingly superficial. They blamed Chuck for the changes I was making, fearful of his influence. He was in an impossible position, taking the brunt of their negativity for my experimentation and growth. I did not discuss my inner feelings or thoughts with either parent and I felt uncomfortable in their presence.

The situation was not much better with my siblings. I had a distant relationship with my brother which mirrored that with my father. My sister and I had tried to avoid Mother's comparing us with each other by dividing up our world of interests, as our parents had done. We thought we had nothing in common, not realizing how competitive we were, or what we were missing. During the infrequent times we were together, our conversation degenerated into criticism of Mother. This focus on her, rather than on ourselves, effectively prevented us from developing an adult relationship with each other.

I took Chuck along when I visited them, hoping that he would solve the problem; yet my remaining in the middle, without taking initiative to state my own position, kept the triangle active. Mother continued to make uncomplimentary remarks about Chuck, Dad remained silent, and Chuck withdrew. This went on for 20 years. After one especially dismal visit, Chuck finally took a differentiating step, saying to me: "I'm not going to try to get along with your parents anymore. You can continue to do whatever you want with them — go there, invite them here. I may or may not be here at the time, and I do not intend to go there."

I was stunned and could think of nothing to say. As I thought it over, resentment began to build at his unfairness. I stomped back and said: "I'm nice to your mother."

He was adamant. "I don't care if you're nice to my mother or not. Do as you please."

I turned his words over and over in my mind during the next few weeks. Although I had completed a successful psychoanalysis five years before and had grown in many areas of my life, my relationship with my original family members had not changed. Now I began to feel alone with my parents for the first time in years. I realized I had relied on Chuck to be a buffer between them and me. I could not put him between us anymore; the next move was up to me. I felt scared, yet excited, because I was longing for change.

PROCESS OF CHANGE

Thus began the slow and painful reintegration of myself — pulling together the adaptive child my family knew with the effective adult I could be away from them. My plan was to talk about the unspoken tensions with each of my parents, to establish firmer boundaries with my mother, and to move closer to my father and siblings on a one-to-one basis.

As I talked with my sister, I found she was also groping towards a closer bond with me. Early in the period of change we agreed to talk only about ourselves and our own concerns and not to criticize Mother. I sent her an audiotape of a talk Bowen had given at the Family Institute and, later on, a copy of one of his early papers. We found we shared attitudes and interests and began to rely on each other for support, a move I had never thought was possible. Early moves with my brother were designed to develop common interests. Although he did not often take initiative, he was warmly responsive. I grew to know him as a quiet, dependable man, a listener like our father.

Examples of letters and visits will provide a sense of the process of change. My first intervention, after Chuck's ultimatum, was a letter to Mother telling her about my frustration when she tried to change my ideas about church, smoking, and drinking. Since she had also taught me to be honest, it was a dilemma for me, and I wanted to talk honestly with her. At first when I wrote such letters to Mother, Dad answered, addressing the letters to my office and trying to smooth things over. I felt scared when I saw his envelopes; the message was clear that I should protect her as he was doing. I wrote back to her, and for two years, when I wrote a direct, personal letter telling her my feelings, he would write back to my office.

When I asked about dates in order to understand the continuity of past events — for example, when I was ill and when Mother was ill — Dad shut me off in a typical letter: "After a third of a century I see no point in trying to unravel the details of family history. We had our ups and downs. You were happy — who could ask for more?"

I started telling family members ahead of time what I planned to do and topics I wanted to discuss when I visited. This forced me to confront differences openly, a skill I had not learned in my family. There was more estrangement with my parents because I was talking about things no one usually talked about. Before one visit I wrote:

"I discussed with Betsy some of the hangups I've had in communication with each of you and I really think it's time to do something about it. There has seemed such a wall and I find myself literally speechless when we're together unless we're talking about something you are doing or I am doing. It's an effort to keep the conversation going, and if this is so for me, it must be equally so for you. So maybe if we talk about it, we can roll back the years and start to understand — if not to approve of — each other. . . . I am certainly very different from the little girl who lived with you. I am a woman — and a rather strong-willed one at that — ready to take responsibility for my behavior and opinions — not under your thumb or Chuck's. I have hesitated to talk to either of you because I have felt that Dad didn't want me to say anything controversial for fear it would affect Mother. But I've felt this for years; time is running out, and I don't like our present relationship. I need to get to know you each separately again because my hangups are different with each of you. Betsy said you also would like to explore beyond the wall that divides us. We should be able to remove at least some of the barriers."

During the following visit I brought up Mother's illness with her for the first time. I told her how my adolescence was shaped by my fear of causing her death. She had not known of Dad's warning or of my reaction to it. She told me she had known she would recover and that she had started to get well when she had placed herself in God's hands. Yet I had been blaming her all those years for the way I had limited myself. I realized that Mother had not forced Dad to protect her; that he had played his part and I had accepted his fears as my own. I also discussed these issues with Dad so that I could understand his position.

I thought I was making headway, and that Mother and I were corresponding openly, when another letter came from my father:

"We did appreciate your visit and consider it as an expression of your love and interest . . . While our discussion may not have solved all the past problems, it at least provided a much better understanding of our respective positions. Upon this basis, we think that further discussion of the past and its difficulties would be of no avail, hence we propose that we close and seal that chapter and begin a new one, unfettered by the past."

I wrote back immediately to both:

"One thing I really can't understand is how you can compartmentalize your lives, tying up years into neat little bundles saying 'Don't touch.' I've played that game by your rules too long. I want us to have a real relationship based on our feelings, our love, our interaction . . . Since I saw you, I've felt warm and accepting of you . . . and then Dad proposes 'we close and seal that chapter.' On reading these words, I felt restricted by your fears of saying what we think when we think it. . . . I hope we can continue in open dialogue with each other. . . . "

Dad answered immediately and backed down, saying he had not meant to shut me off. He invited me to come again.

When I visited my parents I was now more objective and able to see the process. I was aware that Dad and I rarely spoke directly. I would start out talking to him about an area of common interest. As he was slow in answering, Mother would speak for him and I would end up talking to Mother. As I saw this process develop, I commented on it to both of them, telling them I wanted a direct relationship with Dad. I invited him to go for a walk so we could talk together and get to know each other again. I told Mother that I would share with her anything we talked about, that it was not sharing secrets that I wanted but a personal dialogue with my father. The next time I visited, Dad and I started talking and Mother sat and listened without saying a word for an hour and a half.

I was learning to make a plan, wait for a response, accept the response, and hold to my plan. An example occurred the following summer when I decided to spend a week of my vacation with them. Since Mother had not seen her older sister on the East Coast for a number of years, I proposed that the three of us visit her as my gift. When Mother remained uncertain, I set a time limit for the decision. It was only after the deadline had passed, and Dad and I had decided to work on genealogical charts of his extended family, that Mother said she would rather have us take the trip East. Without getting embroiled in controversy, I held to my second plan and we spent the week in their home.

When our parents were 80 years old, Betsy and I went home together to spend a weekend with Dad, Mother, Bob, and Bob's wife Ruth, for the first time in several years. The weekend became a miniature life cycle for me. On Friday evening Betsy and I found ourselves together in the double bed we had shared as children and I was drawn back into the old regressive role of adaptive child. On Saturday I made up the bed in my father's office, establishing a room of my own. As the day progressed, I felt like an adolescent, fighting my way out of the adaptive role, competing with my sister, and into unresolved battles with my parents. The power struggle was subsiding by evening and I felt relief.

I was my adult self on Sunday when I awoke, able to say what I was thinking and to relate comfortably to each member. We spent time in various pairs, enjoying each other. The competition and struggle were gone; we were not so preoccupied with ourselves. The visit ended in a spontaneous group hug for the first time. We felt ourselves to be peers together. Immediately following, I received a letter from Mother:

"It was a good, profitable weekend. We were honest and not trying to protect each other. For the first time in 25 years I had the feeling of real old-time happiness with you. I'm waiting for your return. Your mask is lifted. You are your dear, sweet self."

Six months later I spent another weekend with my parents and Betsy. The bitterness I had felt with Mother was gone. As we cried together, I found myself forgiving her for all the things I had held against her all those years.

LEARNINGS

I learned many things in interaction with my family:

1) To untangle one member from another. I had been angry at Mother, while Dad had been the "good guy." I learned that people who stay in relationships bear equal responsibility for the outcome.
2) To make the covert overt; to talk openly about matters no one talks about.
3) To make myself vulnerable while remaining in control of myself. This meant being able to tell Mother or Dad about problems without having to accept their solutions.
4) To stop being oppositional and live the same way with family members as I did in the rest of my life.
5) To use humor to get my point across, and to laugh at myself and at my own seriousness.
6) To respond immediately when an answer was called for — for example, in answering Dad's shut-out letter.
7) To make decisions carefully and then to stand firm, expecting reactions and therefore not being overly affected by them.
8) To enlarge the field when I reached an impasse by adding family members. My sister provided insights from a different perspective; I was beginning to plan interventions involving aunts, uncles and cousins.

THE VIDEOTAPED WEEKEND

In the spring of 1973, Chuck asked to go with Betsy and me to visit my parents for the first time since he had made his differentiating move eight years before. During the visit, as all five of us were sitting at the breakfast table on the last morning, we evolved a plan together for a three-generation weekend reunion. We had varying motives. Mother had always wanted to have a family reunion which included the children. Betsy, a university-based nutritionist who was already in the process of collecting food habits of family members, wanted to gather more information. I was interested in exploring our family patterns. It was also an opportunity to include our brother actively and to cooperate on a joint project that would enlarge the field. We decided to invite the 22 members in the three generations to a videotaped "Food Weekend" to be held at my house in June.

Fifteen attended, including all the members and spouses of my original family and seven of the 13 members of the next generation (Figure 18). As we met in two-hour blocks of time, the process developed a life of its own. Although members were acutely aware of the videotaping at first, they soon became comfortable. Small talk did not develop; there were few multiple conversations. No one family member emerged as leader; instead, the camera itself become the leader/therapist. Its presence seemed to hold the family within the drama that was taking place.

We started tentatively, feeling each other out, talking about such topics as favorite foods, snacking, and food preparation. As momentum built, however, it became apparent that the subject of food was an entree to talking about a wide range of concerns. As videotaping continued, we were able to keep focused on relationship issues in a way we had never experienced before. Many of the important differences between the generations that had never been openly discussed were now aired. We explored the "shoulds" and "should nots" in the family, competition and complementarity, dependence and independence, power and control, the effect of illness, the use of alcohol, which was a charged subject, and issues around sex and changing mores — living together before marriage, expectations of marriage, and jealousy. I was surprised by my parents' willingness to communicate with us and our sons and daughters about controversial issues. Emotions ebbed and flowed. When feelings got too intense or we started going around in circles, we went back to the subject of food.

During the last 15 minutes of recording, Mother's illness was discussed openly in the family for the first time:

Jan: It all started after Bob was born. I had been the youngest child and then Bob came along and he took an awful lot of time and effort in the family. I think I was jealous at that point. Bob was usurping all the attention I'd been getting.

I led the conversation into the taboo area by describing my feelings at the beginning of those painful years.

Mother: I didn't give you the attention I wanted to give you.

Mother responds empathically.

Jan: I should have been old enough to take a back seat, but I'm not sure I was willing to. (to Mother) That was when the struggle started between us.

I identify a struggle between Mother and myself.

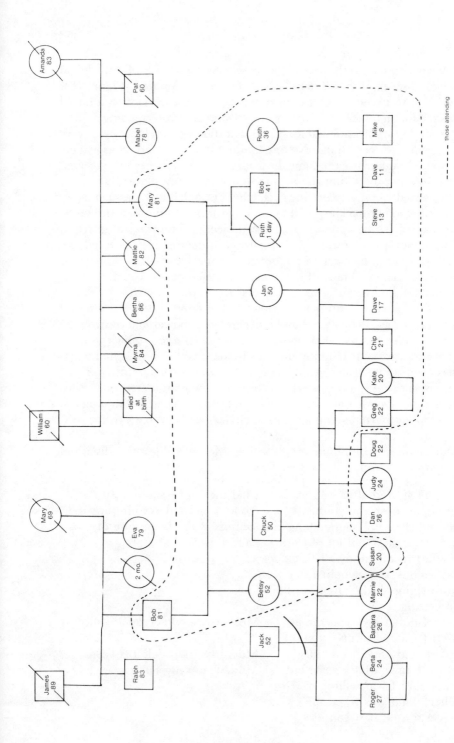

Figure 18. Jan's Family at Time of "Food Weekend," 1972

----- those attending

Mother: You're exaggerating more than it really was, though.

Jan: Up until I was nine, I remember everything being rosy and great. I'm not exaggerating April until September when I didn't get out of that room. That was a very heavy thing for me.

Mother: Well, I got in bed, too.

Mother denies the importance of those years.

I stand my ground, remembering how it felt when I was confined to bed for five months.

Mother's comment sounds competitive. She is caught between denying the pain and wanting to acknowledge it.

Jan: I know it — we were all in a cycle at that point.

I accept her statement and broaden it to include all of the family members.

Mother: (turning to Dad and patting his arm) Not Dad, he wasn't.

Mother pointedly excludes Dad.

Betsy: He was under terrible strain at that time, finishing his doctorate. It was the same.

Betsy speaks strongly for Dad, stating his part in the cyclical interaction.

Jan: Bob had a whole different time when he was a baby growing up than we did. It was like a different family. There was more stress and strain.

I speak for Bob, contrasting his childhood years with those when we were growing up, nine years earlier. Note that neither Betsy nor I ask the men how they experienced it. We were too caught up in our own drama with Mother. Our interchange is still a rebalancing and reintegration among the three women.

Mother: Illness does that in any family. Illness will change the atmosphere. Everybody is under a strain when someone at the head of the family is ill . . .

Mother continues the discussion. This surprises me because I expect her to again discount the importance of that period. She shows her ambivalence between sharing her feelings and shutting them off.

Betsy: And particularly when

Betsy brings up the taboo topic

they're out of the family for six months.

Mother: That's right.

Jan: It was scary—scary for me.
Betsy: I was sure I had caused it. I kept arguing with you, Mother, and we would fight.
Mother: I think you exaggerate all this.
Betsy: Don't you think it was a hard time for you?
Mother: Yes, but I think we came through it beautifully and I don't dwell on the hard times. I wouldn't be where I am today if I had dwelled on the terrible things, like you're talking about them now. (reaching towards Dad) But he always had the atmosphere and I didn't give in to it. I knew we would turn out all right. It was a tragedy in our lives and we lived through it and I don't see why we have to live through it again. Why you can't forget it and, if you feel you've been hurt, forgive! (She is close to tears.)
Jan: Yes, but it's been helpful to me in the last few years to be able to talk about these things with you—for me to understand my part in it so I can put them away.

of Mother's hospitalization in the context of Mother's last statement. This is evidence of Betsy's and my ability to work together, that we are now cooperating, not competing.
Again, I am surprised that Mother allows this topic and that Dad is not shutting it off.
Betsy and I describe our early reactions.

Mother backs off again.

Betsy persists.

Mother gives an eloquent plea to leave the past in the past. She defends her position, underscoring her dependence on Dad. Her pain is evident. Dad is still not protecting her, although she is trying to pull him in.

I empathize with Mother's pain, but I know this moment has been long in coming. Betsy and I are now working together to mend the old hurts. I reaffirm what I have said before to Mother in letters and in person,

that it has helped me to talk to
her.

Mother reiterates her position.

Mother: (still close to tears) It's
been very hard on me to do it
and to live over some parts of
my life that were ill parts, so
let's forget it now.

Jan: But in the doing we have
gotten closer.

Mother: Well, I hope so. But I'm
not sure.

Jan: I think so. I feel much
closer.

I underline my feelings that it
has helped us to get closer.
Mother is still not sure that anything will help.
The moment is pregnant with
possibilities. The room is quiet.
I am leaning forward. I want to
go and comfort Mother, as I
have before, yet something is
holding me back. No one stirs or
speaks. After a while Betsy
moves across the room to
Mother and takes her in her
arms, the first time Betsy can remember spontaneously hugging
Mother. As Betsy moves back to
a seat beside Dad, he takes her
hand and holds it tightly. Now I
am free to move to Mother. As I
kneel on the floor to hug her,
Betsy motions to Bob to join the
inner family circle, surrounded
by in-laws and children.

Betsy: (to Bob) It's funny—you've
gotten bigger and bigger and
bigger.

Chuck: He's not a shrimp anymore. (Bob laughs.)

Betsy: You're not! (to Chuck) I
told him yesterday I had thought
of him as younger than Susan,
my youngest child. (to Bob)
You've grown up.

Betsy now acknowledges her
growing realization of Bob as an
adult, as one of us.
Chuck is referring to Bob's childhood nickname, Shrimp.
Betsy is acknowledging that her
role as the 14-year-old "mother"
of Bob, which started when
Mother was in the hospital, had
continued until recently, preventing an adult-to-adult rela-

Jan: (turning to Bob) We haven't been able to show to each other some of the parts of us that are there. I've felt there was a lot to get to know in you, but I didn't know where it was or how to go about finding it. I hope we can spend time together, both as families and as people. It's very important to me. (Bob nods.)

tionship between them. I also admit my distance from Bob and my hope for more closeness in the future.

Jan: (to Mother) I think we've buried a lot of the past.

Mother: To me, I think we've come up blossoming. (She looks around the circle, ending with Dad.)

I turn to Mother, referring back to her wish to let go of the past. Now Mother agrees. There is a poignancy in this moment and a feeling of connection.

When a family shares their painful experiences together, untapped support may emerge for those who have felt isolated or alone. Betsy and Mother had both longed for a connection they had not been able to make. Betsy's changes had started before the weekend, as she had allowed Mother to hold differing opinions without arguing with her. Her opposition decreased when she gained enough faith in her own beliefs so she did not need to convince Mother and obtain her approval. This allowed her to embrace Mother spontaneously.

During the weekend Mother was active, standing firmly for her beliefs and showing tolerance in listening to dissenting opinions. Dad's usual role was to keep feelings from escalating by stopping the action or changing the subject. He did not protect Mother, however, allowing the process to develop and remaining primarily a listener. Both Betsy and I recognized Bob's maturity and humor. He admitted that he had always felt left out, not knowing how to change his position. He and Betsy began planning their first shared family camping trip.

The rebalancing in the family had powerful reverberations for me. I felt calmer, more able to "be" in the family. Just being with original family members had always seemed either too intense or too boring; I had felt a constant necessity to move away from them and to become engaged in "more interesting" projects. As I took an active part in promoting a happening within the family, I saw that the boredom and intensity were within myself, and that I could alleviate them by being direct and involved.

Feelings in our family had always been dominated by the women, with the men operating at a less intense level. Once the triangle between the women was resolved, there was space for me to invite and accept more closeness from the men at a less intense level, with a growing interest in getting to know my father and brother. This set a model for me for a less intense relationship with my husband and sons, who were also there as witnesses.

MOURNING MOTHER'S DEATH

When there is a death in the family, a void is created which changes the family's homeostatic functioning; emotional forces shift to compensate for the loss. This is a time when a family can become dysfunctional or members can reintegrate on a higher level. When Mother died suddenly of a cerebral hemorrhage eight months after the videotaped weekend, I went through an acute period of mourning unlike anything I had experienced before.

The morning before she died I felt like I was in an altered state, disconnected and lost, and crying without knowing why. In a supervision group Chuck and I co-led that morning, we speculated about my inexplicable behavior and feelings, ending in a group discussion about death. I felt steadily worse as the day and evening progressed, yet I awakened before dawn feeling at peace. Later that morning my sister called to say that Mother had started feeling unwell the morning before, entered the hospital in the evening, and died early that morning. I left immediately with Chuck to join my family.

This was the first immediate family death in my adult life and I allowed myself to experience it fully. I awoke each morning in my parents' house about 4 a.m. during the week following her death, which was an uncommon experience for me. Each day, upon awakening, a new gestalt would emerge, calling for me to progressively rebalance myself in the family. The first night I awoke feeling the aching loss of Mother's ongoing presence in my life and I wept for those lost years when I had been distant from her. As morning came, I felt more connected, glad that she and I had made our peace with each other.

The following night I again awoke at four with a headache, feeling tense. I went to Betsy, who was also awake, and we comforted each other that day. In the evening, while she cradled my head and held me, I was racked by sobs. I became chilled; my hands were icy. I said: "I feel like death, I am so cold." She covered me with blankets and, as I became warm, my headache and tension faded and I had a sense of peace and rebirth. I knew that Mother's death had left room for me to be close to Betsy as I had been that day. We had rarely touched or cared for each other before.

Correcting Inequities

The next day Dad showed us Mother's and his Wills, which were identical. As I read them, I noticed an inequity: When Bob died, his share would go to his wife, Ruth, and then to their children, while my share would bypass Chuck and go directly to my children. The issue was not money but belonging and trust. I saw my husband being shut out again.

That night I woke up feeling tense and what emerged was my need to be free of the tensions between my parents and myself about my husband's place in the family. I resolved to talk to Dad at breakfast. Although I felt resistant, I told Dad that there were still areas that I wanted to resolve, despite the progress we had made in our relationships while Mother was alive. Although I had given them pictures of Chuck over the years, Mother and Dad had never put them on the wall with the family pictures. Now the inequity of the Will was added to the inequity of the pictures; those feelings were likely to be perpetuated. I knew that Mother's Will could not be changed, but he could change his to make it equal. I did not care how he corrected it — whether he put Chuck's name in or left Ruth's name out — but I wanted it to reflect fairness to all of his children for our children to see.

My mother's nonacceptance of my husband had roots in triangles in the past generation. Mother had disliked or distrusted the spouses of my father's siblings and Dad had neither challenged her nor continued to deepen those relationships by himself. My sister's serious boyfriends, including the man she married and divorced, were not accepted. Betsy and I had married men who were not adaptive, and Mother was never able to shape them to her liking. She completely accepted Ruth, Bob's wife, who had a unique position. It seemed to me that Ruth was the adult embodiment of Bob's twin sister, the baby Ruth who had died at birth. In this role, Ruth had always belonged in the family.

Dad said he would not want to perpetuate the situation, that he would talk to his lawyers about the Will. He also said that if I could find the picture I had sent, he would put it up with the others. When I found the picture, he said to Chuck: "Do we need an installation?" Chuck replied: "No, just a holding of hands." They embraced, and it felt to me like Chuck could now enter the family.

As we were sitting together reminiscing that evening, Dad told us that

Mother had wanted to die first so she would not be left without him. Chuck observed: "She got her way, like she always did." Dad chuckled and said, "Yes, she did." As we talked of the tensions between us, Chuck said: "I know what was the matter. She and I were both in love with the same woman." My father smiled and said, "And you got her!"

Early the next morning when I awoke, I found myself reflecting on my relationship with my adult sons and daughter and my part in divisiveness between us. I resolved to refrain from telling them news of each other, pulling back further from the switchboard role. There was a light under Betsy's door. She had been thinking along the same track, writing to her ex-husband that she realized she had filled the spaces between him and their children and that she wanted to relinquish that role.

The next day I again woke early, with a headache and a feeling of heaviness. As I breathed more and more deeply, I was convulsed with sobbing. The feeling was of being split. I recognized that the split was now within myself. I saw myself swinging between two poles — striving for perfection, yet feeling inadequate and helpless. I had tried to be perfect, smoothing things over and focusing more on others than on what seemed right for myself, and the result had been a holding back of my creative drive.

The next morning as I awoke, I was thinking how Mother had filled the spaces in the family and how, to balance this, I had filled my spaces with busyness so it would be easier to resist her intrusiveness. As an adult I had evolved a life where I was closely scheduled and I often did not make the time to do the things I wanted to do or to be with those I wanted to be with. I became aware that during the week of mourning I had not been outwardly busy, instead allowing myself time to be. Within that framework I had learned more about myself and accomplished more than in any other week of my life. I saw my inner life and outer life flowing together, with energy moving between the two.

Shifting of Emotional Forces

As the gestalt experiences emerged, a healing process was set in motion that developed a life of its own, facilitating the healthy realignment of the emotional forces in the family. If Betsy and I had not been working together before Mother's death, it would have been easy for her to move into the void and become the switchboard for the extended family. If she had filled that role, I would have moved still further away. Our joint efforts during mourning, however, prevented that role replacement from happening and again underlined for me the importance of siblings in family change. Thus, Mother's death left a void that we all filled by many small moves, setting the stage for a growth experience for the remaining family members.

Grieving for Mother that first day after her death allowed me to make room for Betsy the following day, and to share with her an experience of renewal. This gave me strength to challenge the inequities with my father concerning his acceptance of my husband. Dad's readiness for resolution of the old triangular situation, involving the united front of my parents, Chuck, and myself, then became apparent. I was surprised when he acknowledged the triangle by saying to Chuck: "And you got her!" I had not appreciated the extent of my father's insight. Then, as the splits were healing with the older generation, my thoughts went to my sons and daughter in the next generation, to avoid perpetuating the dysfunctional patterns.

The next step was a focus on the splits within myself, an internal representation of the external struggle in the family between protecting the status quo and allowing individuality to blossom. I had felt responsible on some level for my parents' happiness, yet I had resisted the responsibility, keeping myself busy as a defense. This internal struggle had interfered with my own life and my creative process.

Completing the Gestalt

The gestalt experience was completed a week after Mother's death when I awoke, scared, after a dream which called for resolution. In the dream I was in the back hall of my parents' house with the back doorbell ringing persistently. Neither Mother nor I, who were in the house alone, knew who was ringing the bell. I went towards the back door with Mother following and she stood at the kitchen door, framed in the light of the kitchen, as I stood part way down the back stairs. There was a shadowy black shape outside the door and the bell was still ringing. I was gripped with fear, not wanting to open the door. I looked back at Mother, expecting her to be afraid, but she was calm. I knew I should open the door, but I was paralyzed, unable to move. The feeling was one of waiting, in an empty void, for something to happen.

As I awoke, feeling the fear, I got out of bed; I knew this dream was important. I closed my eyes and became the different parts of the dream, accepting each one as part of myself. I became the reactive part (the bell) which did what others wanted; the protective part (the door) that stood solidly between me and the future and that perpetuated my splits; and the familiar safety (the stairs) that I took for granted. Those three parts had kept me locked and unable to fully acknowledge and use my power.

As I played out the drama between Death (the figure outside the door), Mother, and myself, two levels were operating. On one level, I was resolving my fear and accepting Mother's death. On another level, however, I was completing an internal resolution of the old triangle of Dad, Mother, and myself. Death, with his calm strength, was the Dad-part of me. The Mother-part in the dream was also calm, had been preparing, and was ready to move on. While I remained in the child-part, persisting in my early role in the family, I continued to feel the triangle closing in. I looked from Death (Dad) to Mother, waiting to be told what to do. There was a discrepancy between my need to hang onto the past patterns and my parents' readiness to move on. The action was up to me. As I was able to open the door myself, I accepted Death as an eternal, abiding presence in my life and reclaimed my Mother in myself, accepting her readiness to move on.

FAMILY REBALANCING FOLLOWING DEATH

When I started changing my relationship with my parents, my goal had been to achieve balance: to be more distant and less intense with Mother and closer and more involved with Dad. This was valid, but simplistic: I also wanted a different closeness with my mother so I could incorporate loved parts of her and accept myself as like her. In a parallel way, I needed distance from my father so we could struggle with controversial issues and define ourselves to each other.

An early objective was to develop a mutually satisfying interaction with Dad in which both of us could mourn together and share our feelings and views. I wanted to understand his life as a man and my life in respect to his. In exchange, I was willing to help him stay in charge of his own life and his aging process. I talked to Dad about his future, planning ahead so he would not be taken by surprise. I found myself admiring his steadfastness, his ability to look at himself, and his wry humor.

Changing the Will

In the years before Mother's death, most of my problems had been with her. Now I wanted to work out a viable issue with my father. Changing his Will, which would correct an imbalance in the family, was such an issue. Dad had assured me after the funeral that he would talk to his lawyer about it. Yet weeks and months went by and he kept putting me off. Since words seemed to have no effect, I wrote him a letter seven months after Mother's death, asking that we meet with his lawyer:

"The basic problem I want to change is the split in our family. This is important to me because the split has been there for years and our children have grown up with it and I see it being perpetuated in your Will. I am referring to the inclusion of Ruth and the omission of Chuck as members of the family.

"I do not want to change the financial intent of your Will. I do, however, want to know if you really wish to perpetuate this split after your death. I don't think this matters moneywise, but it makes a lot of difference in my feelings. Chuck felt a part of our family during the week we spent together. I want to incorporate him in my new relationship with you; so far, these relationships have mostly been separate.

"If you don't want to change the Will, Dad, and you specifically say so, then I am willing to accept it, but I do want it to be clear and to understand it. I am sending a copy of this letter to Bob and Betsy and am enclosing a copy for you to send to your lawyer so he understands the background before our meeting."

Bob and Ruth thought I was blowing the situation out of proportion and tried to smooth it over. This became an issue to work out with them, as well as with my father.

Dad visited me before we met with the lawyer and he still did not seem to understand. He began talking to me about the way he and Mother made decisions. He said that, although he made decisions on big issues, he went along with her on day-to-day affairs when she had strong feelings. The Wills had seemed a day-to-day item to him. As I understood his thinking, we were then able to deal with an underlying issue: his loyalty to Mother as reflected in his past decision vs. his present wish to heal the divisions in the family. As he saw the situation from this new perspective, his resistance subsided and he changed his Will.

Altering the Context

One of my projects was to help Dad reconnect with his own siblings who were both in their eighties, relatively healthy, and living in their family homes. The families had spent little time together over the years since none of their in-laws had liked each other. Nevertheless, there had always been warm feelings, especially between Dad and his older brother Ralph, a widower for the last seven years. When I went with Dad to see his brother, the three of us then traveled together to visit my aunt, their younger sister. I was seeing my father in a new role. There was an intimate, poignant, yet lighthearted quality to our time together. The trip was the beginning of a renewal of contact between the siblings.

Broadening the family support system with a visit to Dad's brother and sister fitted in with one of my goals: to find a mutual project for us to enjoy together. Reconnection with his siblings gave him continuity with his own generation and gave me an understanding of their life together. His brother Ralph had had experience as a widower and could share his skills and his endurance. He was the best guide for Dad in the new life that had been thrust upon him. The reconnection of the two brothers and sister in Dad's generation paralleled that of the two sisters and brother in my generation who were encouraging the process.

I was also changing my communication with Dad. I, like Mother, spoke quickly and had often left him out. Since I was aware of this shortcoming in myself, I consciously planned silences and waited for him to fill them. One time which stands out in my mind was a two-hour layover at the airport when he was enroute to visit my sister a little over a year after Mother died. I had decided I would not initiate any subject, only respond and try to be comfortable with silence. If he did not talk, I would accept it.

First, he began to tell me about a group his church had organized to talk about grief, loss, and death for those who had suffered recent losses; no one had specifically asked him to go, so he had not gone. He said the only person he was really ever close to was Mother, and she had died so suddenly; he had never really cried for Mother, although he knew it was good to do; he had always held back his real feelings. I answered that if he could not cry in a group, maybe he could with me or with Betsy; that it helps me to cry. And so, as the crowds at the airport came and went, this patient, private man — my father — talked of the important areas of his life and cried, as I sat silently by and held his hand.

Despite our efforts, he became more frail and forgetful, needing help at home, then help around the clock, and, finally, nursing home care. I talked to him as each stage was approaching, giving him as much choice as possible about his own care. Mother's sudden death, without warnings or goodbyes, was a contrast to Dad's slow deterioration, with endless chances for contact, but no way to stop the downward slide. There is no ideal way to end a life. If one can see death in a transgenerational context, however, one can keep the emotional forces fluid, allowing growth to occur.

CHAPTER 10

Understanding Connections

Therapist and family members meet and test each other's boundaries and, if therapy is to occur, form a new therapeutic system and struggle for power and control. Therapy takes place in this interface, that area family members and therapist share. An interlocking of dysfunctional patterns between therapist and family may bring about a therapeutic impasse. When implicit rules from both systems are similar and dysfunctional, they will probably interfere with the therapeutic process, especially if the therapist is not aware of the possibility that they may interfere. If she adapts to the family and fits into its structure and rules, no change takes place. If the therapist confronts the family's system without testing its boundaries and without sensitivity to its own way of being, the family will have trouble trusting the therapist, may withhold important parts of themselves, or refuse to continue.

When the therapist is able to see her own contribution to the therapeutic impasse, she has more options for correcting the situation and can turn it into a learning experience for both herself and the family. She can explore her interface reactions by herself or in supervision, invite a consultant to a session, or add a co-therapist. She may or may not explain to the family her understanding of the problem, based on whether she thinks sharing the dynamics with them will promote therapy. Her decision will be influenced by the length of time she has been working with the family, the strength of the therapeutic alliance, the psychological aptitude of the family members, and her understanding of her own family interfaces. As the therapist resolves such a dilemma, the family members will feel safer and can be more open. The safety, however, includes the therapist's willingness to experience the way her own family patterns can be triggered in the therapeutic interface.

CHARTING AN INTERFACE ISSUE

In my adolescent and early adult life I had not entered into authentic dialogue with members of my family of origin, focusing instead on peer group, school, and community, where I was continuing to grow and to become a competent person. However, that part of me that felt helpless was tied to my fear of asking those questions that were not to be asked and voicing forbidden thoughts that were on my mind, which might cause a catastrophe. The connections between my family and myself were constricted by unspoken rules. There was discomfort and tension, yet always with a polite "happy family" façade that I felt restrained from commenting about. I sometimes felt helpless with rage.

As I identified interface issues, I became aware of problems stemming from a family myth that emerged following the period of trauma during my childhood. Table 3 conceptualizes one such issue. The myth—"Mother is fragile: she may die if she does not get her way"—evolved

TABLE 3
Interface Issues

TRAUMA	Mother's depression and hospitalization.
MYTH	Mother is fragile; she may die if she does not get her own way.
DECISION	Not to disagree with or question Mother.

System	Problem	Action to Take
Family of Origin	I had no way to confront differences.	Express opinions directly to Mother to test out myth.
Nuclear Family	1) When I differed with husband, I did not express it and the issue remained unresolved. 2) I had difficulty setting limits for children.	1) Express differences to husband so he knows where I stand. 2) Set specific limits and carry through on them with children.
Client Families	1) I was afraid family members were fragile; not sure how far I could probe/confront. 2) I felt helpless when family members were angry and expressed differences.	1) From work with my own family of origin, I have a good sense of how deeply to probe and when to "let it be." 2) As I was able to initiate and confront differences in my own family, I could work with differences in client families and help them resolve issues.

out of the traumatic, life-threatening experiences the family shared around Mother's depression and hospitalization following my father's inaccessibility and the deaths of my paternal grandmother and baby sister. These traumas elicited a shared decision — "Not to disagree with or question Mother" — that had survival value at the time. As the family continued to live by it, however, it became outmoded and hindered the emotional and psychological growth of family members. As I did not question the myth, it continued to dominate my life, interfering in my interactions with my husband and children.

The decision also impeded my work as a therapist with certain client families. When a family member was considered fragile, I had a tendency to become anxious and overly protective. When members became locked in angry exchanges, I sometimes found myself helpless and passive. Since there are similar processes between family of origin, nuclear family, and work with client families, it is useful to look for parallel problems in each of these areas. This method of organizing interface data has helped me to be aware of the isomorphic quality of both the process and the resolution.

The interconnectedness of patterns of change is shown in Figure 19. When the therapist takes action to modify earlier patterns, arenas for continued practice appear in many areas of her life. The family of origin work does not have to be done first. One can start with a crisis where the situation is already in flux or at an interface where there is a certain degree of comfort to experiment with more congruent ways of being. Eventually, however, if one wants to be the same person in all areas of one's life, changing dysfunctional patterns with the family of origin carries the most promise.

I needed to express opinions directly to each person in my family of origin in order to reclaim that helpless part of myself and to feel whole. I needed to accept each one for him/herself, to listen, not only to the words but to the anxiety, pain, and love behind the words, and to find a way to reconnect so I could integrate myself into a working whole. The process of doing this, imperfect though it may be, has helped me accept and be open and direct with the diverse family members in the families I treat. As I have understood my vulnerability, I have found that I can change myself in any of the different areas of my life — with family of origin, nuclear family, client families, co-therapist, supervisor, etc. — and that, with each change, there is a reverberating effect into parallel interfaces.

STRUGGLE AGAINST INDUCTION

A three-year treatment of the Martin family — John and Carol, their 17-year-old daughter Sara, and seven-year-old son Gilbert — became a basic educational experience for me in working on my own interface is-

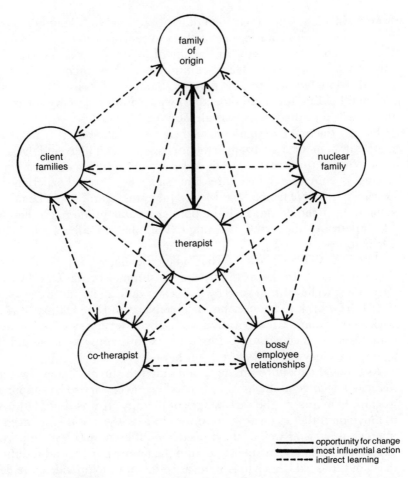

Figure 19. Interconnectedness of Patterns of Change

sues early in my training. Although outwardly unlike my family of origin, Carol and John's relationship hooked me back into my childhood
feelings of anxiety and helplessness around life and death issues. The
couple's roles matched my parents', with Carol depressed, needy, and
intense like my mother and John careful, protective, and walled off from
his feelings like my father. There was an added element of violence that
I had not experienced in my family, and I found myself becoming passive
when I needed to intervene actively.

Our work together covered two phases: During the first two years I
treated them alone, with supervision; in the last year I asked Chuck to
join me as co-therapist. The presenting problem was the angry aftermath

from an incident when their son Gilbert happened to fall out of a second story window during an episode of physical violence between the spouses. Carol ended up in jail at the instigation of John, who was desperate and saw this as a way to get Carol committed for treatment. Gilbert was scared, triangled between his parents. Sara, who was in a parentified role and holding the family together, was planning to leave for college in the fall, and the family was already feeling her loss.

During the first two years I helped each spouse to be less reactive and more autonomous, to detriangle themselves, and to understand their process. When Carol was depressed, however, and John became overly protective, pushing me to take care of his sick wife, I would experience an evocative feeling of foreboding: Maybe John was right; I might be missing something; I should not rock the boat or a catastrophe might happen. I kept detriangling myself, learning to keep the action between the two of them.

After two years of work they had a better balance but periodic escalations continued. In the spring before the summer break, Carol was on edge. I was feeling intimidated by her; it was difficult for me to stay objective; I drew back to a more comfortable place and she felt my drawing back as rejection. Any separation was difficult for her; she had avoided coming to any last session before a break in therapy and she did this again, thus leaving me before I left her.

As I thought about resuming sessions after the break, I knew I wanted to make a change in the format. It had been necessary to be supportive to gain their trust in the early stages of therapy. It was time, however, to move on if therapy was to continue. I knew I was still influenced by my own past. I, as well as they, needed a different and less supportive experience. I had been able to get into the family but I found it difficult to get out. I asked Chuck to join me as co-therapist to provide more flexibility to move in and out of the therapeutic system, and for me to learn more about limit-setting with this crucial case that was so tied in with my own family experience.

Adding a Co-therapist

Chuck moved in slowly, establishing rapport before he began confronting Carol when she overrode him. He was also modeling a firmer stance for John. I could see how Chuck's style contrasted with my softer, supportive approach. As limits were set more firmly over the next seven months, there was more acting-out, calling for more limits. Carol came to our home office without an appointment and I saw her in the hall. It was clear that she was escalating out of control and she talked about wanting to be hospitalized. In the following session Chuck said he would not respond to such gestures. He told her she was able to control herself and that he would not see or talk to her between sessions. I had been available to them between sessions over the years and I hesitated to draw a firmer limit. She tested me by ringing the doorbell in the middle of the night when she was drunk, with Gilbert clinging to her skirt. She drove her car across the lawn and into a tree. I was sucked back into my helpless role.

The next session was a showdown. Carol was angry at Chuck and at the structure he had set, and she forced a confrontation. She also asked him to hospitalize her. He stood his ground, saying he would see her in our regular sessions, that she was not psychotic and that she was stronger than she gave herself credit for. We both said we would terminate the sessions if there was another destructive incident like the one during the previous week. She said Chuck was very important to her because he told her what he thought, but she would not let him break her. She left the room, presumably to go to the bathroom, and drove off in the car. John was desperate; Sara wanted to commit her mother. Chuck said it was all right if they wanted to find someone else to hospitalize her. He would not do it, adding that we could only control the sessions; they would have to control their lives.

They found a doctor to hospitalize Carol. She was subdued when John brought her from the hospital to our next regular session a week later. She walked into Chuck's arms and he held her; she had been afraid she would be rejected. She was aware of feeling caught in the middle between us and John, like she used to feel when she was caught between her parents. She said she had been changing and doing so well, yet John did not want her to change and we did want her to change so that either way she lost and would be rejected.

During those last two sessions I had been primarily a spectator, also feeling caught in the middle. I had been hooked, feeling intimidated, like John. I knew it had started when I was afraid to set the firm limits Chuck had set. When I did not do what I knew I should do, I became helpless. I decided to talk to Carol and John about the way I was hooked, in order to unhook myself.

Carol started the next session by telling us about a discovery she had made about herself.

Carol: It's like I have two people inside me — one who's very confident and strong and the other one who isn't — does that make sense to you? And sometimes one takes over and sometimes the other takes over.

Chuck: And how has that operated in here with us?

Carol: Well, I think it's when you have tremendous confidence in me —
that's when I lose mine. All of a sudden, when you say, "Good!"
Chuck: When was it that we had great confidence in you?
Carol: It was in February. It's a combination of things — it was the mara-
thon for families and we spoke of letting go. That was part of it.
But I get apprehensive.
Jan: How do you handle it when you get apprehensive?
Carol: I run away.
Jan: How else?
Carol: I'm no good at the job I am doing. I fight with you. I'm appre-
hensive now.

The Therapist Unhooks Herself

As Carol described the two parts in herself, she gave me an opening
to explain to her how I had lost my objectivity as a therapist and had
become helpless.

Jan: I'm relating to you this morning in two different ways — with both
my competent and my helpless parts. I became aware after the night
you rang the bell and I saw you alone that I've been sucked into
what's been going on with you. I've not been as objective as I usually
am. Afterwards, I began to realize what was happening with me,
and that it is related to what you have been talking about. I had
an experience as a child that got keyed back in when you got depressed. My mother was very depressed when I was 12 and what
she did when she got depressed was not to eat.
Carol: She was punishing herself.
Jan: She was punishing herself, and you're also putting yourself in a victim position. She was in the hospital for a winter. My father didn't
think she was going to live through it and when she came back, he
said to us, "Don't upset your mother or she may die."
Carol: That's a terrible burden.
Jan: I was very good during my adolescence because if I rebelled, I
thought she might kill herself. I thought I had it all worked out,
but it's been creeping back in. That night you came here I was feeling like it was up to me to save you, yet there was nothing I could
do if you wanted to hurt yourself. I have to stay objective to be helpful. If I feel intimidated, like John does, that's no help to you. And
that was where I was last spring, feeling the heaviness of it without
being able to stay outside of it. That was when I backed off and
you felt it as rejection. But I didn't realize the tie-in, so I couldn't

tell you what it was. All I knew was that I had to back off. I told you what I knew at the time.

Carol: But I didn't understand that.

Jan: I didn't understand it either. That's why I wanted Chuck to join us because his vulnerabilities are not the same as mine. So when I'm vulnerable, he's not. Then we don't both get sucked in at the same time. The other thing I want to say is that when you were talking about your fears and how helpless you felt, there's a piece of me in that, too. The biggest fight Chuck and I ever had was last fall when he knew I could do something and I was feeling like I couldn't do it. I am remembering this really helpless feeling.

Carol: At first I was scared of having two "me's" inside of me, but now I don't feel so scared, since you told me.

Chuck: We've all got more than one "me" inside.

Carol: That's what I was apprehensive about.

Chuck: One of your jobs is to put all those "me's" together.

Carol: Yeah, I would like to blend them. They have good qualities.

Chuck: We have some good ways we can help you do that.

Carol: I knew I was onto something.

As soon as I began describing how I was sucked into a regressive position with Carol and John, my feeling of competence returned. As I spoke of my competent and helpless parts, Carol listened closely, understanding the connection. When she said, "She was punishing herself," I drew the parallel between my mother's and Carol's victim positions. After speaking of my early years when I felt responsibility for my mother's life, I again drew the parallel to my position with Carol when she was depressed and needy, when I had felt overly responsible for her, and I had backed off. I made it clear that this was why I had wanted a co-therapist. I felt relief as it was all out in the open and I was back in my competent role. Carol's response was also one of relief and a diminution of her scare. As I identified with her helplessness, then she was able to identify with my strength. She felt hopeful that she could blend her "me's" together.

The Couple Meets the Challenge

I turned to John to draw him into our dialogue:

Jan: (to John) What's your reaction to all this?

John: (to Carol) I'm worried about how you come across to me when you're out of control, and what you feel your motivation is.

Carol: I know I place myself in a victim position and I'm trying to think why and I only came across one reason and if its true, I want to nip it in the bud. I felt I was losing John. It was like I was getting all A's and John was getting C's and D's and therefore he didn't want to talk to me. When I place myself in the victim position — when I fail and get an F — then he's very kind to me, soft and tender like he wasn't before. So I would like you to be tender to me without my having to resort to that. I want to stop it.

John: Are you saying that I kind of like you because you are a failure, too, like me — is that it?

Carol: You act different to each part of me. You act tender to the helpless part, and to the competent part you act like, "She can do everything; she doesn't need me."

John: I don't know. There's something that you do — there's maybe something to it that you do that makes me feel you do need me and I can help, where the other way I don't know if I feel inferior or incompetent.

Carol: I was feeling depressed and you helped me. I was making a list that did not overwhelm me. You came home from a trip and everything was done and instead of being happy, you were distant.

John: Yeah — the feelings I had then — you came across as happy, exhilarated, and I was cautious. Carol is too happy, too high, and she's going to come down — what then? I wasn't trusting this competent feeling of yours. *I* was apprehensive.

My speaking openly of myself moved the interaction between John and Carol to a new level. As John spoke of his worry when she was out of control, Carol followed my lead in looking inside herself and described the process with a metaphor from the classroom, with grading from A through F. They were then able to explore their reactions to each other in an open, nondefensive way and explore how the process had kept them in their old circular game.

Aftermath

In a month Carol was out of the hospital. Sara, home for the summer, reported that there was a different feeling around the house and that she did not have to feel so responsible. There were a number of sessions with the children, dealing with Gilbert's reactions to their changes. Carol saw Gilbert's testing and acting out as similar to her own provocation to get us to abandon her, and she was able to be firm with Gilbert as Chuck had been with her. A new balance was forming in the family; we evaluated their progress and talked about Carol's cyclical swings and how to prepare for them.

In another two months, however, Carol was again escalating. John was depressed, scared, anxious, in tears. Carol did not want to listen; she said she was not coming back. She and John got into a physical scuffle in our front hall. She tore his coat, grabbed Gilbert by the hair, then picked up two floor plants, one after the other, and hurled them across the hallway. Chuck told them they would have to leave.

We had one final session. Carol brought a friend with her, kept her hat on, and stood in the middle of the room. Chuck said he would not put up with violence, that we had already told them that. I said that I had asked Chuck to work with me as co-therapist because I had gone as far as I could alone, that we were all going around in circles now. It was clear we were no longer being helpful. I said they already had the tools they needed; they could use them themselves.

I felt sad when they left, as well as anxious about what Carol might do. I also remembered that she always avoided the last session before a break in therapy, leaving us before we left her. Then I thought: Maybe making us kick them out is the only way they can stop. Three years is a long time.

My hunch was borne out a year and a half later when Carol called, saying she was sending the rest of the money they owed. She reported that there had been no real upsets between them since they had left therapy. They were enjoying each other, going out to church affairs and parties. John was not afraid of her anymore. He was now second in command in his office and had gotten a raise. Carol said she had had no further depression and was now a volunteer at a museum, teaching school groups. Sara had graduated from college and was applying for graduate school. Gilbert had won first prize at the School District's Science Fair. She said he was no longer frightened when she got angry; they were both able to live and let live.

I asked about her relationship with her father who had abused her as a child and had turned up just after therapy had started. She said he had come over at Christmas to give the children money. She told him they did not want his money; that if they went out for dinner with him, they would pay half of the bill; that he could come and visit, but he could not come and yell. She admitted she was still a little afraid of him, but she said, "He's 71. I'm sorry for him. I won't deny him the kids. John is 100% behind me. I know my father can't do anything to us."

She ended by saying: "I had a dream about both of you about three months ago. Chuck was like he is, with a little grin, like the clock in your kitchen with his face on it. In the dream I came over to see you and told you about the good things that are happening to us. Sometimes I dream and I can't find people, but you were all there."

Interface Connections

Treating Carol and John kept me focused on the therapeutic interface over an extended period. During the three years that this family was in therapy, I was working actively in changing my relationship with my parents; Mother's death occurred two years after the Martins' treatment began. I could not ignore the connections and I was forced to struggle through them. Thus, I was able to test out new ways of handling myself in both arenas. I learned to recognize the physical clues — the way my heart beat at a faster pace and a queasy feeling beneath my ribs — that told me I was hooked. I also became familiar with the interpersonal signs, such as my talking too much or telling others what to do rather than deciding what I would do for myself.

I found myself being repeatedly provoked; I learned to take a stand and hold the limits. I confronted the family myth — "Carol will go crazy unless the family handles her carefully" — which was close to the myth in my own family about my mother.

The trauma, family myth, and decision in the Martin family, shown in Figure 20, can be compared to my own family's in Table 3. In addition, I have shown their chronic cycle (Feldman, 1976). As Carol was helpless, depressed, and anxious, John became protective and overly solicitous. As she felt smothered by him, she began fighting back and holding her own. He became scared that she was going out of control and he tried to control her, withdrawing his emotional support. She began to depreciate herself and again became depressed, starting a new cycle. This is a cycle similar to the one my parents had been in when I was a child, with psychosomatic illness taking the place of violence.

While my family's differences had been covert and hidden, with a stricture against uncovering them, this family's conflicts were blatant, often hiding hurt and fear. Carol as a person seemed totally unlike my mother. Yet when she was depressed, there was a pull for me to believe she was fragile. Although John, also, was unlike my father, his belief that Carol was sick and could not recover paralleled my father's belief about my mother. John's belief colored the way he perceived and dealt with Carol and became an interlocking piece of my interface. When I joined John, I accepted his fears about Carol as my own in the same way I had accepted my father's myth about my mother.

When I tried to protect or save Carol, however, I was treating her

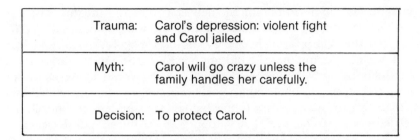

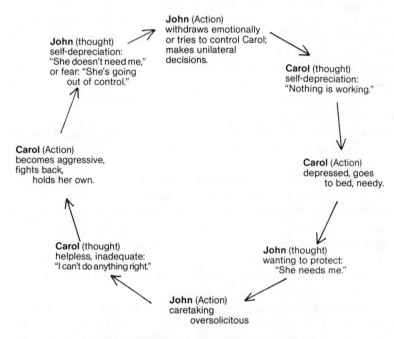

Figure 20. Patterns in the Martin Family

like a victim and she was, as she said, getting all F's. When Chuck made a strong stand that she was not psychotic, that she could be responsible for herself, and that her competent part was able to stay in control, they were in a power struggle, she to prove that she could not handle herself and he to show her that she could. There was a "high noon" quality to their confrontation. John and I were sidelined, watching the battle, since neither of us was certain that she could handle herself. Only Chuck stood firm that she could keep her competent part in control.

Carol felt caught in the middle between John and the therapists, as she had said during the first session after she was hospitalized. As she was changing and pleasing herself and us — getting all A's, as she put it — John withdrew, thinking she did not need him. She took that to mean that John did not want her to change. Then she would let herself go out of control — using alcohol and drugs if necessary, running away, fighting with us, getting all F's — and John would be soft and tender. She felt she needed John and could not live without him. So either way she lost and would be rejected, either by John or by us. Having John in the sessions to see Chuck believe in her strength and competence and to see her respond made it possible for John to change.

When I spoke of my competent and helpless parts, it made us all human together. I could reveal, because of my background with my depressed mother, that I had doubted that Carol could take care of herself and that I had needed to protect her, at times, like John did. This linked me with John giving him a model for seeing her strengths as I continued to acknowledge them. It also gave Carol a model for combining her helpless and competent parts.

Chuck was able to handle this family objectively. His formula was simple: "Get them to 'fall in love with you'; then start setting limits. When they break the limits, hold firm." When we differed on the limits about contact between sessions, however, it was predictable that Carol, a skilled triangler, would use that split and play us against each other. The more anxious I became, the cooler and more deliberate Chuck became, commenting on my being hooked and predicting I would remain quiet in the session.

When a therapist is caught up, as I was, in the interface between her own and the client family, the act of talking about it in the session can be freeing both for self and for the family. The way it is handled, however, is crucial. First, the therapist needs to understand the dynamics and what will be helpful for members to know. Disclosure should be a way of opening doors rather than of placing a further burden on the family.

The timing is important. When one is hooked into a family early in therapy, the place to discuss it is in supervision, not with the family. When the family is in the middle phase of treatment with a working therapeutic alliance, however, then the struggles of living are the subject of therapy and the therapist's own struggles may be pertinent. There is more flexibility to move in and out of the therapeutic system when there are co-therapists. When Chuck was confronting, I was there to support; at other times our positions were reversed. When I talked about my interface issues and feelings of helplessness, he was there as a balance. He could hold Carol in his arms with John and me present.

Once I had talked about my helpless feelings, I felt relief and my anxiety was defused. To put into word those feelings that family members sense but do not know how to interpret opens the door for more honest dialogue and gives both the family and therapist permission to identify further hooks when they happen. It becomes a form of modeling, showing them that the therapist is human and that all are struggling with the problems of life; that it is not the godlike therapist and the suffering patients; all are in the same boat.

I had some afterthoughts about our termination. I usually like terminations tied up neatly, so this was a learning experience. Carol and John kept a connection well beyond the end of therapy by keeping a small amount of money outstanding until after Carol's call. I was delighted with the way she had handled her unpredictable father. She had used the same limit-setting methods with him that we had used with her, repairing their relationship. Her matter-of-fact comments about the children's successes and her recent dream told me that she had incorporated us and our "tools" inside of herself, where she could continue to use them.

I could see the rightness of the ending for this particular family. Carol had been so fearful of abandonment that she needed to abandon us first and then prove that she had been right by staying in control of herself. In setting our limits and sticking to them, we had become trustworthy. They knew they could trust that we would do what we said and stop the therapy if she went over the line we had set. Carol had not only gotten her and John out of therapy, but she had also managed to help me get out of their family with more of my interface issues laid to rest.

INTERFACE WITH STEPHEN AND MARY

It was years later when I treated Stephen and Mary* and by this time I was much more in control of myself. Stephen had interface problems with his family of origin similar to my own, although his were more toxic, producing more dysfunction in his siblings. We both had united-front parents and both had seen our mothers as the problem. He had also been unaware of the part his father played in his mother's domination.

I could empathize as he became anxious when the barbs flew between his wife and mother and I could understand the predictable fight that would result between the spouses. I had heard my husband say, when I returned home from a visit with my parents, "Jan is not herself where her mother is concerned," which was the same thing Mary said about Stephen. My statement to him in the first session, "Your mother believes

---

*See Chapters 2–4 for the account of their therapy.

either she is influencing you or Mary is influencing you—that you cannot stand up as an adult by yourself," was straight out of my own family experience.

Stephen's distance from his siblings paralleled the way mine had been,
with his mother controlling the family switchboard and no one challenging her. Even the way he saw his younger sister, as less responsible than
she actually was, was a replay of my former view of my younger brother.
Mary's talk of Stephen's "look," along with his realization that it was a
recreation of his mother's "look," was also familiar to me. My mother
had such a look, setting her face tightly, turning away in her chair, and
staring into the distance when a family member raised a subject she did
not want to talk about. Then everyone would be silent, I would feel
queasy, and tension would fill the room.

If I were to state an important myth and decision that followed the
trauma in Stephen's family of origin, I would formulate the following:

> *Trauma*: Mother's hospitalization with depression, after which the fam-
> ily split in two.
> *Myth*: If conflict and anger are expressed directly, a catastrophe will
> happen.
> *Decision*: To stay loyal to Mother.

The above are similar to those I have formulated in my own family of
origin. Stephen uncovered in therapy a number of family rules that followed the trauma and myth:

> *Those rules similar to mine were:*
>
> Avoid conflict at all cost.
> Allow women to manipulate.
> Do not talk directly to the person you have a problem with.
> Let things go on and on.
> Adapt when visiting parents.
> You can be efficient as an individual outside the family, but not inside.
>
> *Those rules dissimilar to mine were:*
>
> Mother comes before spouse.
> Approach others expecting anger.
> Rush, yet never be on time.

Bringing the rules into conscious awareness is important because, when
they are known, the individual can decide if he wants to follow them or

not; if not, she can then decide how to change the rule for herself.

Stephen's relationship with Mary was the reverse of my relationship with my husband, who had been triangled through me to my mother, as Mary was. Even though I had chosen my husband over my mother, I had still been dominated by her and she was jealous of and antagonistic towards Chuck. After changing the process, I realized that Mother was allowed to be intrusive by both her husband and children and often was not even aware of the effect of her domination, since no one challenged her. I could see the leverage Stephen had, and I could encourage him to use it. I also identified with Mary in a number of ways. I had struggled through the pitfalls of carrying a full-time job while bringing up a family. I planned ahead as she did, and helped her in her planning, encouraging her to hire outside help. I could identify with Mary's position vis-à-vis Stephen through having painfully recognized that of my husband and his inability to do my job for me.

Those areas I have referred to in their therapy, however, were only a small part of the therapeutic interface I was aware of and have commented on here. Since Stephen and Mary were motivated, understood what I was saying, and were usually successful in carrying out their plans, speaking of my own family was, for the most part, unnecessary. I talk about my family of origin or my marriage in therapy sessions only when there is a particular reason to do so: when speaking of my family helps me to join the family; when members are naive and do not realize how common their problems are; when they need an example to understand what I am saying; when I see value in modeling for them; or when I have been hooked into their system and want to unhook myself. When an example from my own family first comes into my mind, I usually do not use it. If it keeps coming back, however, I consider it more seriously and may talk about it.

I liked working with Mary and Stephen as a couple and wished that my husband and I had had such an opportunity early in our marriage. Psychoanalysis for each of us was a lonely voyage, keeping us far apart and unable to understand each other while we struggled with our own issues. Both of them wanted to do as much as possible on their own and I respected and encouraged this. My definitive changes had come after my analysis was completed, when I was free to turn the energy, which had been focused inward, outward towards the important people in my life. Later, when I decided to change with my family of origin, I did my own planning, using reading, lectures, supervision, consultation, and having and doing therapy as a base.

Many problems thought of as technical are actually interface issues; getting further information on technique is not likely to help if the problem is the therapist's blind spot. When that therapist is able to understand the connection between her early family experiences and her current reaction in the therapeutic session, then she can sort out whether her impasse results from a lack of knowledge or if the situation in the family she in treating is aggravating an unresolved family problem of her own. As she is able to identify and resolve such issues, she will find that she is better able to both empathize with client members and to help them resolve their problems.

CHAPTER 11

Therapist's Use of Self

As the therapist joins the family, testing its boundaries and rules, a therapeutic system comes into being, growing stronger as trust builds. Much of what the therapist comes to know is arrived at from his experience as he interacts with family members. As he connects with each one, they then have the opportunity to connect with him. His authenticity in this encounter will invite honest response by the members. Self-disclosure by the therapist is a means to an end, not an end in itself. If the therapist wants to stimulate thoughts and feelings in others, an effective way to do it is to model for them.

His genuineness, as he relates in the therapeutic situation, is measured by how his words and actions reflect his feelings and values. Since he cannot see and participate except through the filter of his own perception, he needs to be aware that each family member's perception may be different from his and that the awareness and understanding of those differences may be the key to change. I ask family members at the beginning of the second session to give their reactions, positive and negative, to the first session, following which I give mine. This interchange sets the stage for repeated mutual feedback and evaluation throughout therapy. How much I disclose at any one time depends on the acuteness of their crisis and how much the family may be ready to hear. At the beginning of therapy when members are engrossed in their problems, short statements are all that are needed. In the middle phase, however, the therapist can become a role model as he sifts what is happening through his own awareness, reflects back to the family what he experiences in his interaction with them, and is open to their points of view.

Family therapy is a learning process wherein family members acquire new models for feeling, thinking, and action. The process gives the members new information about both life in general and problem-solving.

As trust builds, the therapist can carefully disclose relevant aspects from his own life. A small amount goes a long way; disclosure will hinder therapy if the therapist talks too much about himself. If he tells only the good things that he has already resolved, the family may see him as smug, unreal, or condescending. As he walks the fine line between disclosing too much or too little, he needs to ask himself whether it will promote the therapy or be an interference or burden for the members, monitor the effect of each episode, and modulate his behavior accordingly. Effective self-disclosure can undercut the idea of the omnipotent therapist, demonstrate empathy, and gradually build trust.

First, however, the therapist must care about and take care of himself. Therapists who have been parentified as children in their families of origin often care for others instead of caring for themselves. A therapist who is overresponsible or burned out is not an effective model for the client family. He needs to set a structure he can live with, maintaining control of the session, while leaving family members in charge of their lives. He also has the right to receive something for himself out of each therapeutic session, to hone his growing edge (Napier & Whitaker, 1973). When the therapist believes that each family is significant to him in his own maturation and that he can test out his authentic feelings in the session, then therapy holds excitement and growth for both therapist and family.

A series of examples will illustrate various ways the therapist can use himself to mobilize the therapy.

MODELING USE OF SELF

The Conrad family was in therapy when the oldest son made a suicide attempt. Chuck and I, as co-therapists, continued to meet with the family in the hospital. In the first post-hospital session, Chuck referred to a previous session as he spoke to the wife, Mary Lou, about her husband Lester's reactions:

Chuck: Mary Lou, the other night at the hospital we started out talking about weaknesses and strengths, and Lester talked about some of his weaknesses. I was wondering what your reaction was as you heard him talk about his weaknesses. You said it seemed more real.

Mary Lou: Yes.

Chuck: What kind of an internal reaction did you have? I'm asking because I couldn't tell by looking at you what your internal reaction was.

Mary Lou: Something like . . . I don't know. Give me an example, such as?

Chuck: I don't want to put words in your mouth.

Mary Lou: I know you don't, but . . . I don't know. Give me an example. Such as?

Mary Lou had difficulty giving her reactions and she asked for help. Chuck did not immediately offer to help nor did he pressure her. As she insisted, however, he identified this as a problem for him, and then gave a personal example.

Chuck: Well, this is always my hangup with you. I don't want to put words in your mouth. Well, when Jan and I have been in . . . let me give you an example. Jan and I have been in sessions together in groups — marathons, weekends, and whatnot. And one of the hardest parts of those things is for me to get into my weaknesses and hangups and my symptoms. I get pretty emotional, just as Lester was the other night. My emotions come from pretty deep, and when they come up, they almost overwhelm me. When that happens, Jan has a tremendous reaction to it. (to Jan) You can say more about how it is for you.

Jan: Well, I just feel my insides moving towards him. (to Lester) I was feeling the same thing for you the other night. Really, I could have just gone over and put my arms around you. I had a feeling like I was flowing that way. I feel that way when Chuck has really tremendous emotions. And I couldn't tell, Mary Lou, how you were feeling at that time.

Mary Lou: Ah . . . I guess what I was feeling was, "Well, it's about time! It's about time!"

Lester: That's a reaction I would expect. (Both laugh.)

Mary Lou: I would like to say that my emotions are flowing, too, but it takes this conversation to come up with what was really happening. This is one of the biggest difficulties for me, to get in touch with what is going on with me.

Chuck's example described a parallel process in which he placed himself in Lester's shoes when he disclosed his own weaknesses, and then drew me in to parallel Mary Lou's position. I described my reactions towards Chuck and then moved on to describe my feelings about Lester during that last session. When Mary Lou was able to get in touch with her own response, we were then able to discuss the varying reactions.

Jan: When you say, "It's about time"—that's the history of his not showing those feelings over a long period of time—is that it?

Mary Lou: Yeah.

Lester: It's irritation.

Chuck: Isn't it also a bit of a putdown to him?

Mary Lou: It probably is.

Chuck: A little bit like there's no way you can be satisfied? You've been wanting him to have these feelings and he finally has them and you can still be critical about him because he didn't have them sooner.

Mary Lou: I don't think so, because I know he has them. (She turns to Lester.) You're the one who says that I don't come out with any feelings. This has gone on and on and on.

Chuck: Obviously, you both have deep feelings.

Mary Lou: Many times I don't come out with anything (again, she turns to Lester) and there's this pressure from you.

Chuck: And you end up defending yourself.

Unspoken Feelings Emerge

Self-disclosure can be valuable when properly timed, although more than timing is actually involved. The therapist needs to have enough self-assurance and self-acceptance to be able to risk revealing those pieces of self when they might be judged and/or not be accepted, or even ignored. Self-disclosure may reveal a therapeutic interface which then allows the participants to discuss the process on a deeper level, which happened when I spoke to Carol* of my induction into the Martins' marital system. A meta-communication—"some things in life are universal"—is implied which, in addition to timing, gives its impact.

The therapist may consciously encourage a family member to get in touch with feelings, as Chuck did with Mary Lou. Or a different, less focused process may emerge as the therapist relaxes and allows deeper forces to surface in self. Carl Whitaker approaches therapy as a growthful experience for himself as well as for the family. He gives himself permission to fantasize and tell his fantasies and to say the unsayable to the family. Knowing him and watching him work have had a powerful effect on me, giving me permission to clarify the therapeutic arena for myself, to practice breaking my family's rules of protection, and to keep therapy moving by helping family members identify family rules and decide if they are rules they still want to follow.

---

*See Chapter 10.

Interface reactions are complex, not simply the result of the therapist's unresolved issues. When a therapist's feelings are aroused in a session, it can be productive to explore the possibility that his reactions reflect heightened feelings in client family members. Exploring such feelings can provide significant data about difficulties in that family system. I especially like co-therapy because it allows time for a deeper process to emerge. As one therapist is involved in interaction with a family member, the other is free to backpedal out of the arena and fantasy, connect, or reverberate to the tensions in the room and then bring those fantasies, hunches, or feelings back into the treatment room.

In a middle phase session, the husband Everett was talking to Chuck in an intellectualized way about his situation at work. His wife Polly and I had been sitting quietly, listening. I began feeling empty and drained and I had an almost uncontrollable feeling of being overtaken by sleep. As I described these feelings aloud, there was a silence. Then Everett's expression changed. When he spoke again, his voice had lost its intellectualized tone. He admitted that he was in a rage about his situation at work where there was no clear authority; that he was feeling put down, trapped and bypassed. As he expressed his helpless rage, I felt lighter.

Later in the session Polly was talking to Chuck and again I was listening. She was intellectualizing, fussing about their social schedule and complaining about sex. Again I felt, and then spoke of, a similar feeling of overwhelming sleepiness rolling over me in waves. There was a silence; then all of a sudden Polly buried her face in her hands and burst into tears. When she was able to speak, she said there was something she did not know whether to talk about — a feeling she had recently had of extreme loneliness, as if Everett were no longer alive. She said Everett kept himself so busy there was no room for her or for sex and that she had felt helpless and unable to bring it up. As she sobbed, my overwhelmed feeling lifted.

I believe I was able to connect with the unspoken feelings buried underneath their words because I was sitting quietly each time, relaxed and attentive. Since I had had ample sleep, I knew that the feelings I had belonged in the room in the therapeutic interface, and my simply stating them allowed the blanketed emotions to emerge.

MAINTAINING THE STRUCTURE

Therapy works best if the therapist stays in charge of the session, leaving the family members in charge of their lives. The therapist then knows where responsibility lies and will be able to identify manipulation when it occurs. The way he sets the structure models for the family members how they can take responsibility for themselves. It is essentially the same task a parent has — to help the other help himself. As the therapist deals with violations of the structure, issues that were being avoided are heightened. As they are resolved, the therapeutic alliance deepens.

For example, Janie and Hank Meyer were in the middle phase of therapy. Hank came alone 10 minutes late to a session when Janie was vacationing in New York. The following week Hank was 15 minutes late, explaining that he had had to talk with his stockbroker because the market was fluctuating. Janie, who had said she would be back for this session, was not with him; she had called him the night before, saying she was coming 24 hours later, thereby missing the appointment. As I waited for them, I reviewed our therapy and was ready to talk about it when he arrived:

Jan: You gave me the opportunity to do some thinking when you were late. I'm conscious of the fact that we've started late several times recently. And what I'm concerned about, irrespective of the individual reasons, is that the same thing is happening in therapy that happens in the rest of your life, which is: not using time well, and marking time, and not making decisions that need to be made. And if that continues, then the therapy does not provide a growing edge — it becomes just a part of the rest of your life.

Hank: Uh huh.

Jan: One of my questions to myself was: how to stir things up? I was thinking of various possibilities. One would be to take a break in therapy; one would be to move to a time earlier in the day; one would be to have the two of you join a couples group; one would be to make new goals to work on — all or any of the above.

Hank: The new goals part — I think that is definitely the bottom line. I was feeling resentment for Janie's not being here. I have a way — I could have told my broker, "I have to go and I'll call you back." But if I had done that, then I would have missed the opportunity to change the option I had out, which would correspond to my putting things off. But by not saying, "I'll call you back," I also chiseled on this therapy. That's true.

Jan: The same thing was true last time when you were talking to your mother. It was an important call, as was this call. But it was at the wrong time.

Hank: It was at the wrong time.

Jan: The point is not, "Which is more important?" They're all important. The point is whether we are to meet at this time. There's resentment in me if I'm here and you're not. I'm not interested in babysitting, if we're not really working together.

Hank: What do you think about Janie's not being here?

Jan: I think it has to do with the therapy, just as I think your being late has to do with the therapy. I think you both, in your own peculiar ways, are dragging your feet. And putting important things in its place doesn't change the fact that you're dragging your feet.

Hank: Exactly. And it also doesn't change the fact that I feel anxiety coming in here without Janie. And I feel resentment that, instead of coming back yesterday, she said, "I'm going to take the same flight 24 hours later."

Jan: We're falling into a rut. And it's not just you and Janie who are doing it, but I'm doing it, too, because I'm allowing it to happen. So I'm in this with you. But I'm getting impatient. We need to start work or take a break if you want to coast for a while. You don't need me to coast.

Hank: Right.

Hank, although agreeing with me, tried three times to put the emphasis on Janie. I included her as a full partner in the lateness, but did not fall into the trap of focusing on her. Instead, I included myself and stated that I would not let the current situation continue.

When both attended the next session, I repeated my evaluation to get Janie's input. I recognized that, as I played around with the different kinds of changes that could be initiated, I was experiencing a renewed sense of excitement in the process. In confronting their lateness as a sign that the therapy was moving into a secondary position in their lives, I admitted it was doing the same in mine. Then we could move forward to clarify our contract so that it reflected our mutual goals.

When the therapist maintains a clear structure, it sets a model for clients. Rose, a therapist in therapy with her husband, commented on the effect of the structure of the therapy on her professional life:

Rose: (to Jan) Another thing I'm doing differently — and your role model has been good for me, seeing how you operate — is that I have set specific times when I see patients. Last night they were trying to get me to agree to a Tuesday or Friday night appointment and I said, "No, that's it!" I didn't even go into an explanation why. And that's been a real struggle for me — learning to say "no" to clients. What amazes me is that a few years ago I would have been seeing all these people at night and at five o'clock, which are terrible times for my family. The same type of people are now coming in at 1:15

and 2:15 in the afternoon because they heard I was good and they want to see me. It's like when I'm definite about it and say, "This is the time I have," people will fit themselves in, just like we fit ourselves into your schedule.

USE OF SELF DURING THE FIRST PHASE

Revealing relevant aspects of one's own life not only helps the therapist join the family, but also is a modeling process. How much to make known and when to reveal are important decisions. Disclosure is only useful insofar as it promotes the therapeutic process. The therapist's sharing of his reactions and his own life is more likely to happen as time goes by and the therapeutic alliance deepens. Nevertheless, self-disclosure can be an important aspect of an initial interview or the first phase of therapy.

Chuck and I met in consultation with the family of a depressed patient, Mrs. Mills, and the staff of an inpatient unit. Mrs. Mills, although doing well in the hospital, regressed during home visits. Present in the interview were Mr. and Mrs. Mills and two of their five grown children — a married daughter, Corrine, and a 25-year-old retarded daughter, Annie, who lived at home.

A Modeling Process

We joined the family by paralleling our own family's developmental stage, living arrangement, and marital cooperation with theirs in order to help them develop new ways of thinking about the changes that needed to be made in their lives.

Chuck: I want to shift just a bit to ask what things are like between the two of you now that the kids are gone — all but Annie.
Mr. Mills: I don't know what you mean by that.
Chuck: I'm thinking of our situation, where our kids have been gradually moving out the past few years and we don't have them to think about so much anymore. We have each other to think about, and sometimes we get into scraps about that and sometimes we have to make some adjustments to each other. It's like we're starting over again, in a sense.
Mr. Mills: Well, and you see, she's in the back. We have an apartment in the back. I have this little store in the front. And I'm busy here and whatever she's doing there, I don't know, most of the time.
Jan: And you work during the days and the evenings? Seven days a week?

Mr. Mills: That's right.

Jan: So really you're in different spaces all the time.

Mr. Mills and Mrs. Mills: That's right.

Mr. Mills: There is a lot of work for her. She could really help me, but . . . (His voice trails off.)

Chuck: So the arrangement you have really keeps you separate. You're in the front and she's in the back. Is that satisfactory? Is that the way you want it?

Mr. Mills: It's also on a one-story level. I'm in and out. We see each other. But I am eating on the run. She could go up front and relieve me and I could go back and relax.

Mrs. Mills: I give him his meal in front. It's better if customers have one person to deal with.

Mr. Mills: I have no success getting her to change.

Jan: Do you feel resentment because of that?

Mr. Mills: No. I worked hard all my life. It's in me to accept this. I'm used to being down and come up again.

The Mills were not aware that their children's moving out of the home required compensating moves from each of them. As Chuck raised this issue, Mr. Mills described their divided lives and expressed his wish that his wife would help him in his store. When Mrs. Mills did not see any advantage in changing their engrained roles, Mr. Mills accepted her refusal with a martyr's stance. Later in the interview, Corrine talked about their past life, when the children were young.

The Children Give Input

Corrine: Mom never really expressed her feelings. I appreciate my husband coming home and taking care of my son. And when we were all home, my Dad worked hours upon hours and Mom had five kids at home and she was tired of work and she wanted to go out for a sandwich, but she was stuck with this, seven days a week. They should have worked something out.

Mrs. Mills: Nobody would babysit for my Indians.

Jan: You're sounding nostalgic about not having the Indians around.

Chuck: Well, that was what I was trying to get at when I asked: What's it like, now that the kids have moved out? Because if, for 25 or so years, things have been as you described, Corrine, then Mom and Dad have not really spent a lot of time working things out together. And we certainly had to recommunicate and reconnect when our kids moved out, so I'm really very familiar with the situation.

Jan: (to Chuck) It sounds like they each had a 24-hour-a-day job that they had to do by themselves and (turning to the Mills) that you were each in your own worlds trying to do what you had to do, and now you're in a different space. And it sounds like you don't know how to reconnect back in to what's going on.
Mrs. Mills: Oh, I see. I see what you mean.

As the children grew up, the parents had continued growing apart, each caught up in the endless routine of their lives — he in the store and she with the children. As the children, except for Annie, left, Mrs. Mills had become increasingly depressed.

Chuck: Do you understand what we're trying to say? That you and your husband need to do more talking, planning, arguing, negotiating, and fighting.
Mrs. Mills: Now that I'm in the hospital . . .
Chuck: Tell him that. I'll listen. (All laugh.)
Mrs. Mills: (to husband) Now that I'm in the hospital, we'll never get together.
Mr. Mills: I'll have to get a little rolling pin that will bust when you hit me so you can stop me. (All laugh.)
Chuck: (to wife) What do you think about what he said?
Mrs. Mills: Well, we never physically fight.
Annie: I know. Fight. I in kitchen. Open door.
Mrs. Mills: And you hear us arguing?
Chuck: I'm sure glad you came, Annie.
Annie: Yeah! Dad, brother-in-law fight. No like him. Mama brother-in-law. Dad he no like brother-in-law.
Chuck: And that's what they fight over.
Annie: Yeah.
Mr. Mills: That was good expressing.
Annie: I know!

Annie provided another key to her mother's depression — a long-standing, unresolved conflict between Mr. Mills and his wife's family. Corrine filled in the details: When the Mills had married, Mr. Mills had joined his wife's brothers in a small business and Mrs. Mills had enjoyed the close connection with her family of origin. When a fight erupted between her husband and brothers, Mr. Mills cut off from his wife's family and opened his own store. This move effectively cut Mrs. Mills off from her family and she became increasingly alienated from both her own family and her husband by her divided loyalties.

The Impasse Becomes Clear

Chuck: (to Annie) And you listen to them fight.
Annie: I listen.
Chuck: And it's upsetting to hear them fight.
Annie: Yeah.
Chuck: (to parents) Maybe that's why you avoid each other, so you don't fight and upset Annie.
Annie: (crying) Fight! (Father gives her a handkerchief.)
Jan: (to mother) Yes, but you have to be able to say what's going on with you and what you need.
Mrs. Mills: Right. It's so quiet nobody would know I was there. I have to open my mouth sometimes.
Jan: Are you caught between wanting to talk to your husband but being afraid to, because of Annie?
Mrs. Mills: I always keep her in mind. I say, "Let's not talk about this — Annie's listening."
Jan: So that holds you back. Maybe there are ways you can talk to your husband and tell him things you want to tell him and not scare Annie.
Mrs. Mills: We shouldn't raise our voices because that scares her.

Now the current problem became clear. Mrs. Mills and Annie confined themselves to the apartment while Mr. Mills watched the store, as both parents avoided the central conflict in their lives to avoid upsetting Annie. Mrs. Mills could express her resentment through non-cooperation with her husband, which increasingly cut her off from human interaction and increased her depression. Chuck suggested a way out.

Chuck: One way to do it would be to come in here and talk to the social worker together, just the two of you, and figure out how you're going to live when you go back home. Because it really comes back to the two of you — husband and wife, because the children are mostly gone and Annie's going to be there, listening.
Mrs. Mills: And you two have the same problem with your children being gone?
Jan: Yes.
Mr. Mills: But you're both here working together — you're involved more or less in the same field.
Chuck: Yeah, sometimes.
Jan: I think that's one of the reasons we started working together. It's only since our children have left that we've been working together, like this.

Mr. Mills: You haven't done this before?

Jan: No. We were working in different areas.

Chuck: We live above our store. (All laugh.)

Jan: That's true.

Mrs. Mills: You work in . . .

Jan: We have an office in our home. It's downstairs and we're upstairs. I know what you mean.

Mr. Mills: But you two have more in common.

Jan: We had to work at it. It wasn't all that easy. But I won't bore you with the details.

Chuck: I'd like to know what each of you think about the suggestion I made.

Mr. Mills: What suggestion?

Chuck: I think there would be a value to you coming in and having sessions at the hospital talking together.

Mrs. Mills had not responded when Chuck first raised the question of developmental changes. Later she indicated that she had not only been listening, but was looking for parallels with her own situation. My comment that we had started working together after our children left further aroused her interest. Mr. Mills predictably discounted the connection, saying we both worked in the same field and had more in common than they did. Mrs. Mills, however, had caught a glimpse of a different way of being.

The Mills were willing to meet together several times with the social worker on the unit. When she made a follow-up call five months later, she was surprised by Mrs. Mills' voice and manner; at first she was not sure she had the right person on the phone. Mrs. Mills reported that the family interview had been very meaningful; that she had been struck by the way the two of us worked together. She had not been aware, until that time, of how she and her husband did not interact. She began taking care of the store while her husband ate lunch and she also helped him post the books. They had been going out regularly on rides or to a movie while Corrine's in-laws took care of the store.

A Couple Joins a Couple

We followed a similar process of joining with Cathy and Edward, a young couple who were feeling hopeless about the possibility of change after two years of marriage. They had contrasting styles of approach and decision-making. Cathy talked first and then immediately took action; Edward thought first; he then needed to understand; action for him came last. Edward felt he had to hold back since Cathy moved so fast. They explained themselves during the first phase of therapy.

Cathy: I don't want to hear him when it's going to come out that I'm the Big Bad Wolf. I think I can hear it if it comes out in more deliberate doses.

Chuck: You mean it really comes out hard when Edward comes out with something?

Cathy: Uh huh.

Edward: There are two things. I'm not very sensitive to how I come across and I know there are times I could be brutal.

Chuck: Brutally frank.

Edward: The other thing is that I experience you, Cathy, coming at me in waves and waves and waves.

Cathy: I get it out all the time. I never store it up. It probably does seem like that. I don't make any effort to keep it inside.

Chuck: But there's some value judgment — with Cathy feeling it's *better* to get it out and Edward feeling it's better *not* to get it out.

Cathy: There's another thing that goes on. There are times he tends not to look at me, picks his nails, looks at TV but doesn't look at me, I feel like I have to do something dramatic to get his attention.

Edward: I do feel my involvement must be limited.

Cathy and Edward described how they got stuck, with Cathy overwhelming him with words and drama and Edward clamping down to protect himself. Since we, as married co-therapists, had experienced the same frustration in our marriage, Chuck introduced our parallel roles to initiate a same-sex joining process and to shift the interaction to a new level.

The Therapists Take Over the Struggle

Chuck: (to Jan) I'm very empathic to this because you and I have struggled with this.

Jan: Yes, I'm in your shoes, Cathy, and (turning to Edward) Chuck's in your shoes. It's pretty much a middle ground now, although we still get into it sometimes.

Chuck: Sometimes I need to get away when you need to get me to pay attention.

Jan: Uh huh.

Chuck: We're better at doing it now, but we were in this a long time before working it out.

Jan: I think out loud. A lot of the things you were saying . . .

Chuck: You don't know what you're thinking until you say it.

Jan: And when I said it, it used to tick him off and he'd go whusst! (motioning out)

Edward: I'd probably be better off if I talked up more.

Chuck: Well, over the years Jan and I have managed to learn something from each other and it's been helpful. It's taken a long time to do. There's a certain amount of pride in standing there and not being influenced and not being controlled. My thoughts were very controlling and I didn't realize it for a long time.

Cathy: It's nice to know we're not the only two people in the world who ever had a relationship where we can bring out the worst in each other as well as the best.

Chuck: I think it's extremely common — this kind of disparity between how you each approach things. It affects the way you think, it affects the way you feel, and it affects how you eventually behave.

Jan: (to Chuck) It's one of the reasons they were attracted to each other to begin with. That's where some of the excitement came from, but you still want some comfort along with the excitement.

Chuck: You could be good for each other.

As they listened to us take over their conflict, Edward moved from the statement "I do feel my involvement must be limited" to testing out a new stance, "I'd probably be better off if I talked up more." Chuck then joined him and pointed towards a middle ground where spouses can learn from each other, following it with a nostalgic reference to his former stubborn pride in not being controlled. Cathy felt relief at being understood and we encouraged her hope.

Feedback from Clients

The next week they reported that the tensions between them had eased, and Cathy began to explain:

Cathy: I think one thing that has helped is . . . it seems so corny, but you feel like you're the only people in the world who have been in your position and there has been great comfort that the two of you — not that our paths will be identical to yours or have been in the past — but I somehow did feel myself — how could I have been the only woman in the world and somehow picked out the characteristics of this guy, and that it only happened to me and no one else quite had that experience. And if they *had*, which I questioned, that they could have it work. So . . .

Chuck: So hearing a little bit about us was useful.

Cathy: It was useful. It wasn't intrusive, but just useful.

Chuck: That's good feedback because sometimes we have to find out if telling about ourselves is just a burden and intrusive or if it is really useful.

Edward: It's been helpful to me for just sort of . . . survival. When I tend to see conflict, I tend to think this marriage must be doomed. I most often can be pretty optimistic, but sometimes this doom becomes more pervasive and I feel really helpless about the whole thing.

Cathy: Hearing from you that it doesn't have to be hopeless — that it's what you make of the situation.

Jan: It's a challenge to somehow master this difference in style.

Edward: If I'd heard you were perfect, then it would become very different. I'm not under so much pressure now. It's my own pressure.

Cathy: Well, I think one of the reasons I found it helpful is that I admire, respect, look to your generation, my parents' generation, for people who can express themselves and lend the benefit of their experience — especially when they've been able to make tough things work out. I don't feel like I've had those kinds of people to watch. I've tried to latch onto them.

I see our joining as an effort to educate the couple. Cathy and Edward, although intellectually and professionally competent, were naive about relationships and had few successful models in their families of origin. They did not know how common their predicament was or that the very characteristics which attracted them to each other when they married would later be those areas they would fight over. Experiencing a therapist who will titrate disclosure to the situation helps those who represent both polarized ends to move towards the middle.

The Therapists Switch Alliances

Joining a family is a process that occurs in stages. Co-therapists usually join with the spouse of the same sex as therapy begins. Therapists need to be able to change their alliances, however, in order to model flexibility and stimulate change. The Dorans, a family in the launching phase, were referred to Chuck by a specialist from another state. The children were aged 23, 21, and 18, with the middle daughter anorexic. The father, Donald, ran his own successful business; Delores, the mother, was dissatisfied with what she was getting from her husband.

When Delores called Chuck to set up an appointment, she told him of all the psychiatrists who had failed them over the previous seven years, and of her hope, since he was so highly recommended, that they would finally find a resolution for their daughter. His comment to her was, "Then I wonder how we are going to fail you." In the first session with the entire family, Donald focused on Chuck who ran the interview. I did not compete; instead, I joined Delores and the children, observed the interaction, and made process comments about family roles and rules. I watched for an opening in which I could effectively engage Donald and be taken seriously by him.

We saw the parents alone in the fourth session. Delores began by saying she felt she was heading for a depression. She said: "Something is lacking in the marriage. Soon I'll be too old to ever experience it." Chuck told her of his experiencing her warmth towards him and of Donald's warmth towards him, and commented on how they missed conveying warmth to each other.

Donald: I can't be mushy and romantic and phony. I have to be myself.
Delores: I give him high scores for honesty. I respect him.
Jan: (to Delores) You're in a bind. You have grown up, become independent and changed in twenty-five years. You love him. Yet something is missing. If you are to please yourself, you will have to rock the boat you like. (Delores agreed, nodding her head.)
Donald: I don't understand.

As Delores started to explain, she became more intense and began to speak of all of her disappointments in a blaming stream of words. I broke in by saying to Donald:

Jan: My hunch is—you feel she is insatiable.
Delores: Oh, that's not true.
Donald: (really looking at me for the first time) Yes, I do.
(Delores challenged him.)
Jan: (to Delores) I experience you as insatiable—even today—*now*. You don't want to resolve things but to go on and on.

Donald was now paying attention and taking me seriously as he heard me saying what he would have liked to say, but had not dared to. Delores was also having a different experience with me; I had moved from a supportive to a confronting role. This altered the alliances and allowed Chuck and me, as co-therapists, to shift our roles and to set in motion a process of unpredictable interchangeability as support bases for the spouses. When the therapists can each model their capacity to see both sides of the situation, they can then demonstrate that no one needs to conform to one role all the time. When the therapists can mix it up, the family has a model to also mix it up. Eventually Donald could let down his guard and begin to explore fears and hurt as Delores settled down to build in consistency and control.

USE OF SELF DURING THE MIDDLE PHASE

Therapy takes place within the personal relationship between the therapist and the family members. Ongoing encounters reflect the internal experience and value systems of all those present. How much a family reveals depends on the therapist's ability to create an arena in which each member can trust that he will be understood and supported. This personal relationship, although only one aspect of the therapy, is a crucial one, especially during the middle phase of long term therapy, and it fuels the family's trust in the process and their willingness to risk.

As spouses who have been enmeshed and reactive to each other begin to change, they feel they are on shaky ground. They have lost the old, rigid security that, though stifling, was predictable; yet they have not found a new footing. Personal support from the therapist can help them over the hump at this juncture.

Dealing with the Overadequate Spouse

During Jenny's and Bill's 10-year marriage, Bill had taken on the role of provocative child, mirroring his earlier scapegoated function when he had kept his parents focused on him so they could avoid having to deal with each other. Jenny had played the parent role, blaming their lack of intimacy on Bill's actions, and wanting Bill to change. In the middle phase of therapy, Bill gradually stopped having affairs, taking drugs, and drinking excessively and began to deal with his underlying anxiety. Yet they were still only occasionally able to experience intimacy with each other. The part Bill played was obvious; Jenny's role was less apparent.

Jenny: I've been thinking about how I feel when I'm not with Bill — driving my car, walking down the street.
Chuck: How do you feel?
Jenny: Better. It's like he's a drain on my energy.
Chuck: When he's walking alongside, there's some energy that's going to what he's doing? How am I relating to him? Is it OK between us? How about when you're walking through the aquarium?
Jenny: I was thinking about the fish.
Chuck: Somehow you could just walk and not have this feeling or bad

vibes. It's possible. It happens maybe a few minutes out of a month.
Jenny: That's right.
Chuck: I remember that feeling. It's terrible.
Jenny: You remember the feeling? I don't believe that! (She laughs nervously.)
Chuck: You don't believe that! (to Jan) We ought to have some old tapes to show people because they never believe us. (to Jenny) You only believe what you see now, but you don't believe all the misery we went through.
Jan: You don't see how it was at one point.
Jenny: I was talking to a friend who's separated from her husband. She left him two years ago, took her house plants and split. We were trying to figure out anyone we knew who had a happy marriage. It was difficult to come up with — whether we knew they were happy or not.
Chuck: Even the ones that look happy.
Jenny: That's really disgusting, I think.
Jan: It's hard work, making a happy marriage. It doesn't just happen. Even though you're drawn together and have things in common, the things that draw you together also push you apart. I figure we've had four marriages — four times we could have split. And what we did — instead of changing partners — was to change ourselves.
Jenny: Did you go to attorneys?
Chuck: We didn't get that far.
Jan: We got pretty distant at times, though. And each time was different. I'd come through it and I'd think: Aha! We've made it. And then one of us would grow one way or one grow the other.

We joined the couple in speaking of ourselves, placing their struggle in a developmental continuum of normal experience, since we had already gone through it. We gave them few details, yet what we said was true. Bill's contribution to the problems had been blatant, yet Jenny had not been able to leave the marriage. She was beginning to realize that she did play a part but she did not really understand what her part was, since she was so focused on Bill.

Focusing on Change in Self

One of the most difficult transitions for spouses to make is to focus on changes in *self*, rather than on change in the other. In an enmeshed relationship, each feels that self is controlled by the other, as if one's independent functions must be funneled through the other. Bill had already made important changes in himself and with his family of origin. Now it was Jenny's turn.

Jan: One of the things you contribute is that huge expectation that Bill should be one particular way.

Jenny: Yeah, I have expectations. I think my expectations are perfectly reasonable.

Chuck: That's part of the problem.

Jan: If he's watching tennis, you expect he should drop what he's doing to be with you.

Jenny: I didn't expect him to do that.

Bill: Yes, you did. You didn't tell me that you did. You showed me that you did.

Jan: I don't think there was anything either one of you could have done that night that would have felt all right to the other.

Chuck: It's like they were ready for a fight.

Jan: Yeah. It sounds like one of those provoking conflict points where it was more important to provoke conflict . . .

Bill: Yeah, I agree.

Jan: . . . than it was to settle it.

I had been setting the stage to give Jenny a new perspective on her expectations. Bill joined me as Jenny became quieter and withdrew. Chuck, however, recognized her opposition and spoke of it.

Chuck: I don't think Jenny's buying it.

Jenny: I'm not. Because I don't do that. I didn't feel that way . . .

Jan: But you do have expectations of the other person that he be the way you want him to be.

Jenny: OK.

Jan: And it is something that the most straight, moralistic, righteous person can expect that can drive another person just up the wall.

Bill: Uh huh. Yep.

Jan: I know what it feels like because I used to do this and I still do it sometimes.

Chuck: Um.

Bill: Huh.

Jan: Because you're so damn right that the other person should be doing it and there's no way they can know what's in your head. And if they did know what's in your head, all they'd be would be a puppet.

Bill: Right on. Amen.

Jenny: OK, I don't think it's unreasonable to ask someone to come
home . . .

Jan: When you pick any part of it, you're right. So it's not that you're
not right. It's the attitude of being so intent on the other person
rather than being intent on what *you're* going to do because this is
the way you think is right. It's like you're Big Mama up there, knowing how all the pieces should go on the board. But the problem is
that people like you and me pick people who don't want to do what
we say and we'd probably be bored with someone who would do it.

Jenny: I don't think so.

Jan: I don't say he's the one for you. I don't necessarily know. But you
want to know what you contribute, and I think that's part of what
you contribute.

Jenny was still caught up in whether what she was dong was "right."
As I said, "I know what it feels like because I used to do this and I still
do it sometimes," followed by afffirmative grunts from the men, I felt
a jolt of energy and my voice grew stronger as I described the righteous
feelings I had carried for so long. Jenny was still protesting, but now she
was listening.

Jan: And he contributes his own share. He's provocative in a way that
keeps you doing this thing. As long as you have those strong energy
pulls toward him, where what he does is more important than what
you do, you're going to be vulnerable to him. If you didn't react
so much, if you really didn't care what he did and just went on with
your life, you'd have more times like yesterday, walking in the
aquarium.

Jenny: It's like Bill does all these things. He acts like the naughty little boy.

Jan: So you can be the Big Mama.

Jenny: And I'm trying so hard to unhook myself and he's jumping up and
down and getting me to respond and react.

Jan: You don't have to bounce along to his rhythm. You really don't.
You like it when you walk down the street by yourself.

Jenny: Uh huh.

Jan: You could even be in his presence sometime and not be reactive
to what he's doing.

Chuck: (to Jan) One thing that may happen is that if she stops being Big
Mama to him, he may increase his trickiness for a while . . .

Jenny: He already has.

Chuck: And that will draw you back in again and you'll be back where
you started. So that at the point he increases his trickiness, you have
to hold your position.

Jan: (to Chuck) Or if he doesn't increase his trickiness, it may get very dead between them — empty.

Chuck: Then it would get very boring.

Although it was difficult to get through to Jenny, I persisted. I had felt that frustration she was feeling in my own marriage — the bitter realization of being *right*, and yet still not winning. I had also experienced the relief of giving up my expectations of Chuck and learning to trust that he could handle his own consequences. I knew the joy of following my own path and letting him follow his, and the intimacy that then comes in precious moments of connection.

When Chuck knew she had heard me, he then extended the scenario, anticipating the next step, which Jenny said had already started. Chuck continued to predict that Jenny would be drawn back in and regress, and gave her a strategy to follow. I then proposed an alternative outcome for them to be aware of — the probable next stage for couples who decrease their enmeshment.

Strengthening the Therapeutic Alliance

As the therapeutic alliance deepens, many choices become possible. In the co-therapy format, with a couple treating a couple, a balanced relationship exists that allows for exploration of intimate issues during the middle phase of treatment. Very few relationships outside of the family have the possibility of being more personal and intimate than therapy, and self-disclosure by the therapist promotes self-disclosure in family members.

Amy and Gene, described earlier in the book,* had difficulty being intimate with each other. Amy was initially resistant to connecting her attraction to older men to her father's disappearance when she was a child. Gene had been unable to establish a direct and personal relationship with members of his family of origin. These unresolved problems from their earlier lives contaminated their marriage and were the tough issues we struggled with. We had another arena in the couple/couple format, however, in which Chuck and Amy could explore their transferential relationship.

I had been trying for 20 sessions without much success to get Amy and Gene to see the connection between their current problems and their relationships with their families of origin. I wanted to open up as many options as possible and not approach their resistance head-on.

---

*See Chapters 5 and 7.

Jan: (to Amy) I see many different ways of going about changing what you want to change about yourself and your relationships. I see your relationship with your mother as one, and your father as one, and both being directly related to what goes on here — and with other people, too, including Chuck and me. And if you're doing it at the same time in all these different relationships, then there is more opportunity for it to work. (turning to Gene) And I see the same thing with you — to change your relationship with important people in your family, in the same way. The focus is not all on Amy at all. We just happened to be talking about her.

Chuck: (to Amy) One of the advantages of our co-therapy with you both is that we not only can be aware of how we react to each other, or any other pair, but we have a couple of observers who can tell us what they see. And I'm not averse to saying what my reactions are and exploring my side of it, because they go hand in hand. And the more we can understand my attraction to you, the better we can understand your attraction to me, and the better that can be applied anywhere it's applicable. You're young enough to be my daughter, and I have a daughter not far from your age, and I think that's a factor. And the circumstances of our working together in a quite intimate way sets the stage for natural reactions to occur that are repetitions from the past. So there's a repetition for me going on, too, that I haven't really stopped to think about until right now, in relation to you. I was trained in the tradition of presenting a mirror and I've really changed that in the last few years. I can't think of any time when I was revealing any of my reactions or my history where it created problems. I suppose it would create a problem if I went on and on about it. But I'm willing to share with you what happens to me.

Amy: Well, that would be helpful, because I think you can create more problems by not sharing that kind of information. One of the problems my analyst and I had was that I think he was reluctant to share things I knew were going on with him as well as me, and there gets to be a kind of hypocrisy or situation that lacks integrity when that's going on, with one person not taking responsibility for his or her part of it.

Chuck: I don't think that necessarily means that it wasn't appropriate at the time, or that it couldn't have been helpful to you at the time. But this is a different format, so we can learn different things. We can sit in the same kinds of chairs and look at each other eyeball to eyeball and have much more of a person-to-person type of interaction that should be closer to what happens to you in real life. So . . . I'm for that.

I started out by broadening the context for Amy by including possible work within the therapeutic interface, balancing it by speaking to Gene about work with his original family. Chuck enlarged on my comments, pointing out the advantages of the co-therapy format in focusing on Chuck's and Amy's attraction to each other as parallel to her attraction to her father and to Loren, an older man with whom she was having an affair. When Chuck spoke of his earlier analytic training and practice, Amy spoke of her attraction and reactions to her former analyst. Chuck did not allow himself to be drawn into a comparison; instead, he focused on the advantages of the current format at the present time.

The Spouse Joins the Deepening Alliance

Gene was now ready to talk:

Gene: It's so perfectly complementary in here. When Amy was talking about her past, I was just thinking about my past, which seems vaguer to me. But I know the feeling of how upset I get when someone else I'm close to gets close to somebody else. And it's always made me upset. And I know it isn't the way everyone else reacts, because when I was young, I knew I was getting irrationally upset.

Chuck: We're talking about a basic triangle, really — how a person is feeling about the relationship to two others and their relationship to each other.

Gene: It's really an issue with me because it's one area where I really know I get upset, because last week that happened to me more than once.

Chuck: You must suppress it, because it seemed to me you've taken this whole business of Amy's affair relatively calmly in the last few weeks. I can imagine a husband getting violent.

Gene: I don't think it's just suppressed. Well, maybe it could be, with everything just sealed over.

Chuck: A delayed reaction?

Gene: I was really mad the first week. I think I'm dealing with this better than in the past. When we first talked about it, I reacted. It wasn't until later that I realized the similarities of other situations that were really apparent.

Jan: What was the earliest situation like this that you can remember?

Gene: I can remember back in grammar school, just among the children my own age. I thought I had one friend who was mine exclusively, a boy friend. And he changed his mind. In high school and college, that's how I felt about a girl.

Jan: Did you have that feeling in relationship to your parents?

Gene: I don't think so.

Amy: In recent times, you and your brother were so . . . rather com-
    petitive . . . I wondered if you and Philip didn't each want your
    parents exclusively to yourselves.
Chuck: If so, you each picked different ways to get it.
Amy: His brother got it by being a problem and Gene by being successful.
Jan: In that way, competition doesn't show itself. It's underground.
Gene: Well, that may be true.

Amy's talk with Chuck stirred feelings in Gene of upsetting triangular relationships he was in as a boy and which had now culminated for
him in Amy's affair with Loren. He recognized how upset he got in such
relationships, but somehow, this time, found himself handling it better
as he realized the similarity to the other situations. Although he did not
see any competition with his brother for his parents' attention, Amy recognized and pointed it out, which underlines the fact that it is much easier
to see patterns in one's spouse's family than in one's own.

Jan: (to Amy) Where were you when I got, quote, "off the track"?
Amy: I was upset because I thought everyone was hassling over the fact
    that I said I didn't want to find out from my mother whether my
    parents' quarrel and my father's leaving really happened on the same
    weekend or not. But then I was relieved, Chuck, when you said
    this was a place we could watch something develop between you
    and somebody else. You made it very asexual when you talked
    about it in relation to your daughter and I was glad to see you do
    that because even if you talk about the thing with Loren and me
    as being a sexual thing, and though it is to a certain extent, I don't
    believe that. I think the issue is around me getting close with any-
    body.
Chuck: I agree.
Amy: I'm glad to have that come out clearly.

When I spoke of getting "off the track," I was referring to Amy's comment, made earlier in the session, when she became impatient with questions about her family of origin. Amy was now much less defended, and
relieved that she could experience and examine her feelings in a safe,
four-way situation. Gene was also experiencing the complementarity of
the two-couple format. We now had a contract to explore the therapeutic
interface and, in the journey, to discover together the essence of both
autonomy and intimacy.

Self-disclosure can be effective in bringing out into the open hidden
feelings and thoughts. Since most of us were raised by parents who were

poor self-disclosers, participating in therapy with a therapist who is willing to be open can be a corrective emotional experience, rectifying both the therapist's and the members' misperceptions as they arise. When both therapist and family members can be open about negatives, they can then allow positives to surface and intimacy to grow.

The therapist's prime instrument is himself—the feelings, thoughts, and actions that he introduces into the therapeutic system. When he uses himself and his own reactions in a congruent and consistent manner, awareness is heightened and intimacy is encouraged. His genuineness establishes trust in the relationship. He can build a framework so that spontaneity and freedom are possible within the structure for both therapist and family members. He can use his own experience to help members get in touch with their reactions and understand each other's responses, beginning a modeling process which allows for reciprocal interactions.

PART III

Work with Therapists in a Group

CHAPTER 12

A Structure for Change

Assisting trainees to be aware of interface issues that impede their work with client families is an important consideration in the training of family therapists. Bowen (1978a) has pioneered in this area, developing both a theory and a cognitive method to enable therapists in training to differentiate themselves in their own families in such a way that they can also remain differentiated with client families. Bowen seeks to integrate the two opposing life processes within each person — towards togetherness and towards individuation — so that the person can feel and express feelings and also use her intellect. Such an individual can then function in much the same way in all parts of her life, including her family of origin.

Individuals, however, take in information in different ways. The more methods of presenting information the leader of a training session has at her disposal, the more able she is to tailor an approach that the trainee can comprehend and use. Bowen's method of training is tilted toward the intellect and away from the emotions. In his work as coach, he maintains a cognitive stance and a built-in disengagement from the process, expecting the trainee to feel and express her feelings only with her family members and not in the training session.

Although I think in terms of Bowen's theory, I use an interactive format for training groups, working back and forth between a cognitive and an emotional approach. Each supplies different kinds of information and relates to different individual styles of learning. For a trainee who learns through action, a gestalt or sculpture technique may help make the connection she needs to understand not only her position, but how she wishes to change; however, if the person lacks data or is unclear, she may need to organize information in a more ordered fashion and diagramming may help her see the situation in context.

I encourage emotional engagement in the process, then a backing off and cognitive awareness of that process, and vice versa. I believe that it may be necessary for some trainees to have an emotional experience which can alter their perspective before they can change their intellectual understanding. The Gouldings (1979), who use a combination of transactional analysis and gestalt with individuals in a group context, taught me how to create such an experience. I work from impasses participants describe that usually, but not always, surface in work with the individual's family of origin. I look for an uncomfortable or painful pattern or feeling that encompasses repetitive overtones from earlier situations in her life, or for a discontinuity between her life in the outside world and her experience within her original family's boundaries.

If a trainee can replay in the present her impasses with her family of origin through an experiential technique and find a different solution, then she is freed to actively use that solution with family members. Overcoming such an emotional block leads to cognitive understanding. For other trainees intellectual understanding through diagramming and discussion comes first, which then allows them to have the emotional experience if they deem it necessary.

QUESTIONNAIRE STUDY

During the last six years I have led four or five Therapist's Own Family Groups per year with a total of 140 therapists participating. The trainees take part voluntarily and pay their own fees. The data presented pertain to 23 groups with two different time-related plans, each totaling 20 hours. Twelve groups were 20-hour Therapist's Own Family Seminars in the Center's Short-term Program Series, meeting for four hours once a month for five months, with four to eight therapists per group. Eleven groups were 12-hour Preceptor Groups of five or six participants that met for two hours every other week for six sessions during a quarter in the second year of the Center's Two-year Training Program. Although the 12-hour groups were shorter, students also attended eight hours of classes in which I presented theory, technique, and videotaped examples from my own and client families.

The training groups were based on Bowen theory but used a multifaceted approach, which fit into the eclectic Two-year Training Program at the Center for Family Studies/The Family Institute of Chicago. Participants set their own learning goals. Both discussion and group process were included; action techniques used were family diagramming, family sculpture, gestalt methods, roleplay, and rehearsal. Most of the therapist-trainees developed plans for changing themselves with their own family members.

Participants filled out a pre-questionnaire when they arrived, before introductions. It included data on age, professional degree, and order of sibship. In the profile that emerged, 71% were female and 29% male, with a mean age of 38, and a range from 23 to 62 years. Master's degrees were held by 79%, 13% were physicians or had doctorates, and 8% had varied backgrounds. Firstborns accounted for 40%, 32% were middle children, 23% lastborns, and 5% only children.

Post-questionnaires were given to all 140 participants, with 98% return. The last 114 trainees received, in addition, pre- and six-month post-questionnaires. Self-report data, used as illustrations throughout Part III, are taken primarily from post-questionnaires although, in a few examples, quotations from six-month follow-up are used. The results from the Therapist's Own Family Seminars and Preceptor Groups were analyzed separately and, since the results reported here were not significantly different, they were pooled.

My goal was to examine the impact of brief, small group training on each therapist's understanding of and change in her own family and the families she treated. The post-questionnaire* included 11 questions ranked, where possible, from 5–1, with space given for examples and elaboration. Areas covered were:

1) Goals and issues.
2) What else did you accomplish not listed originally as a goal or issue.
3) The most significant event in the group that happened to you personally; why was it significant?
4) Methods of work in the group that had impact for you (12 items).
5) Impact of the group on your understanding of interface issues; also, on your actions.
6) Impact of the group on your relationship with members of your family of origin; list changes with each member and describe impact.
7) Impact of the group on your relationship with your nuclear family members or intimate other; list changes with each member and describe impact.
8) Has the group improved/hindered your therapy with client families? In what ways?

---

*See Appendix B.

9) How did you like the format of the group? Describe changes to enhance the format.
10) Give your reaction to the leader's facilitation; specific things the leader did which facilitated/hindered.
11) Give a global assessment of the experience.

In their global assessment of the experience, 72% of the 138 therapists who returned post-questionnaires rated it as having strong positive impact. 28% as having some positive impact, and no one rated it as having negative or no overall impact.

Fifty (36%) of the 140 trainees who participated in the groups had 62 additional experiences with me in a context where family of origin and/or interface issues were addressed. Of these 62 additional contacts:

- 19 (31%) were in therapy with me, either individually or with family members
- 18 (29%) were in supervision with me
- 14 (22%) were in a second Therapist's Own Family Group
- 8 (13%) were in extended groups, either for a week or a long week-end, with Chuck and me
- 2 (3%) were in consultation
- 1 (2%) was in both a second and third Therapist's Own Family Group

Those who chose to have two or more such experiences were usually clearer about their area of focus the second time. Some wanted to continue working on issues they had already identified. One member wrote:

"The initial five sessions over four months were simply not long enough to wrestle with and come to an understanding of my functioning in my family."

To solve this problem, two groups negotiated to continue meeting together for another series. Others entered a new group when a different focus emerged and they wanted additional input. One woman wrote that she was "applying the same effort to a new person — my brother."

There is usually not enough time in supervision groups to focus as explicitly as some may wish on their functioning in their own families. A number of students in the second year of the Two-year Training Program have used the Preceptor Group for this purpose. Others use the group as a jumping-off place, later entering therapy to continue the work they have started. One woman, who used a combination of therapy with her husband and two Therapist's Own Family Groups, wrote that the extended experience provided "overall growth and maturity over a period of time."

THE GROUP'S STRUCTURE

A variety of experiences with a diverse group of teachers* shaped my approach to engaging family therapists in the mastery of their interface dilemmas. The theories and procedures of my mentors were dissimilar, with some using only cognitive methods and others broadening the context to include experiential approaches. I wanted to encourage deutero-learning (Bateson, 1976), the ability to learn how to learn, especially in identifying meaningful sequences, such as patterns and rules in the original family, and to help trainees understand the purpose for and consequences of changing patterns and breaking rules. A focus had been developing: to place Bowen's theory in a clear, goal-oriented, time-limited framework using family diagramming, gestalt techniques, and sculpture while allowing time for teaching, discussion and group process.

Members are at different levels in their family of origin work when they enter the group. Some have worked extensively on their families, understand their own interface issues, and know the areas in which they want help. Others are beginners and do not know in what area they want to start. The majority are at some point in-between, sometimes blocked or confused. A group member can start from any interface which is currently uncomfortable and then explore parallels in different interfaces. This gives wide latitude, and in order to preserve this freedom, the group format and its boundaries must be very clear.

After group members fill out pre-questionnaires and exchange brief introductions, I explain that I audiotape sessions, that anyone who misses a session is expected to listen to the tape before the next session to preserve continuity, and that members can also arrange to listen to their own work. We discuss confidentiality and I ask if any members have known each other previously and, if so, if there is unfinished business between them that might interfere with their openness. When a past conflict or misunderstanding surfaces, time is taken to make explicit plans for resolution.

I set forth my objectives: to provide a group experience that can be useful to each individual in whatever changes they want to make, and

---

*Described in the Introduction.

to shape interventions and mini-lectures to each member's unique situation so that we are working with specifics rather than with generalities. I also have expectations of group members: to each take responsibility for themselves, volunteering when they want to work; to plan how to use the time between sessions to continue their own work; and to speak out if they do not understand, or disagree with, what is going on. I state my underlying premise — that work with family of origin is an ongoing process. Our short time together is a chance to get perspective and set a course, or to continue with work already in progress.

Group members have already thought about and written goals in pre-questionnaires. Now I ask each member to describe where they are in that process and what they want to concentrate on in this group, and then to explain their goals to the members and write them on the flip chart. I let them know they will get to know each other through their goals, which usually are more specific this second time around. Those with the most clearly thought-out goals often volunteer first and become models for the group.

After goals are taped to the wall, I describe different ways to start: exploring patterns in a three-generational family diagram, sculpting the family at a crisis point in the past or currently, or roleplaying or using an empty chair to confront an unfinished family situation. A member can plan strategies to use with original family members: relating one-to-one; taking an "I" position; reconnecting with cutoffs; taking advantage of natural crises, planning a reunion, etc. Homework projects include carrying out planned strategies with family members, and/or collecting dates, facts, and stories for an extensive family diagram going back in time for as many generations as the family has records. Each group member, however, makes his or her own plans for homework; I do not assign tasks, although I and others may make suggestions.

Because we have a choice of ways to work, we can suit the method to the participant and the situation. Some learn best experientially, others through discussion or diagramming, and some through observing the work of others. Some know how they want to proceed and feel safe using familiar methods. If the person is moving forward on both levels of learning — giving the group pertinent content and also information about the nature of the situation (its structure and process), I allow her to continue. If a discussion seems to go on and on without new learning emerging, however, I may propose a different technique, based on my belief that if a familiar format is changed, one's point of view can often be altered. Most members prefer to start with their families of origin; some, however, begin from an interface issue they are aware of in their work with a client family, in their agency, or with a nuclear family member.

Each member has the task of acquainting the group with her unique situation in a time-effective way which has the possibility for providing new information about the relationships involved so that a plan for change can be developed. The choice of how to work is often made by the participant from suggestions I offer. For example, "Would you rather do a diagram or a sculpture to understand what is currently happening in your family?" or "Would it work better for you to imagine your father in an empty chair, or to have a group member sit in the chair and role-play him?" Individuals make different choices.

A specific technique, tailored to the goal, can usually clarify the issue. For example, if the goal is "To understand my siding with males in conflictual couples in marital therapy," then sketching a family diagram in which the member can become aware of male/female patterns from previous generations can serve as a backdrop to the member's understanding of and change in current alignments in the family.

If the goal contains space or action words, such as "How to get closer to my mother and brothers without becoming the caretaker and without having to run away," I might suggest a sculpture of the current situation, which could help her discover new information for herself—for instance, that family members always operate as a group and never meet in meaningful dyads—which could provide an avenue for change. Or if the goal is "What slows me down in looking for my father?", I might suggest an empty chair technique to focus the issue as the group member talks to her father (or perhaps her mother) about her reluctance, which she has never expressed to that person before. If her goal is "To unfreeze the distancing impasse with my parents," I may start by asking how she relates to each parent separately and the effect this has on the other parent, uncovering her pattern of seeing her parents as a "we." There are also members who are not yet ready for action. They may need to say aloud those things that were unsayable in their families, validating their own reality. Some members, in seeing others work through issues, make decisions on their own and begin to carry out their plan.

Before each session I tape members' goals and other flip chart work—family diagrams, lists of rules, sketches of cyclical interaction—on the walls, so we can keep in mind the work they have done and the goals they still want to accomplish. Anyone is free to change goals as they go along. As the second and each succeeding session begins, we start with rounds. Each member in turn gives reactions and afterthoughts from the preceding session, reports on any work done between sessions, fills the group in on current issues such as an upcoming family visit or a death in the family, and states if she wants time to work and how much time, if she knows.

The agenda is set by the end of rounds and time is apportioned accordingly. I discovered, working with the Gouldings (1979) that it is possible to do a life-changing piece of work in 20 minutes. I also learned that when a group member is stuck in a dilemma, it is useful to define her impasse clearly and leave her with it, rather than continuing to press for change. One can always come back to it later.

I am continually aware of those who have not worked recently and the imbalance that may result. I comment on this fact, but do not pressure anyone. As the sessions continue, the members' work overlaps and they learn from each other's actions. Towards the middle of the seminar I ask them to check their goals, and again in our termination meeting as we evaluate the group. Since this is a time-limited format, participants know from the beginning when the end will be and are continually preparing for it. An ongoing necessity is built in to condense the process and focus into short time frames, which then need to be balanced by the amount of time necessary to complete each important piece of work. Some groups have so much to accomplish that they prefer to work almost up to the end. Others want to take more time in the last session to say goodbye since they have shared intimate parts of their lives and many have started important changes.

I make process notes after each session, taking time to allow insights to surface. As I read the notes before the next session, additional aspects may emerge which I then feed back to the members during rounds. Following the final session I hand out post-questionnaires, which help members integrate their changes after the group ends, as well as supply information for me. Six-month post-questionnaires provide a further reminder of their ongoing process.

THE LEADER'S INVOLVEMENT

The results of the questionnaire study emphasize that the leader's task is to balance three crucial factors — safety, stimulation, and structure — to effect a change-experience. When responsibilities are clearly defined and the group's structure has explicit and predictable boundaries, then a safe arena emerges for self-disclosure and experimentation. The task, however, in the Therapist's Own Family Group is complex, since the leader is both participant and observer. When I add an evaluative component, then I am also studying a group of which I am a part. Tomm (1983) points to the dangers of such involvement, a warning that is especially pertinent when the subject is interface. He writes:

One thing seems to be quite clear. We need to become more consciously aware of our own active involvement in the phenomena we study. We need to be more explicit about the conceptual categories we use, the assumptions we make and how we ourselves are part of what we are observing. We need to realize we are the ones drawing the distinctions we apply. Those distinctions are not necessarily "out there." (p. 41)

I am aware that my method of collecting data is circular in itself, as I lead the groups and also receive and evaluate the self-report questionnaires. As I began this study, I wanted a hands-on experience: to integrate all parts of the project myself so I could connect my concepts with my internal experience and with the experiences the group members described. To cut down on bias, I have quoted from participants, letting them speak for themselves, yet I am also aware that I choose which quotations to use. The very fact that questionnaires ask for changes with family of origin, nuclear family, and client families shows my expectation that transfer of learning will occur.

Of the 446 items clustered in answer to the questions: "What specific things did the leader do which were facilitative/which hindered?" (Table 4), 375 (85%) covered facilitative items and 65 (15%) related to items that hindered. Three clusters emerged from the data. Of the facilitative items, 176 (47%) clustered under the category of safety/support; 150 (40%) under stimulation; and 49 (13%) related to structure. Of the items that hindered, 8 (12%) clustered under the category of lack of safety/support; 15 (23%) under lack of stimulation; and 42 (65%) under dissatisfaction with structure. It is interesting to note that the facilitative and hindering items cluster in reverse order, indicating that I was most successful, from the participants' point of view, in creating safety/support, and least successful in establishing an effective structure, with the ability to foster a stimulating arena in between.

The high percentage of facilitative items raises the question: Were the members trying to please me? It may be so, in some cases; some mentioned in questionnaires a positive transference and that they used me as a model. Yet I do not see the participants as adaptive followers. They are professionals in their prime, with a mean age of 38 years. Most have had considerable therapy themselves and treat families regularly in their practices.

Safety and Support

Safety/support had the highest rating for specific things the leader did which were facilitative, with 112 items clustered from post-questionnaires describing the "establishment of a trusting atmosphere." I take a strong

TABLE 4
What Specific Things Did the Leader Do Which
Were Facilitative/Which Hindered?

| | Facilitated | | | Hindered | |
	No.	%		No.	%
Number and % of 446 items	**375**	**85%**		**65**	**15%**
Clusters					
Safety/support					
Established trusting atmosphere	112	30%	Lack of safety/support	8	12%
Involving self personally, including sharing self	64	17%			
Total	176	47%			
Stimulation					
Used enabling techniques	71	19%	Lack of stimulation	15	23%
Focused issues with direct intervention and feedback	53	14%			
Conceptualized a transgenerational approach	26	7%			
Total	150	40%			
Structure					
Established a structure with clear limits	49	13%	Dissatisfied with structure		
			Lack of structure	34	52%
			Too much structure	8	13%
			Total	42	65%

and active leadership role, but one which gives responsibility for each group member's actions to that member, since all have chosen to participate and thus have a reason to be there. I make explicit my belief that personal and professional change can come through change with family of origin, but I do not press this belief on members. Members volunteer when they want to work and I monitor the process to make sure they are able to stop when they wish. This allows members to experience themselves in new ways:

"The group made it possible to become aware of process—learning through experiencing. I discovered that I could have others disagree with me, or set limits on me, without feeling criticized or rejected, and therefore I didn't have to become defensive. I feel I am able to be more sensitive and also more self-accepting as a result of this experience."

The other cluster under safety—"that the leader involved herself personally, including sharing herself"—was composed of 64 items. Those members in the shorter preceptor groups in the Two-year Training Program already know about my struggles in my family of origin and my interface issues, since I have shared them in class. Thus, a model has already been set and an equalizing process is at work: they know me better than I know them—an imbalance that gives them permission to be vulnerable. The longer groups have an additional eight hours, with the total group time extended to five months; this allows for trust to build gradually and for a majority of the members to reach the stage where they can be open about their concerns. One member described the process:

"The leader's facilitation was subtle but through modeling and empathic responses to members, she created a safe climate to look at oneself and to risk making changes. She gave the group freedom and responsibility to support and confront each other."

One characteristic of my groups is the apparent lack of hostility, either seen directly in the group (anger, challenging the leader, refusal to work) or indirectly (coming late, not following through on plans, dropping out of the group, not returning questionnaires). I have some thoughts about this, although I am not sure I know all the reasons.

I do not try to catalyze transferences in the group; some report in post-questionnaires that they work them out without the group's knowledge.* Robert Goulding has commented on the lack of hostility in his groups where both transference reactions to the leader and group process are ignored. When hostility first begins to develop, I look for its roots in that individual's original family. Thus, I bypass transferences in the group by going back to its origins; since our subject matter is family of origin, I have their permission to focus there. Members tend to concentrate on their own goals and, when they have a strong emotional response, to look for reference points for their trigger reactions in their own family of origin rather than to use the group time in working out relationship problems with each other. One man described the process for him:

---

*See Chapter 15, p. 303.

"Most significant was my sense of rage at a woman group member when she was being helpless, and my gradual learning to control and work with it. It was significant because my rage at female helplessness began with my mother and my helplessness to meet my obligation to her. It is frequently present in my relationship with some women, particularly in my family."

I listen for negatives and respond as honestly as I can. When one woman took a stand with me and I acknowledged the validity of her position and made a change, it was a learning experience for her:

"Taking my stand with the leader is leading me to an increased acceptance of myself — and my husband — because I was forced to struggle with my concept of her as 'less than perfect.'"

In a supplementary note, the same woman described how she was also able to take a stand with her family:

"Just after our last session, my biological father's mother died. I spent an afternoon with his sister and we have become friends as a result. This, in particular, is the result of my 'taking a stand' against a strongly internalized dictum to have no contact with 'that side' of my family — and the courage to do that is an outgrowth of the group."

I walk a fine line between safety and stimulation; the very act of making the group safe may keep underlying feelings and thoughts from surfacing. One member expressed frustration:

"At times I felt the leader didn't want to hurt feelings or push when it might have been useful to ask harder questions or suggest harder tasks."

Stimulation

The possibility that the changing of one's dysfunctional relationships with original family members can reverberate positively into one's current relationships and can enhance effectiveness as a therapist provides powerful motivation to begin to change relationships that group members have despaired of ever changing. One woman expressed the deep meaning this subject holds:

"It is very hard to pinpoint a single most significant event — many things happened while I worked and watched others work that have resulted in a strong belief in a multigenerational approach to families and all forms of therapy. So the biggest effect was a change in philosophy which will affect my own personal development as well as my professional style."

Since members make their own goals, the issues they deal with are meaningful and become the glue that makes the Therapist's Own Family Groups so powerful. Goals listed on both pre-questionnaires and the flip chart clustered into six categories. Out of 584 goals and issues, 35% were focused on better understanding of interaction with family of origin and 15% were centered on changing self in the original family. These two categories made up 50% of the goals. In addition, 24% were concentrated on professional aspects, 16% on self, 8% on the member's nuclear family, and only 2% were focused on the group experience itself.

In terms of action by participants, 95% of 138 respondents validated the premise that change had occurred. To the question on post-questionnaires, "How much impact had this group had on your *actions* in terms of interface issues?", 33% rated strong positive impact; 62% some positive; and 5% no impact.

When one looks at how the group members saw change occurring, 71 items clustered under the leader's "use of enabling techniques." Stimulation is provided both cognitively and experientially, with change often coming through an alternating sequence of understanding and action. People have different styles of changing. Some want to understand before they can act; diagramming or planning strategies for change are productive ways to involve such participants. Others want to act and then understand; experiential techniques may engage them. When I can tune into an individual's natural rhythm and her own creative energy, movement, and focus, then the power of the member's pacing and timing can work for her. One member described the process:

"Facilitation: the way the leader worked with each individual group member—use of support, empathy, roleplaying, empty chair, confrontation, intensifying (not letting person off the hook), focusing, eliciting from other group members or allowing them to contribute at will."

There is also the chance that I will say too much, interfering with an individual's own pacing:

"With my personal work I felt overly directed, particularly in dealing with sensitive areas where I needed space/time to sort out the feeling."

Fifty-three items clustered under the leader's "focusing issues with direct intervention and feedback." One woman began to understand the need for stimulation:

"What I really learned is that new patterns have to be tried in families
for change to occur and for this change, things have got to be shaken up.
It was significant because to really shake things up is hard for me but it
has to be done for new patterns/behaviors to emerge."

Twenty-six items were clustered under the leader's "conceptualizing a
transgenerational approach." Understanding family patterns can translate unto current behavior change:

"The most significant event for me personally was when the leader told
me to examine the pattern of male and female relationships in my family. I then recognized why the women grew up to be independent and competent while the men grew up to be passive and alcoholic. With this insight, I examined the way I treated my son and daughter and changed
some of our interactions. I'm giving my son more age-appropriate responsibilities."

Structure

The structure of the group, described earlier in this chapter, makes
it easier for those members who are ready to move ahead in their own
behalf. In some groups, when members are fearful or unclear about their
goals, there is a pull to induce me to do their structuring for them. Getting the process started can be a struggle. Thirty-four items were clustered under "lack of structure," which had the highest rating for specific
things the leader did which hindered. One woman described her point
of view:

"I strongly think the leader should structure it more and be more active.
The whole first time I felt was too rambling and unfocused. I was often
bored just because some people didn't know what they wanted and what
some did was off the point and tedious. Maybe we could each be given
a turn every session to work on something."

The push-pull that develops, when I do not meet such expectations,
is necessary if members are to own their place in the group and take
charge of the work they do. The struggle is reminiscent of Whitaker's
"battle for structure" with a family (Napier, 1978, p. 28). Taking initiative in the group is prelude to taking initiative in their own lives. When
they lead the way, then my leadership can be active:

"The leader challenged each group member to reexamine perceptions of
their family situations to see their own involvement in the pattern and
challenged group members to do something different."

We can then work as partners, not only on their own changes, but in their learning how to learn to change, so that they can continue the process and use it in their therapy with clients. Forty-nine items were clustered under "established a structure with clear limits." Such a structure is necessary if there is to be freedom within for creative work. One member described her group:

"The leader structured the time — divided it up and stuck to the agreements we made — tried to see to it that people who wanted to work got a chance and those who didn't weren't forced to."

The time-limited structure is a constant pressure. Group members have an average of two hours each for their personal work, divided into several shorter time frames, with the beginning of each new segment of work carrying with it the possibility for making an attitudinal or behavioral change. One member described the pressure that this structure created:

"Sometimes the scarcity of time created undue frustration for individuals working on heavier issues — at the same time the 'crunch' of time caused us to organize our time more."

IS THIS TRAINING OR THERAPY?

The question needs to be raised: "Is the Therapist's Own Family Group a way to do therapy with students under the guise of education?" There is a thin line between the two, especially in working with families. Mendelsohn and Ferber (1973) clarify the issues:

Family therapy, because of its immediacy and aliveness, much more than individual therapy, elicits therapist responses which relate to the therapist's own family of origin or family of procreation . . . we see this as an inevitable and natural process and one which the therapist will be encountering throughout his professional lifetime. The supervisor's task is not to help the therapist "solve" his family problems, but to teach him to be aware of, and to cope with, the secret presence of his own family in the treatment room. (p. 441)

It is the influence wielded by the "secret presence" of the therapist's family that is so important for the therapist-in-training to understand and to learn how to deal with. There is a difference between a therapeutic experience and therapy. For instance, a movie can be therapeutic, but the intent is entertainment. In like manner, an educational experience can be therapeutic, but the intent is on education. It is the contract one has that defines the difference. Once the contract is made, whether it be therapy or education, then both partners to a consenting agreement are working towards a common goal. Every family therapy educational effort is, in some way, an intervention into the family system of the student. The Therapist's Own Family Group approaches the situation directly and openly, addressing only those parts of the student's life that the student is ready to work on.

Therapists who volunteer for these groups have themselves had varied therapeutic experiences. Ninety-two percent have been in one or more forms of therapy:

84% in individual therapy, with a range between one and "thousands" of sessions; 51% of those in individual therapy had had between 11 and 100 sessions.

53% in couple therapy, with a range between 1 and 200 sessions; 48% of those in couple therapy had had between 11 and 50 sessions.

35% in group therapy, with a range between 2 and 1,000 sessions; 54% of those in group therapy had had between 11 and 50 sessions.

21% in family therapy, with a range between 1 and 80 sessions; 71% of those in family therapy had had between 1 and 10 sessions.

Sixty-one percent had been in either couple or family therapy or both, and only 8% had never been in therapy. Twenty-nine percent were continuing in therapy when they filled out the pre-questionnaire.

The question of how unresolved issues from the original family becomes a secret presence in the therapy room is not one which is usually addressed in personal therapy. Supervisors of therapists-in-training are the most logical individuals to address such interface issues, yet they are often hesitant. Thistle (1981) writes:

Most supervisors admit the value of focusing on this area but often feel that to do so would be taboo because they wish to respect the privacy of the student and avoid being intrusive. Ultimately, however, the majority of supervisors do broach the topic . . . but they do so indirectly, hesitantly, and delicately through a discussion of the student's process recordings. (p. 248)

Analytic institutes have always required analysts to undergo training analyses, starting with Freud's self-analysis, to learn to deal with transference and countertransference. Other trainers have experimented with ways to help trainees get a sense of the therapeutic process from both sides—that of patient and therapist. The Gouldings (1979), who are group therapists, have developed a unique method in which therapists-in-training take turns being both patient and therapist, under supervision, working within a contract developed jointly by the patient-therapist and supervisor. In my training with them, I became comfortable in working by contract and with the exchange of roles with other therapists in a training context.

Since 1967, when Bowen presented his own family of origin at the Family Research Conference (1978a), he has been the foremost proponent of training family therapists by helping them differentiate themselves in their own families. As early as 1971 he had incorporated this method into his postgraduate training programs. He writes: "No single development in almost twenty-five years in family research and family therapy has changed me and my approach to families as much as that one" (1978a, p. xvi).

Feld (1982) who reviewed the literature on countertransference in family therapy, states that

> . . . there is a great need to involve the family therapist as a person and a family member in his or her own learning about this most exciting and difficult treatment modality. All the above authors (Whitaker, Framo, Ferber, Bowen) present interesting ways of accomplishing this, paralleling their own treatment techniques. (p. 12)

Boundaries for Training

The way I work with interface issues with therapists also parallels the way I work with client families. The boundaries in training, however, are specific and task-oriented. I believe a training experience that focuses on the person of the therapist and includes family of origin work can be clearly labeled and directly approached. My recommendations are:

1) That the experience be voluntary and offered in a group setting.
2) That the plan for the training experience be clearly stated with connections to family of origin and client families defined.
3) That members set their own contracts, which must also be acceptable to the leader, so they can choose to focus on those interface areas that have current meaning.
4) That members be explicitly given responsibility for their own work —starting, continuing, and stopping each piece of work.
5) That work with the nuclear family be included only if requested by the member and that it then be discussed only if it can be defined as a connecting part of the member's transgenerational issues.

Problem Areas in Training

Interventions into the family of origin are powerful and can have negative consequences as well as positive. Too much material may emerge and the member may feel overwhelmed. One member, although coping, realized the danger:

"I guess the overall feeling I have from these last months and from this seminar specifically is shakiness. The most significant event was to see and conceptualize my family prescription for craziness, going back two generations. To see all my family's identified patients and to realize that they exist on *both* sides of my family was a tremendously frightening realization because it did suggest: 1) one of my family's norms and maybe even rules, i.e., 'In order to relate to us, you have to buy into craziness'; 2) how easy it would be because it is a transgenerational process. But I also can use those understandings to free me from that prescription. I *can* make choices. Without the knowledge of *what* I was reacting to, I'd be doomed to continue only that: to be reactive to family patterns.

"As I'm writing this, I see that I have this more synthesized than I'd thought. This one construct, more than any other, seems important for me to come to grips with. Because I've just realized in the last week that going crazy, giving in to craziness, is my catastrophic fear."

When asked to describe any changes she thought would enhance the format, she replied:

"None. I liked it. Any longer or more frequent sessions (since this was my first in-depth attempt to understand my family of origin) would have been too intense. I needed the time and space to digest. If I hadn't been so sure that this was what I wanted to do, it would have been oppressive. So *more* intensity could have been an overload."

A few group members sign up who are not ready to work on original family issues. It is important for the leader to recognize this early and to help other trainees become comfortable with that member's decision. Such an understanding enables the process of the group to continue and all participants to have a productive experience. One woman wrote:

"When I originally signed up for the group, I was at a particularly bad point in my life and marriage. I believe (in retrospect) that I began the seminar looking for a 'cure' to my predicament. Although I was not really ready to deal with my family of origin, I was able to use the experience for other purposes: 1) to see my own pathology more clearly and to go into intensive individual treatment; 2) to use the group for support (this was very important to me); and 3) to use the leader as a role model — as a therapist, mother, and human being — this was probably the most important element. More and more I am aware of my own assumptions about women as being hostile, cold, distant, and non-caring (i.e., my mother), and for me the leader was a role model of all the opposite traits. I feel I made a big stride in being able to trust her, be open, and believe her.

"The most significant event, oddly enough, was the realization that other members found me to be a loving, sensitive, and caring person. I think I felt so low that their caring was important, and I could hear it."

Occasionally a participant does not appreciate the distinction between training and therapy. Such a person may be in such pain as to be unable to recognize the necessary boundaries. Such a situation is a challenge to the leader, who needs to be sensitive to the individual's cry for help and fear of rejection, as well as to the educational needs of the group as a whole. I have not had a situation explode nor has anyone walked out. I am prepared, if necessary, to make an explicit distinction in the group between therapy and training if I feel the demands of one person are interfering to too great an extent in the learning of the group.

First, however, I prefer to see if the individual can join the group as it is set up by contracting for an appropriate goal and negotiating for time like everyone else. I was aware of one woman's lability in the beginning session and did not encourage her emotion, while being distantly supportive. In this interaction I saw her telling me verbally what she wanted/needed and me telling her nonverbally that it was inappropriate. In rounds in the second session, she waited until last to state that she had had a transference reaction to me in the first session; that she knew her intense feelings were inappropriate; and that she realized that this was a seminar, not a therapy group. In the final session she told the group she had gone into therapy during the seminar.

How the leader handles such situations signals whether it is safe for members to be open and to accomplish the purpose of the group. The "appropriateness" is what I monitor. My criterion is their ability to pick some specific interface area they want to change. When a participant discloses personal information, it needs to be connected to the group's purpose, not just to air feelings or to tell about their personal problems. The way this is handled by the leader may be the most important learning for group members.

When a therapist-trainee takes responsibility for her own participation and its timing, there is an increased possibility that change will occur. If she is ready to see her impasse in relation to the broader system, then she becomes a partner with the leader, or with other members of the group, in exploring her dilemma and discovering transgenerational patterns that influence her feelings, thoughts, and behavior. As other group members understand her view of the world, her images and language, she also begins to understand theirs and the shared reality expands the points of view of all those who are open to new experiences.

I have described a structured group, with a format designed to provide stimulation and support, where therapists can risk and change, with the possibility for concomitant change with their families of origin. Once involved in this process, the members can begin to monitor their own reactions in whatever interface they occur, becoming more knowledgeable in a self-corrective, lifetime process.

CHAPTER 13

Bridging Theories

Seemingly disparate theories come together in my mind as I lead Therapist's Own Family Groups and study the changes that participants report. How do I converge different perspectives and weave these ideas together? I have a need to develop a model which offers a range of cognitive and experiential concepts, bridging theories of both short-and long-term change. It would combine the cognitive understanding of Bowenian theory (1978a), Boszormenyi-Nagy and Spark's approach (1973), and second-order change concepts (Watzlawick et al., 1974), along with the experiential awareness of gestalt and sculptural techniques, all within a group context.

I may seem to be combining radically different elements which do not quite fit together, and it may be premature to force a fit. However, I utilize them all, as a clinician, and I experience their integration as I work. What links them is the possibility for second-order change through viewing one's own family of origin from a changed perspective. Such a shift can happen in a number of ways; the more techniques the leader can draw on, the greater the possibility of finding a useful fit. Such interventions range from exploring the powerful influence of the family's myths and rules to reliving an experience from the past in the present. Such a model can help group members integrate their present understanding of their transgenerational history and their inner world of experienced meanings with their cognitive awareness of systemic interaction. Bateson's concepts (1972) of deutero-learning (learning how to learn) and double description (1979) (seeing a relationship from all points of view simultaneously) set the stage.

Bowen's theories form the base, underlining the importance of the influence of the continuing relationships with original family members into the adult years. Boszormenyi-Nagy's concepts of transgenerational loyalty

251

and obligation add an important link for recognizing how injustice from past generations can be rebalanced by a family member in the present. Since aspects of these theories have been described earlier in the book, I will move on to contrasting concepts.

Watzlawick et al.'s second-order change theories (1974) contrast with Bowen's family of origin approach. Watzlawick et al.'s short-term schema focuses exclusively on the here and now, while Bowen's concepts for long-term change are concerned with historical knowledge of the family's past and with making personal changes in the present vis-à-vis that past. The question of time, therefore, will also be addressed in bringing these varied concepts.

LEARNING TO LEARN

As we grew up in our families, we adapted to the interactional demands. We not only took in information, we also learned how to learn, according to the family's pattern. We each developed a world view within our family, shaped by its context and the sequences of behavior that were rewarded and punished. Throughout life, the patterns we perceive are a consequence of our own learned habits by which we clarify meaning.

Bateson (1972) has defined orders of learning including the first order in which perceived choices are within a single set of behavioral alternatives. Second-order or deutero-learning is on a higher level and deals with learning about a particular context and how to punctuate and organize one's actions as part of that context — in other words, learning how to learn. Wynne (1976) wrote:

> As the communication of any family . . . begins to become patterned, deutero-learning . . . establishes a relationship in which the participants come to have deep feelings and convictions (usually not verbalizable) about the meaning of what goes on between them. In this process, the form of experiencing and organizing communication becomes stabilized and relatively resistant to change. To some extent, this stabilization of patterns of behavior, and of associated expectations and belief systems, requires that certain "concrete" details of behavior and experience have to be ignored or dissociated. Thus, the observable events in communication and the implicitly agreed upon relationship context may become more and more internally inconsistent with one another. (p. 246)

As long as an individual stays within the behavioral alternatives allowed by his family, he sees only one reality and is not aware of the broader relationship context which may be exhibiting internally inconsistent parts.

When two people interact, each punctuates and gives meaning to the ongoing interaction. If an observer puts together the views of both, an understanding of the system will begin to reveal itself. Bateson (1979) called this juxaposition of two or more views of the relationship "double description." By focusing on double description, the observer can discover different orders of patterns. Keeney (1983) writes: "As two eyes can derive depth, two descriptions can derive patterns and relationship" (p. 38).

The practice of family therapy provides the therapist with multiple perspectives about any one family since each member brings his own point of view to the therapeutic session. To get a sense of the whole system, the therapist must be able to construct patterns connecting these differing views. When the therapist can turn his understanding of double description back into the interfaces in his own family of origin, then he can begin to see that the views he has held of the previous generations or of his siblings are not necessarily the only reality. One group member described his change in perspective:

> "My realization that I wanted my family to change but resented them trying to change me was the most significant event. I am now trying to give them the same freedom I expect from them. This has helped me stop fighting my family and start enjoying them."

When the family member can learn to hold on to his own perspective as a partial view while acknowledging that the perspectives that the other member holds have equal validity, then a more open dialogue can emerge in which the therapist can learn to respect the diverse perspectives of other family members.

A SHIFT IN PERSPECTIVE

When I first read Watzlawick, Weakland, and Fisch's (1974) description of second-order change, I recognized it as an important process in family of origin work. In first-order change the individual tries harder, working from the same premise he has used before. This is effective for situations in which additional effort is required. When adults are caught up in adaptive or rebellious stances with original family members, however, their view of reality is skewed or narrowed so that they are not aware of the possibility of multiple perspectives. They are locked into mind-sets, perceiving only a limited number of solutions and a necessity to choose among them. They have an internal experience of entrapment and paralysis, seeing no way out. Trying "more of the same" only digs them deeper into the rut, and the solution they continue working towards then becomes the problem, forming a self-regulating loop.

In second-order change there is a logical shift to a higher class of learning in which the individual is able to step out of the old familiar cyclical game and no longer just follow or oppose the family rule that dictated the attempted solution. In his shift to a broader perspective, he is able to see multiple realities, even though the situation remains the same. More choices are possible or it may not even be necessary to choose.

I had not consciously planned to stimulate the occurrence of second-order change in the Therapist's Own Family Groups. My goal had been to lead a fast-paced, experientially-oriented group in which participants could make changes in their families of origin which would reverberate into their clinical practices. I had set up a format which included structure, safety, and stimulation to reach this goal. Yet 116 out of 138 therapists (84%) described in post-questionnaires a shift in perspective which seemed to be a second-order change. As I reread Watzlawick et al.'s criteria, I applied them to my groups, looking for similarities and differences:

Watzlawick et al.'s (1974) Criteria for Second-Order Change

(a) "Second-order change is applied to what in the first-order change perspective appears to be a solution, because in the second-order change perspective this 'solution' reveals itself as the keystone of the problem whose solution is attempted.

(b) "While first-order change always appears to be based on common sense (for instance, the 'more of the same' recipe), second-order change usually appears weird, unexpected, and uncommonsensical; there is a puzzling, paradoxical element in the process of change.

(c) "Applying second-order change techniques to the 'solution' means that the situation is dealt with in the here and now.

Therapist's Own Family Groups

(a) In helping participants get to the core of their problems, the focus is on how the currently-maintained problem parallels patterns in the family of origin, what solutions have been attempted, and the positive or negative results of those attempts.

(b) Participants described their experiences as shifting their perspectives in unexpected ways so that alternate choices became available.

(c) Since Watzlawick et al. deal only with the current situation and not with presumed causes and my focus is family of origin,

These techniques deal with effects and not with their presumed causes; the crucial question is what? and not why?

how can these two frameworks be compatible? The effects I deal with are the participants' dysfunctional solutions at self-regulation in the present, based on their world view, which they learned in their families. Discovering themes and patterns provides current insights and changes in attitude. Experiential techniques provide a change-experience in the here and now. The context provides a new experience through the group process itself and also in members who may be stimulated to change through the work of others.

(d) "The use of second-order change techniques lifts the situation out of the paradox-engendering trap created by the self-reflexiveness of the attempted solution and places it in a different frame." (pp. 82–83)

(d) Even though group members may have intellectually understood their predicament, they have still remained trapped within it. The freeing-up that group members described attests to the changed framework they experienced. Ensuing changes made with original family members indicate their ability to follow through.

Of the 84% of group members reporting a shift in perspective, 82 members (59%) described a focus shift in their family situation that helped overcome an emotional block, leading to changes in other interfaces. An additional 34 members (25%) reported a shift following group interaction, also leading to interface changes. Many described these experiences as unexpected, clarifying, and freeing. Those who detailed shifts used the following or similar phrases:

> . . . providing perceptions and linkages . . . changing my outlook . . . bridging where I started and where I am now . . . viewing from a new, less threatening framework . . . discovering why . . . opened a new perspective . . . freed me up and gave me permission . . . discovered the

pattern . . . made me viscerally aware . . . put a new light on an old problem . . . helped me with a blind spot . . . opened up some closed off dimensions . . . helped me lift an impasse . . . received a first-hand, gut-level experience . . . clarified the process I undergo . . . triggered insights into . . . helped me get unstuck . . . produced a picture of the family system and my role never experienced before . . . I could see what I was struggling with . . . I could connect . . . I saw how I set myself up . . . I learned what I contributed . . . very important shift. . . .

There is no history in Watzlawick et al.'s schema; it is focused on how the problem is maintained, rather than on its etiology. I am interested in history, but primarily in terms of unfinished business from the past that has a controlling influence on the present. I want to understand the group member's world view, which he learned in his original family, and how the patterns from the past are limiting his choices in the present. Where some strategic therapists use observers behind the mirror for multiple input, I use the member's family of origin, as they are clustered in his head, and also feedback from other members of the group. The process of raising awareness is heightened when one chooses to confront issues in a group of peers where there can be strong support and also feedback from multiple perspectives; thus I combine the old and familiar (family of origin) with the new and unfamiliar (short-term experience in a group of peers).

To accomplish the task, I use varied methods to both highlight the member's stuck position and to give him the opportunity to break out of the self-regulating cycle and to shift to a broader perspective that includes other realities he has not previously allowed himself to be aware of. Examples of such methods are: diagramming to help him explore isomorphic patterns which constrict him; sculpting the family so that the group member can discover how he limits his own movement; encouraging a participant to rehearse a conversation with a family member in an empty chair so he can become aware of his own projections and how he maintains a self-fulfilling prophecy; and suggesting homework with original family members designed to shift the group member's position in the family. An example will illustrate a common shift.

Freeing Energy and Memory: An Example

Teresa's goals were: "1) changing my role as the disengaged member of the family and 2) working on how my memory problem fits into this." Teresa was an only child, conflictual with her mother and distant from her father, having always gone through her mother to reach him. She was focused on changing the relationship with her mother, yet was stuck because she had no hope of changing it. From the beginning she was picky and testy in the group, saying "yes, but" to any suggestion given her, playing the same role in the group that she played in her family.

In response to her request for ideas as to how to improve her relationship with her mother, I suggested that she ask her father to do something alone with her that they would both enjoy. By the third session she had still not arranged it. With a person like Teresa, who was an expert at proving that an idea would not work, a group was the right setting. I left her alone, while staying connected; she could observe the process until she was ready to move since others were interested in using the time.

Teresa's demeanor was changed when she arrived for the fourth session. The push-pull power struggle she had been in with the group had vanished. She and her father had gone to the zoo. Her mother had not fought it as she had expected. She wrote in her post-questionnaire:

"As a result of getting together with my father, my energy level and productivity have increased dramatically. I never realized there was a connection between my blocked energy and my undeveloped relationship with my father. Now I can work on developing the relationship, aware of the direct effect it has on my own abilities. . . . My memory is better and I am accomplishing more tasks. There are many cutoffs in our family. From having a family reunion I learned that all the others have been communicating. My parents cut us off."

When a family member is locked in an intense relationship, he or she needs to focus somewhere else to loosen up the system. Teresa's intense focus on her mother had kept the system locked. A clue to the tightness in her parents' relationship comes from the new information she learned at the family reunion—that her parents had cut themselves off. Their action had more firmly imprisoned her, an only child, in their tight system. The group experience allowed her to take the necessary step herself and focus on her father, the uninvolved one, and on other family members—moves that shifted the system and freed up her energy and memory.

THE GESTALT POSITION

Gestalt theory defines change in the same struggle between opposites that Bowen describes. The goal of the gestalt process is neither separation (individuation) nor union (togetherness), but the urgent and often painful movement between them. Gestalt techniques, although used with individuals and families, are most often used in group settings.

I see sculpture as a marriage of gestalt techniques and family systems.

Since sculpture is a technique, not a theory, I see it as an experiential and largely nonverbal method for discovering patterns, including alignments and cutoffs; for exploring boundary and power issues; and for depicting diverse views of the same situation. Through sculpting techniques, one can depict in the present memories from the past, a situation in the present, or test out possible options for the future.

Contact, in gestalt theory, is at the interface where self and other converge, involving the boundaries of each and the necessity to find ways to contact the other which allow each to experience the "we," without either indvidual losing self in the joining. When a person is able to be aware of self in the present, then he has a continuing means of monitoring his own experience. He then knows whether he prefers to stay as he is, with the concomitant awareness of what he gains and loses by his position, or whether he is ready for change. In his ability to make this decision, he discovers his own reality and can plan independent action.

Beisser (1970), a gestalt therapist, describes a paradoxical theory of change that he believes is at the heart of gestalt therapy and that I believe applies to family of origin work: " . . . that change occurs when one becomes what he is, not when he tries to become what he is not" (p. 77). When an adult is not comfortable in his original family, he is in conflict between what he "should be" according to his family's rules and what he believes he "is." Where he is stuck, despite his chronological age, is in a delayed developmental shift from an adolescent in the family of origin to an autonomous adult. When he sees his only choices in remaining emotionally connected with his family of origin, as following their rules or changing the family members to accept his, then he remains stuck. As he abandons trying to change the other and is what he is with them, then he has a base to move forward on an adult level.

One participant described the changes she experienced after a gestalt experiment:

> "I participated with the leader in an empty chair exercise that looked at myself in different stages of my growth. By dividing my life into different stages, I could see what I was struggling with — I can't explain why, but I feel more integrated as an individual woman. In a sense, participation in the group helped me in the process of separating from my family of origin."

After six months she reported:

> "I have developed more insight into my boundaries and my ability to maintain the boundary in my marriage. Also was more able to realistically accept my parents and siblings as they are and not as I have always wanted

them to be. Being more realistic has reduced my anxiety and freed me up to start my own family."

The gestalt experiment is an attempt to bring the person's experience into the here and now so it can be explored through current action since some individuals are more apt to make discoveries by participating in experiences than by talking about them. The gestaltist keeps the focus on a never-ending series of polarities, with the expectation of aiding each part to experience itself to the fullest while recognizing its polar equivalent. If the experiment unfolds as an exploration, there can be no failure because whatever emerges gives the group member new information.

THE UTILIZATION OF TIME

Time is a nonspatial continuum in which events occur in apparently irreversible succession from the past through the present to the future. Therapists focus on different aspects and combinations of this continuum, depending on their theoretical framework. Bowen, Watzlawick et al., and the gestaltists view and use time in different ways. My groups include aspects of each: for example, I use Bowen's method of gathering data by diagramming the family's past to discover such patterns as alliances and cutoffs; Watzlawick et al.'s intervention of reframing to facilitate second-order change in the present; and the gestaltists' focus on reliving traumas from the past so that a new decision for the future can be made in a group setting in the present. When I am able to use these varied approaches, each one enhances the other and they extend my ability to move across the parameters of time.

When an individual is bound by constraints from the past, such as unacknowledged rules, then he is unable to see the choices that are possible in the present. My focus is on emotional or mythic patterns, using not only facts from the family's history but also nodal points from the past, as gestaltists do. Discovering belief systems and loyalties uncovers the mythic power that explains the family member's opinions about how he should behave in the world. I use both cognitive and experiential methods to heighten such discoveries in the present, so the member can become aware of how his current behavior is reactive to these patterns. Such knowledge gives him choices for the future that were not available before.

The past carries a special power when its patterns hold sway over the present, locking members into roles. Psychotherapy has had a long history of talking *about* the past in the present, as if change will occur if one understands enough about the past situation. It is sometimes true that change occurs with such understanding; often, however, individuals need to have a more incisive and penetrating experience in order to shift their perspective so that the part of the past that is unfinished and still influencing the present can be seen in a new, less threatening way. It is then possible to make a change in the current situation; often the past repetitive pattern will lose its power to govern the individual's current actions. One member described such a shift with his mother:

> "Most significant was doing my own family chart and receiving feedback because I could see the system for both myself and my mother. I could see her conflicts, fears, pain, and care about her through changing my expectations. When I saw her this fall I related differently—she responded more easily and it was a really good visit. Phone calls have been easier."

The issue is not past vs. present, but how to resolve in the present what is unfinished from the past in order to move on to the future.

The Time Cable

When I discovered Hoffman's Time Cable (1982), these varied approaches fell into place. She constructed the Cable as a metaphor to illustrate diagrammatically the time aspects of the Milan Associates' systemic approach to family therapy. The Cable provides a framework for understanding presenting problems within the context of time and family relationships, as well as a way of looking at rings of interfacing systems. I have adapted the Time Cable (Figure 21) by changing the interfaces to those appropriate for family of origin work.*

Hoffman (1982) stated, in discussing the Milan group's approach:

> Their theories seem to imply that understanding the precursors of behavior in the past will make it possible to change it in the present. . . . But these hypotheses are always pointing backwards and forwards at once and seem to collapse time. . . . In brief, one gets the impression that there is no such thing as the simple present. It is always being influenced by expectations of the future. . . . Equally, there is no such thing as the simple past. Everyone in the family has a different depiction of previous events, or different feelings about them. (p. 10)

Her words express the thoughts I have as I search for family patterns from the past that seem to have a bearing on the current impasse and its resolution.

---

*Hoffman's original model (1982) included the following Rings: Ring One—Internal Family Dynamics; Ring Two—Family/Team Interface; and Ring Three—Referring Context Interfaces.

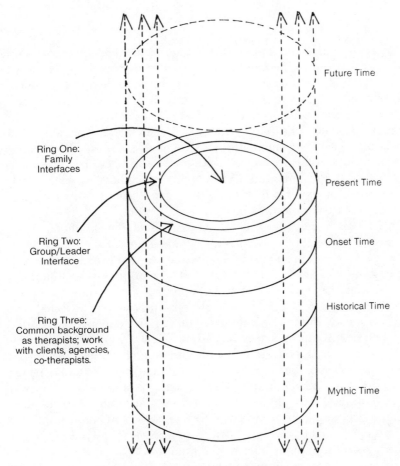

Figure 21. The Time Cable*

Identifying Aspects of Time

Each "time slice" of the Cable refers to that impasse the member is currently experiencing. His choice of goals is reflected in Future Time, while his inability to move on those goals is in Present Time. As I search for patterns by diagramming, sculpting, or early decision work, an Onset Time may emerge which is linked to Historical Time and to myths in Mythic Time that have been alive in the family for years or for generations, affecting the member's choices in the present, both in his original family and in other aspects of his life, including his work with client families and his interaction in his nuclear family, and sometimes in the group.

Future Time is that indefinite period that has not yet arrived, the hy-

---

pothetical time that one can fantasize about or plan for by constructing goals in the group. One can use sculpture to test out various ways to change actions with family members, or one can rehearse for a future conversation.

Present Time embodies the here and now, when the impasse is felt in the family member's inability to make the connection he desires. He may be afraid to change the status quo, feel unable to make himself heard, or be paralyzed in his wish to find a different approach. Feelings can be experienced in Present Time and thoughts which have never been said in words can be expressed. Decisions and redecisions can be made; it is a time for exploration, experiment, and action.

Onset Time identifies a time in the past, usually in childhood or adolescence, when the family member was in an impasse similar to the one that is causing him problems in the present. At that time he made a decision about what he was going to do. There are many such points in his past when he reaffirmed that decision and they form a sequence of repetitive behavior that can be traced backward as one follows a thread, to his earliest decision. The connecting link in such a sequence is his feeling when he attempted a specific action. Such a decision, appropriate to survival in childhood, may include shifts in allegiance, and is often inappropriate when the individual is an adult and need no longer be subject to the family's rules and messages. Using techniques developed by the Gouldings (1979), the leader can help the member relive the situation as a child and clarify his early decision so he can create a different and more satisfactory ending. Then, coming back to the present, he can make a redecision about his current situation.*

Historical Time encompasses facts (such as names, dates, places), nodal events (such as successes, traumas, developmental milestones), and the family member's sense of past relationships in the family (such as alignments and cutoffs). When a member reconstructs Historical Time, usually by diagramming or by sculpture, then he can begin to build a framework for seeing his family from the inside out, without blame. If he can place himself in the shoes of a parent or an extended family member during an earlier traumatic time, he is more able to accept such a member as he is, as a flawed human being who did the best he could.

Mythic Time is important in understanding the emotional map of the family, including catastrophic expectations that evolve out of shared traumatic experiences, as well as heroic aspects the member may attempt to emulate. These events are internalized by the family to guide their actions, restraining members from breaking out of old roles and mak-

---

*See Chapter 6, pp. 97–103 for an example of redecision work.

ing new choices. Such myths are passed down through the generations through patterned behavior that influences the family's history, even when the danger is no longer relevant and may even interfere with the psychological growth of members. When I work with a group member to explore original family issues, I am looking for rules and patterns, usually not spoken about or questioned, that govern the family's interactions and which form such myths, embodying the family's belief system.

Use of Time Aspects: An Example

In the following example, a powerful myth, growing out of a grandmother's suicide, evolved into rules which allowed women to dominate and men to remain passive and distant from the family. Discovering the myth and rules allowed Roger, a young man in a group, to plan a course of action which helped him begin to rebalance the male/female roles.

Roger, who was locked in an impasse with his mother, appeared sleepy-eyed and constrained. His goals were: 1) to understand his father better; and 2) to get a better grasp of male/female patterns in his family. Roger was the only son, with an older and younger sister. The contrast between his father's and mother's families became evident upon diagramming. His mother and her two sisters were raised by his maternal grandmother and his grandmother's twin sister, who had never married. His paternal grandfather raised his five young sons alone after Roger's paternal grandmother hung herself. Roger had always been distant from his father and his father's all-male sibship and close to his dominantly-female mother's family.

The family rules were: "Don't approach Dad about important things" and "Mother will protect Dad." Although everyone knew about his grandmother's suicide, no one ever talked about it. Thus, the family myth could be understood: "Talking about important events is dangerous." Roger had followed the myth, not knowing how to get close to his father. He had not allowed himself to be curious either about the past when his grandmother had cut herself off from the family by suicide, or about the present, when his father had cut off his older sister's husband and would not allow them to visit. He was virtually isolated from the men in his family.

Soon after we diagrammed his family, he made a holiday visit to his hometown where his parents and two married sisters lived. It was the first time he had taken charge of his own time with family members. He turned down invitations both from his parents and older sister for the holiday dinner, sidestepping their competitive moves and arriving after the meal, dividing his time equally.

In the last session Roger did two sculptures, the first when he was 19 when he left for college. His father, mother, and younger sister drove him to school, with his mother reaching out to him, then pulling in, ambivalent about his leaving. His father was preoccupied and anxious to leave. His sister was involved in her own life. Roger felt scared and uncomfortable, not sure if he was dressed right. Feedback from the group described an uptight, emotionally inhibited family, with Roger caught up in the primary triangle.

The second sculpture was of his recent visit home. Although his older sister was cut off from his father, and his father and younger sister still did not want to get involved, Roger claimed the freedom to spend time alone with each one in his family. He recognized that his mother was also moving freely, with a life of her own, inviting his father to join her, but going anyway, even if he refused.

During the group Roger had begun dealing with his family in a more balanced way, refusing to leave anyone out. In the post-questionnaire he reported continuing his one-to-one connection with his father and also initiating contact with two paternal uncles, one of whom was willing to provide information about the events in the family that fueled the myth. He described his most significant event:

> "Seeing, on the diagram, the two arms of my family, one rich and full and mostly women and the other vague, full of mystery and pain — male pain of five boys for their mother who deserted them on a rope — I realized that I needed both arms. And that I have struggled in the past to find healing and conflict in the female arm, when I must find it in the other arm."

In this example, the suicide generated a myth, "Talking about important things is dangerous" and rules that both separated Roger from other males in the family, and allied him with his mother. Diagramming historical data allowed him to see the imbalance between males and females through the two preceding generations and to understand his isolation. In the first sculpture he chose, as Onset Time, the developmental stage when he left home for college, which illustrated the primary triangle he had been involved in. His actions took place in Present Time. During the group he initiated moves with his family that kept him out of the triangle, making one-to-one contacts with his father as well as with other members. He also made goals for Future Time and carried them out, according to his post-questionnaire, further defusing the myth.

The Interfacing Rings

Hoffman (1982) described the interface which contains the most tension and energy between therapist and family as the "presenting edge" (p. 15), that area most accessible to intervention. Detecting this "presenting edge" means, for her, sensing where this persistence relative to the therapist's probe seems to lie. Often . . . it is not located in the family alone, but in an arc that includes family, therapist and other professionals as well. (p. 15)

She illustrates the presenting edge by another spatial metaphor, the three interfacing Rings of her Time Cable (see p. 261).

Although Hoffman was writing of therapy with families, the same concept applies in my work with therapists in a group, where I also find that I must search out such a presenting edge, which usually is a dominant transgenerational theme that emerges from the member's family history. It may also, however, be triggered by the work of other group members, by leader/ group interchange, or through the shared backgrounds of group members.

Ring One, the central cylinder, encloses the family interfaces for each member. It is composed of the myriad family interrelationships going back in time, and reflects the themes, values, and expectations as they have been passed down through the generations. The diagramming of a member's family with the explication of patterns and imbalance, the experiencing of one's family through gestalt techniques, and the planning of change with family members belong in Ring One. One member described this process:

"Doing my family diagram with others making observations and recreating a past scene with the leader coaching were the most significant events. I was freed emotionally — able to see other viewpoints and feelings of family members of which I had been unaware; able to look at childhood incidents from an omniscient narrator point of view which increased my ability to empathize. This gave me knowledge and understanding of family history in a dynamic way, enabling me to conceptualize family patterns and individual responses. Very useful in therapy."

Ring Two is the group/leader interface. Support and safety are essential in this Ring so that participants can trust enough to expose their inner concerns to the group. It is the leader's task to insure safety by both building outer boundaries and preserving the freedom within. The group's safety will need to be tested before some of the members will be willing to reveal their vulnerabilities. Sharing intimate family history, working together experientially, feedback between participants, watching others work, and the process in the group emerge in this Ring and interface with adjoining Rings. One woman described how her experience reverberated to that of another member:

"When one of the members roleplayed confrontation with his mother and did this in a somewhat blameful, unsupportive manner, I later recognized similar elements in my attempts to confront my own mother in a roleplay. I, like him, was not appreciating that some of the behaviors that I dislike that she has are reactions to me. The leader's remark that I needed to learn to say no to her before I could say yes had particular impact as I do assertive training and preach this to others, yet have trouble practicing it in intimate relations."

Ring Three, the outer Ring, represents the participants' common, cohesive background as family therapists, including their work with client families, with co-therapists, and in their work settings. Many report, in pre-questionnaires, a wish to explore their interface with client families, and there is open feedback between members as therapists. Support and challenge are both provided by this outer Ring. One woman put into words her internal experience of her group:

"The experience of knowing the other people intimately (what matters most to them in their life and what issue they are working with) and over time has a profound impact which forms a bond of understanding and concern. The members of the group become an extended family to each other. To know another person (especially another professional who is willing to work on their issues plus utilize their training and skills in the group, share their experience, examine their history) is an unforgettable experience."

Change over time can be seen as a gradual evolution or as taking the form of a transformation, happening in sudden and startling ways. The way Therapist's Own Family Groups are set up depends on the leader's concept of time and view of such change, with formats varying from time-limited to groups which may go on for years. Meetings can be spaced evenly, with long or short intervals between, or patterned by several hours or days of intensive work and then a long period without meetings. The leader's expectation about members' abilities to take responsibility for their own changes is reflected in the way format and time are utilized.

Bowen is pessimistic about quick solutions, defining change in small increments over long periods of time. I have a more hopeful outlook on the process of change, including a belief in second-order change through seeing members of the family of origin from a new perspective. The training group has its parallel in the family group where both levels of communication — content and relationship — are operating. The group itself is a structure in which the members can view themselves and each other in an interactional context, which reflects how each member deals with his own world, outside the group.

As possibilities for change are catalyzed in the group, members become aware of how different individuals, viewing the same situation, experience different realities. When such shifts occur, they can impact on group members in important, system-altering ways, with new gestalts emerging which can then, in their turn, be dealt with.

CHAPTER 14

Shaping Interventions

In finding the "presenting edge" (Hoffman, 1982, p. 15) — that area most accessible to intervention — I gather information, continuing to increase my knowledge of how group members initiate and react, first through their written goals and questionnaires and then through their behavior within the group — how each joins, who volunteers to work, how they prefer to work, and what they reveal. I want to make sense out of how they view their world, to understand their basic premises.

When members present goals, I am looking for repetitive patterns in which their positions have become uncomfortable or painful, yet they are continuing to follow or oppose the system's rules. In order to find the crucial area that is ripe for intervention, I start where the group member is focused, where there is the most tension and energy, which is usually with the original family. If the member's attention is elsewhere, however, I start there — with a man's uneasiness with dominant women in therapy or with how a woman copes with her best friend's death — and then move backward through time to the family of origin to find repetitive patterns that affect the current issue.

As a member volunteers to work, I start where she feels discomfort because there is motivation behind discomfort. I track how she has struggled to solve her problem, which usually has dug her deeper into the status quo. As her dilemma becomes clear, I conceptualize it as multifaceted, although she is usually presenting self as having limited choices. The selection of image and language is crucial since I need to join her in order to extend her horizons. I want to juggle the information that she has kept carefully compartmentalized, or help reorganize information that she has confused. I highlight her position, saying, in effect, "Look at how you're dealing with the world," and, in the process, nudging her

267

toward a broader view that includes other realities, including aspects she may not know or recognize.

My mental image is of a mountain climber who has run into a wall of rock. If she sees the only possibility as going up that one face of the mountain, she may try and try again in an abortive first order change effort. If she sees the possibility of scaling other faces, however, then she widens her view to multiple realities, her task becomes plausible, and she can continue by herself. I see my job as helping her to see that there are other paths so that she can then test this new reality for herself.

As I connect the participant's current problem with patterns from her original family, a number of ways to intervene emerge for me. I am searching for transgenerational dynamics, such as cutoffs, triangles, secrets, and unresolved grief, which are likely to interfere with the current life flow. If she wants to focus transgenerationally in order to understand confusing or contradictory patterns, then the intervention needs to have a broad scope, which usually leads to diagramming or sculpture. If, however, the member has discomfort with a specific person or situation, a role-play or empty chair enactment can bring the incident to life so that group feedback can more accurately assess the person's involvement. Often members' goals encompass both broad and specific aspects; then it becomes necessary to determine which one the member wishes to experience first.

The structure of the group contributes to the leader's ability to locate the point for intervention. With the time frame limited and a tightly structured boundary inside which each participant has maximum freedom, the responsibility is shifted to the members, who react in their typical styles. Early in the group, the most effective intervention is an active one; if a climate for current change is to be fostered, the invitation to be open to new experiences is essential. Discussion can be effective later; at the beginning, however, until an expectation for change is established, discussion often tends to go around in a circle, becoming "more of the same." As long as I stay within the familiar frame set by the group member, we are working on her turf and not on mine. If she is just repeating an old story, I want to get her off center, like a judo maneuver. That old story is not just a familiar story but is often part of a repetitive family game in which the member is following a family rule which determines what is permitted and what is not permitted. She needs to become aware of the power those rules exert on her life because, when she knows the family rules she is following, she is then free to choose whether she will be bound by them.

As each dilemma unfolds, we have the possibility of discovering together how family rules limit the member to what is permitted by the family. It is important for her to experience that situation in a way she has not been exposed to before. This gives her the chance to use different pathways in thinking and to change the way she communicates. If the member is quite verbal, I would prefer sculpture so she has to change the way she expresses herself. If she is unclear, a diagram will help her organize her thoughts. If she talks *about* issues in a practiced way, I consider setting out an empty chair so she will have to alter her thinking and talk *to* the family member. As she shifts her focus in the group context, it then becomes easier for her to also modify her thought process in a similar context outside the group.

Those who are more naive or less trusting may wait until they see changes in others before they risk. In a few groups no one volunteered to work at the first session; by their holding back they were telling me that it was not yet safe enough, and we continued our discussion. The longer the group goes with each member waiting for someone else to make a move, the less the process builds. I encourage members and offer ideas, but I do not step in and assign tasks, although some of those who were in such groups reported that they wanted me to do so. If a group does not claim its own process, there is a feeling of restraint, even though individual members accomplish their goals. What is lost is the group-at-work; the setting becomes more dyadic, that of teacher/student working in the presence of observers.

REFRAMING

Reframing, an interpretation of the context, is often an intervention of choice. Watzlawick et al. (1974) describe the term:

> To reframe, then, means to change the conceptual and/or emotional setting or viewpoint in relation to which a situation is experienced and to place it in another frame which fits the "facts" of the same concrete situation equally well or even better, and thereby changes its entire meaning. . . . What turns out to be changed as a result of reframing is the meaning attributed to the situation, and therefore its consequence, but not its concrete facts. (p. 95)

The process of reframing emerges from the transgenerational context as I begin to understand how the family member has allowed herself to be trapped in the patterns of the past: "Successful reframing must lift the problem out of the 'symptom' frame and into another frame that does not carry the implication of unchangeability" (Watzlawick et al., 1974,

p. 102). I said to a woman who considered herself the black sheep in her family: "It seems to me you are like a pioneer — the one who forges ahead and breaks new ground." She accepted my reframe, and commented in her post-questionnaire:

> "Thank you for labeling me a pioneer rather than a black sheep. In the family, my pioneering efforts have been labeled 'black sheep' or, at least, nonconforming. Not realizing it, I believe I have always challenged the family rules. I have never accepted emotionally the family cutoffs."

I feed back to the working member and the group my understanding of the process as it emerges so that she can correct my assumptions and begin to own the process herself. One woman described such an experience while viewing a videotape of herself with her parents, four years after her father died:

> "After viewing with the group a videotape of my Dad and Mom, the leader gave me feedback re how much my Dad cared for me. It was a segment in the tape where he expressed concern over my chosen field and problems with my spouse. I always tuned out my Dad's lectures. I always heard them as him trying to sell me on what he wanted me to do. Now I could hear the caring, paternal, protective quality, too. It was important because it had been difficult for me to 'hear' positives from my father, particularly, and from men in general."

If there is an exploratory process in motion, I stay with it. One woman reframed her situation through group discussion, in which members highlighted her situation by examining the messages she had incorporated from her family:

> "When I discussed my fear of marriage, I became very aware of how much I'd bought into my family's belief that men are no good and how I was setting up my boy friend to be no good. Realizing from comments others in the group made that I was doing this helped me to watch out for this and to more easily catch myself when I started thinking the worst about ambiguous situations."

Occasionally members prefer to start by exploring their therapeutic interface. For example, Thomas's goals were: 1) Explore interface of family of origin/therapy; and 2) Work through blocks in therapy with certain types of patients. His specific problem was dealing with authoritarian males. He found himself working too hard and trying to outdo the men. The analogy used was that his male patient had his big guns out and

Thomas tried to use even bigger guns when he was not even good with guns; his strong area was knives.

When I asked Thomas who was authoritarian in his family, he said, "No one." What emerged from his family diagram, however, was a strong message from his father: "Follow the rules; don't get in trouble; don't confront authority." As he understood that in breaking his father's rule he was overdoing the confrontation, he was then able to relax. He said it particularly helped him when a group member reframed the behavior of authoritarian males as demonstrating vulnerability (rather than attack) on their part. It helped him outside of therapy as well, where he was able to deal with his authoritarian boss in a friendlier, assertive, and more relaxed manner, receiving an "outstanding" evaluation. He reported:

"Most significant was viewing authoritarian people from a new, less threatening framework and feeling much less responsible and overinvolved in therapy. I find it easier to be assertive rather than passive or passive-aggressive, which only punishes me in the end. There is much less tension at the end of the day for me."

In reframing, the leader can take the following steps:

1) Help the member to define the current impasse or discomfort so the group can see how the member is caught in her situation.
2) Conceptualize the situation as multifaceted and watch for other facets as the exploration continues.
3) Heighten the situation by discussion, diagramming, or an experiential technique, so the situation becomes very clear.
4) Reframe the situation, giving it a positive connotation which is compatible to the person's style of thinking.
5) Devise a way (by discussion, reenacting a scene, etc.) so that the group member can see how *she* wants to change, even if others in the family never do.

DISCOVERING PATTERNS THROUGH DIAGRAMMING

Bowen theory provides the cognitive base, a consistent and logical thread supplying a continuing guide to make visual a family's emotional system. In 30 or 40 minutes, the leader can diagram a three- or four-generation family and, together with the family member, discover the recurring patterns that are interfering with the member's goals. Although trainees already have knowledge about their families, they are often unable to put it together in a way that makes sense to them. Diagramming can clarify the patterns:

> "When I diagrammed my family to look at patterns, rules, and roles, it clarified my relationship with my sister and the triangling that goes on between my mother, sister, and myself. It helped me to see how my mother pulls me into taking care of my sister and how some of the anger that I directed towards my sister was displaced."

Diagramming becomes an invaluable tool for gathering transgenerational information until a paradigm emerges that encapsulates the relationship rules of preceding generations that influence the present. New information can be uncovered which clarifies the member's understanding of self. Such new information can then be used to fuel future exploration, understanding, and change. One woman wrote:

> "Family diagramming delineated multigenerational trends about how my choice of spouse fits the pattern. I discovered reasons for cutoffs within my family and my spouse's and therefore what we have cut off within ourselves and were looking for within the other. Began exploration of my invisible loyalties to my family and how these affect my current behaviors and decisions."

Sometimes a member is able to see her role in her family in a different way, without even trying to change, when she acquires a transgenerational perspective:

> "In doing my family diagram I saw that I was much more powerful in my family and in myself than I was previously aware of. In the past, my position had been one of 'family clown' or distractor. This position has changed. What I say and who I am seems to be more significant to other members. I'm not sure how this happened."

PLANNING FOR DIFFERENTIATION

Many participants saw the Therapist's Own Family Group as a place to plan strategies for their own differentiation. Bowen (1978a) writes:

> Differentiation begins when one family member begins to more clearly define and openly state his own inner life principles and convictions, and he begins to take responsible action based on convictions. . . . When the differentiating one defends himself, or counterattacks, or falls silent, he slips back into the old emotional equilibrium. When he can finally stay

on his own calm course, in spite of the togetherness forces, the accusations reach a peak and quickly subside. (p. 437)

Some group members knew where they wanted to start in the differentiation process; others knew only that it was a problem for them. Ruth, an unmarried woman of 40, was in a group that elected to continue meeting for four additional sessions of six hours each, over the following year. When she entered the group she appeared rigid and guarded, spoke slowly and carefully, and did not know how to start. I accepted her initial goal, "More objectivity in assessment of problems — especially re divorce," wondering what she would do with it, yet not wanting to press her.

Ruth was an only child and belonged to a closely knit extended family, whose members on both the maternal and paternal sides lived nearby. Ruth had become responsible for her mother when her father left home when she was 13. She was greatly admired by her aunts and uncles for her constant devotion.

As I kept her focused on what she wanted for herself, for the first time her suppressed anger began to emerge, and then the hurt of always having to be strong and never being able to ask for help. She reported a dream in which she was so angry at her mother that she was trying to kill her. The dream shocked her, but she found she was no longer overprotective of her mother; that she could come and go as she wished and could think about putting her mother in a nursing home with less guilt. As she became comfortable in the group, she changed her goal to "How to get in touch with Ruth." She described a discussion in the group when she recognized that her need for immediate resolution was connected to the Onset Time when her father left the family:

"There was discussion around a person's feeling compelled to do something about an immediate solution to a problem. Ensuing conversation pointed out there are situations where the most feasible solutions would be to do nothing. It was significant because of my tendency to feel badly if no effort was immediately made to try to handle all problems. Longstanding orientation unconsciously has been trying to repair the break in parental relations."

She spoke of her awareness of the togetherness forces when she began to make choices for herself instead of adapting in the old way:

"Becoming aware of the subtle pressures (past and present) exerted by both paternal (especially) and maternal relatives to place me in roles of their choice."

I predicted the above process, which helped Ruth to follow her plan. I told her that there was no point in her even starting a differentiating process until she was clear that she was ready to hold to the direction she had chosen. Then, when she was met with such pressures, instead of being surprised and crawling back into the old role, she could stay on her predetermined course and realize that their opposition was a sign that she was having an effect on the system. She described changes with her mother and in herself:

"I made a more realistic appraisal of our relationship, i.e., that I cannot be all things for her. I recently made arrangements for additional help in her care. There has been an easing of negative or guilt feelings about my shortcomings or failures to conform to the family's expectations for me."

As Ruth gave up her role as her family's therapist, she made a plan to spend time with individual family members rather than go to the family reunion as she always had done. She changed her role with her cousin, with whom she had the closest relationship, and with her aunt, the family matriarch:

"Attempting to gradually change or modify my cousin's view of me as a person who can do everything. Making her aware of my frailties. More ease in expressing feelings with my aunt, rather than remaining silent."

Eventually, as her family members realized that she was seriously living her life according to her own principles, they began to see her as more mature and in charge of herself. As Ruth left the group, she was softer, more open, and more spontaneous.

REFRAMING THROUGH SCULPTURE

I may offer to coach a member in a sculpture (Duhl, Kantor, & Duhl, 1973; Duhl, 1983), a technique to make the time and space dimensions in a family's life visible. Sculpture is an alternate language, primarily nonverbal, which places the family member's experience in a different context, thus encouraging exploration and insight. We can all participate in it because it represents the nonverbal world we lived in as children, when spatial perceptions and affect were intimately connected.

The family member becomes the sculptor or stage manager, with the leader coaching. Group members are chosen by the sculptor to play designated roles and can either accept or refuse. The sculptor is responsible for the content and works with the leader, who is responsible for the safety of the arena and for the process as it evolves. The leader supports the sculptor's right to create her own vision and to start and stop as she chooses. If the sculptor loses herself in her sculpting, the leader can bring her back to the group by asking, "How are you *right now?*", and then deciding with her in the present how to proceed. After the sculpture, the leader helps the sculptor and players to process their roles before allowing feedback from the rest of the group. An example will illustrate how a sculpture can move a group member towards her goals.

Defining the Impasse

I suggested a sculpture to Harriet, an unmarried woman in her thirties, when her family entered a transitional phase after her grandmother's death. Harriet's goals were: 1) to explore closeness/distance and 2) to look at her caretaking role in the family. Harriet had learned to keep distance from her family members in order not to be "swallowed up," while still maintaining a caretaking role. She also distanced herself in other relationships and saw herself doing it in the group. As the oldest child, she had always mothered her two younger sisters and was close to her blind maternal grandmother. When her grandmother died early during the group, she experienced the loss deeply and felt even further isolated from her family.

When her next sister Lois delivered the family's first grandchild, Harriet was aware of her dead grandmother, Mother, Lois, and the baby as important in the family. The baby had been very ill and the family was focusing on her in the same way they had focused on Grandmother. I suggested that Harriet do a three-part sculpture (Figure 22): 1) before Grandmother's death; 2) after Grandmother's death; and 3) after the baby was born.

In the first scene Grandmother was central, with all family members taking entrenched positions. Only the women of the family were visible in the room; Father was hiding behind a curtain and both of Harriet's sisters' husbands were outside the room, widely separated from each other. Only Mother and Harriet could move — Mother from a hidden position to circle her chair near Grandmother, not stopping until she was once again hidden behind a curtain on the opposite side of the room from Father. Harriet stood equidistant from all family members except when she moved in to care for each member, one at a time.

In the second scene, the ghost of Grandmother was in the chair Grandmother had previously occupied, with Mother, Lois, and Penny, Harriet's youngest sister, on the floor, tightly encircling Grandmother's ghost.

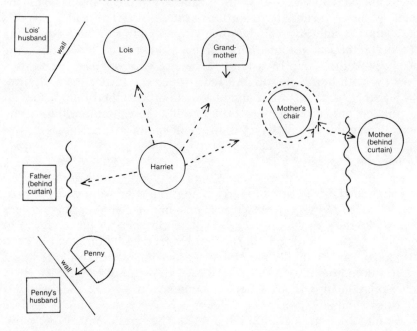

A. Before Grandmother's Death

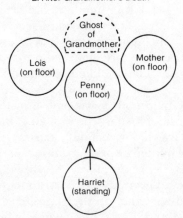

B. After Grandmother's Death

Figure 22. Harriet's Three-Part Sculpture

C. After Baby was Born

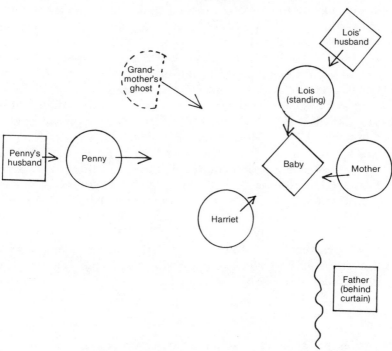

Figure 22 (continued)

Harriet was standing at a distance outside the circle, feeling uncomfortable. The men were nowhere in sight.

In the third scene the baby was now in the center with Grandmother's ghost on the side, reaching toward the baby. The women were still occupying the main arena, with Lois and Mother touching the baby, and Harriet farther away than before, more or less equidistant, and not moving. Father was still behind the curtain, although both young husbands had moved in, behind their wives, facing the baby.

Reframing the Impasse

As Harriet and the group processed the sculptures, we saw the system in the first scene as rigid, with Grandmother occupying the center and Harriet responsible for all the connecting. Mother's and Father's relationship had not flowered, with Grandmother and the children coming between them. By the third scene, the baby was occupying the central spot that Grandmother had occupied. The alignments had shifted twice, with death and then with birth. I commented that since there had already been shifts, there was the possibility that more shifts could be made and that Harriet looked like the person in the system most able to move.

I suggested to Harriet that the roleplayers go back to their places in the third scene and that Harriet try out different ways she might move in order to keep the system more fluid—perhaps she might take on a mysterious role as the one who comes and goes. She immediately knew what she wanted to do: She first went to Father behind the curtain and pulled him out; then, to Mother and connected with her; and finally to Lois, taking the baby and walking around, showing her to the others.

In the next session Harriet reported that she was experiencing a feeling of ease and comfort as she moved in and out of her family. She was more conscious of their rigid positions and found herself able to move to her own rhythm—not just complying or rebelling. She had actually found herself in her family one day holding the baby and moving as she had done when she explored her options in the sculpture. She was also feeling at ease and comfortable in the group, roleplaying a grandmother for one member and a sister for another.

Acquiring Self-knowledge

In the last session of the group Harriet felt exhausted, resistant, and caught up in the pain in her family. She reported having a visual image of standing her family members up in front of her and telling them off, allowing them only to listen and not respond. We set it up as a roleplay, with the same group members playing her family members. She was angry, frustrated, and overwhelmed with all of them except Penny; her anger turned to understanding as she realized Penny needed distance, like Harriet did. What emerged from her diatribe and from the roleplayers' feedback was how Harriet allowed herself to be triangled by Lois, listening endlessly to Lois' complaints about Father, Mother, and Lois' husband, while Harriet took on Lois' pain. She was also angry at her parents for not listening to her, yet Harriet did not tell them or Lois of her own problems and pain. As observing group members gave feedback, she saw how she stayed in old familiar patterns by being the switchboard, not admitting any problems of her own, but taking on theirs. In seeing how she was contributing, she also saw how she could change her part. These were the same issues facing four other members in the group who were also caretakers, which is a very common role for family therapists: how to interact with family members in a growth-producing way rather than taking the assigned caretaking role, and also how to move in and out from closeness to distance and back again at their own pace. These two areas had been Harriet's goals.

Resulting Changes

In the post-questionnaire, Harriet described the sculpture and roleplay as her most significant events:

> *The sculpture*: "Arranging people before and after Grandmother's death was significant because I learned I was not standing still — I could move from person to person. It helped me put the whole dying before/during/after experience together and gave me closure."

> *The roleplay*: "Saying what I wanted to say to family members in the last session was significant because I felt more separate from them and their pain. Afterwards I felt very adult. It was a great help in dealing with the issue of my overresponsibility. I see myself in a somewhat new and positive role in relation to my family — 'the mysterious one' who comes and goes."

Of her changes in the various interfaces, she wrote:

> *With sister Lois*: "When she makes crisis calls now, I picture myself as a large piece of blotting paper, soaking up her pain. It's comical, so I don't get hooked. I now tell her when I am under stress and can't listen."

> *With parents*: "Above true, also. I tell them when I am upset — no long discussions, just a statement. I used to say, 'I'm fine!'"

> *With male friend*: "This relationship is changing in that I feel less responsible for his pain. It is better for me, but makes for problems in our relationship since a big part of it has been based on my caretaking."

> *With client families*: "The biggest improvement is that I'm aware of my capacity to soak up pain with my clients, too. I am doing less overresponsible stuff with them; I feel less burdened; they do better. I am also more sensitive to individuation struggles."

A focus on action, in and out of the group, maintains a continuing stimulus. Such a focus, while using aspects of Bowen's method, also encompasses much more. When I reframed Harriet's role as the "mysterious one who comes and goes," she was immediately able to try out that role in the sculpture within the group, giving herself a different experience. Subsequently, she was able to transfer that role into her family. Six years later she reported it as the most important reframe.

When, during a group, there is a death of a close relative of a member, that person often uses the group for support in their grief. Harriet found the group supportive in dealing with her grandmother's death and did not really start working on her goals until the initial group meetings were almost complete. The group she was in, however, was the same one Ruth (see p. 273) was in, which chose to meet four times the following year for continuation sessions. It was during that time that she was able to do the sculpture and roleplay.

OVERCOMING AN EMOTIONAL BLOCK

A number of group members have reported blocks in the areas of competence, energy, and memory that have interfered in their personal and professional lives. It is my impression that such participants often have intense and conflictual relationships with one parent and are distant and uninvolved with the other. Rebalancing the relationship by spending time alone with the distant parent and limiting contact with the intense one so that the contact itself can be affirming seem to help restore energy and purpose. The most common pattern is that the mother is intense and conflictual and the father distant and uninvolved, although this is not always the case. It was true, however, of Teresa (see p. 256). In the following example, an empty chair technique was used to restore the connection with the distant parent, when that parent was no longer living.

Following Family Rules

Roy's goals were: 1) making changes in relationships with his family and 2) freeing energy and competence. Recently divorced, he reported drifting in his life. He knew his lack of purpose was tied to his family of origin although he did not know how. Since he had few memories of his early years, it was difficult for him to understand how he was allowing transgenerational patterns to control his life.

Roy asked me to diagram his family in the first session, since he was planning a visit home. His father had been a Marine until 30. Then, following a religious conversion, he had become a missionary in a foreign country, dying of cancer when Roy was 16. Early conflict between his parents had gone underground following his father's conversion. His mother, who had been controlling, had become a model minister's wife as Roy had become a model older son. Since his father had died, his mother had developed a successful professional career and now lived with his maternal grandmother and his younger invalid brother. There was an intense relationship between Roy and his mother, with Roy succumbing to her control and then distancing, in a cyclical pattern. Rules in the family were: 1) Don't talk about anything important in the family; and 2) Don't talk about feelings, especially good feelings.

He had broken the rules by the second session by talking to his grandmother and mother. By the third session, waves of memories were coming back to him, along with the realization that he was always calm. I put out a chair, suggesting he talk *to* his "calmness" rather than about it. In doing so, he discovered that he was only able to be calm and never showed strong feelings. When I asked what he did to liven things up, he said, "I can pick a fight in a real covert sort of way. Basically, I liven up the other person"; and then he gave us a demonstration. It became obvious that his role was to provoke others into strong feelings while he remained calm, a maneuver in which he was able to follow the family rules. Group members gave him feedback on how he had provoked or bored them. Before the session ended, I said: "My suggestion would be that between now and the next session you become aware of how you provoke others to do your liveliness for you. Don't cut it off—just be aware."

Strong Feelings Emerge

In the fourth session, he reported in rounds being scared on his way to the group and feeling fear as he spoke. He did not ask for time early in the session. After several members worked on issues with their fathers, I turned to Roy:

Jan: Where are you with your fear?
Roy: I've had a whole range of very heavy feelings. I've been doing a lot of internal work and spacing out, inside my head. The suggestion you made to me last time was to be aware of how I suppressed my feelings. Whenever tears have come out, at the same time there will be a series of anxieties and fears that will come into focus and then the tears have left.
Jan: So it's the sadness that gets overpowered.
Roy: Right, and submerged.

Roy had followed my suggestion and discovered sadness was the trigger, allowing anxieties and fears to surface. In not letting his sadness come out, he was also holding down his liveliness.

Roy: I have become aware I am not skillful in groups. It's like ten years ago. Yet, since college, in the last five years I've developed good friends and real social adeptness. (pause) I have less social skills now.

I presume this went way down deep inside. I'm aware there's a layer I'm really skilled at and a layer I don't know much about. When I try to work I get a lot of anxiety. (tears) I haven't gotten a lot of support in my life. I never really had much brains until the last couple of years.

I was listening for clues as to how he cut off his sadness. His reference to "ten years ago" pinpointed his father's death. When he said "I have less social skill now," he was referring to his drifting since his divorce, another loss. His confusion was surfacing. He was telling us he had social skills but he was not allowing himself to use them; his fear of sadness interfered.

Jan: Stay in touch with the sadness.
Roy: (low voice, full of tears) Not very much support. (sigh) So when I try to do something which takes internal structure, I fall apart. I can't get myself to do something that's very hard — I fall apart and rest awhile, watch television. We moved all the time while I was growing up — we moved at least every year and I was in various strange places.
Jan: Talk again about "how I never felt any support." That feels like the core of it.
Roy: That didn't come from my family.

When I asked Roy to stay with his sadness, it led him to his lack of support when he felt his internal structure falling apart. He then described his drifting, which was reminiscent of his childhood years when he lived in various strange places.

Talking to Father

I sidestepped his denial of family involvement and posed a direct question:

Jan: To whom do you want to say: "I never feel any support?"
Roy: To begin with, my father. I never felt any support.
Jan: (setting out a chair) There's your father.
Roy: (to Father) You just could never make connection with me at all. There was something wrong with me. (sigh) I would retreat into books and you thought that was really weird. You never had conversations with me. All you did was make derogatory comments

about how weird I was and that people would think something was wrong with me if I didn't act more normal. You were so far out — you had no idea there were good possibilities for me and strengths and things I was headed for. Anything I accomplished was in spite of you.

Jan: Tell him what you did when you had feelings.

Roy: The only time I can remember having feelings on the surface when I was around you was when I was asking for something. I was asking you to give me a gun. I started crying. I couldn't ask you for what I wanted and you didn't say anything — sort of listened to me for awhile and drifted off.

Jan: What are you saying to him, inside your head, while you are crying?

Roy: (tears) You know, I really want this thing. Why can't you put your arm around me and talk to me about this thing. The gun really isn't the issue. I want your love. I want your companionship. I want to have a dad and you were off somewhere else. (There is a pause, then suddenly he becomes lively.) There was a time when I was real little, about up to the time when I learned how to talk, when you played with me and I remember you teaching me some words and we laughed together, and after that you were gone from my memory. I remember you relating to my mother and other people, but not to me after I learned how to talk.

Jan: Do you try to get his attention?

Roy: Yeah, by doing things, by being like a little man, learning how to talk real well. I still use the dictionary.

Jan: What do you do with your feelings? What do you decide about that?

Roy: I don't talk to anybody about that. I keep them all inside.

Jan: You hold those feelings, like tears, inside? You are going to show him?

Roy: Right.

Roy poured out his anger and frustration to his father — words that he had been unable to say then and that would help free him to understand now. When I asked him to tell his father what he did when he had feelings, he went back to an earlier onset time when his father had not responded and had "drifted off," a word Roy had also used to describe his current state. Having expressed his anger, however, he was then freed to remember pleasant memories of his father at an even earlier time when they had played and laughed together before he had learned how to talk. His early decision became clear: to be a little man; to be intellectual and hold his feelings inside.

Reframing the Past

I brought him back to the present by asking, "Where are you now?" He was relieved that he had the capacity to show his feelings. As he described how he had kept himself from getting support over the years, I began to look for strengths:

Jan: So one of the big changes you've made in your life in the last five years has been to allow yourself to let people in.
Roy: I began having some buddies in college. I got married—but she was perhaps in worse shape than I was, not able to give. (pause) It's a new thing to view my life as actually having some strange things about it that weren't exactly normal. My parents really didn't deal with feelings in a natural way.
Jan: So you learned early not to deal with feelings in natural ways so now, as an adult, you're having to learn how to do it. (pause) So you're really the leader in the family in terms of feelings.
Roy: There were no other models.
Jan: A pioneer always does have difficulties deciding which path to take. He has to hack it out.

Before I asked the group to join us, I wanted to look at his current situation and help him see more clearly where he was. I had begun by speaking of the social skills he was using. His acknowledgment led to a thoughtful questioning, for the first time, of the normality of his life with his parents in terms of the expression of feelings. I reframed his role as that of leader or pioneer, having to learn skills on his own. After the group members joined us, giving supportive feedback, I turned to Roy:

Jan: What's happened to your fear?
Roy: I feel a lot more relaxed. There are certain things I'm still concerned about—a lot of work to do. But it feels solid. My chest has loosened up a lot. I feel like I'm at a beginning.

Correcting Distortions

In winding up the group in the fifth session, Roy spoke of his changes:

Roy: I've had a nice thing happen with my grandmother. I never had much of a relationship with her at all before six months ago. She was always standoffish. Over the phone we got into some nice conversations. It's obviously because I make myself available. I don't think she's doing anything different. (pause) My mother's kind of resentful I'm not cooperating by giving more to her. She'd like me to go back there to live.

Jan: Does getting reconnected with your grandmother affect your relationship with your mother?

Roy: I hadn't thought of that.

Jan: It could be a loyalty thing. Is it disloyal to your mother to go directly to your grandmother? In my family, my mother had to be the switchboard. To get to anyone in the family I had to go through Mother and if she didn't give me permission, I felt like I was doing something I shouldn't be doing. I had to become aware of that pattern before I could decide what I wanted to do.

Roy: I don't spend enough time with my brother, as far as she is concerned. Last night, in talking to a friend, I got into a little kid frame of mind talking about Mother and I said: "You're supposed to like your mother better than anybody in the world!" And this woman said: "Hey! I never got that message from my mother — that she was supposed to be first." And I realized, as a person, I don't like the way she is. Although she is my mother, I have a lot of feelings about that.

Roy was building his support system, starting with his grandmother. When he spoke of the start of their relationship six months before, he was referring to the visit with her and his mother, after we diagrammed his family during the first session. He realized that the change came from him, not from her. As he spoke of his mother's resentment, I connected it to his new and direct relationship with his grandmother, which bypassed his mother. Her resentment sounded like a triangulating move on his mother's part. I used my relationship with my mother as an example, framing a suggestion as a story. His reply was to also admit disloyal thoughts about his mother. As the group ended, Roy looked at his goals taped to the wall.

Roy: The big anxiety I came with — freeing energy and competence and moving on professionally — has a lot to do with how it was in the family. The more support I have, the more competence seems to come as a function of having support, so the unused ability that I have has to do with getting more support. I'll be starting graduate school next fall to get my doctorate. (He has since completed his doctorate.)

The context of the original family is a key area for second-order change. Family members like Roy learn the family rules as children when they feel their survival depends on following them. Such rules form the basis for many of their actions; they are their most compelling frame of reference, having been a major factor in decisions throughout their earlier and most impressionable years. If they can become aware of and learn to question the rules that are currently confining them and choose for themselves those they wish to follow, then they will have tools to help take charge of their own lives.

CHAPTER 15

The Influence of the Group

The impact of the group itself and its process should not be under-estimated in accounting for the high percentage of change reported by members. Important aspects of the group are represented in the Time Cable (see p. 261) by Ring Two (group/leader interface) and Ring Three (common background as therapists) which are reinforcing interfaces. The interpersonal learning and shared themes that become possible upon involvement with other members is both a stimulus and a universal factor. This is especially true for therapists who may feel unsure in dealing with client family problems as "expert professionals," when they are conscious of similar personal problems in their own relationships.

My groups start out as leader-focused since I set the structure and work individually with members, using various techniques. As common themes emerge, the group becomes more interactive, with members sharing and learning from each other; then I am able to move back and forth between the roles of technical expert and model-setting participant. If members do not discover shared themes, they are more likely to continue to interact primarily with me. The norms for the group are formed early in its life and, once established, are difficult to change.

CURATIVE FACTORS IN THE GROUP

Yalom (1970) provided provisional guidelines when he described 10 interdependent curative factors which he found to be actual methods of effecting change and which were also remarkably similar across groups. These factors are: instillation of hope; altruism; development of socializing techniques; imparting of information; imitative behavior; catharsis; interpersonal learning; group cohesiveness; universality; and the correc-

287

tive recapitulation of the primary family group. Depending on the goals and composition of a particular type of group, these factors become important in different ways. In addition, members of the same group may be helped by different clusters of curative factors.

I will discuss first those I consider to be underlying factors in Therapist's Own Family Groups, leading up to those which are most influential — interpersonal learning and universality. Universal concerns reveal themselves in shared themes, since the subject matter is family of origin and group members share a common background as family therapists. The corrective recapitulation of the primary family group is illustrated in the last part of the chapter, "Learning Through Transference."

Underlying Factors

Instillation of hope is crucial in all therapeutic groups, with members watching each other's progress and applying it to themselves; reframing encourages this process. Altruism — the concern for the welfare of others — sets the therapeutic influences in motion as members help one another. The development of socializing techniques operates in all groups, including the Therapist's Own Family Groups, even though social learning is not an area of focus. Imparting of information goes on continually as I teach Bowen theory, suggest strategies, and give mini-lectures as needed or requested.

Examples of imitative behavior — the modeling after other group members or the leader — turn up again and again in the questionnaires, especially among those who are uncertain. Caroline, whose mother had been mentally ill for years, was quiet and unsure of herself as she entered the group, and had difficulty competing:

> "The leader trusted some of us to know what we needed and then to ask for it. I seldom knew what I needed, and therefore couldn't specifically ask. However, I often picked out my areas as others worked, but then we were short of time."

Those who volunteer first stimulate competition among others as they negotiate for time. Caroline, turning the disadvantage she reported to her advantage, used the work of another to learn more about herself:

> "Watching another group member work through a grief issue with her father was significant because I respected the clinical ability she evidenced and I respected her self-confidence and self-assured manner; yet I discovered that such characteristics and qualities were not incompatible with a traumatic childhood and current conflicts in family of origin. I felt that I was given permission to have problems and admit them. It doesn't make

me bad to admit that I have needs,too, which I think I've unconsciously thought."

When Caroline did work in later sessions, she enjoyed the expertise of her fellow participants:

"I felt that, in working myself, I had 10 therapists as opposed to one; therefore, no stone was left unturned in that process."

Catharsis, the release of emotion, is a potent part of the group experience but it is a part process and, in itself, does not bring about lasting change; something else is needed to make the change endure. In Therapist's Own Family Groups the necessary step is to return to the family of origin and make a relevant shift in behavior or attitude. Catharsis in the group is usually connected to the expression of feelings about family members or to a member in an empty chair, letting out blocked negative feelings so that positive ones can also emerge. One woman described her experience:

"Doing my family diagram and exposing some extremely painful issues from the past was most significant because this was the first time it was ever out in the open in over 20 years. I've always felt this as a heavy load; I've been fearful of rejection, and had much guilt. I feel more positive about my sharing feelings with clients and families than before."

Catharsis can be a first step towards exploring previously avoided or unknown parts of self. After the release of feelings, the member may be able to see self's part in the process:

"The most significant event was when a workshop member responded to my diatribe against my family by saying "Every family needs a saint." It made me realize how I was cutting myself off from them (my "sainthood") and why (so that I could avoid their unhappiness and failure and maintain my lack of responsibility for "growing up" and making myself happy)."

Those who have expressed strong emotions are more likely to feel cohesion in the group; the events they identify on post-questionnaires as "most significant" are often turning points which have an affective component.

Interpersonal Learning

Interpersonal learning is a primary factor in allowing members to gain knowledge. The group is a structure in which the members can view themselves and each other in an interactional context, with a focus not only on factual information but also on information about relationships. The training group has its parallels to the family group where both levels of communication — content and relationship — are operating. One woman described the process for her, leading to a changed relationship with her brother:

> "I was able to have a very meaningful visit with my brother because I had already discussed my feeling of rejection and my desire for closeness in the group. The members were able to help me seek a sort of closeness with my brother that would not demand a decision on his part between his loyalty to his wife (who has expressed much dislike and distrust of my parents and even of my own nuclear family) and to his relationship to me. I felt much better about working towards a closeness that was not demanding, competitive, or more than either of us wanted."

What goes on in the training group reflects how each deals with his own world, outside the group. If, through interaction with the group, with the leader, or in observing the work of other members, a participant can see his own dilemma from a new perspective, then alternatives may become possible. In sharing their similarities and differences, many members are able to change their perspective in the context of the group and then transfer it to their original family and to other interfaces:

> "Understanding the family dynamics of other group members and seeing the similarities and differences from my own helped me gain a sense of normality about the processes in my own family, enabling me to capitalize on my family's strengths, rather than the craziness."

I believe, with Yalom (1970), that members, through self-observation and feedback,

> "become aware of significant aspects of their interpersonal behavior: their strengths, their limitations, their parataxic distortions, and their maladaptive behavior which elicits unwanted responses from others. . . . The depth and meaningfulness of this awareness is directly proportional to the amount of affect associated with the transaction. . . . As a result of this awareness, the patient [group member] may gradually change or may more abruptly risk new types of behavior and expression." (pp. 30–31)

Such affect often surfaces when experiential techniques are used, and can give the participant a gut-level awareness of her position in the family:

> "Most significant was a sculpture of moving from my family of origin to my new family due to my upcoming marriage. I felt a vivid pull between

Father and my husband-to-be, in which I experienced intense awareness of anxiety and conflict. It was so current, it really enabled me to structurally 'see' and feel this pull and acknowledge the difficulty. I have a much clearer and experienced understanding of the issues involved in my 'leaving' or separating from my family of origin to begin my new family."

Yalom (1970) believes that the likelihood that change will occur is a function of:

a) the patient's [group member's] motivation for change; the amount of personal discomfort and dissatisfaction with current modes of behavior;
b) the patient's [group member's] involvement in the group, his need for acceptance by the group, his respect and appreciation of the other members;
c) the rigidity of the patient's [group member's] character structure and interpersonal style. (p. 31)

In the Therapist's Own Family Group, the focus is narrowed to the common shared experiences of the members of having each been part of their own early family group, including shared themes and the processes in the group itself that arise from that experience. For this particular group I would add:

d) the group member's willingness to explore his own family patterns, to see parallels between them and his current discomfort, and to change in the group and with his own family members.

The actual changes that result may generate a new cycle of interpersonal learning for group members through self-observation in the group and in their own families as they realize, as Yalom notes, that the calamities they feared did not materialize.

Group Cohesiveness

Depending on shared goals and themes and the support that is felt, group cohesiveness, the attraction a group holds for its members, varies in Therapist's Own Family Groups. The more curative factors that are operating in any group, the more cohesive the group will be. In some groups cohesion was felt by some members and not by others. In one group of one black man and five white women, the individual members' evaluation of the group's cohesiveness varied widely. The man changed his original goals, which had related to his father, brothers, and peer relationships with men, to his relationship with aggressive women and then found there were none in the group. He wrote:

"I found that it is difficult for me to learn from white females. I was uncomfortable being the only male in the group. From my vantage point everything felt watered down. The world I live in is more control-conflictual and hostile. I feared being attacked by females who presented themselves as soft and (possibly) with little appreciation for what it is like being a black male. This statement is not to put the group down; but an acknowledgment of what I felt."

Two women in the same group had positive views of the group's interaction. One wrote:

"The way in which we were able to reach out in a trusting, supportive way and really give each other helpful ideas was the most significant factor, rather than one event, because it allowed us all to stay open and receptive to working and feeling."

Although the man faded out of the group and missed two of the five sessions, the differences in reported group cohesion can be understood because he was forthright about his dilemma, described his family background, and was supportive to the other members.

Curative factors such as hope, altruism, and universality lead to group cohesiveness early in the group. Many members feel safe enough to allow themselves to experience affect that they have not allowed themselves with their original family members, and then are able to move towards those family members in new ways. Others have different needs: If they are already emotionally involved, they may need to stand back, become more objective, and see what they contribute to the process. Even those who did not share common themes often were able to work directly on family of origin issues, gaining support from the group and leader.

THE IMPORTANCE OF SHARED THEMES

The universality of the group's focus — the original family — creates shared themes based on family patterns, life stages, and life styles. Mutual exchange with others helps members see their own lives from a more realistic perspective:

"I gained a greater understanding of the universality of issues — how, in particular, so many of us are engaged in the process of growing up (differentiating) well into our adult years. It was encouraging for me to see this. (I thought I was the only one!)"

An added bond is the fact that the members are therapists. They are often fearful as they contemplate exposing their issues, afraid they will be seen as inadequate or be rejected. When one person is willing to reveal her concerns, her openness gives permission to other group members to talk about themselves. When the first volunteer is joined by another, their sharing becomes a common bond. When two group members share a common theme, they are able to support each other and the bond deepens. When three, four, or more share a theme, the group begins to feel like an open family and, for some participants who come from closed families, this may be their first such experience with co-professionals and, for a few, their first such experience ever.

Themes that emerge from the family's historical past are of vital concern when they are still exerting their influence in the present. Transgenerational themes include unresolved mourning, over-responsible caretakers, cutoff members, unbalanced male/female patterns and parent/child issues. These are underlying concerns, causing conflict in intimate relationships, which bring couples and families into therapy. Another important theme emerges for those who come from dysfunctional families which may include mentally ill, suicidal, or alcoholic members.

Current themes fall under the categories of life stages, including separation from family at time of marriage, the birth of children, children leaving for college, and care of aging parents; alternate life styles, including divorce, marrying into a blended family, live-in partners, and homosexual or bisexual issues; and current life events and trauma, such as the death of an important family member and changing careers. Future themes are usually concerned with differentiation and planning strategies for change.

If group members have not yet gone through later life stages or encountered certain life events, they may have difficulty feeling rapport with a client family member's experience. Exposure to life struggles of other therapists increases their empathy:

"I know everyone is different, but I have never experienced the differentness to such a degree. It's something everyone knows, but I still can't get over it. It is significant because of the infinite variety of coping (coping in many cases well) but more important, the knowledge of patterns of behavior that one carries on unconsciously that are very destructive."

CARETAKING THEME

Six out of eight participants in one group were single, overresponsible caretakers, ranging from 25 to 60 years of age. I use the term "overresponsible caretaker" to describe that person whose degree of concern keeps their primary loyalty focused on the original family. Some caretakers do not allow themselves to marry and have children; others, although married, retain their earlier loyalties at the expense of their nuclear families. The overinvolvement of all six affected both their personal and professional lives. All were ambivalent about this role; they had strong family bonds and were also striving for individuality. They were asking: How can I fulfill my role as family caretaker without having to sacrifice my own life to do it?

The profile that emerged was of someone parentified early in life who still places others before self. As he began his career he felt he was fulfilling self in the caretaking role. As he continued this role, however, it became increasingly burdensome as others' expectations increased, his own sense of self diminished, and he found himself overcommitted to his practice and working harder than the patient or family he was treating.

Such therapists need an experience of sharing their own vulnerabilities — first, perhaps, in the group, but this is usually not sufficient unless it is followed by an equal sharing with their original family members. When they stop being the expert in their own families and instead ask for help when they have problems, it shifts the family system into better balance and allows underadequate members to show their competence, as the overadequate ones are able to show their weaknesses.

Because of the difficulty in changing overresponsible roles quickly, one group contracted to meet for four additional six-hour sessions over the year following the five-month group. Experiences of two members, Ruth (p. 273) and Harriet (p. 275) are described elsewhere in Part III. One man described his changes, which were typical of those experienced by the other overresponsible members:

> "I initially had difficulty 'seeing' my family as a system. I now not only have been able to see much of our dynamics but also have been able to test out its reactiveness and strategize a plan to increase my person-to-person contact in my family, to become better differentiated, and to do my own style of caretaking that I am comfortable with. I was able to celebrate my disengagement from my overinvolved position at the Agency. I discovered much strength in clarifying my work role, eventually resigning, and traveling before taking another job. I think I have been able to negotiate my current job more effectively than I would have previously. I have seen, over the past year and a half, a gradual unfolding of issues and individuating moves by all members of our group. It has been comforting to learn that change takes time and will come by confronting difficult and hurtful issues and by methodically staying true to yourself and continuing along a pre-decided course of action."

One woman who was not a caretaker had been overinvolved with her severely dysfunctional family and learned to erect the same kinds of boundaries that the caretakers did:

"Most significant was telling the group that my mother and I had a very limited, superficial relationship and I did not want to spend any more of my time trying to make a change. The group supported me which really surprised me but helped confirm my thinking. I decided to move my center of attention from my family of origin and focus more on myself as a developing person and on my relationship with my husband. It feels good to have a structure on the relationship with Mother; I don't get anxious that I will be overwhelmed by her. As I move my focus to myself, it feels strange. I feel lost. I feel there are parts of myself that I need to discover."

FATHER/SON THEME

In one 12-hour preceptor group composed of three men and two women, two of the men, Mathew and Randy, reported distant relationships with their fathers and the third, Henry, was in a helpless position with his. The three men developed a synergy, which is a common process in the groups; when one volunteered, it stimulated action by another and vice versa, so that a process was set into motion with the result that group members were able to delve deeper together and look more critically at their own behavior than any one of them could have done alone. What eventually emerged for each was released energy in their lives and increased intimacy in their primary relationships, both of which were directly related to their release of inhibition with their fathers. Since their interaction is the focus of this theme, I have not included the work of the women.

Henry reported feeling scared in the first session when Mathew wrote his goals, because of the parallels he saw. Mathew, who cared deeply about his nuclear family but did not like his father at all, wanted: 1) to look at different ways to relate to his father so as to be better able to accept him, and 2) to look at how his original family affected his nuclear family. Henry then realized that his original family situation had not changed since he had gone into therapy in graduate school when he was having difficulty separating from his family. There had always been a family expectation that he get a Ph.D. as a rite of passage. As he talked, he realized that his sister, who now had physical problems necessitating her moving back home, had started studying for her Ph.D. when her problems began. Henry was serious about change when he wrote his goals: 1) decide whether or not to get a Ph.D.; and 2) see parallels between family of origin and personal life issues.

Randy was divorced, the father of two sons, and had recently started living with Elaine. His parents had always fought, but stayed together, with his father passive and his mother in control. He could only remember spending time alone with his father once; they had gone fishing and afterwards his father had "caught Hell" from his mother. His goals were: 1) to make plans for his parents' 50th wedding anniversary; and a plaintive 2) "Why am I what I am?"

In the second session, Randy reported that his parents refused to celebrate the anniversary unless he stopped living with Elaine. He had reacted by picking fights with Elaine, and she had almost decided to move out that morning. Following this, Mathew was ready to talk about his anger at his father for being the way he was and not living up to Mathew's early hero image. I diagrammed his family as he talked; he was the parentified older child who had taken sides between his father and his mother, who was now dead, deciding who was right and wrong. When he got stuck in therapy, he was also trapped into deciding who was right and wrong.

Henry found himself continually in a one-down position with his father, who hooked him into giving advice, and then made fun of him for his "dumb" ideas. I said it was clear he wanted his father to change; it sounded as if he kept stepping into his father's traps in the same way, over and over. He could keep quiet or even give his opinion if he did not expect his father to like what he said. The group's feedback was that he gave his power away; that the parent cannot give a child permission to grow up; that the adult child has to take charge of himself.

By the third session Henry reported three decisions he had made. He and his wife had decided to have a child whether or not he went to graduate school. Once that had been decided, he became clear that he did want to get a Ph.D. for himself, not for his father, and that he would start when the time seemed right to him. He had also decided not to give advice in the family, telling his father to "handle it." Mathew was confused and feeling uncentered and did not want any time. Randy was sad and depressed. His family had not celebrated his parents' anniversary at all and his relationship with Elaine was rocky. Her parents did not approve either. Since I would be on vacation at the time of our next meeting, we decided to meet for a four-hour session in a month.

This double session provided a breakthrough. Mathew had said in rounds that he wanted to complete his family diagram; now he wanted to work on something more immediate, although also tied to his family of origin — his relationship with his wife. He had been telling her he wanted to be closer, yet he had discovered his actions did not match his thoughts and words. She had confronted him about a recent incident in a way she had never done before and told him how it really felt to her when what he said and what he did were not congruent; that she was not sure she could count on him; and that she needed to do things for herself and not depend on him. He had listened without being defensive.

I pointed out that he had already done something different in listening to her without getting into a "right or wrong" position. I said I thought his relationship with his father was influencing his relationship with his wife and suggested he talk to his father without being defensive and accept what Father said as his father's opinion, as he had accepted what his wife had said.

Henry was affected by Mathew's experience. He had planned to talk about the "good things" he had done with his family of origin but instead talked about his relationship with his wife and the way he thwarted his own wish for intimacy. He spent very little time alone with her; he was seeing that it was necessary to be comfortable alone together before having a child. He had realized, as Mathew talked, that they always went out socially and spent vacations with friends and relatives. I told how my husband and I had planned four weekends a year to go away alone together when our children were small; that I thought marriage required a changed context from time to time so the couple relationship could evolve away from the problems at home. The trust level in the group was now very high.

Randy, who had been quiet and troubled and had not wanted any time that day, was now able to divulge his secret fear—he had always wondered if he was his father's son. His father had been gone around the time he was born and he felt that there was something odd about it all. He wondered if that was why his mother kept him away from his father. We explored whom he could talk to. I suggested that his sister, who was 12 years older, must know a lot more than he.

In the sixth session Randy reported that he had hurried home after the last session and called his sister to ask if his father was really his father. She convinced him, describing his father as very happy when his mother brought him home from the hospital. If anything, she said, his mother was jealous of his father. His sister asked him if he had ever wondered why their father did not have any men friends; her opinion was that their mother would not let him. That same evening Randy had taken Elaine with him to his parents' house to drop off some genealogical material his father had requested. His mother and Elaine had talked comfortably together, to his surprise. Later in the session he said his father was 74 years old and he really wanted to get to know him before he died.

Mathew had bought a rose and taken it home. His wife was excited, then asked, "Is there anything wrong? What's up?" He told her he had felt good about their conversation the weekend before and he wanted to tell her he had heard her and loved her. They had been talking on a different level since then. He had not started his change with his father, but was planning a visit.

Henry had applied for and gotten the position of Program Director in his agency. He told his boss in the interview when he would be leaving to go back to graduate school for his Ph.D.

Resulting Changes

All three men reported personal and professional gains. Mathew told of his most significant event:

> "An insight during the second to last session when I realized I was using my anger at my father to avoid looking at my present marital and family relationships. I also recognized that the areas I disliked about my father I was beginning to duplicate in my own family. It helped me focus my attention on my nuclear family and thereby took some pressure off my relationship with my father."

Mathew described his changes:

> *With father*: "I realize I have blamed him for all the family problems and have secretly wanted him to admit his responsibility and repent. I am now starting to be more open with him about my own feelings rather than waiting for him to open up to me. This continues to be a very slow and difficult process."
>
> *With wife*: "I had not been open with her about myself. In fact, in some respects, I behave similarly as my Dad did with Mother. I am working at being more open and more considerate and trying to let her know how special she is to me. So far, the results are favorable."
>
> *With client families*: "I have a greater appreciation and understanding of how family of origin issues affect and influence nuclear family relationships. I am more understanding of parents and give them the benefit of the doubt as I hope my children will give me the benefit of the doubt."

Henry described his most significant event:

> "I realized that I was waiting for my parents to see me as an adult and not assuming that responsibility for myself in spite of them. This was a major turning point in my life. I realized I was giving my parents my power. I placed the responsibility on myself."

Henry related his changes with family members and with client families:

> *With father*: "As I've made myself powerful, my father has begun to accept me as a knowledgeable peer. I am able to see him as a person and

not an all-powerful being. I am more relaxed with him and we are talking more together. Last Saturday I called him and asked for his advice on a problem without feeling defensive."

With mother: "I went through a period of anger with her for setting up my father to be the heavy and me to be her 'therapist.' I have more patience with her."

With sister; "I have refused to act like a teenaged brother with her and defined our relationship as being adults or no relationship. I still get angry with her when she tries to hook me into brother/sister fights. I am able to see this and back off."

With client families; "I am more objective. I don't get into as many power struggles to prove myself as being powerful. I don't get triangled as easily into marriages as I did. I am able to treat adults in therapy as equals as opposed to parent/child relationships."

Randy described several events as most significant:

"1) Securing my sonhood with my father; 2) being an adult with my parents, which opened up their acceptance of me and Elaine; and 3) I understood the 'we' rule in the family and how I still can get caught up in it."

Randy wrote of his changes in his different interfaces:

With father: "Discovered I am my father's son. He sees me in an adult role and I feel stronger about our relationship."

With mother: "I try not to get involved in her craziness."

With both parents: "I have begun a program of taking one of my parents to breakfast each month. It's lots of fun."

With Elaine: "Elaine and I got married."

With client families: "My own family of origin issues are very important for my own well-being. As I have begun to deal with them, it has helped me to be freer to encourage the same with clients I see. I use family of origin material more directly in my clinical work by: 1) charting family diagrams; 2) giving them homework assignments pertaining to family of origin work — 3) after making link-ups in connection with blocks."

This group provides a good example of synergy at work. Henry's ability to admit his fear, as he described how long he had been stuck in the same position in his family, allowed him to get in touch with the reality of his adolescent behavior and to make several important decisions by the third session, when Mathew and Randy were both still floundering. At the beginning of the double session, Mathew was feeling safe enough to alter his agenda and share his confusion about the double messages he was giving his wife. This encouraged Henry to look more closely at himself in his marital relationship. The process was building; Randy was then able to say the unsayable and, in saying it, to receive permission to ask questions and to secure his sonhood with his father.

PROTECTION AS A THEME

Most groups have several common themes, although they are not always as obvious as the two I have described. In one group there seemed to be little group cohesion and the usual themes binding members together did not emerge as shared issues. All the members felt the slowness and commented on it in their post-questionnaires. I explained the lack of cohesion to myself on the basis of the diversity between group members (three of the five were foreign-born, all three from different cultures) and their relative inexperience in working with original family issues. Yet I know that such diversity and inexperience need not impede bonding.

As I have since studied the group's process, through my notes and their questionnaires, the theme that emerged was protection — not in the form of the overresponsible caretaker, but more subtly, as in a united front family. This gave me the clue I needed; the special mix in the group re-created my own family of origin, although I was not aware of it at the time.

Richard was in an impasse with his parents, having believed for years that his father was fragile. His protective strategy required that he go through his mother to reach his father, thereby remaining angry at his mother. An older woman, Helena, had had multiple losses as a girl, before she lost extended family in the holocaust. She had felt she "had to protect" her parents, and only recently had she been able to open up to her children and not protect them.

A younger woman, Anna, had been protecting her mother since her father's death four years before. When she discovered in the group that her family had solidified into dyads since that loss, she began making plans to intervene one to one into the various dyads. Cora was engrossed in the cognitive goal of making a genealogical chart of her family, tracing through the generations both the enmeshment and the emigration which had led to the isolation of those who had moved away. The youngest member, Roberta, appealed to the group from what seemed a helpless stance, which contrasted with her history of emigrating alone to Chicago, thousands of miles from her family.

As I reconstruct it now, Richard became my father (who protected my mother, whom he considered fragile) and Helena, my mother (who had had losses, but who expected to survive). Anna and Cora stood for two sides of my older sister (Anna taking a protective role and Cora filling in with cognitive questions whenever there was unspoken-for time). Roberta was my younger brother (whom the family had felt needed protection and treated as younger than he was).

The group started out as other groups did, with members willing to talk about themselves and their goals. In the first session Helena confronted Richard when I asked if there was any unfinished business from earlier contacts. They had been in the same supervision group the year before; he had given feedback to the members at the very end of the group when there had been no time left to process it, which had upset her. Their interchange established a norm of openness.

In the third session, Richard pointed out how all of us were giving Roberta advice, like her mother gave her advice, which did not help. He noted that the feelings she was inducing in the group members she probably also brought out in her mother. I thought it was an astute observation and told him so. All the women, including myself, were acquiescing to his male authority and failing to check out or challenge his statements. I should have asked Roberta and the group if they agreed, and looked more specifically at my own functioning. Only later did I realize that he was beginning to take over the role of group processor at the expense of the work he had mapped out for himself and was resistant to doing: to find a way to test out if his father was, in fact, weak and fragile.

By the fourth session, Cora was questionning whether she wanted to commit the required time and effort over a period of years to achieve more than a superficial historical/demographic understanding of her family system. Richard asked why she was doing it. She replied that it was for her daughter, to change the pattern of mother/daughter relationships in her family. Her protection was towards her child. In the ensuing discussion, many issues were raised in terms of enmeshment/isolation/child centeredness. She was seeing the value of her own autonomous reconnection as insurance for the future.

In the fifth session the group was noticeably slowing. Richard offered to do a sculpture of his current family of origin, probably as much to keep the group going as to experience the sculpture. It reinforced his impasse; no alternatives seemed viable to him. Again, I did not challenge him; we were unwitting partners in keeping the status quo and not moving to a deeper level.

By the sixth and final session, when Richard asked if our group was less active than the usual ones, I answered yes, and we discussed the process, without any real insight. Individual members, however, had made changes. Cora had made many discoveries about the relationships between her family members. For Helena, connecting the early traumas in her life with the present gave her a changed point of view. Anna had become aware of patterns, alliances, and cutoffs, and was realizing the role she could play in helping to cause a shift in alliances in her family. She also realized that she had the power either to maintain the homeostasis or to work toward change. Richard's accomplishments were all concerned with group interactions; he reported no change at all with his family of origin.

When curative factors are applied to this group, important areas, especially in interpersonal learning and universality, were missing since I did not deal with the theme that the members and I were struggling with. Individual members felt hope, but not to the same degree as if I had figured out my interface issues and shared them with the group, giving us a common, interpersonal experience. There was valuable information imparted in terms of work with original family members, but not about the group's interfaces.

The group was cautious and intellectual from the beginning, with little catharsis. There was, for me, a dysfunctional recapitulation of the primary family group as I was sucked back in; since I did not recognize my interfacial contagion, it did not become a learning and the group did not experience cohesion. There was little imitative behavior reported, except for Richard's sharing of the leader's role. My impression is that Richard was monitoring the group, while I structured individual work with the other four members. In this way he could bypass dealing with his father and I could avoid the interface connection with my father.

If I had been able to see how I was caught up in the protection racket, I could have spelled it out to the group, relating my interactions to theirs and vice versa (as I have here), which would have been a way to attend to the process without attacking, blaming, or withdrawing. Such a move would model for each group member how to deal with his or her own issues around protection as I would have been dealing with mine. Not seeing the larger picture, I withdrew to working individually with those who volunteered to work, which, under the circumstances, was a functional, although non-group-oriented process.

LEARNING THROUGH TRANSFERENCE

The corrective recapitulation of the primary family group is not a focus I consciously make; nevertheless, the early experiences members had in their original families permeate the group and give it power. Transference operates in the groups, often without being discussed, surfacing in post-questionnaires. As long as the leader keeps himself unhooked or is aware and ready to discuss his part, such working behind the scenes can be useful. There is little time, in a short-term group, to concentrate on intragroup issues, even though the group interface is an important learning situation.

In one group of eight members with an age span from 27 to 57 years, five of the women were working on mother/daughter issues. Two of the women reported in questionnaires transference reactions which they had experienced early in the group: from Ellen to Miriam, from Miriam to Lorraine, and from Miriam to the leader. Neither Ellen nor Miriam spoke of their transference in the group, yet their feelings formed a base for important work with their own family members.

Miriam was the oldest group member. She was cut off from her daughter and was focused on the pathology in her family. She had never thought of examining her extended family's strengths or using them as a resource. Both Ellen and Lorraine were young enough to be her daughters. Miriam, the first to volunteer, presented generalized goals in an anxious, rambling manner, describing psychoses and cutoffs in her family. I tactfully but firmly kept her on course.

During rounds in the second session, Miriam said she felt embarrassed, acknowledging her anxiety and verbosity the time before. By the third session she was clearer and more focused, admitting that this was the first group she had ever been in. She told us that when she had spoken of her embarrassment the time before, she had felt accepted and understood. By the fourth session Miriam's extended family was becoming alive for her as she visited, wrote letters, and planned to attend a reunion. She was seeing the strengths in her father's family and realized how she had automatically disregarded his family because her mother had not considered them important.

I discovered, when reading the questionnaires, that much of the process had gone on internally. Ellen described her reaction to Miriam and then her change with her mother:

"Most significant was an argument with someone (Miriam) to whom I had a negative transference. No one rescued me, no one criticized or blamed me; I was left to deal with my feelings in and out of the group and I survived the experience and felt stronger. Then, later, I heard some accepting and educative statements made by this same woman which opened me up to hearing and considering certain feelings and points of view that were/are very helpful to me in my work with my mother.

"With my mother, the relationship is now more negative or, rather, more real, with more negative feelings beings expressed. I have more confidence in my ability to survive negative expression about self. I see my mother as slightly less powerful."

Miriam reported her reactions to Lorraine, another woman in the group:

"Most significant was my change from an initial negative reaction to Lorraine to a warm and loving one. I appreciated her feedback to me and positive response which 'validated' me as a mother who couldn't get through to her 'frozen' daughter. Her negativism to her mother paralleled that of my daughter toward me, though for different reasons. It was significant because my transference to her as an oldest daughter-surrogate facilitated my confidence that I could get close to and become more intimate with my oldest daughter — which did happen three months later."

Miriam described the breakthrough with her oldest daughter three months after the final meeting of the group:

"A most significant event was the marriage of our middle daughter. She was ambivalent about having a wedding vs going to the justice of the peace. The seminar convinced me of the importance of a wedding (neither we nor our oldest daughter had had one). I pressed for a small family wedding; it occurred and was the beginning of a positive change in my relationship with my husband. My oldest daughter came home for the week and I was able to talk to her about intimate issues we were not able to discuss before. I feel closer to her than I have in ages and see her more clearly as my daughter (not as a mother or older sister)."

Miriam wrote of her competition and change in relation to myself as leader, who was close to her age, and the parallel changes she made with her sister:

"I initially felt quite competitive with the leader. I admired and respected her. She had done many things I had done, but in this situation, she was in charge of me, which is what my sister had always been. Her obvious confidence in her role as leader helped me to resolve this without her making an issue of my behavior. I felt relaxed and a genuine group member by the last session.

"Most of my work has been in the relationship with my sister. We are peers, now, but in the past I was required to be the dependent little sister. The impact of our new-found intimacy and role change is that I have better (less competitive) relationships with peers, and clearer differentiation with my daughters."

Throughout the group there were many meaningful mother/daughter interactions and discussions, including one woman talking to her mother in an empty chair. Not all members, however, are able to utilize the group to identify and understand their transference reactions. Donna was not significantly affected by the other members' focus on mother/daughter issues. She ended up disappointed, still seeing her mother as causing her negative feelings, and the group not providing enough insight:

> "I am frustrated because I still do not understand why my mother makes remarks that cause such a negative reaction in me. I want to respond more positively and handle my negative feelings better but I did not gain enough insight from the course and I am still groping. This was the thing most important to me, and while I learned some positives, I thought there would be much more."

Donna's disappointment could also have been, in part, a transference reaction to either myself or Miriam which she was, as yet, unable to identify and learn from. Lorraine wrote to me four years later when she identified her own transference reactions after reading this segment for the book. Her comments throw some light both on her own view and on Donna's possible situation:

> "I remember what you write about quite well. I found Miriam's rambling painful (is this how my mother might be in a group?) — I wanted you to *more* firmly keep her on course (who can control my mother for me?) — I am trying to decide if I should identify with Lorraine (I used the 'frozen' label) or Donna (because I recall my frustration with the workshop). If Donna, I needed to rage at Miriam (at my mother) and couldn't/wouldn't. At the end of the group I remember feeling pleased for Miriam and the progress she had made, but *still* embarrassed by her — and I guess I find that there are times when my mother is self-revealing that I am embarrassed by her.
> "I am just tonight identifying my negative transference to Miriam and thinking that perhaps my way of coping with it was to freeze myself so that nothing could come in (did not gain enough insight) or go out (rage)."

REPORTED FOCUS SHIFT

Most participants come into the group centered on themselves and their family of origin issues. Only 2% of 584 written goals and issues related to the group or the group process. As each group continued, however, the focus shifted to include observation of and participation in the work of others and to learning from the process of the group itself.

Thus, in the post-questionnaires, the group assumed more importance. When asked, "What else did you accomplish that you did not list originally as goals or issues?", 19% of the 316 items centered on the group. In answer to the question, "What was the most significant event in the group that happened to you personally?", 24% of 136 items were focused on the individual's experience with group members. When asked, "Of the following methods of work, which had impact for you as you worked on your goals and issues?", 98% reported positive impact to feedback from the group; 99% reported positive impact to group discussion; and 97% reported positive impact to watching others work.

Although participants come into the group focused on themselves and their families of origin, powerful interactions occur with other members which increase their interpersonal learning and their self-understanding. When the leader is aware of and able to use his own interface issues effectively, additional learning from the group itself becomes possible. Shared themes can create a common bond, encouraging more openness, and thus increasing the possibility for understanding and change.

CHAPTER 16

Developmental Stages: The Individual and the Group

When I work with individuals in a group, I am aware of individual developmental issues as well as family transitional stages. Erikson's (1963) eight ages of man is a conceptual schema that describes the process of the child's development as well as the stages of an individual's life. All of us go through the stages Erikson describes, with each stage building on the stage before and preparing for those stages to follow. All families must cope with unpredictable external forces and transgenerational trauma, which combine to give rise to the patterns and rules that influence the way the family member developed during the childhood years. The gaps in her developmental learning, based on her unique experience in her family, follow her into adulthood to become the interface issues that are the subject of this book.

Erikson's schema forms a cyclical, developmental spiral, connecting a member of one generation to a member of the next. Although his epigenetic chart is linear, his thinking is at least in part systemic as he quotes Webster's Dictionary to connect the first stage with the last, noting that

> Trust (the first of our ego values) is here defined as "the assured reliance on another's integrity," the last of our values. . . . And it seems possible to further paraphrase the relation of adult integrity and infantile trust by saying that healthy children will not fear life if their elders have integrity enough not to fear death. (1963, p. 269)

We are used to connecting parts of our lives to other parts that have meaning for us. In describing his first stage, Basic Trust vs. Mistrust, Erikson (1963) wrote:

> Parents must . . . be able to represent to the child a deep, an almost somatic conviction that there is a meaning to what they are doing. (p. 249)

The subject of the group — differentiation from family of origin — carries that kind of meaning. As parents demonstrate to the child a belief in the meaning of their actions, so also the adult child has reason to express to the parent the meaning that differentiation holds, so that an adult-to-adult connection may be fostered.

The group can provide a safe arena with both the controls and freedom that foster such tasks, paralleling the controls and freedom in a nurturing family. In those groups where participants share common themes, the group can become an alternate family for a short space of time, in which unsaid thoughts can be spoken and untried actions can be practiced. Members can rework in the group a developmental stage that had never been resolved, as a preliminary to resolving that stage with actual family members.

When the group (family) context provides enough trust (Stage 1), then individuals can move at their own pace (Stage 2), to take initiative (Stage 3) to apply themselves to their goals (Stage 4). They can clarify their identities (Stage 5), explore difficulties with intimacy (Stage 6), focus on transgenerational issues (Stage 7), or deal with the way they accept their own finite life cycle (Stage 8). Descriptions of the life stages follow, with examples from participants' questionnaires.

BASIC TRUST VS. BASIC MISTRUST

Trust, which forms the basis for the child's sense of identity, is a mutual and interactive process between the baby and parent. Consistent nurturing over time provides a connection between the baby's inner experience and the outer world. Group members, in the same way, need to feel safe and supported in the group before they can risk exposing their inner concerns.

The adult child needs to convey to her parent that there is meaning to the changes she is making on her own behalf, just as the leader conveys to group members her convictions about the importance of interface change. A cautious man, who did not trust easily, decided to risk in the group and then was able to risk changing his behavior with his enmeshed parents:

> "Most significant was my internal recognition that I would need to expose myself in spite of lack of trust in peers if I was to gain what I wanted from the experience. I particularly mistrusted one group member and felt much of what she did was inappropriate. It was significant because it runs against my cautious style. I felt I trusted myself and the leader to handle whatever came up.

"The group helped me recognize the merger of my parents and my difficulty relating to each separately. Each has spent time with me, if only on a long walk. Both have begun letting me call and talk separately with them. I am also hearing each express a wish for time apart. I have increased sympathy, tolerance, understanding of Mother. My anger at her for her manipulation and 'depression' has subsided. My search for my roots opened up my mother's interest in her family and she has begun contacting them. It's been very gratifying to watch her interest grow — like a part of her has been reclaimed. I had Father help me work on my summer cabin. We are beginning to experience the specialness of our relationship, especially since his stroke."

AUTONOMY VS. SHAME AND DOUBT

The child is caught between holding on and letting go, needing firm and comforting parental control so that she does not scare self by her own untested feelings. If not allowed the gradually expanding experience of her own free choice, she may obsessively repeat what she has learned; if undercontrolled and not firmly reassured, she doubts self and feels exposed. The group also needs firm outer control, at first, so there can be freedom within. Members need to decide their own pace, and experiment with how far they want to go. The leader must see that no one is forced to do anything against their will; that no one "loses face."

One woman used the group for a rehearsal, testing herself and increasing her autonomy by revealing her doubts. After this experience, she was able to also share her doubts with her family members:

"The most significant event was letting myself expose all my anxiety initially, particularly my continuous questioning and demandingness of myself professionally. I was concerned that if I exposed myself, the group members would not respect my work. Instead I felt respected and appreciated. I'm starting to share with Mother, Father, and my brothers some of my self-doubts and the fact that I don't want to continue to always present myself as having no problems professionally. I have begun to give myself permission to be a beginner as a consultant — this has been and continues to be a difficult process."

INITIATIVE VS. GUILT

When the child feels protected and able to move freely in her family, she is then ready to take initiative with others, including identification with the same-sex parent and competition for the opposite-sex parent. If she is overregulated, she will not feel pleasure in her energy as she charges ahead; if she reaches this stage without enough regulation, she will feel guilty and overregulate herself. In the group, members take initiative for themselves, volunteering to work. I caution them to go slow and to not take the first step until they have thought through the consequences of that step and the next one and are prepared to follow through. I underline that, although they cannot change the other, they have the right to decide what they need to do for themselves and to take responsibility for their moves.

One woman, whose parents had divorced when she was ten, had remained loyal to her mother and cut off from her father. Although she felt vulnerable in sharing with the group, when she took the initiative and contacted her father, it changed her family system and modified her feelings of guilt. She wrote:

"I experienced tremendous vulnerability in telling the group about my relationship with my father. I experienced wanting to take in and receive support vs. trusting/not trusting that it was OK to share. My experience of my father was that he was a 'stranger' to me. Since that time I've developed a continuing relationship with him, shared old painful feelings and, most important, I've been able to take in that he does care for and love me.

"With Mother I've come to separate my projections of so many, many people as being directly related to her. I have come to see 'my mother' in myself. During the time of the workshop I described my mother as critical, overresponsible, defensive, and hiding feelings with a defense of 'I'm competent' and 'I'm strong.' As I reviewed the list, I was struck with more negative responses than positive. Presently, this surprises me. And then I realize I have reclaimed and owned many of the above as my own and 'what I do to me.' I see myself as more separate from my mother, have been able to share with her my anger and hurt about not knowing my father, and presently share my feelings which I currently experience with my father — with her.

"In the past I felt some guilt over getting to know 'Dad.' Now I've reowned my birthright and sense of who are my parents. With client families, I appreciate and understand more fully the impact of 'mothers and fathers' on children's lives."

INDUSTRY VS. INFERIORITY

As the child is ready for the give-and-take world of play and school, she begins to apply self to more structured skills of learning and social interaction. The danger lies in her not being prepared and feeling inferior to the tasks she or others set for her. The group is task-oriented, a place to learn important therapeutic and personal skills where participants can also have the experience of being productive group members. There is a back-and-forth movement between group and home, with members developing strategies, moving out to put them into action, back into the group for further input, and then out again to test their plans in reality.

Laura's problems at home were hindering her at work, where she was feeling the same inadequacy that she had felt in her original family. In making a plan and carrying it out, she began to feel effective in both settings. Laura's primary goal was to explore why, at various points with clients, especially when nothing was being said or there was conflict, she became numb. She related this to the same feeling she had experienced with her family of origin. Laura was the fourth of six children, caught in a triangle between her mother and her oldest brother Sam, and isolated from her father. She decided to tell Sam that she did not want to be in the middle anymore and to write her mother saying she loved her, but also loved Sam, and did not want to hear negatives about Sam from her mother.

Two months later she had changed both relationships and found herself not feeling as numb. We talked about her next steps. She had always tried to please Sam; not doing anything at all would be a change. She was beginning to see that the moves were up to her. She also planned to contact two sisters to whom she felt inadequate. Laura reported three most significant events:

1) "I began to see myself as an equal person with my family of origin for the first time. Having a talk with my mother through gestalt work — then being able to tell her I loved her. Being able to perceive myself as adequate and good and competent instead of the underdog has been a tremendous help."

2) "The sculpture done with another group member in which various parts of her life were given form and she role played her life in miniature in front of us was significant because it reminded me of myself and how I sometimes trap myself with too much 'busy-ness.' It helped me reflect on how I want to spend my time and what is important to me. I became more organized instead of devoting so much time to my inner anxiety."

3) "The leader's response to my statement that various members of my family intimidate me. She switched it around: 'You allow them to intimidate you.' Her comment helped me to feel in control of myself. I became more comfortable and relaxed with myself, not so anxious inside."

Laura reported changes in the following interfaces:

With mother: "I am now feeling freer to disagree with her and give her support without paralleling her behavior."

With father: "For the first time in my life I have been able to hug my father."

With Sam: "I have been able to see Sam in a new light. I still love him and respect his opinion, but I don't need his approval in order to feel good about myself."

With client families: "I no longer become numb in the face of conflict. Before, I had a tendency to become aligned with one client or the other. I am much more comfortable in de-triangulating myself, which is a relief to me and a help to my clients. And I don't feel as panicky or as responsible for clients' problems or whether or not they always respond to me."

IDENTITY VS. ROLE CONFUSION

Adolescence is a time when all that has come before is questioned and there is apprehension about the fit between how the young person feels on the inside and how she appears to others. The identity search includes coming to terms with earlier idealized images of parents and with occupational choice. The problem is role confusion, sometimes sexual, but often in terms of occupational identity.

One woman, who felt herself validated in the group, experienced sadness in accepting the loss of her idealization of her family. In her search for self-definition, she re-committed herself as a family therapist. She wrote:

"Just being there and sharing with others at increasingly deeper levels of awareness—I felt like all the unexpressed parts of me were valid—that I existed at levels deeper than what I thought possible. I began to care about developing and integrating other aspects of my personality. I began to truly see that the differentiation process is lifelong and feel accepting about that.

"Principally the headwork was helpful—the thinking through of family patterns by charting and deciphering scripting were extremely relevant to my learning about myself. I'm learning that the sadness I've felt within me for a long time is the sadness of knowledge that my family is limited emotionally and intellectually—at times in my youth, severely so. Now, they 'try' to accept me and I'm trying to understand what it was that went wrong—with them and myself—so that I can be more accepting of what there is to get from my family now.

"My career 'crisis' stemmed from a need for greater self-definition. I think, even though I've been undecided regarding where I 'fit' in relation to my career choice, I now feel better about continuing my commitment as a family therapist. I'm approaching a place within myself where I truly like myself—maybe I can relax a little and fight less in behalf of that self."

INTIMACY VS. ISOLATION

Following the search for identity, the young adult is ready to join with a partner and taste the joys of intimacy. The danger is that they will either merge with each other or remain distant and isolated. Intimacy is experienced in the group by members who, when they are able to speak openly, find themselves accepted and validated. A common goal is to learn to regulate closeness and distance with original family members. Such regulation includes transferring primary loyalty from parent to spouse at the time of marriage.

One woman described how she contributed to her dependent relationship with her mother, which kept her from enjoying intimacy with her husband:

"The most significant event was discovering why I close myself off from my husband. He used to complain about my coldness. I knew I became that way but I did not realize it was because I was more hooked into my mother than I was to him. I became aware of how my mother uses money to keep me hooked and my part in allowing, enabling, and making her do that, and how my passivity enables her to take more control. With my mother, I am beginning to take some control and take care of my needs. I have put my husband over my mother. I am learning to stop her when I don't want to hear what she has to say.

"With my husband, I am allowing myself to feel totally close to him, not hooking him into being the perfect son-in-law, and not hooking him into feeling *my* anger at my family of origin. Since I changed, our relationship has doubled in satisfaction."

GENERATIVITY VS. STAGNATION

The stage of generativity encompasses the producing and nurturing of children, as well as the development of a more equal and balanced relationship with aging parents. There can be peer interchange between generations, with older parents learning from their adult children, as well as children learning from their parents. Such transgenerational openness paves the way for productivity and creativity in all three generations. As the older parents continue to age, the way is eased for the reversal of generations. If the generations remain emotionally isolated, stagnation is likely to occur. The group is, by definition, focused on transgenerational patterns and the ways enmeshed and cutoff members can reconnect so that they can enjoy and pass on to future generations more productive ways of relating.

Harry's primary goal was to examine issues related to his father's marginal role in the family. When he was 18, Harry had known his father was not taking care of himself, but he had not known how seriously ill he was. In reenacting with an empty chair a conversation with his father a few months before his father died, Harry realized how he had contributed to their isolation from each other. After this conversation, Harry realized there was a man currently in his life who was like his father and that he avoided him. He decided to get to know him better. He recognized that he had never been willing to get close to or take from men who could be his mentors in his academic community. He described the most significant event:

> "The leader used an empty chair exercise to help me recreate a conversation with my father in which he distanced himself from me and I had felt helpless to bridge the gap and get closer to him. In that conversation, my father had first congratulated me on an academic award, then pointed out how my intelligence made me resemble my mother more than I resembled him; in the same breath, he exclaimed how difficult it was for my mother and him to communicate with each other. The empty chair exercise helped me to realize how the encounter with my father (and other encounters like it) could have had a different outcome; how I shared responsibility for its outcome (rather than just being a victim of my father's withdrawal) and how I might handle such isolation in current life situations. Though I don't want to exaggerate the impact of that one exercise, it had lasting effects."

He reported changes in the following interfaces:

With mother: "Coinciding with my participation in the seminar was my mother's major move into a small apartment, becoming more independent of me and my sister, becoming more socially active, retiring from work and (later in the year) remarrying (following 18 years of being a widow). I have felt a greater affinity with her and, at this time, greater objectivity. I believe that dealing as I did during the seminar with my part in the father (isolated)-mother (overinvolved)-child (me) triad actually freed me up to recognize and enjoy those aspects of my mother's values and style of relating with which I have always identified. She supported me in quitting a good but high pressure job and she shared with me more openly than ever before some core, nonconformist attitudes and early experiences of her own."

With son: "I used the seminar primarily to examine issues of father as emotional outsider in the family process. Simultaneously, however, I'm involving myself in my son's life in new ways. This was a decision my wife and I were making, but being in the seminar helped me develop new ways of talking to both my kids. They both also became more outspoken in making emotional demands on me during the past few months."

With client families: "I've developed improved judgment about timing — *when* to pursue family of origin issues — as a result of greater current comfort and grasp of the subject."

EGO INTEGRITY VS. DESPAIR

Acceptance of one's own finite life cycle and its place in the transgenerational continuum allows one to accept life's order and meaning and also the inevitability of death. Lack of acceptance carries a sense of powerlessness or resignation and a fear of death. The acceptance by the group of all members and their struggles helps them accept themselves, which allows them to accept their parents as they are — as fallible human beings. When one accepts one's family heritage, one can then begin recognizing strengths that have been there all along. As the group ends, in addition to reviewing their goals, members often talk of ways to integrate the various parts of their lives into a more harmonious whole.

William's extended family all lived close together in a closed system with "family" coming first and in-laws only marginally accepted. William, who was unmarried, had been moving away bit by bit — at the time of the seminar he was living 25 miles from home. Many family members had died young, including one possible suicide; they avoided talking to each other about their grief in order to protect each other.

The group coincided with the first anniversary of William's father's death and also with William's graduation from the Two-year Training Program. William was able to talk about his father's death in the group and also to recognize termination issues involved in leaving the Program. He was able to see his family more objectively, observing that they did not relax, have fun, or go on vacations. My image was of a clan huddled together, waiting for death. William was able to see the "living death" both he and his family immersed themselves in, and began to try out new roles with family members, friends, and client families. He wrote:

"The most significant event was when I started to realize the roles that death and responsibility played in my family because I had a tendency to feel depressed and burned out. I felt that it was my 'responsibility' to take on additional roles. I also felt that life was 'dead' serious. With the feedback from the group about getting in touch with people who are better models for me in having fun, I became more aware of the serious and overresponsible positions that I place myself in, like my parents did, and how much of a caretaker I have become. Now, I feel more of a sense of choice, not taking on additional responsibilities and not feeling guilty, as well as learning to have fun."

William reported changes in the following interfaces:

With mother: "I am feeling less responsible towards my mother and more confident that she can handle her life, even though my father died. She can ask me if she needs help."

With father (who died a year ago): "I feel more understanding knowing my father's overresponsible role, rather than feeling cheated out of his life."

With intimate other: "Although I am not quite in an 'intimate' stage, I am more open and willing to have relationships with women, feeling less of a sense of burden trying to please, and am becoming more fun-loving."

With client families: "I still have difficulty with families with mourning issues, but I am more aware of my interface and I am improving in working with them. I have less difficulty dealing with depressed and/or sad client family members; I feel less burden and responsibility and place more on them. I am starting to play and have some fun and humor in my family sessions instead of dead seriousness."

Developmental life stages of individuals in the family and of the family system itself are interwoven. Successive phases of the life cycle compel families to experience new stages, offering members continuing occasions for change and growth. There is a cyclical movement through the stages, with the family's emotional balance subject to interruption by developmental changes. Difficulties emerge when the family is unsuccessful in moving in an expedient way through these natural family crises. Symptoms and anxiety are most likely to occur when the members have difficulty bridging the transition.

The gaps in children's developmental learning, based on their singular experiences in their families, accompany them into adulthood. As the group is able to provide meaning and safety, it can become a shared arena in which developmental impasses from earlier life stages can be identified, allowing group members to rework such experiences currently with their family members and move on in their lives and as therapists.

CHAPTER 17

Transfer of Learning Between Interfaces

When I presented preliminary findings from this study at a Research Conference sponsored by the Center for Family Studies in 1982, Lyman Wynne commented that this was an unknown type of work and a pioneering effort, formulated according to isomorphic principles. His recommendation was that I pin down the connectedness by thinking more about how what is learned in one context can be passed into another.

The transfer of learning from one context to another is an acquired skill which the baby learns from parents and siblings and then transfers to play with other children and adults. The cycle continues, with learning transferred from home to school and back again, and from school to work, to nuclear family, etc., in a spiraling fashion. Dysfunctional as well as functional patterns are transferred and may continue to affect family relationships into succeeding generations. The problem is not so much how to transfer learning, but how functional transfer becomes blocked so that, in specific areas, new learning does not occur and old cyclical patterns repeat themselves in the new situations. One member described how the reenactment in the group of such a transfer allowed her to free herself and her son from continuing to replay her earlier dysfunctional relationship with her sister:

"I role played myself as a child with my younger sister and family of origin and then role played myself with my son and the rest of my nuclear family. Although I had had an intellectual understanding of my transfer of feelings of being 'crowded' and clung to and bothered from my younger sister to my oldest child, the roleplay made me viscerally aware of my feelings, how angry and helpless I felt, and how much I confused the two relationships. Both relationships have subsequently improved greatly."

The reenactment, in a changed context (the group), of her "crowded" feelings from onset time in childhood allowed her to subsequently bring the relationship with her sister up-to-date in adult-to-adult interaction and thus separate it from the relationship with her son.

Since children go through developmental stages in their families, how each child masters these stages becomes part of that family's developmental process, affected by and affecting both the events and the emotional tone at any particular time. Decisions made as children or adolescents also play into each family's cyclical process. Since members learned how to learn in their original families, their family's perspective colors their subsequent relationships, limiting the way they view their world and thus the choices available to them.

When a family member is able to change his attitude or behavior as an adult and move towards differentiation in his original family, his attitude or behavior towards other aspects of his life that were linked to those original attitudes or actions in his family are then also available for change. One woman described her awareness of this process operating in therapy:

"As I have seen how my sisters and I interact, I have become more aware of how members within families that I work with are interacting, i.e., as the fog 'lifts,' or I change, I feel that my perception and effectiveness with families increase to the same degree."

A shift in perception may happen over time or suddenly, as with one man who worked with adolescents in an agency. He succinctly described his shift in thinking:

"In the family of origin sculpture I realized the powerful-confronting position I had in my family (not a victim), and suddenly began seeing adolescents as having too much control and parents not enough. If I sense myself getting into a battle with a parent for control, now I back off; before, I would move ahead."

Such seemingly spontaneous transfer of change does not just happen; the individual's readiness, the context of the group, and the intervention allow it to occur. When identified attitudes or behaviors are amenable to change within the group, they can then be tested out in a transfer to other interfaces. I believe that transfers to family of origin are most likely to anchor the change.

THE GROUP AS CONTEXT

The setting of the group is where the process begins which allows for transfer of learning. The interfacing aspects of the Time Cable (see p. 261) are present in the group, providing challenge and support: Group members combine shared professional backgrounds with the common task of changing in their original families. All have some degree of competence in feedback. There is the opportunity to compare one's unique view of the world with others' world views through both observation and discussion, and to discover how others, as well as self, are caught up in automatic patterns that limit choice. It is possible, in the group, to try on a new attitude for size, as one goes shopping and tries on dresses or suits. One may try a reframe, grasp an unfamiliar concept such as the need to talk to family members one-on-one, or find ways to say "no" to members and still maintain contact.

The first few "pieces of work" in the group are extremely important, since they set the stage for the series of meetings. The group needs at least one motivated risk-taking member with a specific goal, and I, as the leader, need to develop rapport with this volunteer and find a mutually acceptable intervention. Helen asked me to chart her family diagram so she could become aware of family patterns. She described her shift:

> "Looking at my own family role in relation to my mother's family of origin — in particular, her relationship with her sister — and my functioning as a conflict absorber in my parents' marriage was most significant. It validated for the first time my intuitive experience of my family role and my perceptions of my experience — which helps me feel less crazy. It begins to explode a painful myth for myself that I would never be acceptable to anyone because of being fat. Helps me to take my decision re losing or not losing weight out of the arena of pleasing or not pleasing my parents and of being a prerequisite for love. Helps me begin to believe that I could be loveable. Very significant, in short."

If at least one of the first several pieces of work is thought-provoking and galvanizes the members' interest, the group is off and running. Other members can observe and learn that it is not only safe but also productive to try a new experiment. Such work may provide a shift in perspective, pointing to a change that can be made in another interface outside the group. The process, however, may unfold more slowly. Even though the volunteer may not immediately see value in his own work, it may strike a familiar chord in another member and begin a process for him which can then reverberate in later sessions back to the first volunteer.

The first change for some may be an attitudinal shift in which the member sees change in others like himself. "If he can do it, so can I" may be the first transfer. As others see a member develop a specific plan, they can decide which of their goals they want to pursue. As another member volunteers to work, he may be a self-starter like the person before him, he may have gained courage from the first one's success, or he may have been stimulated by a common family theme, which is already a transfer from the context of the first member's work to that of the second. As they learn from each other, the group members begin to extend their boundaries, developing intermember interfaces as they recognize their common issues. Irene was stimulated by Helen's work:

> "Hearing Helen talk about the impact of her parents on her self-esteem and on her accepting a self-defeating role in her family of origin was the most significant event, because the projection process she described from her parents to her, and her struggle to achieve her own autonomous identity, had meaning for me in relation to my own children and my messages in relation to their individuation."

As the members who worked in the first session report on the effects of their work in rounds in the second session, then others can begin to see the process in action. As the changes in the group impact on the members' systems outside the group, an awareness grows of the interconnections of the process.

FROM ONE CONTEXT TO ANOTHER

Bowen (1978a) has written about the application of differentiation precepts to other interfaces. He states that "differentiation of self principles apply in all areas of relationships whether it be within the family or in social or work relationships" (p. 461). Yet Bowen does not deal with group process, focusing exclusively on the trainee's role in his own family system. I believe, in contrast, that attention to group process is compatible with a focus on differentiation in family of origin and that Bowen, in not allowing the process to emerge in his groups, ignores an important area for transfer of change.

Beck (1982) has written of his attempts to integrate family of origin changes outside the group with the group process inside:

> If separation-individuation is our ultimate goal . . . it stands to reason that the process of change can only be enhanced by a structure that allows for movement towards individuation. . . . The group, a dynamic labora-

tory for change, provides the ideal structure for experimentation and, later, application to the outside. (pp. 233–234)

Yalom (1970) views the interpersonal properties of the group as giving it a unique power for change. His concept of the social microcosm is bi-directional:

> . . . not only does outside behavior become manifest in the group, but behavior learned in the group is eventually carried over into the patient's social environment and alterations appear in his interpersonal behavior outside the group. Gradually an *adaptive spiral* is set into motion, at first inside and then outside the group."

When members can learn to transfer such change from the group to their original family and then into other interfaces, there is increased possibility that the adaptive spiral will continue and will influence their lives when the group is no longer meeting.

Factors that Increase the Transfer of Learning

I. Subject: Focus on a subject with universal meaning: differentiation in family of origin qualifies as such a subject.
II. Format for Intervention:
   A. A structure providing safety/support and stimulation
   B. Group of peers with similar professional backgrounds encourages:
      1) a high level of pertinent feedback
      2) learning about functional and dysfunctional patterns in own family of origin
      3) parallel learning about all families, which is applicable to client families
   C. Emphasis on self-responsibility and self motivation by:
      1) voluntary commitment to join the group
      2) formulation of specific goals by each member
      3) agenda arrived at by group consensus, with members requesting time
      4) time-limited format requiring consensual agreement when more members want to work than there is time
      5) variety of methods and roleplayers available for addressing an issue, with a format to be arrived at by group member/leader
III. Intervention:
   A. Process of intervention by focusing on:
      1) current situation: what is the current impasse?

    2) past patterns relevant to current situation: identifying other ways of viewing the situation

    3) current plans for future change: how can the member change attitude/behavior to test out in family of origin new ways of viewing the situation?

    4) application of personal changes to work with client families

B. Intervention encourages deutero-learning, with focus on:

    1) how a group member's world view reflects the original family's world view; then broadening the perspective and reframing so that multiple realities can be explored

    2) making sense out of sequences of behavior or events by finding patterns of a higher order in the family of origin

Interface Changes Identified

Post-questionnaires from Therapist's Own Family Groups provide information on changes made with their original families, with nuclear families, and in therapy. The specific items clustered into six categories (Table 5), the first four of which have relevance in the transfer of learning between interfaces:

- Changing the relationship through action, including sharing thoughts and feelings
- Establishing clearer limits
- Accepting family member(s)
- Becoming aware of different thoughts and feelings not had before

In many situations, when a group member makes a change with a member of his family of origin, he also reports being able to handle the same issue with client families. For example, when Henry (p. 295) realized in the group that he was giving his power to his parents rather than placing that responsibility on himself, he recognized it as a major turning point in his life. He reported that, as he claimed his own power, his father began to accept him as a knowledgeable peer. He also reported not getting into as many power struggles with his clients to prove himself. Numerous such examples have been described throughout Section III of this book.

Changing Through Action

The largest number (50%) of changes reported were with original family members in the cluster, *Changing relationship through action, including sharing thoughts and feelings.* One woman described how her change affected her family:

TABLE 5
Interface Changes Based on Impact of the Group

Clusters of Items Describing Impact	With Original Family Member	With Nuclear Family Member Intimate Other	With Client Family Members
No. of Items	344	180	195
Changing relationship through action, including sharing thoughts and feelings	50%	29%	18%
Establishing clearer limits	13%	29%	18%
Accepting family member(s)	15%	19%	4%
Becoming aware of different thoughts and feelings not had before	14%	19%	35%
Identifying a situation although not ready to change	8%	4%	2%
Improved techniques			23%
	100%	100%	100%

"I have changed my attitude towards my oldest brother and his role as scapegoat; consequently, other family members are doing the same and I have already seen a change in the system. I feel really good about my family's willingness to change."

There was a lesser, but still substantial, change with nuclear family (29%) in the above cluster. One woman described the transfer from her work with family of origin to her change with her husband:

"Because I've been feeling a 'freeing' separation from my family of origin, I find I have become more in touch with my 'womanly' (grown-up) side. This has brought my husband and me closer; I find he is a friend now. When I am sad about my family of origin, I can own this openly and don't displace into our relationship."

A number of participants noted three-generational patterns, with linkages from grandparent to parent to child:

"Experiencing my 'part' in what happened between my mother and myself in an empty chair communication gave me a better understanding of my mother, and me as her daughter. I do have the feeling now that I am a person and not only a daughter and we can relate on that basis. During the group discussion I saw how I manipulate my daughter so that she is doing the same as me. It was significant because I have to get frustrated with myself and not with my daughter. That freed both of us and the manipulation is gone."

The category, *Establishing clearer limits*, was larger for nuclear families (29%) than for either original or client families. Clearer boundary setting for a child by the middle generation often follows a shift in attitude towards or behavior with original family members. A woman, who was angry with and distant from both her parents, did a gestalt with her father in an empty chair and realized that her wish to have him change his *past* way of behaving was unfulfillable and unfair. This work with her father tied in with one of her goals: "As a therapist, identifying with rebellious teenagers, not parents." In seeing the parallel between her anger at and unrealistic expectations of her father and her identification with rebellious teenagers, she also saw a need to change her relationship with her oldest daughter:

> "I am clearer about the need to set clear, simple limits on her behavior, use pat formulas and phrases if necessary, and not engage in long conversations, explanations, and arguments with her. I see that guilt keeps me relating to her in situations where walking away would be most caring."

Correcting Attitudinal Distortions

When group members correct attitudinal distortions about original family, they increase their ability to change, irrespective of other people's changes. Such learning can also translate directly into increased therapeutic competency as the member frees self from similar distortions with client families.

The category, *Accepting family members*, was also larger for nuclear families (19%) than for either original or client families. I make a distinction between the words *approval* and *acceptance* as a way of relating to family members. Approval carries with it an aspect of admiration and the right to judge. Acceptance is a less loaded word and means receiving as adequate or satisfactory. The word acceptance, when used by an observing family member, acknowledges the reality of other adult members' needs and wants and their responsibility for their own actions. One may not approve of what one cannot change, but one can accept it.

Lawrence, who was angry with and dependent on his mother, talked to her in person after he had rehearsed a conversation with her in an empty chair, receiving feedback from the group. As he was able to relax with and enjoy her in the months following that first talk, he found himself changing with his nuclear family:

"I am markedly less intrusive and controlling of the children (also my wife) and expect them to be more accountable for their own behavior. This gives my wife and me much more time and energy for ourselves."

Lawrence described his change with his college-age son in moving from a stance of trying to control him to accepting what he could not control. This paralleled his movement with his mother to a more independent and self-controlled position. As Lawrence backed off, he left his son alone to face himself, instead of fighting his father:

"I have finally gotten it clear to myself that his behavior is in his hands and not mine. I feel a certain emptiness about this but also a certain calmness. He, on the other hand, seems quite a bit more anxious and on edge —but a little less depressed. He is definitely doing much less drugs."

Group members identified *Becoming aware of different thoughts and feelings* as the largest cluster of improvement in their therapy with client families (35%). The connection can be understood: changes made in original families freed them to become aware of parallel processes in the families they were treating. Lawrence described the changes for him, which paralleled those with his mother and with his nuclear family:

"I see client interaction more objectively and am more aware of what is going on. I am, thus, better at maintaining a neutral stance and not taking sides. I am not as emotionally involved; I feel less need to solve clients' problems for them."

Transfer to the Work Setting

Some participants described how their changes had transferred into interfaces not identified in post questionnaires, such as their work situation and relationships with co-therapist, supervisor, or friend. The largest number of such transfers took place in the work setting. It is not unusual to have a participant rethink career goals when loyalties are freed up with original family members:

"Most significant was developing insight into how my choice and feelings about my career were related to loyalty to my father. Using the group to say goodbye to him (in the empty chair) and work through his death more completely allowed me to reconsider what career I want for myself and to finally bury my father and move on."

A participant who had been a caretaker in her original family found herself rethinking her role as a therapist:

"This sounds strange, but while I have unhooked from my overresponsible saving fantasy, I have also developed some feelings of resentment at the 'burden' of dealing daily with people's problems — a situation I've not encountered before. It's like a pendulum swinging — and I'm hoping that an interval of time will put me back in more comfortable balance."

When group members develop a growing ability to see themselves in their original families from a transgenerational point of view, a multifaceted perspective becomes possible, which allows the members to correct attitudinal distortions, reconnect in ways that allow them to retain their autonomy, and thus to feel and act more congruently, whether their family members change or not. Such learning and action translate directly into increased therapeutic competency.

There is an almost automatic release of energy when a person confronts a catastrophic expectation in the family of origin and moves beyond it. When tensions with the original family lessen, such family members find themselves freed to use their abilities and energies in creative ways that had not seemed possible before. The power of the family rules to keep members locked into old roles is matched by the strength individuals can reclaim for themselves when they stand up to their families and take responsible action based on their own convictions.

Changing Self with
Family of Origin:
A Checklist*

The following is a checklist of strategies for changing oneself in one's family of origin.

I. Become an astute observer of your family:
   A. Learn all the facts you can
      1) Emphasize who, what, when, where, and HOW, not why.
      2) Ask yourself questions, such as:
         a. Do you know and relate to all members in all branches of your family?
         b. Are you equally fair to all, including self?
         c. Do you accept all members, although not necessarily approving of what those members do?
   B. Become aware of:
      1) Your family process: the traumas, myths, patterns, rules, and binds.
      2) The part you play in the process — the myths you believe and the rules you follow — and decide, of those rules you follow, which ones you like and want to continue following and which ones you want to change.
II. Make a plan which can be implemented slowly in an ongoing campaign:
   A. Contacting members
      1) Contact family members on a one-to-one basis. When you spend time with your family in a group in its usual setting, there is a patterned way of relating which keeps a homeostatic

---

*Based on theoretical concepts of M. Bowen, M.D.

balance. When you meet with each member alone, you are less likely to become stuck in the patterns.

2) It is often easier to contact peripheral members first, to gather more information and gain a richer perspective on your origins, before making contact with central figures, especially if there are long-term cutoffs. It is most important, however, to develop a person-to-person relationship with each parent and sibling.

3) Any cutoff member in the extended family is very important, well worth getting to know and forming your own opinion about. A cutoff member is often one who broke the family rules, and knowing this person gives you important information. Also, it shakes up the rest of the system when you contact a cutoff member.

B. Letters, phone calls, visits

1) Writing letters can open up emotional issues from a distance. If you predict the response you expect in a letter, it may diffuse some of the intensity.

2) Writing to one parent at a time about one emotional issue can focus your effort. Then you can follow up in a visit.

3) Take responsibility for writing or calling, asking yourself if you are following dysfunctional patterns or saying honestly what you think and feel.

4) Initiate both the beginning and ending of phone calls.

5) Plan each visit, determining how long you will be able to relate without getting sucked back into destructive patterns.

III. Beginning of change:

A. Take an "I" position in the family

1) Take responsibility for and make clear statements about your own feelings, thoughts, and actions without blaming the other for the way you are.

2) Control your own emotional reactiveness. Stay between serious and humorous so that you can move either way, like the zoom lens on a video camera moves in to a close-up and out to observe the whole group.

3) Humor, fantasy, and the recognition of the absurd can be valuable allies in detoxifying tense situations.

4) Keep yourself detriangled in the family

a. Insist on one-to-one communication.

b. Avoid taking sides.

c. Avoid listening to negatives about a third person.

5) If you become locked into an emotional triangle with your parents:

    a. Move laterally and focus on others who are emotionally important to your parents in their generation — aunts and uncles.

    b. Move vertically and focus on those in the generations above and below your parents (i.e., your grandparents, great uncles and aunts, or your siblings or cousins.)

    c. Connect with someone cut off from the family.

6) Find ways to communicate clearly and openly about matters which are barely or never referred to, making the covert overt. Secrets are often withheld or differentially shared, forming a boundary between the secret holder and the unaware family member which can perpetuate mystification and foster cutoffs.

7) Use your feelings as signals to yourself that you are getting sucked in when old feelings, such as anxiety, hurt and anger, surface.

8) Take advantage of birth, marriage, divorce, illness and death as prime times for family contact. It is easier to change one's actions in the family when the family is in crisis or transition.

9) Be aware of the realignment of emotional forces following death, and how the family balance shifts to fill the void. This is a time when new emotional alliances can form or members may cut off, or those who have cut off can rejoin the family.

B. Differentiation is a three-step process:

1) You make a differentiating move.

2) You expect opposition from the family togetherness forces.

3) You know what you will do in response to the opposition forces in the family so you are not taken by surprise.

If you keep on your own calm course, eventually the family members will give up their struggle and accept that "that's the way you are." At that point, another family member, following your example, may make a differentiating move.

C. Bowen's three rules for communication with family of origin:

1) Avoid counterattacking when provoked

2) Do not become defensive

3) Maintain an active relationship with other key members without withdrawing or becoming silent.

APPENDIX B

Post-Questionnaire:
The Therapist's Own
Family Seminar

TO: Date:

FROM: Jan Kramer

RE: Follow-up Evaluation of *The Therapist's Own Family Seminar*

This questionnaire is part of an evaluation of *The Therapist's Own Family Seminars* which have been held since January 1977. I hope you will be as candid as possible since your answers will have an effect on our plans for the future. For certain questions I have provided space for three answers (A, B, C or 1, 2, 3). If you have fewer, list what you have; if you have more, use the back of the page.

1. These are the goals and issues you listed at the beginning of the Seminar. (Mark 5-1 beside each goal or issue: 5 = Very satisfied; 4 = Somewhat satisfied; 3 = Neutral; 2 = Somewhat dissatisfied; 1 = Very dissatisfied).

2. What else did you accomplish which you didn't list originally as goals or issues?
   A.

   B.

   C.

3. A. What was the most significant event in the Seminar that happened to you personally?

330

B. Why was it significant?

4. Of the following methods of work in the group, which had impact for you as you worked on your goals and/or issues? (Mark 5-1 beside each method. 5 = Strong positive impact; 4 = Some positive impact; 3 = No impact; 2 = Some negative impact; 1 = Strong negative impact).

_____planning strategies for change

_____group discussion

_____working yourself

_____watching others work

_____feedback from group

_____charting family tree

_____becoming aware of patterns, alliances and cut-offs in own family system

_____rehearsal

_____sculpture

_____role-play

_____playing a part in another's sculpture or role playing

_____empty chair exercise

_____other (describe)

5. We define *interface issues*; how one's own family experiences influence the individual and vice versa, including connections one makes with members of one's family of origin, nuclear family, intimate other, with co-therapists and with client families.

A. How much impact has this Seminar had on your *understanding* of interface issues?

5	4	3	2	1
Strong positive impact	Some positive impact	No impact	Some negative impact	Strong negative impact

B. How much impact has this Seminar had on your *actions* in terms of interface issues?

5	4	3	2	1
Strong positive impact	Some positive impact	No impact	Some negative impact	Strong negative impact

6. A. How much impact has this Seminar had on your relationship with members of your family of origin?

5	4	3	2	1
Strong positive impact	Some positive impact	No impact	Some negative impact	Strong negative impact

B. List (in order of importance) each family of origin member you are changing your relationship with, and describe impact for you:

1)

2)

3)

7. A. How much impact has this Seminar had on your relationship with your nuclear family members or intimate other?

5	4	3	2	1
Strong positive impact	Some positive impact	No impact	Some negative impact	Strong negative impact

If no nuclear family or intimate other, check here

B. List (in order of importance) each nuclear family member you are changing your relationship with, and describe impact for you:

1)

2)

3)

8. A. Has this group improved/hindered your therapy with client families?

5	4	3	2	1
Greatly improved	Somewhat improved	Neutral	Somewhat hindered	Greatly hindered

B. In what ways?

1)

2)

3)

9. A. How did you like the format of the group you attended?

5	4	3	2	1
Strongly positive	Somewhat positive	Neutral	Somewhat negative	Strongly negative

B. Describe any changes you think would enhance the format.
1)

2)

3)

10. A. Give your reaction to the leader's facilitation of the Seminar:

5	4	3	2	1
Strongly positive	Somewhat positive	Neutral	Somewhat negative	Strongly negative

B. What specific things did the leader do which were facilitative?
1)

2)

3)

C. What specific things did the leader do which hindered?
1)

2)

3)

12. Give a global assessment of the experience.

5	4	3	2	1
Strong positive impact	Some positive impact	No impact	Some negative impact	Strong negative impact

13. Please add any other comments or suggestions on the back of the page.

Bibliography

Altshul, V. (1977). The so-called boring patient. *American Journal of Psychotherapy, 31*(4), 533–545.

Aponte, H. J. (1982). The person of the therapist: The cornerstone of therapy. *Family Therapy Networker*, Mar.–Apr., 19–46.

Armstrong, R. H. (1974). Reversals: Their care and feeding. In F. D. Andres & J. P. Lorio (Eds.), *Georgetown family symposia* (Vol. I) (pp. 136–148). Washington, D.C.: Georgetown Medical Center.

Bank, S., & Kahn, M. D. (1975). Sisterhood-brotherhood is powerful: Sibling subsystems and family therapy. *Family Process, 14*, 311–337.

Bank, S. P., & Kahn, M. D. (1982). *The sibling bond.* New York: Basic Books.

Bargo, M. (1977). Self-disclosure as a growth-inhibiting agent. *Voices, 13*(3), 53–54.

Barnett, J. (1971). Narcissism and dependency in the obsessional-hysteric marriage. *Family Process, 10*(1), 75–82.

Barnhill, L. R. (1979). Healthy family systems. *The Family Coordinator, 28*(1), 94–100.

Barnhill, L. R., & Longo, D. (1978). Fixation and regression in the family life cycle. *Family Process, 17*, 469–478.

Barwick, R. W., & Wepman, B. J. (1982). Siblings as healers. *Voices, 18*(1), 53–57.

Bateson, G. (1972). *Steps to an ecology of mind.* New York: Ballantine Books.

Bateson, G. (1976). Double bind, 1969. In C. Sluzki & D. Ransom (Eds.), *Double bind: The foundation of the communicational approach to the family.* New York: Grune & Stratton.

Bateson, G. (1979). *Mind and nature: A necessary unity.* New York: E. P. Dutton.

Beck, R. L. (1982). Process and content in the family-of-origin group. *Int J. Group Psychotherapy, 32*(2), 233–244.

Beisser, A. R. (1970). The paradoxical theory of change. In J. Fagan & I. L. Shepherd (Eds.), *Gestalt therapy now* (pp. 77–80). Palo Alto, CA: Science and Behavior Books.

Berger, M. (1982). The strategic use of "Bowenian" formulations. *The Journal of Strategic and Systemic Therapies, 1*(4), 50–56.

Bodin, A., & Ferber, A. (1973). How to go beyond the use of language. In A. Ferber, M. Mendelsohn, & A. Napier (Eds.), *The book of family therapy* (pp. 272–317). Boston: Houghton Mifflin.

Boszormenyi-Nagy, I., & Krasner, B. R. (1980). Trust-based therapy: A contextual approach. *American Journal of Psychiatry, 137*(7), 767–775.

Boszormenyi-Nagy, I., & Spark, G. (1973). *Invisible loyalties.* New York: Harper & Row.

Bowen, M. (1978a). *Family therapy in clinical practice.* New York: Jason Aronson.

Bowen, M. (1978b). Family reaction to death. In M. Bowen (Ed.), *Family therapy in clinical practice* (pp. 321–335). New York: Jason Aronson.

Bradt, J. O. (1980). *The family diagram: Method, technique and use in family therapy.* Washington, D.C.: Groome Center.

Braverman, S. (1982). Family of origin as a training resource for family therapists. *Canadian Journal of Psychiatry, 27,* 629–633.

Braverman, S. (1981). Family of origin: The view from the parents' side. *Family Process, 20,* 431–437.

Bregman, O. C., & Schur, T. J. (1976). Space and systems: A brief suggestion for a profound interface. In R. W. Manderscheid (Ed.), *Systems science and the future of health.* Washington, D.C.: Groome Center.

Cain, A. (1981). The role of the therapist in family systems therapy. In G. Berenson & H. White (Eds.), *Annual review of family therapy* (Vol. I). New York: Human Sciences Press.

Carter, E. A. (1978). Transgenerational scripts and nuclear family stress: Theory and clinical implications. In R. R. Sagar (Ed.), *Georgetown family symposia* (Vol. III). Washington, D.C.: Georgetown University Medical Center.

Carter, E. A., & McGoldrick, M. (Eds.). (1980). *The family life cycle.* New York: Gardner Press.

Carter, E. A., & Orfanidis, M. M. (1976). Family therapy with one person and the family therapist's own family. In P. Guerin (Ed.), *Family therapy* (pp. 193–219). New York: Gardner Press.

Caust, B. L., Libow, J. A., & Raskin, P. A. (1981). Challenges and promises of training women as family systems therapists. *Family Process, 20*(4).

Charny, I. W. (1972). Injustice and betrayal as natural experiences in family life. *Psychotherapy: Theory, Research and Practice, 9*(1), 86–91.

Christofori, R. H. (1978). Survival and the family of extinction. In R. R. Sagar (Ed.), *Georgetown family symposia* (Vol. III) (pp. 122–140). Washington, D.C.: Georgetown University Medical Center.

Constantine, L. (1978). Family sculpture and relationship mapping techniques. *Journal of Marriage and Family Counseling, 4*(2), 13–23.

Dell, P. F., & Appelbaum, A. S. (1977). Trigenerational enmeshment: Unresolved ties of single-parents to family of origin. *American Journal of Orthopsychiatry, 47*(1), 52–59.

Dies, R. (1977). Group therapist transparency: A critique of theory and research. *International Journal of Group Psychotherapy, 127*(2), 177–200.

Drye, R. C., Goulding, R. L., & Goulding, M. E. (1973). No-suicide decisions: Patient monitoring of suicidal risk. *American Journal of Psychiatry, 130*(2), 171–174.

Duhl, B. S. (1983). *From the inside out and other metaphors.* New York: Brunner/Mazel.

Duhl, F., Kantor, D., & Duhl, B. (1973). Learning, space, and action in family therapy: A primer of sculpture. *Seminars in Psychiatry, 5*(2), 167–183.

Erikson, E. H. (1963). *Childhood and society.* New York: W. W. Norton.

Feld, B. (1982). Countertransference in family therapy. *Group: The Journal of the Eastern Group Psychotherapy Society, 6*(4), 3–13.

Feldman, L. (1976). Depression and marital interaction. *Family Process, 15*(4), 389–395.

Ferber, A., Mendelsohn, M., & Napier, A. (1973). *The book of family therapy.* Boston: Houghton Mifflin.

Ferber, A., & Whitaker, C. (1973). The therapist's family, friends, and colleagues. In A. Ferber, M. Mendelsohn, & A. Napier, (Eds.), *The book of family therapy* (pp. 468–479). Boston: Houghton Mifflin.

Fogarty, T. (1975). Triangles. *The Family, 2*(2), 11–19.

Fisch, R., Weakland, J. H., & Segal, L. (1982). *The tactics of change.* San Francisco: Jossey-Bass.

Ford, F. R. (1983). Rules: The invisible family. *Family Process, 22*(2), 135-145.

Ford, F. R., & Herrick, J. (1973). Family rules: Family life styles. *American Journal of Orthopsychiatry, 44*(1), 61-69.

Framo, J. L. (1968). My families, my family. *Voices,* Fall, 18-27.

Framo, J. (1972). Symptoms from a family transactional viewpoint. In C. J. Sager & H. S. Kaplan (Eds.), *Progress in group and family therapy* (271-308). New York: Brunner/Mazel.

Framo, J. (1975). Personal reflections of a family therapist. *Journal of Marriage and Family Counseling, 1*(1), 15-28.

Framo, J. (1976). Family of origin as a therapeutic resource for adults in marital therapy: You can and should go home again. *Family Process, 14,* 193-210.

Framo, J. (1982). *Explorations in marital and family therapy.* New York: Springer.

Freud, S. (1963). *The standard edition of the complete psychological works of Sigmund Freud.* (Vol. XVI) (J. Strachey, Trans.) London: The Hogarth Press.

Friedman, E. H. (1971). The birthday party: An experiment in obtaining change in one's own extended family. *Family Process, 10*(3), 345-359.

Garcia Badaracco, J. E. (1982). The family as the real context of all psychotherapeutic processes. In F. Kaslow (Ed.), *The international book of family therapy.* New York: Brunner/Mazel.

Gauron, E. F., & Rawlings, G. I. (1973). The myth of the fragile patient. *Psychotherapy: Theory, Research and Practice, 10*(3), 290-291.

Gilbert, S. J. (1976). Self-disclosure, intimacy and communication in families. *The Family Coordinator, 25*(3), 221-230.

Goulding, M. M., & Goulding, R. L. (1979). *Changing lives through redecision therapy.* New York: Brunner/Mazel.

Goulding, R. (1972). New directions in transactional analysis: Creating an environment for redecision and change. In C. J. Sager & H. S. Kaplan (Eds.), *Progress in group and family therapy* (pp. 105-125). New York: Brunner/Mazel.

Greenberg, G. S. (1979). Review of videotape: Making the invisible visible, therapist P. Papp. *Family Process, 18,* 367-369.

Guerin, K. (1982). Oldest daughters in the family system. *The Family, 9*(2), 80-82.

Guerin, P., & Fogarty, T. (1973). Study your own family. In A. Ferber, M. Mendelsohn, & A. Napier (Eds.), *The book of family therapy* (pp. 445-467). Boston: Houghton Mifflin.

Guerin, P., & Fogarty, T. (1972). The family therapist's own family. *International Journal of Psychiatry, 10*(6), 6-50.

Guerin, P. J., & Guerin, K. B. (1976). Theoretical aspects and clinical relevance of the multigenerational model of family therapy. In P. J. Guerin (Ed.), *Family therapy* (pp. 91-110). New York: Gardner Press.

Guerin, P. J., & Pendagast, E. G. (1976). Evaluation of family system and genogram. In P. J. Guerin (Ed.), *Family therapy* (pp. 450-464). New York: Gardner Press.

Haley, J. (1969). Toward a theory of pathological systems. In G. Zuk & I. Boszormenyi-Nagy (Eds.), *Family therapy and disturbed families* (pp. 11-27). Palo Alto, CA: Science and Behavior Books.

Haley, J. (1973). The family life cycle. In J. Haley, *Uncommon therapy* (pp. 41-64). New York: W. W. Norton.

Hartman, A. (1978). Diagrammatic assessment of family relationships. *Social Casework,* October, 465-476.

Hatcher, C. (1978). Intrapersonal and interpersonal models: Blending Gestalt and family therapies. *Journal of Marriage and Family Counselling, 4*(1), 63–68.

Haverlick, J. J. (1981). The single parent, the therapist and their extended families. *The Family, 9*(1), 3–10.

Hawkins, J. L., & Killorin, E. A. (1979). Family of origin: An experiential workshop. *American Journal of Family Therapy, 7*(4), 6–17.

Hoffman, L. (1982). A co-evolutionary framework for systematic family therapy. In B. Keeney (Ed.), *Diagnosis and assessment in family therapy* (p. 42). Rockville, MD: Aspen Systems Corporation.

Hogg, W. F. (1972). The split field: Relayer system as a factor in the etiology of anxiety. *Psychiatry, 35,* 126–137.

Jackson, D. D. (1965). The study of the family. *Family Process, 4*(1), 1–20.

Jackson, D. D. (Ed.). (1968a). *Therapy, communication and change.* Palo Alto, CA: Science and Behavior Books.

Jackson, D. D. (Ed.). (1968b). *Communication, family and marriage.* Palo Alto, CA: Science and Behavior Books.

Jefferson, C. (1978). Some notes on the use of family sculpture in therapy. *Family Process, 17*(1), 69–76.

Jolly, W., Froom, J., & Rosen, M. G. (1980). The genogram. *The Journal of Family Practice, 10*(2), 251–255.

Jourard, S. M. (1971). *The transparent self.* (pp. 133–152). New York: Van Nostrand.

Kadis, L. B., & McClendon, R. (1980). Project: Family "cure." *Transactional Analysis Journal, 10*(2), 147–152.

Kadis, L. B., & McClendon, R. (1981). Integrating redecision therapy and family therapy. In A. Gurman (Ed.), *Questions and answers in family therapy* (pp. 147–151). New York: Brunner/Mazel.

Kantor, D., & Lehr, W. (1975). *Inside the family.* San Francisco: Jossey-Bass.

Kaplan, M. L., & Kaplan, N. R. (1978). Individual and family growth: A Gestalt approach. *Family Process, 17,* 195–205.

Keeney, B. (1983). *Aesthetics of change.* New York: The Guilford Press.

Kempler, W. (1974). *Principles of gestalt family therapy.* Salt Lake City: Desert Press.

Kerr, M. E. (1980). Emotional factors in physical illness: A multigenerational perspective. *The Family, 7*(2), 59–66.

Kerr, M. (1974). The importance of the extended family. In F. D. Andres & J. P. Lorio (Eds.), *Georgetown family symposia* (Vol. I) (pp. 49–62). Washington, D.C.: Georgetown University Medical Center.

Kniskern, D. P. (1983). The new wave is all wet. *Networker, 7*(4), 38–62.

Kramer, C. H. (1968a). *Psychoanalytically oriented family therapy: Ten-year evolution in a private child psychiatry practice.* (Monograph.). Center for Family Studies/The Family Institute of Chicago.

Kramer, C. H. (1968b). The theoretical position: Diagnostic and therapeutic implications. In C. H. Kramer, B. Liebowitz, R. L. Phillips, S. Schmidt, & J. Gibson (Eds.), *Beginning phase of family therapy* (pp. 1–15). (Monograph.). The Family Institute of Chicago.

Kramer, C. H. (1980). *Becoming a family therapist.* New York: Human Sciences Press.

Kramer, C. H., & Kramer, J. R. (1976). *Basic principles of long-term patient care: Developing a therapeutic community.* Springfield, IL: Charles C Thomas.

Kramer, J. R., & Reitz, M. (1980). Using video playback to train family therapists. *Family Process, 19,* 145–150.

Krell, R., & Rabkin, L. (1979). The effects of sibling death on the surviving child: A family perspective. *Family Process, 18*(4), 417–477.

Kuhn, J. S. (1978). Realignment of emotional forces following loss. In R. R. Sagar (Ed.), *Georgetown family symposia* (Vol. III) (pp. 193-204). Washington, D.C.: Georgetown University Medical Center.

Laing, R. D. (1972). *The politics of the family.* New York: Vintage Books.

Leader, A. L. (1978). Intergenerational separation anxiety in family therapy. *Social Casework, 59*(3), 138-144.

Legg, C., & Sherrick, I. (1976). The replacement child — A developmental tragedy. *Child Psi and Human Development, 7*(2), 113-126.

Lewis, J. M. (1982). Dying with friends: Implications for the psychotherapist. *American Journal of Psychiatry, 139*(3), 261-266.

Lieberman, S. (1979). A transgenerational theory. *Journal of Family Therapy, 1*(4), 347-360.

Lieberman, S. (1979). Transgenerational analysis: The genogram as a technique in family therapy. *Journal of Family Therapy, 1,* 51-64.

Lifton, R. J. (1979). *The broken connection.* New York: Simon & Schuster.

Loewenstein, S. F. (1981). Mother and daughter — an epitaph. *Family Process, 20*(1), 3-10.

Mendelsohn, M., & Ferber, A. (1973). Is everybody watching? In A. Ferber, M. Mendelsohn, & A. Napier (Eds.), *The book of family therapy* (pp. 431-444). Boston: Houghton Mifflin.

McClendon, R., & Kadis, L. B. (1983). *Chocolate pudding.* Palo Alto, CA: Science and Behavior Books.

McClendon, R. (1977). It really is just the same. *Transactional Analysis Journal, 7*(1), 77-82.

McNeel, J. R. (1982). Redecisions in psychotherapy: A study of the effects of an intensive weekend group workshop. *Transactional Analysis Journal, 12*(1), 10-25.

Napier, A. Y. (1971). The marriage of families: Cross-generational complementarity. *Family Process, 10*(14), 373-395.

Napier, A., & Whitaker, C. (1973). A conversation about co-therapy. In A. Ferber, M. Mendelsohn, & A. Napier (Eds.), *The book of family therapy* (pp. 480-506). Boston: Houghton Mifflin.

Napier, A. Y., & Whitaker, C. A. (1978). *The family crucible.* New York: Harper & Row.

Orfanidis, M. (1979). Problems with family genograms. *American Journal of Family Therapy, 7*(3), 74-76.

Papp, P., Silverstein, O., & Carter, E. (1973). Family sculpting in preventive work with "well families." *Family Process, 12*(2), 197-212.

Papp, P. Family choreography. In P. J. Guerin (Ed.), *Family therapy: Theory and practice* (pp. 465-477). New York: Gardner Press.

Pattison, E. M. (1981). The fatal myth of death in the family. In G. Berenson & H. White (Eds.), *Annual review of family therapy* (Vol. 1) (pp. 340-353). New York: Human Sciences Press.

Paul, N. L. (1980). A family need: A sense of intergenerational continuity. *International Journal of Family Psychiatry, 1*(4), 453-460.

Paul, N. L. (1980). Now and the past: Transgenerational analysis. *International Journal of Family Psychiatry, 2,* 235-248.

Paul, N. L., & Grosser, G. H. (1965). Operational mourning and its role in conjoint family therapy. *Community Mental Health Journal, 1*(4), 339-345.

Paul, N. L., & Paul, B. B. (1975). *A marital puzzle.* New York: Norton.

Pendagast, E., & Sherman, C. (1979). A guide to the genogram. *The best of the family, 1973-78* (pp. 101-112). New Rochelle, NY: The Center for Family Learning.

Penn, P. (1982). Circular questioning. *Family Process, 21*(3), 267-280.

Platt, L., & McCauley, J. (1978). Family reunions. In C. H. Simpkinson & L. Platt

(Eds.), *1978 Synopsis of family therapy practice* (pp. 20–35). Olney, MD: The Family Therapy Practice Network.

Polster, E., & Polster, M. (1973). *Gestalt therapy integrated.* New York: Brunner/Mazel.

Rabkin, R. (1970). *Inner and outer space: Into a theory of social psychiatry.* New York: W. W. Norton.

Rhodes, S. L. (1977). A developmental approach to the life cycle of the family. *Social Casework,* May, 301–311.

Roberts, L. (1982). Training: "The infamous Violet Crumble incident." *Australian Journal of Family Therapy, 3*(3), 159–163.

Rosenberg, E. B. (1980). Therapy with siblings in reorganizing families. *International Journal of Family Therapy, 2*(3), 139–158.

Rudolph, E. (1978). Defining a self. *The Family, 6*(1), 25–33.

Satir, V. (1967). *Conjoint family therapy.* Palo Alto, CA: Science and Behavior Books.

Satir, V. (1972). *Peoplemaking.* Palo Alto, CA: Science and Behavior Books.

Satir, V., Stachowiak, J., & Taschman, H. A. (1975). *Helping families to change.* New York: Jason Aronson.

Sevcik, E. A. (1980). Adult sibling reunion as a therapeutic intervention. In *The many dimensions on family practice* (pp. 162–173). New York: Family Service Association of America.

Simon, R. M. (1972). Sculpting the family. *Family Process, 2*(1), 149–157.

Sluzki, C. E. (1981). Process of symptom production and patterns of symptom maintenance. *Journal of Marriage & Family Therapy, 7*(3), 273–280.

Sluzki, C. E., & Ransom, D. C. (1976). Comment on part one. In C. E. Sluzki & D. C. Ransom (Eds.), *Double bind: The foundation of the communicational approach to the family.* New York: Grune & Stratton.

Solomon, M. A. (1973). A developmental conceptual premise for family therapy. *Family Process, 12*(2), 179–188.

Spark, G. (1974). Grandparents and intergenerational family therapy. *Family Process, 13,* 225–237.

Stagoll, B., & Lang, M. (1980). Climbing the family tree: Working with genograms. *Australian Journal of Family Therapy, 1*(4), 161–170.

Stewart, R. H., Peters, T. C., Marsh, S., & Peters, M. J. (1975). An object-relations approach to psychotherapy with marital couples, families, and children. *Family Process, 14*(2), 161–178.

Stierlin, H. (1981). Aspects of transference and countertransference in family therapy. In G. Berenson & H. White (Eds.), *Annual review of family therapy* (Vol. 1) (pp. 148–165). New York: Human Sciences Press.

Stierlin, H. (1974). Shame and guilt in family relations. *Archives of General Psychiatry, 40,* 381–389.

Strassberg, D., Roback, H., D'Antonio, M., & Gabel, H. (1977). Self-disclosure: A critical and selective review of the clinical literature. *Comprehensive Psychiatry, 18*(1), 31–39.

Thistle, P. (1981). The therapist's own family: Focus of training for family therapists. *Social Work, 26*(3), 248–250.

Toman, W. (1976). *Family constellation* (3rd ed.). New York: Springer.

Tomm, K. (1983). The old hat doesn't fit. *Networker, 7*(4), 41.

Tousley, M. M. (1982). The use of family therapy in terminal illness and death. *Journal of Psychosocial Nursing and Mental Health Services, 20*(1), 17–22.

Wachtel, E. (1982). The family psyche over three generations: The genogram revisited. *Journal of Marriage & Family Therapy, 8*(3), 335–343.

Walsh, F. (1978). Concurrent grandparent death and birth of schizophrenic offspring: An intriguing finding. *Family Process, 17*(4), 457–463.

Watzlawick, P., Beavin, J. H., & Jackson, D. D. (1967). *Pragmatics of human communication.* New York: W. W. Norton.

Watzlawick, P., Weakland, J., & Fisch, R. (1974). *Change.* New York: W. W. Norton.

Weakland, J. H., Fisch, R., Watzlawick, P., & Bodin, A. M. Brief Therapy: Focused problem resolution. *Family Process, 13*(2), 141–167.

Weiner, M. F. (1978). *Therapist disclosure: The use of self in psychotherapy* (pp. 46–69). Boston: Butterworths.

Weltner, J. S., & Dym, B. (1980). Shall we dance? Spatialization of couple and therapist-patient relationships. *Psychiatry, 43*, 259–262.

Whitaker, C. (1981, January). Editorial: Value of extended family conference. *AAMFT Newsletter*, 3–4.

Whitaker, C. (1981). The therapist's forced change. *AAMFT Newsletter, 12*(2), 9.

Williams, T. (1955). *Cat on a hot tin roof.* New York: New Directions.

Williamson, D. (1981). Debriefing the past president. *AAMFT Newsletter, 12*(2), 9.

Williamson, D. (1981). Personal authority via termination of the intergenerational hierarchical boundary: A "new" stage in the family life cycle. *Journal of Marriage & Family Therapy, 7*(4), 441–452.

Wright, L. M., Hall, J. S., O'Connor, M., Perry, R., & Murphy, R. (1982). The power of loyalties: One family's developmental struggle during the launching years. *Journal of Strategic and Systemic Therapies, 1*(4), 57–70.

Wynne, L. (1976). On the anguish, and creative passions of not escaping double binds: A reformulation. In C. E. Sluzki, & D. C. Ransom (Eds.), *Double bind: The foundation of the communicational approach to the family.* New York: Grune & Stratton.

Yalom, I. D. (1970). *The theory and practice of group psychotherapy.* New York: Basic Books.

Yalom, I. D. (1975). The therapist: Transference and transparency. In I. D. Yalom, *The theory and practice of psychotherapy* (pp. 191–218). New York: Basic Books.

Yalom, I. D., Lieberman, M. A., & Miles, M. D. (1973). *Encounter groups: First facts.* New York: Basic Books.

Index